Selected Titles in This Series

31 **Ralf Korn and Elke Korn,** Option pricing and portfolio optimization: Modern methods of financial mathematics, 2001
30 **J. C. McConnell and J. C. Robson,** Noncommutative Noetherian rings, 2001
29 **Javier Duoandikoetxea,** Fourier analysis, 2001
28 **Liviu I. Nicolaescu,** Notes on Seiberg-Witten theory, 2000
27 **Thierry Aubin,** A course in differential geometry, 2001
26 **Rolf Berndt,** An introduction to symplectic geometry, 2001
25 **Thomas Friedrich,** Dirac operators in Riemannian geometry, 2000
24 **Helmut Koch,** Number theory: Algebraic numbers and functions, 2000
23 **Alberto Candel and Lawrence Conlon,** Foliations I, 2000
22 **Günter R. Krause and Thomas H. Lenagan,** Growth of algebras and Gelfand-Kirillov dimension, 2000
21 **John B. Conway,** A course in operator theory, 2000
20 **Robert E. Gompf and András I. Stipsicz,** 4-manifolds and Kirby calculus, 1999
19 **Lawrence C. Evans,** Partial differential equations, 1998
18 **Winfried Just and Martin Weese,** Discovering modern set theory. II: Set-theoretic tools for every mathematician, 1997
17 **Henryk Iwaniec,** Topics in classical automorphic forms, 1997
16 **Richard V. Kadison and John R. Ringrose,** Fundamentals of the theory of operator algebras. Volume II: Advanced theory, 1997
15 **Richard V. Kadison and John R. Ringrose,** Fundamentals of the theory of operator algebras. Volume I: Elementary theory, 1997
14 **Elliott H. Lieb and Michael Loss,** Analysis, 1997
13 **Paul C. Shields,** The ergodic theory of discrete sample paths, 1996
12 **N. V. Krylov,** Lectures on elliptic and parabolic equations in Hölder spaces, 1996
11 **Jacques Dixmier,** Enveloping algebras, 1996 Printing
10 **Barry Simon,** Representations of finite and compact groups, 1996
9 **Dino Lorenzini,** An invitation to arithmetic geometry, 1996
8 **Winfried Just and Martin Weese,** Discovering modern set theory. I: The basics, 1996
7 **Gerald J. Janusz,** Algebraic number fields, second edition, 1996
6 **Jens Carsten Jantzen,** Lectures on quantum groups, 1996
5 **Rick Miranda,** Algebraic curves and Riemann surfaces, 1995
4 **Russell A. Gordon,** The integrals of Lebesgue, Denjoy, Perron, and Henstock, 1994
3 **William W. Adams and Philippe Loustaunau,** An introduction to Gröbner bases, 1994
2 **Jack Graver, Brigitte Servatius, and Herman Servatius,** Combinatorial rigidity, 1993
1 **Ethan Akin,** The general topology of dynamical systems, 1993

Option Pricing and Portfolio Optimization

Modern Methods of Financial Mathematics

Option Pricing and Portfolio Optimization

Modern Methods of Financial Mathematics

Ralf Korn
Elke Korn

Graduate Studies
in Mathematics
Volume 31

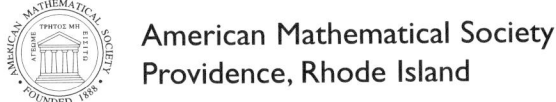

American Mathematical Society
Providence, Rhode Island

Editorial Board
James Humphreys (Chair)
David Saltman
David Sattinger
Ronald Stern

Originally published in the German language by Friedr. Vieweg & Sohn Verlagsgesellschaft mbH, D-65189 Wiesbaden, Germany, under the title "Ralf und Elke Korn: Optionsbewertung und Portfolio-Optimierung: Moderne Methoden der Finanzmathematik. 1. Auflage (1st edition)".

© by Friedr. Vieweg & Sohn Verlagsgesellschaft mbH, Braunschweig/Wiesbaden, 1999

Translated from the German by Ralf Korn and Elke Korn.

2000 Mathematics Subject Classification. Primary 62P05, 91B28, 93E20; Secondary 49L20, 60G44, 60H05.

ABSTRACT. This text covers the typical problems of continuous-time financial mathematics such as option pricing (in particular the Black-Scholes formula and corresponding variants) and portfolio optimization (determination of optimal investment strategies). Further, a separate chapter deals with exotic options and numerical methods.

The required mathematical tools which include Brownian motion, Itô calculus, and stochastic control theory will be presented in self-contained excursions.

The book is suitable as the basis of a course on financial mathematics building up on a basic course in probability.

Library of Congress Cataloging-in-Publication Data
Korn, Ralf.
  Option pricing and portfolio optimization : modern methods of financial mathematics / Ralf Korn, Elke Korn.
    p. cm. — (Graduate studies in mathematics ; v. 31)
  Includes bibliographical references and index.
  ISBN 0-8218-2123-7 (alk. paper)
  1. Options (Finance—Prices—Mathematical models. 2. Portfolio management—Mathematical models. I. Korn, Elke, 1962– II. Title. III. Series.
HG6024.A3 K667   2000
332.63′228—dc21
                                                                                               00-046912

Copying and reprinting. Individual readers of this publication, and nonprofit libraries acting for them, are permitted to make fair use of the material, such as to copy a chapter for use in teaching or research. Permission is granted to quote brief passages from this publication in reviews, provided the customary acknowledgment of the source is given.

Republication, systematic copying, or multiple reproduction of any material in this publication is permitted only under license from the American Mathematical Society. Requests for such permission should be addressed to the Assistant to the Publisher, American Mathematical Society, P. O. Box 6248, Providence, Rhode Island 02940-6248. Requests can also be made by e-mail to reprint-permission@ams.org.

© 2001 by the American Mathematical Society. All rights reserved.
The American Mathematical Society retains all rights
except those granted to the United States Government.
Printed in the United States of America.

∞ The paper used in this book is acid-free and falls within the guidelines
established to ensure permanence and durability.
Visit the AMS home page at URL: http://www.ams.org/

10 9 8 7 6 5 4 3 2 1   06 05 04 03 02 01

Contents

Preface	ix
Frequently Used Notation	xiii
Chapter 1. The Mean-Variance Approach in a One-Period Model	1
Chapter 2. The Continuous-Time Market Model	11
§2.1. Modeling the Security Prices	11
Excursion 1: Brownian Motion and Martingales	15
2.1. Continuation: Modeling the Security Prices	23
Excursion 2: The Itô Integral	26
Excursion 3: The Itô Formula	42
§2.2. Trading Strategy and Wealth Process	56
§2.3. Properties of the Continuous-Time Market Model	64
Excursion 4: The Martingale Representation Theorem	71
Exercises	76
Chapter 3. Option Pricing	79
§3.1. Introduction	79
§3.2. Option Pricing via the Replication Principle	83
Excursion 5: Girsanov's Theorem	93
3.2. Continuation: Option Pricing via the Replication Principle	99
§3.3. Option Pricing by the Partial Differential Approach	105
Excursion 6: The Feynman-Kac Representation	111
§3.4. Arbitrage Bounds for American and European Options	122

§3.5. Pricing of American Options — 129
§3.6. Arbitrage, Equivalent Martingale Measures and Option Pricing — 134
§3.7. Market Numeraire and Numeraire Invariance — 143
Exercises — 148

Chapter 4. Pricing of Exotic Options and Numerical Algorithms — 153
§4.1. Exotic Options with Explicit Pricing Formulae — 155
a) Path independent options on one stock — 155
b) Options on more than one underlying stock — 162
c) Path dependent options — 167
Excursion 7: Weak Convergence of Stochastic Processes — 170
§4.2. Monte-Carlo Simulation — 175
§4.3. Approximation via Binomial Trees — 177
§4.4. Trinomial Trees and Explicit Finite-Difference Methods — 187
§4.5. The Pathwise Binomial Approach of Rogers and Stapleton — 191
Exercises — 201

Chapter 5. Optimal Portfolios — 203
§5.1. Introduction and Formulation of the Problem — 203
§5.2. The Martingale Method — 206
§5.3. Optimal Option Portfolios — 215
Excursion 8: Stochastic Control — 223
§5.4. Portfolio Optimization via the Stochastic Control Method — 236
Exercises — 244

Bibliography — 247

Index — 251

Preface

There are only a few things in daily life which are regarded as a better synonym for uncertainty than security prices. No one seems to be able to predict their exact future values. There are just too many factors and unpredictable events which influence security prices, e.g. the economic situation, political events, company influences, behavior of buyers and sellers, technical innovations,.... So it is natural to describe financial markets where equities and other securities are traded by stochastic models.

The starting point of the history of such stochastic modeling was the dissertation of L. Bachelier [**BACH 00**]. However, the event marking a new period in mathematical finance was the Black-Scholes formula for pricing European options developed some seventy years later; see [**BL/SC 73**]. Modeling financial markets with stochastic models got a major boost from this as the formula became widely accepted by both academics and practitioners. The Black-Scholes formula proved to be so useful in real-life applications that trading in options flourished. Thus, it was natural that R. Merton and M. Scholes were awarded the Nobel Prize in economics for their work contributing to the Black-Scholes formula.

Subsequently, the financial markets introduced (and still are introducing!) more and more types of derivatives often having very complex structures. For their quantitative valuation it is essential to have a sound knowledge of mathematical models for financial markets and to be able to handle the corresponding mathematical toolbox. Here, the most important tool has become the Itô calculus. The impact of the applications of Itô calculus to the finance sector was tremendous. Banks and finance houses all over the world have realized this and have recruited an enormous number of mathematicians, physicists, and economists with the relevant knowledge.

One aim of this book is a fast and at the same time rigorous introduction to Itô calculus. This introduction is tailored to applications in financial mathematics. It therefore forsakes generality which is not needed for the applications. Based on this introduction we build up the standard diffusion type security market model in Chapter 2. The first major problem in finance, the pricing of options, will be treated in detail in Chapter 3. We shall start by introducing the method of option pricing via replication and no arbitrage. This approach is based on the principle that the price of an option should exactly equal the amount of money needed to create the option's payments synthetically. We also present the method to price options with partial differential equations which is the original approach taken by Black and Scholes. In recent years many new types of options, so-called exotic options, appeared at the market and also inspired the research. We shall present numerous examples of such options in this book, some of them with explicit pricing formulas. For obtaining prices for exotic options where an explicit pricing formula cannot be found, numerical methods are needed. Therefore, in Chapter 3 we also describe the basics of Monte Carlo methods, tree methods, and finite difference methods. Finally, another problem in finance is to find optimal investment and consumption strategies, the so-called portfolio problem. This subject will be dealt with in Chapter 5 where we shall describe the martingale method and the stochastic control method for portfolio optimization. As a very recent application we have also included a portfolio problem where only trading in options is allowed.

Although the main parts of this book are based on probabilistic methods and results, we have to emphasize that modern financial mathematics is related to various mathematical fields. After having a quick look through the book you will realize that methods of numerical analysis, partial differential equations, optimization, and functional analysis are also needed.

Required knowledge. For understanding most parts of this book a basic course in probability theory is sufficient. All other tools that are needed will be presented in this book. Of course, knowledge of stochastic processes would be desirable, but only the concept of conditional expectation is definitely needed. As we also introduce the main economic concepts there is no need for having a preknowledge in this area. For a more detailed background on option trading and the economic theory we refer to the books by Hull [**HULL 93**] or Jarrow and Turnbull [**JA/TU 96**].

The concept. With the exception of a short introduction to the Markowitz mean variance approach, we concentrate on the presentation of so-called continuous-time models in this book. Our aim is to give a sound introduction to the mathematical methods of continuous-time finance and thus we present them in detail. We do not simply cite the major results, we also develop concepts like "stochastic integration", "change of measure", and "stochastic control" just at that moment when they are applied for the first time in financial mathematics. So this book consists of a mathematical description of continuous-time finance with extra sections, which we call excursions, which supply the essential mathematical tools in a compact form.

As we meant this book to be a basis of a lecture course, we made some compromises. As we decided not to present stochastic integration in a very general form, we restricted ourselves to Itô processes as integrators. For the applications this is not a severe restriction and it allows us to present the theory without using the Doob-Meyer decomposition. Its presentation would have increased substantially both the number of pages and the degree of difficulty of this book.

How to read this book. Apart from reading the book chapter by chapter – this is what we recommend – there are many other reasonable ways to read it. It is possible to skip the option chapters and jump to portfolio optimization after Chapter 2. A more traditional approach would be to work first through all excursions and then read the mathematical finance parts. On the other hand, a reader with a theoretical background could even skip the excursions.

An introductory book such as ours can only give a first impression of the large area of financial mathematics. Good sources for more details about stochastic calculus are [**KA/SH 91**], [**OKS 92**], [**R/YOR 91**], [**RO/WI 87**] or [**WE/WI 90**]. For recent aspects of portfolio optimization we refer to [**KORN 97**]. In [**KA/SH 98**] you can find recent aspects of various topics of mathematical finance.

Typos and errors. Even good books on graduate mathematical topics contain typing errors and sometimes even real errors. This book is probably no exception. So if you get stuck on a formula, do not despair, it might simply be a typing error. And do not invest millions of dollars relying on a formula or description you found here! Mistakes can be hidden anywhere. We absolutely do not accept any responsibility or liability for losses or damages occasioned through this book.

Acknowledgements. We would like to thank our teachers at the Johannes-Gutenberg Universität of Mainz: Prof. W. Bühler, Prof. H. Mülthei, Prof. C. Schneider and Prof. H.-J. Schuh. Also we would like to thank Prof. C. Klüppelberg of the Technical University of Munich for initiating the original German version of the book. Many others helped in various ways and pointed out typos and minor errors in the German version. We therefore thank Dr. M. Borkovec, Dr. M. Helm, Dipl. Math. H. Kraft, Dr. O. Schein,

Dr. G. Schlüchtermann, Dipl. Math. J. Sutor, Dipl. Math. M. Krekel, and Dipl. Math. T. Volz.

Further the staff at AMS and in particular Edward G. Dunne, Barbara Beeton, and Gil Poulin were very helpful.

Finally the biggest thanks go to our son Uwe being really patient with his always very busy parents.

Ralf Korn

Elke Korn

Stelzenberg, May 2000.

Frequently Used Notation

Abbreviations

w.l.o.g.	without loss of generality
min	minimize
max	maximize
inf	infimum
sup	supremum

Symbols

$\mathbb{N}$	$= \{1, 2, 3, ...\}$
$\mathbb{R}$	set of real numbers
$\mathbb{R}^n$	n-dimensional Euclidean space
$\emptyset$	empty set
$C[0,1]$	set of continuous functions from $[0,1]$ to $\mathbb{R}$
$C^1[0,1]$	set of continuously differentiable functions from $[0,1]$ to $\mathbb{R}$
$C^2[0,1]$	set of twice continuously differentiable functions from $[0,1]$ to $\mathbb{R}$
$C^{1,2}([0,1] \times [0,1])$	set of continuous functions from $[0,1] \times [0,1]$ to $\mathbb{R}$ which are continuously differentiable with respect to the first variable and twice continuously differentiable with respect to the second variable

$f_t(t,x)$, $f_x(t,x)$	partial derivatives with respect to t and x, respectively
$exp(x)$	$= e^x$
$1_A(x)$	$= 1$ if $x \in A$ or $= 0$ if $x \notin A$ ("indicator function of A")
a^+	$\max\{a, 0\}$
a^-	$\max\{-a, 0\}$
$x \wedge y$	$\min\{x, y\}$
$A := B$	A is defined by B
x'	transpose of the vector x
$\underline{1}$	$= (1, 1, ..., 1)'$
∂O	boundary of the set O
$\bar{O}$	closure of the set O, $\bar{O} = O \cup \partial O$
$P(A)$	probability of the set A
$\sim$	distributed according to
$\mathcal{N}(0, 1)$	standard normal distribution with mean 0 and variance 1
$\mathcal{N}(\mu, \sigma^2)$	normal distribution with mean μ and variance σ^2
$E(X)$	expectation of the random variable X
$Var(X)$	variance of the random variable X
$E(X \mid \mathcal{F})$	conditional expectation of the random variable X with respect to $\mathcal{F}$
$\langle X \rangle$	quadratic variation of the Itô process X
$\langle X, Y \rangle$	quadratic covariation of the Itô processes X and Y
$\mathcal{B}(U)$	Borel σ-field of the set U, the smallest σ-field containing all open subsets of the topological space U
$\sigma(X)$	the smallest σ-field with respect to which the random variable X is measurable
$\sigma(\mathcal{F})$	the smallest σ-field containing the collection of sets $\mathcal{F}$
$\mathcal{F} \otimes \mathcal{G}$	$= \sigma(A \times B; A \in \mathcal{F}, B \in \mathcal{G})$, the product σ-field

Chapter 1

The Mean-Variance Approach in a One-Period Model

Before we shall consider continuous-time market models, we start by looking at a simple one-period model. The mathematical starting point of the theory of portfolio optimization is the work of H. Markowitz (see [**MARK 52**]) on the mean-variance criterion to judge investment strategies in security markets. Due to both its simplicity and plausibility, Markowitz's approach quickly became popular in theory and practice. Even today, its use is still widespread. So it was well-deserved that Markowitz gained the Nobel Prize in economics in 1990 (in fact, he had to share the prize with two other economists). However, the simplicity of the mean-variance approach is also a reason for some disadvantages which lead to the consideration of continuous-time models (see e.g. [**MERT 69**]). The model underlying the mean-variance approach is a so-called one-period model. This means that decisions on investment strategies are only made at the beginning of the period. The consequences of these decisions will then be observed at the end of the period, and there is no further action in between. This is the reason why such a model is called a static model.

Description of the one-period model. We consider a market where d different securities with prices $p_1, p_2, ..., p_d > 0$ at the initial time $t = 0$ are traded. The security prices $P_1(T), P_2(T), ..., P_d(T)$ at the final time $t = T$ are not foreseeable. Therefore, they are modeled as non-negative random variables on a probability space $(\Omega, \mathcal{F}, P)$. In the following we shall look at the *returns* of the securities

$$R_i(T) := \frac{P_i(T)}{p_i}, \ i = 1, ..., d,$$

and assume that we know (or have estimated) their means, variances, and covariances

$$E(R_i(T)) = \mu_i \text{ for } i = 1, ..., d,$$
$$Cov(R_i(T), R_j(T)) = \sigma_{ij} \text{ for } i, j = 1, ..., d.$$

We assume that each security is perfectly divisible, i.e. we can hold $\varphi_i \in \mathbb{R}$ shares of security i, $i = 1, ..., d$. A negative position (i.e. $\varphi_i < 0$ for some i) in a security corresponds to a short selling of it (see Section 2.2). To avoid the possibility of a negative final wealth, we shall not allow such negative positions in our one-period setting here. Hence, we require $\varphi_i \geq 0$, $i = 1, ..., d$. Further, we assume that there are no transaction costs in our model.

Remark. The matrix $\sigma := (\sigma_{ij})_{i,j \in \{1,...,d\}}$ is positive semi-definite as it is a variance-covariance matrix.

Definition 1.1. An investor with initial wealth $x > 0$ is assumed to hold $\varphi_i \geq 0$ shares of security i, $i = 1, ..., d$, with

$$\sum_{i=1}^{d} \varphi_i \cdot p_i = x \qquad \text{``budget equation''}.$$

Then the *portfolio vector* $\pi = (\pi_1, ..., \pi_d)$ is defined as

$$\pi_i := \frac{\varphi_i \cdot p_i}{x}, \ i = 1, ..., d,$$

and

$$R^\pi := \sum_{i=1}^{d} \pi_i \cdot R_i(T)$$

is called the corresponding *portfolio return*.

Remark 1.2. (1) The components of the portfolio vector represent the fractions of the total wealth which are invested in the corresponding securities. In particular, we have

$$\sum_{i=1}^{d} \pi_i = \frac{\sum_{i=1}^{d} \varphi_i \cdot p_i}{x} = \frac{x}{x} = 1.$$

(2) If $X^\pi(T)$ denotes the final wealth corresponding to an initial wealth of x and a portfolio vector π

$$X^\pi(T) = \sum_{i=1}^{d} \varphi_i \cdot P_i(T),$$

then we have
$$R^\pi = \sum_{i=1}^d \pi_i \cdot R_i(T) = \sum_{i=1}^d \frac{\varphi_i \cdot p_i}{x} \cdot \frac{P_i(T)}{p_i} = \frac{X^\pi(T)}{x}.$$

This relation justifies the name portfolio return for R^π.

(3) The mean and the variance of the portfolio return are given by
$$E(R^\pi) = \sum_{i=1}^d \pi_i \cdot \mu_i,$$
$$Var(R^\pi) = \sum_{i=1}^d \sum_{j=1}^d \pi_i \cdot \sigma_{ij} \cdot \pi_j.$$

Criteria for selecting a portfolio. Of course, when choosing a portfolio an investor has the aim of obtaining a return as large as possible. If the only criterion to judge this is the mean of the portfolio return, then this will typically lead to investing the whole sum into the security with the highest mean return. However, this could be a very risky security and thus, the return can have big fluctuations. To accommodate this fact, we introduce the idea of minimizing such a risk as a second criterion. As a measure for this risk, the portfolio variance is chosen. The basic idea of Markowitz was to look for a balance between risk (i.e. portfolio variance) and return (i.e. portfolio mean). He considered the problem of requiring a lower bound for the portfolio return ("minimum return") and then choosing from the corresponding set the portfolio vector with minimal variance. Alternatively he considered the problem of setting up an upper bound for the portfolio variance and then he determined the portfolio vector with highest possible mean return from the remaining set. We shall look at both these variants of the mean-variance approach explicitly.

Problem formulation in the mean-variance approach.
(1) We consider the task of maximizing the mean of the portfolio return $E(R^\pi)$ under a given upper bound c_1 for the variance $Var(R^\pi)$.

(1.1) $$\max_{\pi \in \mathbb{R}^d} E(R^\pi)$$
subject to $\pi_i \geq 0$ for $i = 1, ..., d$, $\sum_{i=1}^d \pi_i = 1$, $Var(R^\pi) \leq c_1$

In words: Under all possible portfolios $\pi \in \mathbb{R}^d$, consider only those which satisfy the constraints (which form the "feasible region"), in particular those which have a variance that is below c_1. Then, among those portfolios determine the one with the largest expected return.

(2) The second formulation of the mean-variance approach leads to the task of minimizing the variance of the portfolio return $Var(R^\pi)$ given a lower bound on the expected portfolio return, $E(R^\pi) \geq c_2$.

$$(1.2) \qquad \min_{\pi \in \mathbb{R}^d} \ Var\left(R^\pi\right)$$

$$\text{subject to} \quad \pi_i \geq 0 \text{ for } i = 1, ..., d, \quad \sum_{i=1}^{d} \pi_i = 1, \quad E\left(R^\pi\right) \geq c_2$$

In words: Under all possible portfolios $\pi \in \mathbb{R}^d$, consider only those which satisfy the constraints, in particular those which yield at least an expected return of c_2. Then, among those portfolios determine the one with the smallest return variance.

Solution methods.

(1) Problem (1.1) is a linear optimization problem with an additional quadratic constraint. For such problems there are no special standard algorithms. Of course, we could treat this problem with general methods of non-linear optimization, but this would lead to inefficient algorithms.

(2) Problem (1.2) is a quadratic optimization problem with a positive semi-definite objective matrix, namely σ. This problem can be solved in a very efficient way by using standard quadratic programming algorithms such as the ones of Goldfarb and Idnani, see **[GO/ID 83]**, or Gill and Murray, see **[GI/MU 78]**. The feasible region of the optimization problem is non-empty (i.e. there exists at least one π satisfying the constraints) if we have

$$c_2 \leq \max_{1 \leq i \leq d} \mu_i.$$

If the matrix σ is positive definite and if furthermore the feasible region is non-empty then the problem possesses a unique solution. This is even the case if one of the securities is a riskless one (i.e. the price $P_1(T)$ of the first security is non-random) and the variance-covariance matrix corresponding to the remaining securities is positive definite.

1. The Mean-Variance Approach in a One-Period Model

Although the two problems are not the duals of each other, (1.1) and (1.2) are closely related in the sense of Theorem 1.3 which can be shown by application of non-linear optimization theory (see [**KORN 97**], p. 8).

Theorem 1.3. *Consider the problems (1.1) and (1.2). Let the matrix σ be positive definite and let the constants c_1, c_2 satisfy the following constraints*

$$\min_{1 \leq i \leq d} \mu_i < c_2 < \max_{1 \leq j \leq d} \mu_j$$

$$\min_{\pi \geq 0, \pi' \underline{1} = 1} \sigma^2(\pi) \leq c_1 \leq \max_{\pi \geq 0, \pi' \underline{1} = 1} \sigma^2(\pi)$$

with $\underline{1} := (1, ..., 1)' \in \mathbb{R}^d$. Then we have

(1) *If π^* solves Problem (1.2) with*

$$E(R^{\pi*}) = \sum_{i=1}^{d} \pi_i^* \mu_i = c_2,$$

then π^* also solves Problem (1.1) with $c_1 := Var(R^{\pi*})$.

(2) *If $\hat{\pi}$ solves Problem (1.1) with*

$$Var\left(R^{\hat{\pi}}\right) = \sum_{i=1}^{d}\sum_{j=1}^{d} \hat{\pi}_i \cdot \hat{\pi}_j \cdot \sigma_{ij} = c_1,$$

then $\hat{\pi}$ also solves Problem (1.2) with $c_2 := E\left(R^{\hat{\pi}}\right)$.

Remark. With the help of the above connection between (1.1) and (1.2) we can now construct an iterative scheme for the solution of (1.1), see [**KORN 97**], p. 8. However, we will not go into detail here.

An example for the diversification effect. To illuminate the variance reducing effect of distributing the capital into different securities, we give the following simple example. Consider the case of $d = 2$, a market with only two different securities. Assume that the variance of the return of both securities is positive, $\sigma_{11}, \sigma_{22} > 0$. This in particular means that both security prices fluctuate randomly. We further assume that the two security prices are independent which implies $\sigma_{12} = \sigma_{21} = 0$. Then for the portfolio $\pi = (1/2, 1/2)$ we have

$$Var(R^{\pi}) = Var\left(\tfrac{1}{2} \cdot R_1 + \tfrac{1}{2} \cdot R_2\right) = \frac{\sigma_{11}}{4} + \frac{\sigma_{22}}{4}.$$

In the case of $\sigma_{11} = \sigma_{22}$ this implies that the variance of the return of the portfolio $(1/2, 1/2)$ is only half as big as that of either the portfolios $(1, 0)$ or $(0, 1)$. This reduction of the variance is called the diversification effect. In general, the diversification effect gets more significant as the number d of traded securities increases.

A simple example. In the following, we shall show by means of a simple example that under the mean-variance criterion it can even be optimal to invest in a seemingly bad security. To show this, we have a look at a model with two securities with negatively correlated prices. This means that one price has the tendency to increase when the other one falls and vice versa. We shall also give a graphical illustration of the solution method. The parameters we choose here are

$$\mu_1 = 1, \quad \sigma_{11} = 0.1,$$
$$\mu_2 = 0.9, \quad \sigma_{22} = 0.15,$$
$$\sigma_{12} = \sigma_{21} = -0.1.$$

The problem (1.2) then reads

(1.3) $\quad \min_{\pi} \; Var\left(R^{\pi}\right) = \min_{\pi} \left(0.1 \cdot \pi_1^2 + 0.15 \cdot \pi_2^2 - 0.2 \cdot \pi_1 \pi_2\right)$

$$\text{subject to} \quad \pi_1 + \pi_2 = 1, \quad \pi_i \geq 0, \; i = 1, 2$$
$$E\left(R^{\pi}\right) = 1 \cdot \pi_1 + 0.9 \cdot \pi_2 \geq 0.96$$

At first glance, security two does not seem to be very attractive. Its expected return is less than that of the first one, and also the risk of random price fluctuations (measured by the return variance) is bigger for security two. However, the fact that both security prices are correlated will imply that despite the unattractive features of security two, it can be advantageous also to invest in the second security. We first consider the two portfolios $(1,0)$ and $(1/2, 1/2)$:

$$Var\left(R^{(1,0)}\right) = 0.1, \qquad E\left(R^{(1,0)}\right) = 1,$$
$$Var\left(R^{\left(\frac{1}{2},\frac{1}{2}\right)}\right) = 0.0125, \quad E\left(R^{\left(\frac{1}{2},\frac{1}{2}\right)}\right) = 0.95.$$

We note that the portfolio return variance of $(1/2, 1/2)$ is much less than that of $(1,0)$. However, $(1/2, 1/2)$ does not satisfy the expectation constraint. Before solving (1.3), we look for the portfolio having the least variance under all admissible portfolios when we temporarily ignore the expectation constraint. This problem can be rewritten in the following way if we take into account that $\pi_1 + \pi_2 = 1$:

$$\min_{\pi} \left(0.1 \cdot \pi_1^2 + 0.15 \cdot (1 - \pi_1)^2 - 0.2 \cdot \pi_1 (1 - \pi_1)\right),$$

hence

$$\min_{\pi} \left(0.15 + 0.45 \cdot \pi_1^2 - 0.5 \cdot \pi_1\right).$$

In this case we obtain the minimizing portfolio as

$$(\pi_1, \pi_2) = \left(\tfrac{5}{9}, \tfrac{4}{9}\right)$$

1. The Mean-Variance Approach in a One-Period Model

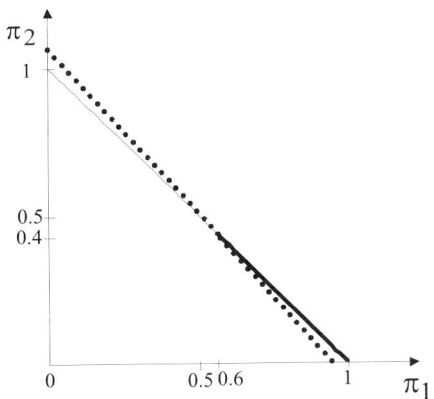

Figure 1.1. Admissible pairs

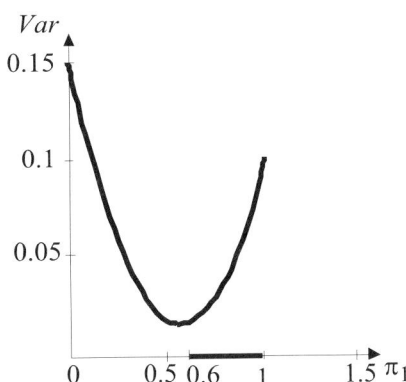

Figure 1.2. Variance of pairs

with portfolio return variance and mean of

$$Var\left(R^{\left(\frac{5}{9},\frac{4}{9}\right)}\right) = 0.0\bar{1}, \qquad E\left(R^{\left(\frac{5}{9},\frac{4}{9}\right)}\right) = 0.9\bar{5}.$$

Again, this is not the solution of (1.3), but we have found a better portfolio than $(1/2, 1/2)$ (i.e. one with a smaller portfolio return variance *and* a higher portfolio return mean). Finally, to solve (1.3) we look at the following two diagrams. In Figure 1.1 all pairs (π_1, π_2) that satisfy the expectation constraint are located above the dotted line. The intersection of this area with the line given by $\pi_1 + \pi_2 = 1$ (and the non-negative quadrant) forms the feasible region of our mean-variance problem (the bold line). The parabola of Figure 1.2 represents the portfolio return variance of all pairs satisfying $\pi_1 + \pi_2 = 1$ as a function of π_1. Its minimum in the feasible region $[0.6, 1]$ for π_1 is obviously attained at $\pi_1 = 0.6$. Hence, we have identified the optimal portfolio in our mean-variance problem (1.3) as

$$(\pi_1^*, \pi_2^*) = (0.6, 0.4)$$

with

$$Var\left(R^{\pi^*}\right) = 0.012, \quad E\left(R^{\pi^*}\right) = 0.96,$$

i.e. the expectation constraint is binding.

For this portfolio we have reduced the variance (the "fluctuations risk") drastically compared to the portfolio $(1, 0)$, but still it obtains an acceptable mean return.

Remark. We do not go into further details of the mean-variance approach and omit the introduction of such terms as the capital market line or the efficient frontier. The interested reader is referred to standard literature on that topic such as [**SHAR 85**] or [**LUEN 98**].

A first stock price model. In the one-period setting presented so far, it was not necessary to make an explicit assumption on the distribution of the security returns, since to solve the mean-variance problem we only needed expectations and covariances. Thus, in this setting we could choose any possible distribution for the returns that matches the first two moments and satisfies some further requirements. Of course, it should be constructed on the non-negative real numbers as the price $P_1(T)$ is non-negative. In discrete-time market models (and in particular in multi-period ones) the so-called binomial model (also called the Cox-Ross-Rubinstein model, see [**C/R/R 79**]) is very popular. To illustrate it briefly, we consider here a one-period model with just one security. This security has the price p_1 at time $t = 0$, with probability q the price decreases by the factor d or it goes up with probability $(1 - q)$ by the factor u, $u > d$. This means, at time T the security may have the price $d \cdot p_1$ or $u \cdot p_1$. For the mean and the variance of the return we get

$$E(R_1(T)) = E\left(\frac{P_1(T)}{p_1}\right) = q \cdot \frac{u \cdot p_1}{p_1} + (1-q) \cdot \frac{d \cdot p_1}{p_1} = q \cdot u + (1-q) \cdot d,$$

$$Var(R_1(T)) = Var\left(\frac{P_1(T)}{p_1}\right) = q \cdot u^2 + (1-q) \cdot d^2 - (q \cdot u + (1-q) \cdot d)^2.$$

This price model can be extended to more than one period with the same parameters. Then after n periods the security has the price

$$P_1(n \cdot T) = p_1 \cdot u^{X_n} \cdot d^{n-X_n},$$

where X_n denotes the number of "up-movements" of the price in n periods. X_n is a binomially distributed random variable with $X_n \sim B(n, q)$. This explains the name *binomial model*.

As an example we calculate the factors u and d in our very simple example explicitly if we choose $q = 1/2$ and want $E(R_1(T)) = \mu_1 = 1$ and $Var(R_1(T)) = \sigma_{11} = 0.1$:

$$u = 1 + \sqrt{0.1}, \quad d = 1 - \sqrt{0.1}.$$

In this book the binomial model will only be considered as a possibility to compute option prices numerically (see Section 4.3).

Some comments on the mean-variance approach. The mean-variance approach (in a one-period setting) is easy to understand and can be implemented in a straightforward manner. This explains its popularity in practice. However, there is only trading at time $t = 0$. No reactions to current price changes are possible, and the risk of an investment is only modeled via the variance of its return. In general, the security price modeling is quite simplistic and it is a purely static model. This absence of dynamics with respect to time in both the modeling of the price evolution and of the possible trading activities has to be seen as the major reason for the development of continuous-time market models. Further, it should be mentioned that the complexity of discrete-time multi-period models increases very rapidly with increasing numbers of periods, and even in times of fast computers they can not be solved in real time.

Chapter 2

The Continuous-Time Market Model

2.1. Modeling the Security Prices

Description of the continuous-time market model. We consider a market where $d+1$ securities are traded. Among them are d risky stocks with prices $p_1, p_2, ..., p_d$ at time $t = 0$ and random prices $P_1(t), ..., P_d(t)$ at times $t > 0$. The remaining security is a riskless one called a *bond* with price p_0 at time $t = 0$, and a deterministic price $P_0(t)$ at other times. We shall see that according to its modeling this riskless security is much more similar to a bank account than to a bond (see below). However, for historic reasons, we shall continue in calling it a bond. We further assume that our model allows for perfectly divisible securities and that no transaction costs occur either for selling or for buying of securities. In the sequel, we shall almost always look at a finite trading interval $[0, T]$. In contrast to the one-period model it will now be possible to trade at each time in $[0, T]$. As we are thus not solely interested in initial and final prices of the securities, we also have to consider the price developments on the whole interval $[0, T]$. A realistic modeling of these price processes will be our next task.

The bond price. As we would like to model the bond price evolution over time similar to that of a bank account, we first have a closer look at it.

Usually, interest on a typical savings bank account is compounded annually; this means interest will be added to a bank account after one year (or more generally: after one period). From that time on, interest will also be paid on that added interest part of the bank account. Thus, in the first year, the bank account grows linearly in time. Consider a bank account of value K and let r be the interest rate per unit of time. If interest will only be paid at the instant $t = 1$, then the value of the account increases to

$$K + r \cdot K = K \cdot (1 + r) \text{ at } t = 1.$$

However, if the interest of $r/2$ is compounded at time $t = 1/2$, then this will accrue additional interest during the period of $[1/2, 1]$. Together with the next interest payment we then have a value of

$$\left(K + \tfrac{r}{2}K\right) + \left(K + \tfrac{r}{2}K\right) \cdot \tfrac{r}{2} = K \cdot \left(1 + \tfrac{r}{2}\right)^2 \text{ at } t = 1.$$

Hence, the capital grows linearly with a slope of $r \cdot K$ during the interval $[0, 1/2]$. On $[1/2, 1]$ it also grows linearly, but now with a slope of $r \cdot (K + r/2 \cdot K)$. In general, compounding of interest r/n at times i/n, $i = 1, ..., n$, $n \in \mathbb{N}$, lead to a bank account having a value of

$$K \cdot \left(1 + \tfrac{r}{n}\right)^n \text{ at } t = 1.$$

By interpreting the limiting case of $n \to \infty$ as interest payments in continuous time, this leads to a final wealth of

$$K \cdot e^{r \cdot 1} \text{ at } t = 1$$

and a running capital of

$$K \cdot e^{r \cdot t} \text{ at } t \in [0, 1].$$

Figure 2.1 shows the different time evolutions of an initial capital $K = 1$ corresponding to the different methods of payment of interest as described above. Here $P_1(t)$ represents the evolution if interest is paid only once (annually), $P_{1/2}(t)$ if interest is paid twice (semi-annually), and $P_c(t)$ corresponds to continuously compounded interest. Obviously, continuous compounding leads to the highest final value given the same interest rate for all ways of compounding interest. Of course, it is no problem to determine an interest rate $\tilde{r}$ such that continuous compounding leads to the same capital as annual compounding at times $t = 1, 2, 3, ...$. Simply choose

$$\tilde{r} = \ln(1 + r).$$

The interest rate r is called the *effective rate* of the period, while $\tilde{r}$ is called the *continuous* or *nominal rate*.

From now on, we assume continuous compounding of interest at a constant rate r leading to a bond price of

$$(2.1) \qquad P_0(t) = p_0 \cdot e^{r \cdot t} \text{ for } t \in [0, T]$$

This can be generalized to the case of a non-constant, time-dependent, and integrable interest rate $r(t)$ resulting in

2.1. Modeling the Security Prices

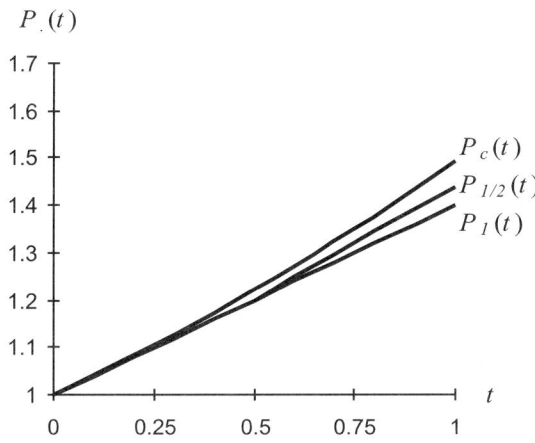

Figure 2.1. Evolution of a bank account corresponding to different ways of compounding of interest

$$(2.2) \qquad P_0(t) = p_0 \cdot e^{\int_0^t r(s)ds} \text{ for } t \in [0, T]$$

as a model for the bond price. By interpreting the following differential equation

$$dP_0(t) = P_0(t) r(t) dt, \quad P_0(0) = p_0 \text{ for } t \in [0, T]$$

as an integral equation

$$P_0(t) = p_0 + \int_0^t P_0(s) r(s) ds \text{ for } t \in [0, T]$$

the bond price $P_0(t)$ given in (2.2) is its unique solution.

The stock price - motivation. We think of a stock price being similar to a bond price but admitting a random behavior. More precisely, the stock price is assumed to fluctuate around an "intrinsic bond component" which has an interest rate different from that of the bond (see Figure 2.2). As a premium for the risk originating from these random fluctuations we would expect the interest rate $\tilde{b}_i$ of the intrinsic bond part being bigger than the usual bond interest rate r.

As in the case of a constant interest rate the logarithm of the bond price is linear (this is often referred to as a log-linear bond price),

$$\ln(P_0(t)) = \ln(p_0) + r \cdot t$$

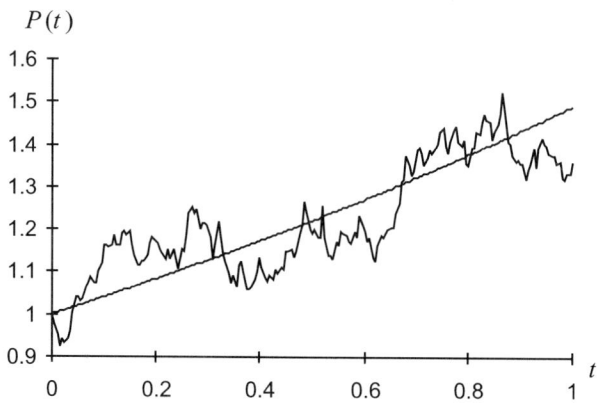

Figure 2.2. Stock price with prediction

this suggests the following log-linear model for a stock price

$$\ln(P_i(t)) = \ln(p_i) + \tilde{b}_i \cdot t + \text{"randomness"}.$$

This "randomness" is assumed

- to have no tendency, i.e. $E(\text{"randomness"}) = 0$,
- to be time dependent,
- to represent the sum of all deviations of $\ln(P_i(t))$ from $\ln(p_i) + \tilde{b}_i \cdot t$ on $[0, T]$.

If we also assume that these deviations from $\tilde{b}_i \cdot t$ are the sum of many similar independent deviations, then the law of large numbers suggests the choice

$$\text{"randomness"} \sim \mathcal{N}(0, \sigma^2 t)$$

for some $\sigma > 0$. By abbreviating the deviation at time t as

$$\ln(P_i(t)) - \ln(p_0) - \tilde{b}_i \cdot t =: Y(t)$$

and choosing

$$Y(t) \sim \mathcal{N}(0, \sigma^2 t),$$

we then have

- $E(Y(t)) = 0$,
- $Y(t)$ is obviously time dependent.

Further, by looking at

$$Y(t) = Y(\delta) + (Y(t) - Y(\delta)), \ \delta \in (0, t),$$

it appears reasonable to require that the distribution of the increments of the deviation $Y(t) - Y(\delta)$ only depends on the time span $t - \delta$ and is independent of $Y(s)$, $s \leq \delta$. In particular, $Y(t) - Y(\delta)$ would then be distributed according to $\mathcal{N}\left(0, \sigma^2(t-\delta)\right)$.

Existence and properties of such a family of random variables $\{Y(t)\}_{t \in [0, \infty)}$ (a so-called stochastic process) will be studied in greater detail in the following excursion on the Brownian motion.

Excursion 1: Brownian Motion and Martingales

> **General assumptions**
> Let $(\Omega, \mathcal{F}, P)$ be a complete probability space with sample space Ω, σ-field $\mathcal{F}$ and probability measure P.

We start by introducing the concept of a filtration. This is the formalization of a model describing the flow of information over time.

Definition 2.1. Let $\{\mathcal{F}_t\}_{t \in I}$ be a family of sub-σ-fields of $\mathcal{F}$, I be an ordered index set with $\mathcal{F}_s \subset \mathcal{F}_t$ for $s < t$, $s, t \in I$. Such a family $\{\mathcal{F}_t\}_{t \in I}$ is called a *filtration*.

The σ-field $\mathcal{F}_t$, $t \in I$, usually models the events which can be observed up to time t. Thus, if a random variable X_t is $\mathcal{F}_t$-measurable, we are able to determine its value from the information given at time t. In the following, the notion of a stochastic process will always be connected with a filtration.

Definition 2.2. A set $\{(X_t, \mathcal{F}_t)\}_{t \in I}$ consisting of a filtration $\{\mathcal{F}_t\}_{t \in I}$ and a family of $\mathbb{R}^n$-valued random variables $\{X_t\}_{t \in I}$ with X_t being $\mathcal{F}_t$-measurable is called a *stochastic process* with filtration $\{\mathcal{F}_t\}_{t \in I}$.

Remark 2.3. (1) In the following, we shall usually choose $I = [0, \infty)$ or $I = [0, T]$ as index set.

(2) If we simply talk of a process $\{X_t\}_{t \in I}$ or X_t, then this implies the choice of the filtration
$$\mathcal{F}_t := \mathcal{F}_t^X := \sigma\{X_s \mid s \leq t, \, s \in I\}.$$
This filtration is called the *canonical* or the *natural filtration* of $\{X_t\}_{t \in I}$.

(3) Instead of $\{X_t\}_{t \in I}$ we often write $\{X(t)\}_{t \in I}$ or (for short) X. For a fixed $\omega \in \Omega$, the set
$$X.(\omega) := \{X_t(\omega)\}_{t \in I} = \{X(t, \omega)\}_{t \in I}$$

can be interpreted as a function of time t. Such a function is called a *sample path* or a *realization of the stochastic process*. According to this interpretation a stochastic process is nothing else than a function-valued random variable.

In some proofs it will be important to decide if two stochastic processes can be identified with each other. We hereby distinguish between two different concepts:

Definition 2.4. Let $\{(X_t, \mathcal{F}_t)\}_{t \in [0,\infty)}$ and $\{(Y_t, \mathcal{G}_t)\}_{t \in [0,\infty)}$ be two stochastic processes. Y is called a *modification* of X, if we have

$$P\{\omega \mid X_t(\omega) = Y_t(\omega)\} = 1 \text{ for all } t \geq 0.$$

Definition 2.5. Let $\{(X_t, \mathcal{F}_t)\}_{t \in [0,\infty)}$ and $\{(Y_t, \mathcal{G}_t)\}_{t \in [0,\infty)}$ be two stochastic processes. X and Y are called *indistinguishable* if we have

$$P\{\omega \mid X_t(\omega) = Y_t(\omega) \text{ for all } t \in [0, \infty)\} = 1.$$

If X and Y are indistinguishable then Y is also a modification of X. The converse is not true. Y may be a modification of X, but both processes may have totally different paths. However, we can state (see Exercise (1)):

Theorem 2.6. *Let the stochastic process Y be a modification of X. Further, if both processes have continuous sample paths P-almost surely, then X and Y are indistinguishable.*

For our purposes the most important example of a stochastic process is

The Brownian Motion.

The real-valued process $\{W_t\}_{t \geq 0}$ with continuous sample paths and
   i) $W_0 = 0$ *P*-a.s.
   ii) $W_t - W_s \sim \mathcal{N}(0, t-s)$ for $0 \leq s < t$, *"stationary increments"*
   iii) $W_t - W_s$ independent of $W_u - W_r$ for $0 \leq r \leq u \leq s < t$,
                                                                                     "independent increments"
is called a *one-dimensional Brownian motion*.

By an *n-dimensional Brownian motion* we mean the $\mathbb{R}^n$-valued process

$$W(t) = (W_1(t), ..., W_n(t)),$$

with components W_i being independent one-dimensional Brownian motions.

Brownian motion and Brownian filtration. Of course, Brownian motion can be associated with its natural filtration,

$$\mathcal{F}_t^W := \sigma\{W_s \mid 0 \le s \le t\}, \quad t \in [0, \infty).$$

However, for technical reasons we shall typically work with the *P-augmentation of the natural filtration*,

$$\mathcal{F}_t := \sigma\{\mathcal{F}_t^W \cup N \mid N \in \mathcal{F}, P(N) = 0\}, \quad t \in [0, \infty),$$

and call it the *Brownian filtration*. One advantage of working with the Brownian filtration is the following: If the stochastic process Y is a modification of X then the $\mathcal{F}_t$-measurability of X_t also implies $\mathcal{F}_t$-measurability of Y_t. Hence, X and Y are measurable with respect to the same filtration.

In the literature, the requirement iii) of independent increments of a Brownian motion with respect to a given filtration $\{\mathcal{F}_t\}_{t \ge 0}$ is typically stated as

iii)* $W_t - W_s$ independent of $\mathcal{F}_s$, $0 \le s < t$.

If $\{\mathcal{F}_t\}_{t \ge 0}$ is either the natural filtration or the Brownian filtration then the requirements iii) and iii)* are equivalent. However, this need not be the case for every arbitrary filtration! A trivial counterexample would be the filtration

$$\mathcal{G}_t := \sigma\{W_T, W_s \mid 0 \le s \le t\}.$$

In this case, requirement iii)* is not satisfied as W_T is obviously not independent of $\mathcal{G}_0$. Of course, requirement iii) - which is independent of the filtration - is still valid.

In the sequel, when we consider a Brownian motion $\{(W_t, \mathcal{F}_t)\}_{t \ge 0}$ with an arbitrary filtration $\{\mathcal{F}_t\}_{t \ge 0}$ we implicitly assume requirement iii)* to be fulfilled.

Remarks on the existence of the Brownian motion. Of course, the existence of Brownian motion as a stochastic process has to be shown, more precisely, the existence of a stochastic process satisfying the requirements characterizing a Brownian motion. There are different methods to construct such a process. All of these constructions and existence proofs are long and technical. A construction based on weak convergence and approximation by random walks can be found in [**BILL 68**]. Another approach consists of requiring the appropriate finite-dimensional distributions (i.e. the joint distributions of $(W_{t_1}, ..., W_{t_n})$ for an arbitrary n-tuple $(t_1, ..., t_n)$, $n \in \mathbb{N}$, $t_i \ne t_j$) having independent, stationary, and normally distributed increments. Then by Kolmogorov's theorem a suitable probability measure on a suitable measurable space can be constructed (see [**KA/SH 91**], section 2.2). The first proof of the existence of such a measure was given by Wiener in [**WIEN 23**]. It is therefore called *Wiener measure*, which is the reason for our use of the letter W and the use of the name *Wiener process* for a Brownian motion.

For technical reasons, in the theory of stochastic integration a filtration is usually required to be right-continuous (see also Exercise (4)).

Theorem 2.7. *The Brownian filtration $\{\mathcal{F}_t\}_{t\geq 0}$ is right-continuous as well as left-continuous, i.e. we have*

$$\mathcal{F}_t = \mathcal{F}_{t+} := \bigcap_{\varepsilon > 0} \mathcal{F}_{t+\varepsilon} \text{ and } \mathcal{F}_t = \mathcal{F}_{t-} := \sigma\left(\bigcup_{s<t} \mathcal{F}_s\right).$$

Proof: see [**KA/SH 91**], section 2.7.

Thus the Brownian filtration satisfies the usual conditions in the sense of

Definition 2.8. A filtration $\{\mathcal{G}_t\}_{t\geq 0}$ satisfies the *usual conditions* if it is right-continuous and $\mathcal{G}_0$ contains all P-null sets of $\mathcal{F}$.

General assumption for this section:
Let $\{\mathcal{F}_t\}_{t\geq 0}$ be a filtration which satisfies the usual conditions.

We now introduce a class of stochastic processes which will be fundamental for our applications in stochastic calculus and financial mathematics.

Definition 2.9. The real-valued process $\{(X_t, \mathcal{F}_t)\}_{t\in I}$ with $E|X_t| < \infty$ for all $t \in I$, where I is an ordered index set, is called:

a) a *super-martingale*, if for all $s, t \in I$ with $s \leq t$ we have

$$E(X_t|\mathcal{F}_s) \leq X_s \quad \text{a.s. } P,$$

b) a *sub-martingale*, if for all $s, t \in I$ with $s \leq t$ we have

$$E(X_t|\mathcal{F}_s) \geq X_s \quad \text{a.s. } P,$$

c) a *martingale*, if for all $s, t \in I$ with $s \leq t$ we have

$$E(X_t|\mathcal{F}_s) = X_s \quad \text{a.s. } P.$$

Interpretation of the martingale concept. Very often, martingales are used for modeling games of chance. If the sequence X_n, $n \in \mathbb{N}$, denotes the wealth of a gambler after his n-th participation in a fair game, then it should satisfy the martingale condition

$$E(X_{n+1}|\mathcal{F}_n) = X_n \quad \text{a.s. } P.$$

So, in the mean the player is as rich after the game as he was before. In this sense a favorable game (in the gambler's view) corresponds to a sub-martingale, while a super-martingale represents a non-favorable one. A typical example of a martingale is the tossing of a fair coin where a gambler receives one dollar if "head" occurs and has to pay one dollar if "tail" occurs.

Theorem 2.10. *A one-dimensional Brownian motion W_t is a martingale.*

Proof. By the usual requirement iii)* the increment $W_t - W_s$ is independent of $\mathcal{F}_s$ for $s \leq t$. Hence we have:

$$E(W_t \mid \mathcal{F}_s) = E(W_t - W_s + W_s \mid \mathcal{F}_s)$$
$$= E(W_t - W_s \mid \mathcal{F}_s) + W_s = E(W_t - W_s) + W_s = W_s$$

for $s \leq t$ P-almost surely. $\square$

Remark 2.11.   (1) More generally we have: each stochastic process with independent, centered increments is a martingale with respect to its natural filtration.

(2) The *Brownian motion with drift μ* and *volatility σ*

$$X_t := \mu t + \sigma W_t, \quad \mu \in \mathbb{R}, \quad \sigma \in \mathbb{R},$$

is a martingale if $\mu = 0$, a super-martingale if $\mu \leq 0$ and a sub-martingale if $\mu \geq 0$.

Theorem 2.12.   (1) *Let $\{(X_t, \mathcal{F}_t)\}_{t \in I}$ be a martingale and $\varphi : \mathbb{R} \to \mathbb{R}$ be a convex function with $E|\varphi(X_t)| < \infty$ for all $t \in I$. Then*

$$\{(\varphi(X_t), \mathcal{F}_t)\}_{t \in I}$$

is a sub-martingale.

(2) *Let $\{(X_t, \mathcal{F}_t)\}_{t \in I}$ be a sub-martingale and $\varphi : \mathbb{R} \to \mathbb{R}$ a convex, non-decreasing function with $E|\varphi(X_t)| < \infty$ for all $t \in I$. Then*

$$\{(\varphi(X_t), \mathcal{F}_t)\}_{t \in I}$$

is a sub-martingale.

Proof. For $t \geq s$, Jensen's inequality implies

$$E(\varphi(X_t) \mid \mathcal{F}_t) \geq \varphi(E(X_t \mid \mathcal{F}_t)) \begin{cases} = \varphi(X_s) & \text{if } X \text{ martingale,} \\ \geq \varphi(X_s) & \text{if } X \text{ sub-martingale.} \end{cases}$$

$\square$

Remark 2.13.   (1) Typical applications of the theorem are given by

$$\varphi(x) = x^2 \quad , \quad \varphi(x) = |x|.$$

(2) The theorem is also valid for d-dimensional vectors

$$X(t) = (X_1(t), \ldots, X_d(t))$$

of martingales and convex functions $\varphi : \mathbb{R}^d \to \mathbb{R}$.

The concept of a local martingale plays an important role in stochastic calculus. To introduce this concept we first need to know more about stopping times.

Definition 2.14. A *stopping time* with respect to a filtration $\{\mathcal{F}_t\}_{t\in[0,\infty)}$ (or $\{\mathcal{F}_n\}_{n\in\mathbb{N}}$) is an $\mathcal{F}$-measurable random variable

$$\tau : \Omega \to [0,\infty] \quad (\text{or } \tau : \Omega \to \mathbb{N} \cup \{\infty\})$$

with $\{\omega \in \Omega | \tau(\omega) \le t\} \in \mathcal{F}_t$ for all $t \in [0,\infty)$ (or $\{\omega \in \Omega | \tau(\omega) \le n\} \in \mathcal{F}_n$ for all $n \in \mathbb{N}$).

Theorem 2.15. *If τ_1, τ_2 are both stopping times then $\tau_1 \wedge \tau_2 := \min\{\tau_1, \tau_2\}$ is also a stopping time.* (The simple proof will be left as an exercise.)

The stopped process. Let $\{(X_t, \mathcal{F}_t)\}_{t \in I}$ be a stochastic process, let I be either $\mathbb{N}$ or $[0,\infty)$, and τ a stopping time. Then we can define a new process, the stopped process $\{X_{t\wedge\tau}\}_{t\in I}$, by

$$X_{t\wedge\tau}(\omega) := \begin{cases} X_t(\omega) & \text{if } t \le \tau(\omega), \\ X_{\tau(\omega)}(\omega) & \text{if } t > \tau(\omega). \end{cases}$$

The stopping time thus determines the moment at which we stop the process and "freeze" it in its current state. The requirement $\{\omega \in \Omega | \tau(\omega) \le t\} \in \mathcal{F}_t$ on a stopping time means exactly that at time t we should be able to decide if we want to stop the process immediately or not.

Remark 2.16. A typical example of a stopped process is the wealth of a gambler who participates in a sequence of games until he is either bankrupt or has reached a given level of wealth. On the other hand, the rule to stop gambling if the wealth in a given time interval has reached its maximum, is not a stopping time. In this case the decision when to stop can only be made afterwards and not in real time (see also Exercise (2)).

The stopped filtration. Let τ be a stopping time with respect to a filtration $\{\mathcal{F}_t\}_{t\in[0,\infty)}$. We then define the *$\sigma$-field $\mathcal{F}_\tau$ of events determined prior to the stopping time τ* by

$$\mathcal{F}_\tau := \{A \in \mathcal{F} \mid A \cap \{\tau \le t\} \in \mathcal{F}_t \text{ for all } t \in [0,\infty)\}.$$

Then τ is $\mathcal{F}_\tau$-measurable. As with τ, $\tau \wedge t$ is also a stopping time, so we can define the *stopped filtration* $\{\mathcal{F}_{\tau \wedge t}\}_{t \in [0,\infty)}$. Note that in particular $\mathcal{F}_{\tau \wedge t} \subset \mathcal{F}_t$.

What will happen now if we stop a martingale or a sub-martingale by means of a stopping time? Will it remain a martingale or a sub-martingale? This will be answered by the following theorem.

Theorem 2.17 ("optional sampling"). *Let $\{(X_t, \mathcal{F}_t)\}_{t \in [0,\infty)}$ be a right-continuous sub-martingale (or martingale). Let τ_1, τ_2 be stopping times with $\tau_1 \leq \tau_2$. Then for all $t \in [0, \infty)$ we have*

$$E\left(X_{t \wedge \tau_2} \mid \mathcal{F}_{t \wedge \tau_1}\right) \geq X_{t \wedge \tau_1} \ a.s. \ P$$

(or

$$E\left(X_{t \wedge \tau_2} \mid \mathcal{F}_{t \wedge \tau_1}\right) = X_{t \wedge \tau_1} \ a.s. \ P).$$

Proof: see [**KA/SH 91**], theorem I.3.22.

Corollary 2.18. *Let τ be a stopping time and $\{(X_t, \mathcal{F}_t)\}_{t \in [0,\infty)}$ a right-continuous sub-martingale (or martingale). Then the stopped process $\{(X_{t \wedge \tau}, \mathcal{F}_t)\}_{t \in [0,\infty)}$ is also a sub-martingale (or a martingale, respectively).*
Proof: see Exercise (2).

With the help of the optional sampling theorem we obtain a useful characterization of a martingale.

Theorem 2.19. *Let $\{(X_t, \mathcal{F}_t)\}_{t \in [0,\infty)}$ be a right-continuous process. Then X_t is a martingale if and only if for all bounded stopping times τ we have*

$$EX_\tau = EX_0.$$

Proof. As τ is a bounded stopping time we have $\tau(\omega) \leq T$ for some $T > 0$ and all $\omega \in \Omega$, i.e. $\tau = \tau \wedge T$. Thus we can apply the optional sampling Theorem 2.17 and obtain

$$EX_\tau = E\left(E\left(X_{\tau \wedge T} \mid \mathcal{F}_0\right)\right) = E(X_0)$$

for a martingale X. To prove the converse direction of the theorem, let $0 \leq s \leq t$, $A \in \mathcal{F}_s$. Then $\tau := s \cdot 1_{\Omega \setminus A} + t \cdot 1_A$ defines a stopping time with $\tau = \tau \wedge t$. This implies

$$EX_0 = EX_\tau = E\left(X_s \cdot 1_{\Omega \setminus A} + X_t \cdot 1_A\right) = E\left(X_s \cdot 1_{\Omega \setminus A}\right) + E\left(X_t \cdot 1_A\right).$$

Further $\tau \equiv s$ is a stopping time with

$$EX_0 = EX_s = E\left(X_s \cdot 1_{\Omega \setminus A}\right) + E\left(X_s \cdot 1_A\right).$$

Hence, for all $A \in \mathcal{F}_s$ we have

$$E\left(X_t \cdot 1_A\right) = E\left(X_s \cdot 1_A\right).$$

Using the definition of the conditional expectation, we obtain

$$E\left(X_t \mid \mathcal{F}_s\right) = X_s,$$

and thus $\{(X_t, \mathcal{F}_t)\}_{t \in [0,\infty)}$ is a martingale. □

With the help of stopping times the notion of a martingale can be weakened.

Definition 2.20. Let $\{(X_t, \mathcal{F}_t)\}_{t \in [0,\infty)}$ be a stochastic process with $X_0 = 0$. If there exists a non-decreasing sequence $\{\tau_n\}_{n \in \mathbb{N}}$ of stopping times with
$$P\left(\lim_{n \to \infty} \tau_n = \infty\right) = 1,$$
such that
$$\left\{\left(X_t^{(n)} := X_{t \wedge \tau_n}, \mathcal{F}_t\right)\right\}_{t \in [0,\infty)}$$
is a martingale for all $n \in \mathbb{N}$, then X is called a *local martingale*. The sequence $\{\tau_n\}_{n \in \mathbb{N}}$ is called a *localizing sequence* corresponding to X.

Remark 2.21. (1) Each martingale is a local martingale.
  (2) If X is a local martingale with continuous paths, then it is called a continuous local martingale.
  (3) There exist local martingales which are not martingales (see e.g. **[KA/SH 91]**). Note therefore also that $E(X_t)$ need not exist for a local martingale. However, the expectation has to exist along the localizing sequence $t \wedge \tau_n$. In particular, the local martingale X is a martingale on the random time intervals $[0, \tau_n]$.

Theorem 2.22. *A non-negative local martingale is a super-martingale.*

Proof. Let M be a non-negative local martingale. Then there exists a sequence $\{\tau_n\}_{n \in \mathbb{N}}$ of stopping times with
$$E(M_{t \wedge \tau_n} | \mathcal{F}_s) = M_{s \wedge \tau_n} \text{ and } \tau_n \xrightarrow{n \to \infty} \infty \quad \text{a.s. } P.$$
Hence, Fatou's lemma implies
$$M_s = \lim_{n \to \infty} \inf M_{s \wedge \tau_n} = \lim_{n \to \infty} \inf E(M_{t \wedge \tau_n} | \mathcal{F}_s)$$
$$\geq E\left(\lim_{n \to \infty} \inf M_{t \wedge \tau_n} | \mathcal{F}_s\right) = E(M_t | \mathcal{F}_s) \quad \text{a.s. } P.$$
$\square$

The following inequalities will prove to be useful later on.

Theorem 2.23 (Doob's inequality). *Let $\{M_t\}_{t \geq 0}$ be a martingale with right-continuous paths and $E(M_T^2) < \infty$ for all $T > 0$. Then, we have*
$$E\left(\left(\sup_{0 \leq t \leq T} |M_t|\right)^2\right) \leq 4 \cdot E(M_T^2).$$

Theorem 2.24. *Let $\{(X_t, \mathcal{F}_t)\}_{t \in [0,\infty)}$ be a non-negative super-martingale with right-continuous paths. Then, for $\lambda > 0$ we obtain*
$$\lambda \cdot P\left\{\omega \,\Big|\, \sup_{0 \leq s \leq t} X_s(\omega) \geq \lambda\right\} \leq E(X_0).$$

Proof. The proofs of theorems 2.23 and 2.24 can be found with the help of theorems 1.3.8 (ii) and (iv) in [**KA/SH 91**]. For this, note that $\{-X_t\}_t$ is a non-positive sub-martingale and $\{|M_t|\}_{t\geq 0}$ is a non-negative super-martingale.

2.1. Continuation: Modeling the Security Prices

Continuation: The stock price. In Brownian motion $\{(W_t, \mathcal{F}_t)\}_{t\geq 0}$ we have found the appropriate stochastic process to model the "randomness" in the log-linear form of the stock price. In the case of $d = 1$ (i.e. a market model with solely one stock and one bond), it is natural to choose a Brownian motion with *volatility* σ_{11} for the "randomness",

$$\ln(P_1(t)) = \ln(p_1) + \tilde{b}_1 \cdot t + \sigma_{11} W_t.$$

Hence, we obtain

$$P_1(t) = p_1 \cdot e^{\tilde{b}_1 t + \sigma_{11} W_t}.$$

In the general d-dimensional case we choose

$$(2.3) \qquad \ln(P_i(t)) = \ln(p_i) + \tilde{b}_i \cdot t + \sum_{j=1}^{m} \sigma_{ij} W_j(t), \ i = 1, ..., d,$$

and consequently

$$(2.4) \qquad P_i(t) = p_i \cdot \exp\left(\tilde{b}_i \cdot t + \sum_{j=1}^{m} \sigma_{ij} W_j(t)\right), \quad i = 1, ..., d,$$

where $W(t) = (W_1(t), ..., W_m(t))$ is an m-dimensional Brownian motion. This leads to a distribution of the logarithm of the stock prices given by

$$\ln(P_i(t)) \sim N(\ln(p_i) + \tilde{b}_i \cdot t, \sum_{j=1}^{m} \sigma_{ij}^2 \cdot t).$$

Therefore, we say that $P_i(t)$ is *log-normally distributed*. Further properties of the stock price given by equation (2.4) follow from the next lemma.

Lemma 2.25. *Let* $b_i := \tilde{b}_i + \frac{1}{2}\sum_{j=1}^{m}\sigma_{ij}^2$ *and* $P_i(t)$ *as in equation* (2.4), $i = 1, ..., d, t \geq 0$. *Then we have*

(1) $E(P_i(t)) = p_i \cdot e^{b_i t}.$

(2) $Var(P_i(t)) = p_i^2 \cdot \exp(2b_i t) \cdot \left(\exp\left(\sum_{j=1}^{m}\sigma_{ij}^2 t\right) - 1\right).$

(3) $X_t := a \cdot \exp\left(\sum_{j=1}^{m}\left(c_j W_j(t) - \tfrac{1}{2}c_j^2 t\right)\right)$ with $a, c_j \in \mathbb{R}$, $j = 1, ..., m$,
is a martingale.

Proof.

(1) We only consider the case $m = 1$. The general case can be proved similarly by noting the fact that

$$\sum_{j=1}^{m} \sigma_{ij} W_j(t) \sim \mathcal{N}(0, \sum_{j=1}^{m} \sigma_{ij}^2 t).$$

Completing the square in the exponent in the following chain of equalities yields:

$$E(P_i(t)) = p_i \cdot \int_{-\infty}^{\infty} \tfrac{1}{\sqrt{2\pi t}} \cdot e^{\tilde{b}_i t + \sigma x} \cdot e^{-\tfrac{x^2}{2t}} dx$$

$$= p_i \cdot \int_{-\infty}^{\infty} \tfrac{1}{\sqrt{2\pi t}} \cdot e^{\tilde{b}_i t + \tfrac{1}{2}\sigma^2 t} \cdot e^{-\tfrac{(x - \sigma t)^2}{2t}} dx$$

$$= p_i \cdot e^{b_i t} \cdot \int_{-\infty}^{\infty} \tfrac{1}{\sqrt{2\pi t}} \cdot e^{-\tfrac{(x - \sigma t)^2}{2t}} dx = p_i \cdot e^{b_i t} \cdot 1.$$

Note that for the last equality sign we have used the fact that the integrand is the density of an $\mathcal{N}(\sigma t, t)$-distributed random variable.

(2) This is proved similar to (1) via computing $E(P_i^2(t))$ in analogous fashion (see Exercise (3)).

(3) Again we only prove the case $m = 1$. Let $t \geq s \geq 0$. Then we have

$$E(X_t \mid \mathcal{F}_s) = a \cdot e^{c_1 W_s - \tfrac{1}{2}c_1^2 s} \cdot E\left(e^{c_1(W_t - W_s) - \tfrac{1}{2}c_1^2(t-s)} \mid \mathcal{F}_s\right)$$

$$= a \cdot e^{c_1 W_s - \tfrac{1}{2}c_1^2 s} \cdot E\left(e^{c_1(W_t - W_s) - \tfrac{1}{2}c_1^2(t-s)}\right)$$

$$= a \cdot e^{c_1 W_s - \tfrac{1}{2}c_1^2 s} \cdot E\left(e^{c_1 \tilde{W}_{t-s} - \tfrac{1}{2}c_1^2(t-s)}\right) = X_s.$$

Here the second equality is implied by the independence of the increments of $W(t)$. As $\tilde{W}_{t-s} := W_t - W_s$ also defines a Brownian motion, we can use (1) to conclude that the last expectation equals 1. □

2.1. Continuation: Modeling the Security Prices

Interpretation of the stock price model. Lemma 2.25 yields a new interpretation of our stock price model:

$$(2.5) \quad P_i(t) = p_i \cdot e^{b_i t} \cdot e^{\sum_{j=1}^{m} \left(\sigma_{ij} W_j(t) - \frac{1}{2}\sigma_{ij}^2 t\right)},$$
$$P_i(0) = p_i, \quad i = 1, ..., d.$$

Thus, the stock price is the product of

- the mean stock price $p_i \cdot e^{b_i t}$ and
- a martingale with expectation 1, namely

$$\exp\left(\sum_{j=1}^{m} [\sigma_{ij} W_j(t) - \tfrac{1}{2}\sigma_{ij}^2 t]\right),$$

which models the fluctuation of the stock price around its mean value.

The vector

$$b = (b_1, ..., b_d)'$$

will be called *vector of mean rates of stock returns*.

The matrix

$$\sigma = \begin{pmatrix} \sigma_{11} & \cdots & \sigma_{1m} \\ \vdots & \ddots & \vdots \\ \sigma_{d1} & \cdots & \sigma_{dm} \end{pmatrix}$$

is known as the *volatility matrix*.

Further, a stochastic process of the form $P_i(t)$ will also be called a *geometric Brownian motion* with drift b_i and volatility $\sigma_{i\cdot} = (\sigma_{i1}, \ldots, \sigma_{im})'$.

Summary: Stock prices. In the continuous-time setting we model the bond price and the stock prices according to

$$P_0(t) = p_0 \cdot e^{rt}, \quad P_0(0) =: p_0,$$

$$P_i(t) = p_i \cdot e^{b_i t} \cdot e^{\sum_{j=1}^{m} [\sigma_{ij} W_j(t) - \frac{1}{2}\sigma_{ij}^2 t]}, \quad P_i(0) =: p_i, \; i = 1, ..., d.$$

Unfortunately, we are not able to formulate a more general form of the model allowing for non-constant, time-dependent, and integrable rates of return $b_i(t)$ and volatilities $\sigma(t)$. In that case the stock prices should look like:

$$P_i(t) = p_i \cdot \exp\left(\int_0^t \left(b_i(s) - \tfrac{1}{2}\sum_{j=1}^m \sigma_{ij}^2(s)\right) ds\right)$$
$$\cdot \exp\left(\sum_{j=1}^m \int_0^t \sigma_{ij}(s)\, dW_j(s)\right).$$

Note the appearance of the yet unknown integral

$$\int_0^t \sigma_{ij}(s)\, dW_j(s) = \ ?$$

To be able to formulate such a model, to describe trading strategies and to judge them, we need the concept of the stochastic integral (also called: Itô integral) and the corresponding rules of the Itô calculus.

Excursion 2: The Itô Integral

Motivation. Consider the measurable space $(\mathbb{R}, \mathcal{B}(\mathbb{R}))$ of real numbers equipped with the Borel σ-field. If F is now a differentiable distribution function and X a measurable, non-negative real-valued function on $(\mathbb{R}, \mathcal{B}(\mathbb{R}))$, then the following integral can be computed with the help of the density $f(s) = \frac{dF(s)}{ds}$:

$$\int_0^t X(s)\, dF(s) = \int_0^t X(s) f(s)\, ds \text{ for } t > 0.$$

If the distribution function F is not differentiable then this integral can be computed in the Lebesgue-Stieltjes sense, if X is continuous, e.g., as

$$\int_0^t X\, dF = \lim_{n\to\infty} \sum_{k=1}^n X\left(\frac{(k-1)t}{n}\right) \cdot \left(F\left(\frac{kt}{n}\right) - F\left(\frac{(k-1)t}{n}\right)\right).$$

(Note that the value of the integral does not change if we replace $X((k-1)t/n)$ by $X(kt/n)$ or any other value $X(s)$ for $s \in [(k-1)t/n, kt/n]$ for taking the limit. This will not be the case for stochastic integrals, see e.g. [**OKS 92**], Example 3.1.)

This can easily be generalized (see [**KA/SH 91**], section 1.4). Therefore, let $(\Omega, \mathcal{F}, P)$ be a complete probability space and $\{A_t\}_{t\in[0,\infty)}$ an increasing process (i.e. $A_0(\omega) = 0$ for $\omega \in \Omega$, the paths $t \mapsto A_t(\omega)$ are non-decreasing, right-continuous functions and $E(A_t) < \infty$ for all $t \in [0, \infty)$).

Let $\{X_t\}_{t\in[0,\infty)}$ be a non-negative process with $\mathcal{B}([0,\infty))$-$\mathcal{B}(\mathbb{R})$-measurable paths $t \mapsto X_t(\omega)$. Then, for each fixed $\omega \in \Omega$ the following integral can be computed in the Lebesgue-Stieltjes sense:

$$I_t(\omega) := \int_0^t X_s(\omega) \, dA_s(\omega).$$

Given that $I_t(.)$ is $\mathcal{F}$-$\mathcal{B}(\mathbb{R})$-measurable (this can always be achieved by requiring certain suitable properties of X), we obtain a new random variable for each $t \in [0, \infty)$, i.e. a new stochastic process. This kind of integral can also be extended to the case where A_t possesses paths of finite variation on each finite time interval $[0, T]$.

There remains the question of whether this approach can even be generalized to the case of the integrator being a one-dimensional Brownian motion $\{W_t\}_{t\in[0,\infty)}$. Is it possible to define the following integral

$$\int_0^t X_s(\omega) \, dW_s(\omega),$$

the so-called *stochastic integral*, ω-wise in a reasonable way?

First, we have to realize that imitating the situation with an existing density is not possible (for a proof of the following theorem see [**KA/SH 91**], p.110).

Theorem 2.26. *P-almost all paths of the Brownian motion $\{W_t\}_{t\in[0,\infty)}$ are nowhere differentiable.*

Hence, a definition of the form

$$\int_0^t X_s(\omega) \, dW_s(\omega) = \int_0^t X_s(\omega) \, \frac{dW_s(\omega)}{ds} ds$$

is *impossible*. Moreover, the next theorem even shows that a definition as a Lebesgue-Stieltjes integral is also impossible (see [**KA/SH 91**], p.35, p.130).

Theorem 2.27. *With the definition*

$$Z_n(\omega) := \sum_{i=1}^{2^n} \left| W_{i/2^n}(\omega) - W_{i-1/2^n}(\omega) \right|, \quad n \in \mathbb{N}, \omega \in \Omega,$$

we have

$$Z_n(\omega) \xrightarrow{n \to \infty} \infty \text{ a.s. } P,$$

i.e. the paths $W_t(\omega)$ of the Brownian motion admit infinite variation on the interval $[0, 1]$ P-almost surely. Even more: the paths $W_t(\omega)$ of the

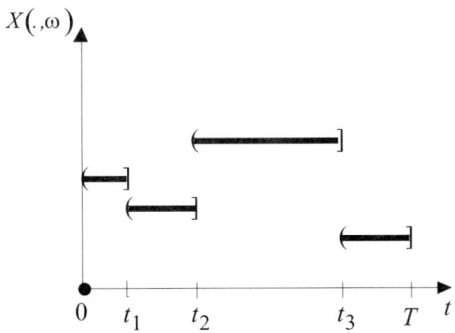

Figure 2.3. Path of a simple process

Brownian motion have infinite variation on each non-empty finite interval $[s_1, s_2] \subset [0, \infty)$ P-almost surely.

Due to the two foregoing negative results, the stochastic integral that we want to define must be a new kind of integral. In the sequel we shall start by constructing it for so-called simple processes X_t. Then, it will be extended to more general integrands with the help of an isometry.

> **General assumptions for this section:**
> Let $(\Omega, \mathcal{F}, P)$ be a complete probability space equipped with a filtration $\{\mathcal{F}_t\}_t$ satisfying the usual conditions. Further assume that on this space a Brownian motion $\{(W_t, \mathcal{F}_t)\}_{t \in [0, \infty)}$ with respect to this filtration is defined.

Definition 2.28. A stochastic process $\{X_t\}_{t \in [0,T]}$ is called a *simple process* if there exist real numbers $0 = t_0 < t_1 < ... < t_p = T$, $p \in \mathbb{N}$, and bounded random variables $\Phi_i : \Omega \to \mathbb{R}$, $i = 0, 1, ..., p$, with

Φ_0 $\mathcal{F}_0$-measurable, Φ_i, $i = 1, ..., p$, $F_{t_{i-1}}$-measurable,

such that $X_t(\omega)$ has the following representation

$$X_t(\omega) = X(t, \omega) = \Phi_0(\omega) \cdot 1_{\{0\}}(t) + \sum_{i=1}^{p} \Phi_i(\omega) \cdot 1_{(t_{i-1}, t_i]}(t)$$

for each $\omega \in \Omega$.

Remark 2.29.   (1) Note that X_t is $F_{t_{i-1}}$-measurable for all $t \in (t_{i-1}, t_i]$.

(2) The paths $X(., \omega)$ of the simple process X_t are left-continuous step functions with height $\Phi_i(\omega) \cdot 1_{(t_{i-1}, t_i]}(t)$ (see Figure 2.3).

Definition 2.30. For a simple process $\{X_t\}_{t\in[0,T]}$ the *stochastic integral* $I.(X)$ for $t \in (t_k, t_{k+1}]$ is defined according to

$$I_t(X) := \int_0^t X_s \, dW_s := \sum_{1 \leq i \leq k} \Phi_i \left(W_{t_i} - W_{t_{i-1}} \right) + \Phi_{k+1} \left(W_t - W_{t_k} \right),$$

or more generally for $t \in [0, T]$:

$$I_t(X) := \int_0^t X_s \, dW_s := \sum_{1 \leq i \leq p} \Phi_i \left(W_{t_i \wedge t} - W_{t_{i-1} \wedge t} \right).$$

Hence, on each interval where X is constant, the increments of the Brownian motion on that interval are multiplied with the corresponding value of X_t, namely Φ_i. (Compare this with the Lebesgue-Stieltjes integral for simple functions.)

Theorem 2.31 (Elementary properties of the stochastic integral). *Let $X := \{X_t\}_{t\in[0,T]}$ be a simple process. Then we have:*

(1) $\{(I_t(X)\}_{t\in[0,T]}$ *is a continuous martingale with respect to* $\{\mathcal{F}_t\}_{t\in[0,T]}$. *In particular, we have* $E(I_t(X)) = 0$ *for all* $t \in [0,T]$.

(2) $E \left(\int_0^t X_s \, dW_s \right)^2 = E \left(\int_0^t X_s^2 \, ds \right)$ *for* $t \in [0, T]$.

(3) $E \left(\sup\limits_{0 \leq t \leq T} \left| \int_0^t X_s \, dW_s \right| \right)^2 \leq 4 \cdot E \left(\int_0^T X_s^2 \, ds \right)$.

Remark 2.32. (1) By Theorem 2.31 (2) the stochastic integral is a square-integrable stochastic process.

(2) For the simple process $X \equiv 1$ we obtain

$$\int_0^t 1 \, dW_s = W_t,$$

and Theorem 2.31 (2) implies

(2.6) $$E \left(\int_0^t dW_s \right)^2 = E \left(W_t^2 \right) = t = \int_0^t ds.$$

This relation is often described by

$$dW_t = \sqrt{dt}.$$

However, this should always be understood in the sense of relation (2.6) and not as equality of two differentials.

Proof of Theorem 2.31.

(1) As Φ_i is $\mathcal{F}_{t_{i-1}}$-measurable and W_{t_k} is $\mathcal{F}_t$-measurable for $t_k \leq t$ we obtain $\mathcal{F}_t$-measurability of $I_t(X)$. Continuity of $I_t(X)$ becomes obvious, if one notes the continuity of the paths of the Brownian motion. Let $t \in (t_{k-1}, t_k]$, $s \in (t_{l-1}, t_l]$ with $s < t$. W.l.o.g. we can assume $k > l$. As Φ_i, $i = 1, ..., l$, and W_r, $r \leq s$, are $\mathcal{F}_s$-measurable, we obtain

$$E(I_t(X)|\mathcal{F}_s) = E\left(\sum_{i=1}^{l-1} \Phi_i \left(W_{t_i} - W_{t_{i-1}}\right) + \Phi_l \left(W_{t_l} - W_s + W_s - W_{t_{l-1}}\right)\right.$$
$$\left. + \sum_{i=l+1}^{k-1} \Phi_i \left(W_{t_i} - W_{t_{i-1}}\right) + \Phi_k \left(W_t - W_{t_{k-1}}\right) \Big| \mathcal{F}_s\right)$$
$$= \sum_{i=1}^{l-1} \Phi_i \left(W_{t_i} - W_{t_{i-1}}\right) + \Phi_l \left(W_s - W_{t_{l-1}}\right)$$
$$+ \underbrace{E\left(\Phi_l \left(W_{t_l} - W_s\right) | \mathcal{F}_s\right)}_{=:A}$$
$$+ \underbrace{E\left(\sum_{i=l+1}^{k-1} \Phi_i \left(W_{t_i} - W_{t_{i-1}}\right) + \Phi_k \left(W_t - W_{t_{k-1}}\right) \Big| \mathcal{F}_s\right)}_{=:B}$$
$$= I_s(X) + A + B.$$

For $i \geq l+1$ and $u \geq t_{i-1}$ we have (note that in this case $t_{i-1} \geq s$)

$$E\left(\Phi_i \left(W_u - W_{t_{i-1}}\right) | \mathcal{F}_s\right)$$
$$= E\left(E\left(\Phi_i \left(W_u - W_{t_{i-1}}\right) | \mathcal{F}_s\right) | \mathcal{F}_{t_{i-1}}\right)$$
$$= E\left(E\left(\Phi_i \left(W_u - W_{t_{i-1}}\right) | \mathcal{F}_{t_{i-1}}\right) | \mathcal{F}_s\right)$$
$$= E\left(\Phi_i \cdot E\left(W_u - W_{t_{i-1}}\right) | \mathcal{F}_s\right) = 0.$$

Further, as Φ_l is $\mathcal{F}_s$-measurable and $W_{t_l} - W_s$ is independent of $\mathcal{F}_s$ and has zero expectation, the two terms A and B in the above sum equal zero. This implies $E(I_t(X) | \mathcal{F}_s) = I_s(X)$. The case of $s = 0$ can be shown similarly by doing some obvious modifications.

(2) For simplicity let $t := t_{k+1}$. Then:

$$E\left(I_t(X)^2\right) = E\left(\sum_{i=1}^{k} \sum_{j=1}^{k} \Phi_i \Phi_j \left(W_{t_i} - W_{t_{i-1}}\right)\left(W_{t_j} - W_{t_{j-1}}\right)\right).$$

First consider the case $i \neq j$. W.l.o.g. we can assume $i > j$:

$$E\left(\Phi_i \Phi_j \left(W_{t_i} - W_{t_{i-1}}\right) \left(W_{t_j} - W_{t_{j-1}}\right)\right)$$
$$= E\left(E\left(\Phi_i \Phi_j \left(W_{t_i} - W_{t_{i-1}}\right) \left(W_{t_j} - W_{t_{j-1}}\right) \big| \mathcal{F}_{t_{i-1}}\right)\right)$$
$$= E\left(\Phi_j \cdot \left(W_{t_j} - W_{t_{j-1}}\right) \cdot \Phi_i \cdot \underbrace{E\left(W_{t_i} - W_{t_{i-1}} \big| \mathcal{F}_{t_{i-1}}\right)}_{=0}\right) = 0.$$

In the case of $i = j$ we have

$$E\left(\Phi_i^2 \left(W_{t_i} - W_{t_{i-1}}\right)^2\right) = E\left(\Phi_i^2 \cdot E\left(\left(W_{t_i} - W_{t_{i-1}}\right)^2 \big| \mathcal{F}_{t_{i-1}}\right)\right)$$
$$= E\left(\Phi_i^2 \cdot (t_i - t_{i-1})\right)$$

due to the properties of the Brownian motion. Consequently

$$E\left(I_t(X)^2\right) = E\left(\sum_{i=1}^{k} \Phi_i^2 \cdot (t_i - t_{i-1})\right) = E\left(\int_0^t X_s^2 \, ds\right).$$

(3) is implied by (1) and (2) and Doob's inequality; see Theorem 2.23. □

Remark 2.33. (1) Integrals with general boundaries can be introduced by:

$$\int_t^T X_s \, dW_s := \int_0^T X_s \, dW_s - \int_0^t X_s \, dW_s \text{ for } t \leq T.$$

With this definition we have for $t \leq T$, $A \in \mathcal{F}_t$:

$$\int_0^T 1_A(\omega) \cdot X_s(\omega) \cdot 1_{[t,T]}(s) \, dW_s = 1_A(\omega) \cdot \int_t^T X_s(\omega) \, dW_s.$$

(2) Let X, Y be simple processes, $a, b \in \mathbb{R}$. Then the stochastic integral is linear:

$$I_t(aX + bY) = a \cdot I_t(X) + b \cdot I_t(Y).$$

As already indicated in the motivation part in the beginning of this excursion, we have to take a closer look at measurability assumptions for the stochastic process X to be able to define the stochastic integral for more general integrands in a reasonable way.

Definition 2.34. Let $\{(X_t, \mathcal{G}_t)\}_{t \in [0,\infty)}$ be a stochastic process. This stochastic process will be called *measurable* if the mapping

$$[0, \infty) \times \Omega \to \mathbb{R}^n$$
$$(s, \omega) \mapsto X_s(\omega)$$

is $\mathcal{B}([0,\infty)) \otimes \mathcal{F}$-$\mathcal{B}(\mathbb{R}^n)$-measurable.

Remark 2.35. Measurability of the process X in particular implies that for a fixed $\omega \in \Omega$, $X(., \omega)$ is $\mathcal{B}([0,\infty))$-$\mathcal{B}(\mathbb{R}^n)$-measurable. Thus, for all $t \in [0, \infty)$, $i = 1, ..., n$, the integral $\int_0^t X_i^2(s)\, ds$ is defined.

Definition 2.36. Let $\{(X_t, \mathcal{G}_t)\}_{t \in [0,\infty)}$ be a stochastic process. This stochastic process will be called *progressively measurable* if for all $t \geq 0$ the mapping

$$[0, t] \times \Omega \to \mathbb{R}^n$$
$$(s, \omega) \mapsto X_s(\omega)$$

is $\mathcal{B}([0,t]) \otimes \mathcal{G}_t$-$\mathcal{B}(\mathbb{R}^n)$-measurable.

Remark 2.37. (1) If the real-valued process $\{(X_t, \mathcal{G}_t)\}_{t \in [0,\infty)}$ is progressively measurable and bounded, then for all $t \in [0, \infty)$ the integral $\int_0^t X_s\, ds$ is $\mathcal{G}_t$-measurable.

(2) Obviously every progressively measurable process is measurable.

(3) It can be shown that each measurable process X possesses a progressively measurable modification (see a corresponding theorem of Chung and Doob in [**CH/DO 65**]).

The following theorem shows that progressive measurability is a generalization of right-continuity and left-continuity. So in particular, simple processes are progressively measurable.

Theorem 2.38. *If all paths of the stochastic process $\{(X_t, \mathcal{G}_t)\}_{t \in [0,\infty)}$ are right-continuous (or left-continuous), then the process is progressively measurable.*

Proof. We assume X to be right-continuous. The case of a left-continuous X follows similarly. Let $t > 0$, $m \in \mathbb{N}$, $k = 0, 1, ..., 2^m - 1$, $0 \leq s \leq t$ and define

$$X_0^{(m)}(\omega) := X_0(\omega),$$
$$X_s^{(m)}(\omega) := X_{(k+1)t/2^m}(\omega) \quad \text{for } \frac{kt}{2^m} < s \leq \frac{(k+1)t}{2^m}.$$

Obviously the mapping

$$[0, t] \times \Omega \to \mathbb{R}^n$$

$$(s, \omega) \mapsto X_s^{(m)}(\omega)$$

is $\mathcal{B}([0,t]) \otimes \mathcal{G}_t$-$\mathcal{B}(\mathbb{R}^n)$-measurable. As the process X_t possesses right-continuous paths, we further have

$$\lim_{m \to \infty} X_s^{(m)}(\omega) = X_s(\omega) \text{ for all } (s, \omega) \in [0, t] \times \Omega.$$

Consequently the P-almost surely limit $\omega \mapsto X_s(\omega)$ is also $\mathcal{B}([0,t]) \otimes \mathcal{G}_t$-$\mathcal{B}(\mathbb{R}^n)$-measurable. □

The following theorem yields an important property of progressively measurable processes, as we will see that the stopped process $\{X_{t \wedge \tau}\}_t$ is measurable with respect to the original filtration $\{\mathcal{F}_t\}_t$.

Theorem 2.39. *Let τ be a stopping time with respect to the filtration $\{\mathcal{G}_t\}_{t \in [0, \infty)}$. If the stochastic process $\{(X_t, \mathcal{G}_t)\}_{t \in [0, \infty)}$ is progressively measurable, then so is the stopped processs $\{(X_{t \wedge \tau}, \mathcal{G}_t)\}_{t \in [0, \infty)}$. In particular, $X_{t \wedge \tau}$ is both $\mathcal{G}_t$ and $\mathcal{G}_{t \wedge \tau}$-measurable.*

Proof. The mapping $(s, \omega) \mapsto X_{s \wedge \tau}(\omega)$ defined on $[0, t] \times \Omega \to \mathbb{R}^n$ is a composition of the mappings $f_1 : (s, \omega) \mapsto ((s \wedge \tau)(\omega), \omega)$ and $f_2 : (s, \omega) \mapsto X_s(\omega)$. f_1 is $\mathcal{B}([0,t])$-$\mathcal{G}_t$-measurable as $s \wedge \tau$ is $\mathcal{G}_{s \wedge \tau}$-measurable and $\mathcal{G}_{s \wedge \tau} \subset \mathcal{G}_t$. As X is progressively measurable, it is obvious that f_2 is $\mathcal{B}([0,t])$-$\mathcal{G}_t$-measurable. Putting these facts together we obtain the $\mathcal{B}([0,t])$-$\mathcal{G}_t$-measurability of $f_2 \circ f_1$. Hence, the process $\{(X_{t \wedge \tau}, \mathcal{G}_t)\}_{t \in [0, \infty)}$ is progressively measurable. To prove the $\mathcal{G}_{t \wedge \tau}$-measurability of $X_{t \wedge \tau}$ it must be shown that for an arbitrary $A \in \mathcal{B}(\mathbb{R}^n)$ we have

$$X_{t \wedge \tau}^{-1}(A) \cap \{t \wedge \tau \leq s\} \in G_s \text{ for all } s \geq 0.$$

In the case of $s > t$ we have $\{t \wedge \tau \leq s\} = \Omega$ and $X_{t \wedge \tau}^{-1}(A) \in G_t \subset G_s$, as $\{(X_{t \wedge \tau}, \mathcal{G}_t)\}_{t \in [0, \infty)}$ is progressively measurable.

In the case of $s \leq t$ we have $X_{t \wedge \tau}^{-1}(A) \cap \{t \wedge \tau \leq s\} = X_{t \wedge s \wedge \tau}^{-1}(A) \cap \{t \wedge \tau \leq s\} \in G_s \cap G_s$ as $\{(X_{s \wedge \tau}, \mathcal{G}_s)\}_{s \in [0, \infty)}$ is progressively measurable and $t \wedge \tau$ is a stopping time. □

Extension of the stochastic integral to $L^2[0, T]$-processes. Based on the above discussion we require integrands to be progressively measurable when we want to extend the stochastic integral to more general integrals than just simple processes. Further, to be able to define a norm for stochastic integrals, we consider the following vector space:

> $$L^2[0,T] := L^2\left([0,T], \Omega, \mathcal{F}, \{\mathcal{F}_t\}_{t\in[0,T]}, P\right)$$
> $$:= \left\{\{(X_t, \mathcal{F}_t)\}_{t\in[0,T]} \text{ real-valued stochastic process } \mid \right.$$
> $$\left. \{X_t\}_t \text{ progressively measurable}, E\left(\int_0^T X_t^2\, dt\right) < \infty\right\}$$

To define a norm on $L^2[0,T]$, we set

$$\|X\|_T^2 := E\left(\int_0^T X_t^2\, dt\right).$$

This is the well-known L^2-norm on the probability space $([0,T] \times \Omega, \mathcal{B}([0,T]) \otimes \mathcal{F}, \lambda \otimes P)$. In fact, it is only a semi-norm as $\|X - Y\|_T^2 = 0$ does not necessarily imply $X = Y$; we can only deduce $X = Y$ a.s. $\lambda \otimes P$. We then say that the process X is *equivalent* to the process Y.

For simple processes X the mapping $X \to I.(X)$ induces a norm on the space of stochastic integrals given by

$$\|I.(X)\|_{L_T}^2 := E\left(\int_0^T X_s\, dW_s\right)^2 = E\left(\int_0^T X_s^2\, ds\right) = \|X\|_T^2.$$

Hence, the mapping $I.(X)$ is linear and norm-preserving and thus an isometry, the so-called *Itô isometry*.

We shall now extend the stochastic integral $I.(X)$ to processes $X \in L^2[0,T]$. To do this, we use on one hand those processes $X \in L^2[0,T]$ that can be approximated by a sequence $X^{(n)}$ of simple processes. On the other hand we also use the statement that by the Itô isometry, the corresponding sequence $I.(X^{(n)})$ of stochastic integrals is a Cauchy sequence with respect to the L_T-norm. It remains to prove that this Cauchy sequence converges and that the limit is independent of the approximating sequence $X^{(n)}$. We shall then denote the limit by $I(X) = \int X_s\, dW_s$. This extension of stochastic integrals to L^2-processes is illustrated by Figure 2.4 (where M_2^c denotes the space of continuous, square integrable martingales).

Please note again that for a simple process $X^{(n)}$ we have:

$$\left\|X^{(n)}\right\|_T = \left\|I\left(X^{(n)}\right)\right\|_{L_T}.$$

To start with the extension of the Itô integral, we give the following approximation result.

Theorem 2.40. *An arbitrary $X \in L^2[0,T]$ can be approximated by a sequence of simple processes $X^{(n)}$. More precisely: There exists a sequence*

Excursion 2: The Itô Integral

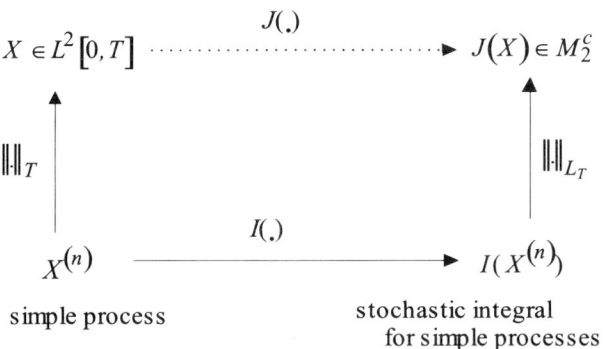

Figure 2.4. Extension of the stochastic integral

$X^{(n)}$ of simple processes with

$$\lim_{n \to \infty} E \int_0^T \left(X_s - X_s^{(n)} \right)^2 ds = 0.$$

Proof. (1) Let $X \in L^2[0, T]$ be continuous and bounded:
Choose

$$X_t^{(n)}(\omega) := X_0(\omega) \cdot 1_{\{0\}}(t) + \sum_{k=0}^{2^n - 1} X_{\frac{kT}{2^n}}(\omega) \cdot 1_{\left(\frac{kT}{2^n}, \frac{(k+1)T}{2^n} \right]}(t).$$

Then the desired convergence is a consequence of the dominated convergence theorem.

(2) Let $X \in L^2[0, T]$ be bounded:
Let $G_t(\omega) := \int_0^t X_s(\omega)\, ds$. Then for $m \in \mathbb{N}$, m sufficiently large such that $t - 1/m \geq 0$, the process

$$\tilde{X}_t^{(m)} := \frac{G_t(\omega) - G_{t-1/m}(\omega)}{1/m}$$

is continuous, bounded, and $\mathcal{F}_t$-measurable. The fundamental theorem of calculus then implies

$$\lim_{m \to \infty} \tilde{X}_t^{(m)}(\omega) = X_t(\omega)$$

for $\lambda \otimes P$-almost all $(t, \omega) \in [0, T] \times \Omega$. Further, the dominated convergence theorem yields

$$E \int_0^T \left(\tilde{X}_t^{(m)} - X_t \right)^2 dt \xrightarrow{m \to \infty} 0.$$

Hence, by (1) we can choose a sequence $X^{(n)} := X^{(m_n)}$ of simple processes with

$$E \int_0^T \left(X_t^{(n)} - X_t\right)^2 dt \xrightarrow{n \to \infty} 0.$$

(3) Let $X \in L^2[0,T]$ be arbitrary:
Define

$$\tilde{X}_t^{(m)}(\omega) := X_t(\omega) \cdot 1_{\{\omega \mid |X_t(\omega)| \leq m\}}(\omega).$$

This process is bounded and satisfies

$$E \int_0^T \left|\tilde{X}_t^{(m)} - X_t\right|^2 dt \xrightarrow{m \to \infty} 0$$

by the dominated convergence theorem as we have $\left|\tilde{X}_t^{(m)}\right| \leq |X_t|$. By (1) and (2) there exists a suitable diagonal sequence $X^{(n)} := X^{(m_n)}$ with

$$E \int_0^T \left|X_t^{(n)} - X_t\right|^2 dt \xrightarrow{n \to \infty} 0.$$

□

For proving the main theorem containing the construction of the Itô integral we need the following technical lemma which says that certain martingales can be modified on sets of measure zero such that they become right-continuous and still remain martingales.

Lemma 2.41. *Let $\{(X_t, \mathcal{G}_t)\}_{t \in [0,\infty)}$ be a martingale where the filtration $\{\mathcal{G}_t\}_{t \in [0,\infty)}$ satisfies the usual conditions. Then the process X_t possesses a right-continuous modification $\{(Y_t, \mathcal{G}_t)\}_{t \in [0,\infty)}$ such that $\{(Y_t, \mathcal{G}_t)\}_{t \in [0,\infty)}$ is a martingale.*

Proof. The assertions follow from theorem I.3.13 in [**KA/SH 91**]. This theorem says that under the above assumptions the process X_t possesses a right-continuous modification $\{(Y_t, \mathcal{G}_t)\}_{t \in [0,\infty)}$ such that $\{(Y_t, \mathcal{G}_t)\}_{t \in [0,\infty)}$ is a sub-martingale if the function $t \mapsto E(X_t)$ is right-continuous. As X is a martingale, its expectation is constant and so it obviously satisfies the right-continuity requirement. Then the modification Y satisfies $EY_t = EX_t = EX_0$ for all $t \geq 0$. Thus, Y is a sub-martingale with a constant expectation and hence is a martingale. □

Theorem 2.42 (Construction of the Itô integral for processes in $L^2[0,T]$). *There exists a unique linear mapping J from $L^2[0,T]$ into the space of continuous martingales on $[0,T]$ with respect to $\{\mathcal{F}_t\}_{t\in[0,T]}$ satisfying*

(1) $X = \{X_t\}_{t\in[0,T]}$ *simple process*
$$\Longrightarrow P\left(J_t(X) = I_t(X) \text{ for all } t \in [0,T]\right) = 1$$

(2) $E\left(J_t(X)^2\right) = E\left(\int_0^t X_s^2\, ds\right)$ \hfill "Itô isometry"

This mapping is unique in the following sense: If two mappings J, J' both satisfy requirements (1) and (2), then for all $X \in L^2[0,T]$ the processes $J'(X)$ and $J(X)$ are indistinguishable.

Definition 2.43. For $X \in L^2[0,T]$ and J as in Theorem 2.42 we set

$$\int_0^t X_s\, dW_s := J_t(X)$$

and call this the *stochastic integral* or the *Itô integral* of X with respect to W.

Proof of Theorem 2.42.
a) First we approximate the process with the help of simple processes. Then we examine the convergence of the corresponding sequence of stochastic integrals. For $X \in L^2[0,T]$ by Theorem 2.40 there is a sequence of simple processes $X^{(m)} \in L^2[0,T]$ with

$$\lim_{m\to\infty} E \int_0^T \left(X_s - X_s^{(m)}\right)^2 ds = 0.$$

This sequence $X^{(m)}$ is also a Cauchy sequence with respect to the T-norm. Due to the linearity of the stochastic integral for simple processes and Theorem 2.31 (2), we have, for $t \in [0,T]$:

$$E\left(I_t\left(X^{(n)}\right) - I_t\left(X^{(m)}\right)\right)^2 = E\left(I_t\left(X^{(n)} - X^{(m)}\right)\right)^2$$
$$= E\left(\int_0^t \left(X^{(n)} - X^{(m)}\right)^2 ds\right) \xrightarrow{n,m\to\infty} 0.$$

Hence, the sequence $I_t(X^{(m)})$ is a Cauchy-sequence in $L^2(\Omega, \mathcal{F}_t, P)$ with an $\mathcal{F}_t$-measurable, square-integrable L^2-limit which we shall denote by $I_t(X)$. As the convergence in mean square in particular implies convergence in probability with respect to P, we obtain for each $\varepsilon > 0$:

$$P\left(\left|I_t\left(X^{(m)}\right) - I_t(X)\right| > \varepsilon\right) \xrightarrow{m\to\infty} 0.$$

By choosing an appropriate subsequence $X^{(m_k)}$, we get P-almost surely convergence to the above limit $I_t(X)$.

In total, we obtain a new stochastic process with respect to $\{\mathcal{F}_t\}_{t\in[0,T]}$, namely $I(X) := \{I_t(X)\}_{t\in[0,T]}$. So far we cannot tell much about this limiting process. In particular, we do not know if $I(X)$ is continuous. Moreover, the L^2-limit is not uniquely determined; it is only unique up to P-zero sets. Also, the subsequences on which we have almost sure convergence can be different for each t.

b) However, we can show that the process $I(X)$ has the martingale property as an L^2-limit:

Let $t, s \in [0,T]$, $t > s$. As the stochastic integral for simple processes is a martingale it follows that

$$E\left(I_t\left(X^{(m)}\right) \mid F_s\right) = I_s\left(X^{(m)}\right) \text{ for all } m \in \mathbb{N}.$$

The definition of conditional expectation yields

$$\int_A I_t\left(X^{(m)}\right) \, dP = \int_A I_s\left(X^{(m)}\right) \, dP \text{ for all } A \in \mathcal{F}_s \text{ and all } m \in \mathbb{N}.$$

Due to the above mentioned L^2-convergence we further have

$$\int_A I_t\left(X^{(m)}\right) \, dP \xrightarrow{m \to \infty} \int_A I_t(X) \, dP$$

and

$$\int_A I_s\left(X^{(m)}\right) \, dP \xrightarrow{m \to \infty} \int_A I_s(X) \, dP.$$

In total this implies

$$\int_A I_t(X) \, dP = \int_A I_s(X) \, dP \text{ for all } A \in \mathcal{F}_s.$$

As $I_s(X)$ is $\mathcal{F}_s$-measurable, this yields the martingale property

$$E(I_t(X) \mid F_s) = I_s(X) \text{ a.s. } P.$$

c) We now construct the mapping J with the help of the L^2-limit $I_t(X)$:

As the filtration $\{\mathcal{F}_t\}_t$ satisfies the usual conditions and $\{I_t(X)\}_t$ is a martingale, then by Lemma 2.41 we can modify the martingale $I_t(X)$ for each t on a P-zero set such that we obtain a right-continuous process $\{J_t(X), \mathcal{F}_t\}_t$ which still is a martingale. Note that $J_t(X)$ is square-integrable.

d) We now prove the continuity of $J(X)$:

Excursion 2: The Itô Integral

The above constructed martingale $J(X)$ is still an L^2-limit of the sequence $I_t(X^{(m)})$. By applying Theorem 2.23, Doob's inequality, we obtain

$$E\left(\sup_{0\leq t\leq T}\left|I_t\left(X^{(m)}\right)-J_t(X)\right|\right)^2$$
$$\leq 4\cdot E\left(I_T\left(X^{(m)}\right)-J_T(X)\right)^2 \xrightarrow{m\to\infty} 0.$$

Hence, there is a subsequence $X^{(m_k)}$ with

$$E\left(\sup_{0\leq t\leq T}\left|I_t\left(X^{(m_k)}\right)-J_t(X)\right|\right)^2 \leq \frac{1}{2^k\cdot k^2}.$$

Application of Chebyshev's inequality then yields

$$P\left(\sup_{0\leq t\leq T}\left|I_t\left(X^{(m_k)}\right)-J_t(X)\right|\geq \frac{1}{k}\right) \leq k^2 \cdot E\left(\sup_{0\leq t\leq T}|\ldots|\right)^2 \leq \frac{1}{2^k}.$$

Thus, by the first Borel-Cantelli lemma the sequence of continuous processes $\{I_t(X^{(m_k)})\}_{t\in[0,T]}$ converges uniformly P-a.s. to a right-continuous process $J(X)$ for $k\to\infty$. As we have uniform convergence for almost all $\omega\in\Omega$, the process $J(X)$ has continuous paths for almost all ω. We can thus w.l.o.g. assume that $J(X)$ possesses continuous paths.

e) We now prove the independence of $J_t(X)$ of the approximating sequence $X^{(m)}$ for X:

Let $X^{(m)}\in L^2[0,T]$, $Y^{(m)}\in L^2[0,T]$ be two approximating sequences for $X\in L^2[0,T]$ with L^2-limits $I(X)$ and $I'(X)$ respectively. Then

$$Z^{(m)}:=\begin{cases} X^{(m)} & m \text{ even} \\ Y^{(m)} & m \text{ odd}\end{cases}$$

also defines an approximating sequence for X, and $I_t(Z^{(m)})$ converges in L^2 to both $I_t(X)$ and $I'_t(X)$. Hence, for all $t\in[0,T]$, $I_t(X)$ and $I'_t(X)$ have to agree P-almost surely. Consequently, they have to coincide P-almost surely with $J_t(X)$, too.

f) Further, due to the L^2-convergence of $I_t(X^{(n)})$ and Theorem 2.31 (2), we have

$$E\left(J_t(X)^2\right) = \lim_{n\to\infty} E\left(I_t\left(X^{(n)}\right)^2\right)$$
$$= \lim_{n\to\infty} E\left(\int_0^t \left(X_s^{(n)}\right)^2 ds\right) = E\left(\int_0^t X_s^2\, ds\right).$$

The last equality is due to the fact that in $([0,T] \times \Omega, \mathcal{B}([0,T]) \otimes \mathcal{F}, \lambda \otimes P)$ the process X is the L^2-limit of $X^{(n)}$.

g) Linearity of J follows by a limiting process similar to the one in f) together with the linearity of the stochastic integral for simple processes.

h) Uniqueness of the mapping J:

Let J' be a linear mapping having all the properties required in Theorem 2.42. Then, by property (1) and continuity of linear mappings, it follows:

$$J'_t(X) = J'_t\left(\lim_{k \to \infty} X^{(m_k)}\right) = \lim_{k \to \infty} J'_t\left(X^{(m_k)}\right) = \lim_{k \to \infty} I_t\left(X^{(m_k)}\right)$$
$$= J_t(X) \text{ a.s. } P \text{ for all } t \in [0, T].$$

As $J_t(X)$ and $J'_t(X)$ are both continuous processes, we have their indistinguishability by Theorem 2.6. $\square$

Theorem 2.44 (Special case of Doob's inequality). *Let $X \in L^2[0,T]$. Then we have*

$$E\left(\sup_{0 \le t \le T} \left|\int_0^t X_s \, dW_s\right|^2\right) \le 4 \cdot E\left(\int_0^T X_s^2 \, ds\right).$$

Proof. The assertion follows from Doob's inequality, Theorem 2.23, and the Itô isometry as $\int_0^t X_s \, dW_s$ is a martingale. $\square$

Definition 2.45 (Multi-dimensional generalization of the stochastic integral). Let $\{(W(t), \mathcal{F}_t)\}_t$ with $W(t) = (W_1(t), ..., W_m(t))$ be an m-dimensional Brownian motion and $\{(X(t), \mathcal{F}_t)\}_t$ be an $\mathbb{R}^{n,m}$-valued progressively measurable process such that for each component we have $X_{ij} \in L^2[0,T]$. Then the Itô integral of X with respect to W is defined as follows:

$$\int_0^t X(s) \, dW(s) := \begin{pmatrix} \sum_{j=1}^m \int_0^t X_{1j}(s) \, dW_j(s) \\ \vdots \\ \sum_{j=1}^m \int_0^t X_{nj}(s) \, dW_j(s) \end{pmatrix},$$

$t \in [0,T]$, where the single terms appearing in the sums are all one-dimensional Itô integrals. Note that

$$\sum_{j=1}^m \int_0^t X_{ij}(s) \, dW_j(s)$$

are again martingales.

Further extension of the stochastic integral. For modeling trading strategies we need an extension of the stochastic integral to an even wider class of processes than $L^2[0,T]$. Therefore we consider the vector space

$$H^2[0,T] := H^2\left([0,T], \Omega, \mathcal{F}, \{\mathcal{F}_t\}_{t\in[0,T]}, P\right)$$
$$:= \left\{ (X_t, \mathcal{F}_t)_{t\in[0,T]} \text{ real-valued stochastic process } \mid \right.$$
$$\left. \{X_t\}_t \text{ progressively measurable, } \int_0^T X_t^2 \, dt < \infty \text{ a.s. } P \right\}$$

As processes $X \in H^2[0,T]$ do not necessarily have a finite T-norm, they cannot be approximated by simple processes as was the case for processes in $L^2[0,T]$ needed in the proof of Theorem 2.42. However, we can localize a process $X \in H^2[0,T]$ with the help of suitable sequences of stopping times. More precisely:

By the sequence τ_n, $n \in \mathbb{N}$, given by

$$\tau_n(\omega) := T \wedge \inf\left\{ 0 \leq t \leq T \,\Bigg|\, \int_0^t X_s^2(\omega) \, ds \geq n \right\},$$

(τ_n is indeed a stopping time with respect to $\{\mathcal{F}_t\}_t$, see Exercise (4)) we define the sequence $X^{(n)}$ of stopped processes via

$$X_t^{(n)}(\omega) := X_t(\omega) \cdot 1_{\{\tau_n(\omega) \geq t\}}.$$

By this, we obtain that the processes $X^{(n)}$, $n \in \mathbb{N}$, are members of $L^2[0,T]$. Thus, for $X^{(n)}$ the stochastic integral $I(X^{(n)})$ is already given by Theorem 2.42. We then define the stochastic integral $I(X)$ via

$$I_t(X) := I_t\left(X^{(n)}\right) \text{ for } 0 \leq t \leq \tau_n.$$

As we also have the consistency property

$$I_t(X) = I_t\left(X^{(m)}\right) \text{ for } 0 \leq t \leq \tau_n (\leq \tau_m),\ m \geq n,$$

$I_t(X)$ is thus well-defined for $X \in H^2[0,T]$. Further, for $X \in H^2[0,T]$, the non-decreasing sequence of stopping times satisfies

$$\tau_n \xrightarrow{n \to \infty} +\infty \text{ a.s. } P.$$

Hence, by construction, $I_t(X)$ is a local martingale with localizing sequence τ_n. This so defined stochastic integral is still linear and possesses continuous paths. However, the properties appearing in Theorem 2.42 (2) (Itô isometry) and in Theorem 2.44 do not necessarily hold any longer as they may contain non-existing expectations.

Excursion 3: The Itô Formula

The basic tool of Itô calculus is Itô's formula in its numerous variants. We shall introduce it here only for the special class of so-called Itô processes.

> **General assumptions for this section:**
> Let $(\Omega, \mathcal{F}, P)$ be a complete probability space equipped with a filtration $\{\mathcal{F}_t\}_t$ satisfying the usual conditions. Further, assume that on this space a Brownian motion $\{(W_t, \mathcal{F}_t)\}_{t \in [0, \infty)}$ with respect to this filtration is defined.

Definition 2.46. Let $\{(W(t), \mathcal{F}_t)\}_{t \in [0,\infty)}$ be an m-dimensional Brownian motion, $m \in \mathbb{N}$.

(1) $\{(X(t), \mathcal{F}_t)\}_{t \in [0,\infty)}$ is called a *real-valued Itô process* if for all $t \geq 0$ it admits the representation

$$X(t) = X(0) + \int_0^t K(s)\,ds + \int_0^t H(s)\,dW(s)$$

$$= X(0) + \int_0^t K(s)\,ds + \sum_{j=1}^m \int_0^t H_j(s)\,dW_j(s) \quad \text{a.s. } P.$$

Here, $X(0)$ is $\mathcal{F}_0$-measurable, and $\{K(t)\}_{t \in [0,\infty)}$ and $\{H(t)\}_{t \in [0,\infty)}$ are progressively measurable processes with

$$\int_0^t |K(s)|\,ds < \infty, \quad \int_0^t H_i^2(s)\,ds < \infty \quad \text{a.s. } P,$$

for all $t \geq 0$, $i = 1, ..., m$.

(2) An *n-dimensional Itô process* $X = (X^{(1)}, ..., X^{(n)})$ consists of a vector with components being real-valued Itô processes.

Remark 2.47. (1) Note that under the above requirements we have $H_j \in H^2[0, T]$ for all $T > 0$, $j = 1, ..., m$.

(2) The above representation of an Itô process is unique up to indistinguishability of the representing integrands K_t and H_t (see Exercise (5)).

(3) Very often the symbolic differential notation

$$dX_t = K_t\,dt + H_t\,dW_t$$

is used for the representation of an Itô process.

Definition 2.48. Let X and Y be two real-valued Itô processes with representations

$$X(t) = X(0) + \int_0^t K(s)\,ds + \int_0^t H(s)\,dW(s),$$

$$Y(t) = Y(0) + \int_0^t L(s)\,ds + \int_0^t M(s)\,dW(s).$$

Then,

$$\langle X, Y \rangle_t := \sum_{i=1}^m \int_0^t H_i(s) \cdot M_i(s)\,ds$$

is called the *quadratic covariation* of X and Y. In particular, $\langle X \rangle_t := \langle X, X \rangle_t$ is called the *quadratic variation* of X.

Notation. Let X be a real-valued Itô process, and Y a real-valued, progressively measurable process. We set

$$\int_0^t Y(s)\,dX(s) := \int_0^t Y(s) \cdot K(s)\,ds + \int_0^t Y(s) \cdot H(s)\,dW(s)$$

if all the integrals on the right-hand side are defined.

Now we are ready to formulate the one-dimensional Itô formula.

Theorem 2.49 (One-dimensional Itô formula). *Let W_t be a one-dimensional Brownian motion, and X_t a real-valued Itô process with*

$$X_t = X_0 + \int_0^t K_s\,ds + \int_0^t H_s\,dW_s.$$

Let $f : \mathbb{R} \to \mathbb{R}$ be twice continuously differentiable. Then, for all $t \geq 0$ we have

$$f(X_t) = f(X_0) + \int_0^t f'(X_s)\,dX_s + \tfrac{1}{2} \cdot \int_0^t f''(X_s)\,d\langle X \rangle_s$$

$$= f(X_0) + \int_0^t \left(f'(X_s) \cdot K_s + \tfrac{1}{2} \cdot f''(X_s) \cdot H_s^2\right)ds$$

$$+ \int_0^t f'(X_s)\,H_s\,dW_s \quad \text{a.s. } P.$$

In particular, all integrals appearing above are defined.

Remark 2.50. By looking at the right-hand side of the first equality, we notice that the Itô formula differs from the fundamental theorem of calculus by the additional term

$$\tfrac{1}{2} \cdot \int_0^t f''(X_s)\, d\langle X\rangle_s.$$

Note that the quadratic variation $\langle X\rangle_t$ is an Itô process.

Differential notation. To state Itô's formula it is convenient to use the symbolic differential notation

$$df(X_t) = f'(X_t)\, dX_t + \tfrac{1}{2} \cdot f''(X_t)\, d\langle X\rangle_t.$$

Proof of the Itô formula in Theorem 2.49.
Step 1: Localization:
First, by localization we ensure that all following expectations exist and that all limiting processes can be interchanged. More precisely, define for $t \geq 0$

$$M_t := \int_0^t H_s\, dW_s,\ B_t := \int_0^t K_s\, ds,\ \hat{B}_t := \int_0^t |K_s|\, ds.$$

Then, for $n \in \mathbb{N}$ we define the stopping times

$$T_n := \begin{cases} 0, & \text{if } |X_0| \geq n, \\ \inf\left\{ t \geq 0 \,\middle|\, |M_t| \geq n \text{ or } \hat{B}_t \geq n \text{ or } \int_0^t H_s^2 ds \geq n \right\}, & \text{if } |X_0| < n, \\ \infty, & \text{if } |X_0| < n \text{ and } \{\ldots\text{see above}\ldots\} = \emptyset. \end{cases}$$

Then we have $T_1 \leq T_2 \leq \ldots \to \infty$ P-almost surely. If we can now prove the Itô formula for the stopped process

$$X_t^{(n)} := X_{t \wedge T_n},$$

then the general result will be obtained via the limit $n \to \infty$ (see Exercise (7)).

Due to the above localization, we can now w.l.o.g. assume that $X_0(\omega)$, $M_t(\omega)$, $\hat{B}_t(\omega)$, and $\int H_s^2 ds$ are all bounded by a constant C on $[0,\infty) \times \Omega$. This also implies $|X_t(\omega)| \leq 3C$. Moreover, the values of f outside the interval $[-3C, 3C]$ are now irrelevant, as under the above assumptions all possible values of X_t are inside this interval. We can thus restrict ourselves to consider only functions f which are twice continuously differentiable and have a compact support. Hence, f, f' and f'' are also bounded.

Step 2: Taylor expansion:
Let $t > 0$ and let $\pi = \{t_0, t_1, \ldots, t_m\}$ with $t_0 = 0$, $t_m = t$ be a partition

of $[0,t]$. Define
$$\|\pi\| := \max_{1 \leq k \leq m} |t_k - t_{k-1}|.$$

By performing a Taylor expansion of each difference in the following telescope sum for fixed ω, we obtain (to simplify the notation we do not explicitly state the dependence on ω):

$$f(X_t) - f(X_0) = \sum_{k=1}^{m} \left(f(X_{t_k}) - f(X_{t_{k-1}}) \right)$$

$$= \underbrace{\sum_{k=1}^{m} f'(X_{t_{k-1}}) (X_{t_k} - X_{t_{k-1}})}_{(*)} + \underbrace{\tfrac{1}{2} \sum_{k=1}^{m} f''(\eta_k) (X_{t_k} - X_{t_{k-1}})^2}_{(**)}$$

with $\eta_k(\omega) = X_{t_{k-1}}(\omega) + \theta_k(\omega) (X_{t_k}(\omega) - X_{t_{k-1}}(\omega))$, $\theta_k(\omega) \in (0,1)$.

We shall now show that the sums $(*)$, $(**)$ converge to the corresponding integrals occuring in the Itô formula.

Step 3: The linear term $(*)$:
We have

$$(*) = \underbrace{\sum_{k=1}^{m} f'(X_{t_{k-1}}) (B_{t_k} - B_{t_{k-1}})}_{A_1(\pi)} + \underbrace{\sum_{k=1}^{m} f'(X_{t_{k-1}}) (M_{t_k} - M_{t_{k-1}})}_{A_2(\pi)}.$$

i) For $\|\pi\| \to 0$, $A_1(\pi)$ converges P-a.s. and in L^1 against the Lebesgue-Stieltjes integral

$$\int_0^t f'(X_s)\, dB_s = \int_0^t f'(X_s)\, K_s\, ds.$$

ii) To examine the convergence of $A_2(\pi)$, we approximate $f'(X_s)$ by the simple process

$$Y_s^\pi(\omega) := f'(X_0(\omega)) \cdot 1_{\{0\}}(s) + \sum_{k=1}^{m} f'(X_{t_{k-1}}(\omega)) \cdot 1_{(t_{k-1}, t_k]}(s).$$

The Itô isometry yields

$$E\left(\int_0^t (f'(X_s) - Y_s^\pi) \cdot H_s\, dW_s \right)^2 = E\left(\int_0^t (f'(X_s) - Y_s^\pi)^2 \cdot H_s^2\, ds \right).$$

By the dominated convergence theorem this value tends to zero for $\|\pi\| \to 0$. This implies

$$A_2(\pi) = \int_0^t Y_s^\pi \cdot H_s \, dW_s \xrightarrow{\|\pi\| \to 0} \int_0^t f'(X_s) H_s \, dW_s \text{ in } L^2.$$

iii) From i) and ii) we obtain:

$$(*) \xrightarrow{\|\pi\| \to 0} \int_0^t f'(X_s) K_s \, ds + \int_0^t f'(X_s) H_s \, dW_s \text{ in } L^1.$$

Step 4: The quadratic term (**):
We have

$$\sum_{k=1}^m f''(\eta_k) (X_{t_k} - X_{t_{k-1}})^2$$

$$= \underbrace{\sum_{k=1}^m f''(\eta_k) (B_{t_k} - B_{t_{k-1}})^2}_{I_1(\pi)} + \underbrace{2 \sum_{k=1}^m f''(\eta_k) (B_{t_k} - B_{t_{k-1}}) (M_{t_k} - M_{t_{k-1}})}_{I_2(\pi)}$$

$$+ \underbrace{\sum_{k=1}^m f''(\eta_k) (M_{t_k} - M_{t_{k-1}})^2}_{I_3(\pi)}.$$

i) As B, M, and f'' are bounded and also $\sum_{k=1}^m |B_{t_k} - B_{t_{k-1}}| \leq \hat{B}_t < C$ is valid, we obtain

$$|I_1(\pi) + I_2(\pi)|$$

$$\leq 2C \cdot \|f''\|_\infty \cdot \left(\max_{1 \leq k \leq m} |B_{t_k} - B_{t_{k-1}}| + \max_{1 \leq k \leq m} |M_{t_k} - M_{t_{k-1}}| \right).$$

As B and M are continuous the above expression tends to zero P-a.s. and in L^1 for $\|\pi\| \to 0$.

ii) Now consider $I_3(\pi)$. Define

$$I_3^*(\pi) := \sum_{k=1}^m f''(X_{t_{k-1}}) (M_{t_k} - M_{t_{k-1}})^2,$$

$$I_4(\omega) := \sum_{k=1}^m f''(X_{t_{k-1}}) \int_{t_{k-1}}^{t_k} H_s^2 \, ds.$$

Excursion 3: The Itô Formula

This yields

$$|I_3(\pi) - I_3^*(\pi)| \leq \max_{1 \leq k \leq m} |f''(\eta_k) - f''(X_{t_{k-1}})| \cdot \left(\sum_{k=1}^{m} (M_{t_k} - M_{t_{k-1}})^2\right).$$

Then the Cauchy-Schwarz inequality implies:

$$E(I_3(\pi) - I_3^*(\pi))^2$$

$$\leq \underbrace{\sqrt{E\left(\max_{1 \leq k \leq m} |f''(\eta_k) - f''(X_{t_{k-1}})|\right)^2}}_{\downarrow \|\pi\| \to 0 \atop 0} \cdot \underbrace{\sqrt{E\left(\sum_{k=1}^{m} (M_{t_k} - M_{t_{k-1}})^2\right)^2}}_{\leq \sqrt{48C^4}}.$$

Here convergence of the first factor is due to the continuity of f''. The boundedness of the second factor is ensured by Lemma 2.51 (1) (see below). Hence we obtain

$$E(I_3(\pi) - I_3^*(\pi))^2 \xrightarrow{\|\pi\| \to 0} 0.$$

By noting that we have

$$E(M_{t_k} - M_{t_{k-1}})^2 = E \int_{t_{k-1}}^{t_k} H_s^2 \, ds$$

and the fact that the mixed terms in the squares occuring below have zero expectation (see Exercise (6)), the following relation is valid:

$$E(I_3^*(\pi) - I_4(\pi))^2$$

$$\leq \|f\|_\infty^2 \cdot E\left(\sum_{k=1}^{m} \left[(M_{t_k} - M_{t_{k-1}})^2 - \int_{t_{k-1}}^{t_k} H_s^2 \, ds\right]\right)^2$$

$$= \|f\|_\infty^2 \cdot E\left(\sum_{k=1}^{m} \left((M_{t_k} - M_{t_{k-1}})^2 - \int_{t_{k-1}}^{t_k} H_s^2 \, ds\right)^2\right).$$

Due to the well-known inequality $(a-b)^2 \leq 2(a^2 + b^2)$, the above relation results in

$$E(I_3^*(\pi) - I_4(\pi))^2$$

$$\leq 2 \cdot \|f\|_\infty^2 \cdot E\left(\sum_{k=1}^{m} (M_{t_k} - M_{t_{k-1}})^4 + \sum_{k=1}^{m} \left(\int_{t_{k-1}}^{t_k} H_s^2 \, ds\right)^2\right).$$

Lemma 2.51 (2) yields

$$E\left(\sum_{k=1}^{m} \left(M_{t_k} - M_{t_{k-1}}\right)^4\right) \xrightarrow{\|\pi\|\to 0} 0.$$

Further, the theorem on dominated convergence implies

$$E\left(\sum_{k=1}^{m} \left(\int_0^t H_s^2\, ds\right)^2\right)$$

$$\leq E\left(\underbrace{\left(\max_k \int_{t_{k-1}}^{t_k} H_s^2\, ds\right)}_{\to 0 \text{ for } \|\pi\|\to 0} \cdot \underbrace{\int_0^t H_s^2\, ds}_{<C}\right) \xrightarrow{\|\pi\|\to 0} 0.$$

In total, $I_3^*(\pi)$ tends to $I_4(\pi)$ in L^2 for $\|\pi\| \to 0$. As we also have

$$I_4(\pi) \xrightarrow{\|\pi\|\to 0} \int_0^t f''(X_s) H_s^2\, ds = \int_0^t f''(X_s)\, d\langle X\rangle_s$$

P-a.s. and in L^1, we get

$$I_3^*(\pi) \xrightarrow{\|\pi\|\to 0} \int_0^t f''(X_s) H_s^2\, ds \text{ in } L^1.$$

Therefore note

$$E\left(\left|I_3(\pi) - \int_0^t f''(X_s) H_s^2\, ds\right|\right)$$

$$\leq E\left(|I_3(\pi) - I_3^*(\pi)| + \left|I_3^*(\pi) - \int_0^t f''(X_s) H_s^2\, ds\right|\right)$$

$$= \underbrace{E\left(|I_3(\pi) - I_3^*(\pi)|\right)}_{\to 0 \text{ for } \|\pi\|\to 0} + \underbrace{E\left(\left|I_3^*(\pi) - \int_0^t f''(X_s) H_s^2\, ds\right|\right)}_{\to 0 \text{ for } \|\pi\|\to 0}.$$

Thus, $I_3(\pi)$ converges against $\int_0^t f''(X_s) H_s^2 ds$ in L^1 for $\|\pi\| \to 0$.

Step 5: The end:
For $\|\pi\| \to 0$, (*) tends to
$$\int_0^t f'(X_s) K_s \, ds + \int_0^t f'(X_s) H_s \, dW_s$$
and (**) tends to
$$\int_0^t f''(X_s) H_s^2 \, ds \text{ in } L^1.$$

In total, for the stopped process there exist subsequences π_k of partitions of $[0, t]$ such that the relevant sums in steps 2, 3, and 4 converge against the correct limits P-almost surely. This means that both sides of the Itô formula are P-a.s. equal for fixed t. However, as both sides are continuous in t, this even implies that they are then P-a.s. equal for all t, and hence indistinguishable. $\square$

Lemma 2.51. *Let X be a martingale with $|X_s| \leq C$ for all $s \in [0, t]$ P-almost surely. Let $\pi = \{t_0, t_1, ..., t_m\}$, $t_0 = 0$, $t_m = t$, be a partition of $[0, t]$. Then we have*

(1) $E\left(\sum_{k=1}^m (X_{t_k} - X_{t_{k-1}})^2 \right)^2 \leq 48 \cdot C^4$

(2) *If X is continuous, we obtain* $E\left(\sum_{k=1}^m (X_{t_k} - X_{t_{k-1}})^4 \right) \xrightarrow{\|\pi\| \to 0} 0$.

Proof.
(1) Let $0 \leq l \leq m - 1$: The martingale property implies

(2.7) $E\left(\sum_{j=l+1}^m (X_{t_j} - X_{t_{j-1}})^2 \Big| \mathcal{F}_{t_l} \right) = E\left(\left(\sum_{j=l+1}^m (X_{t_j} - X_{t_{j-1}}) \right)^2 \Big| \mathcal{F}_{t_l} \right)$

$= E\left((X_{t_m} - X_{t_l})^2 \big| \mathcal{F}_{t_l} \right) \leq 4 \cdot C^2$ a.s. P.

As $|X_t| \leq C$, we have

(2.8) $E\left(\sum_{j=1}^m (X_{t_j} - X_{t_{j-1}})^4 \right) \leq 4 \cdot C^2 \cdot E\left(\sum_{j=1}^m (X_{t_j} - X_{t_{j-1}})^2 \right) \leq 16 \cdot C^4$.

Further,

(2.9) $E\left(\sum_{l=1}^{m-1} \sum_{j=l+1}^m (X_{t_j} - X_{t_{j-1}})^2 (X_{t_l} - X_{t_{l-1}})^2 \right) = E\left(E(\ldots | \mathcal{F}_{t_l}) \right)$

$$= E\left(\sum_{l=1}^{m-1}\left(X_{t_l}-X_{t_{l-1}}\right)^2 E\left(\sum_{j=l+1}^{m}\left(X_{t_j}-X_{t_{j-1}}\right)^2|\mathcal{F}_{t_l}\right)\right)$$

$$\leq 4\cdot C^2\cdot E\left(\sum_{l=1}^{m-1}\left(X_{t_l}-X_{t_{l-1}}\right)^2\right)\leq 16\cdot C^4.$$

Relations (2.8) and (2.9) imply

$$E\left(\left(\sum_{j=1}^{m}\left(X_{t_j}-X_{t_{j-1}}\right)^2\right)^2\right)$$

$$= E\left(\sum_{j=1}^{m}\left(X_{t_j}-X_{t_{j-1}}\right)^4\right)+2\cdot E\left(\sum_{l=1}^{m}\sum_{j=l+1}^{m}\ldots\right)$$

$$\leq 16\cdot C^4+2\cdot 16\cdot C^4=48\cdot C^4.$$

(2) First note that

$$\sum_{j=1}^{m}x_j^4\leq\left(\max_{1\leq j\leq m}(x_j)\right)^2\cdot\sum_{j=1}^{m}x_j^2.$$

Apply this to $x_j:=\left(X_{t_j}-X_{t_{j-1}}\right)$. Then we have

$$\underbrace{E\left(\sum_{j=1}^{m}\left(X_{t_j}-X_{t_{j-1}}\right)^4\right)}_{(\otimes)}$$

$$\leq E\left(\left(\max_{1\leq j\leq m}\left(X_{t_j}-X_{t_{j-1}}\right)\right)^2\cdot\sum_{j=1}^{m}\left(X_{t_j}-X_{t_{j-1}}\right)^2\right).$$

Hölder's inequality yields

$$(\otimes)\leq\underbrace{\sqrt{E\left(\left(\max_{1\leq j\leq m}\left(X_{t_j}-X_{t_{j-1}}\right)\right)^4\right)}}_{\text{a.s. }\underset{0}{P\downarrow}\|\pi\|\to 0}\cdot\underbrace{\sqrt{E\left(\left(\sum_{j=1}^{m}\left(X_{t_j}-X_{t_{j-1}}\right)^2\right)^2\right)}}_{\leq\sqrt{48}\cdot C^2\text{ due to 1.}}$$

$$\xrightarrow{\|\pi\|\to 0}0.$$

Convergence to zero is ensured by continuity of X and by the dominated convergence theorem.

$\square$

Excursion 3: The Itô Formula 51

Some applications of Itô's formula.

(1) $X_t = t$:

This very simple process can be represented as
$$X_t = 0 + \int_0^t 1\, ds + \int_0^t 0\, dW_s.$$
Then for a twice continuously differentiable f, the Itô formula implies
$$f(t) = f(0) + \int_0^t f'(s)\, ds.$$
Thus, the fundamental theorem of calculus can be regarded as a special case of Itô's formula.

(2) $X_t = h(t)$:

In this case, for continuously differentiable functions h, Itô's formula implies the chain rule in the following way:
$$X_t = h(0) + \int_0^t h'(s)\, ds + \int_0^t 0\, dW_s$$
$$\Rightarrow (f \circ h)(t) = (f \circ h)(0) + \int_0^t f'(h(s)) \cdot h'(s)\, ds.$$

(3) $X_t = W_t$, $f(x) = x^2$:

Due to
$$W_t = 0 + \int_0^t 0\, ds + \int_0^t 1\, dW_s$$
we obtain
$$W_t^2 = \int_0^t 2 \cdot W_s\, dW_s + \tfrac{1}{2} \cdot \int_0^t 2\, ds = 2 \cdot \int_0^t W_s\, dW_s + t.$$
Note the additional term "t" compared to the rules of usual calculus. It has its origin in the non-vanishing quadratic variation of W_t.

Theorem 2.52 (Multi-dimensional Itô formula).
Let $X(t) = (X_1(t), ..., X_n(t))$ be an n-dimensional Itô process with
$$X_i(t) = X_i(0) + \int_0^t K_i(s)\, ds + \sum_{j=1}^m \int_0^t H_{ij}(s)\, dW_j(s),\ i = 1, ..., n,$$
where $W(t) = (W_1(t), ..., W_m(t))$ is an m-dimensional Brownian motion. Further let $f : [0, \infty) \times \mathbb{R}^n \to \mathbb{R}$ be a $C^{1,2}$-function, i.e. f is continuous, continuously differentiable with respect to the first variable (time) and twice

continuously differentiable with respect to the last n variables (space). We then have

$$f(t, X_1(t), ..., X_n(t)) = f(0, X_1(0), ..., X_n(0))$$
$$+ \int_0^t f_t(s, X_1(s), ..., X_n(s)) \, ds + \sum_{i=1}^n \int_0^t f_{x_i}(s, X_1(s), ..., X_n(s)) \, dX_i(s)$$
$$+ \frac{1}{2} \cdot \sum_{i,j=1}^n \int_0^t f_{x_i x_j}(s, X_1(s), ..., X_n(s)) \, d\langle X_i, X_j \rangle_s.$$

Proof. The proof of the multi-dimensional Itô formula is very similar to the one-dimensional case. However, in step 2 we have to consider (for simplicity let $n = 1$):

$$f(t_k, X(t_k)) - f(t_{k-1}, X(t_{k-1}))$$
$$= [f(t_k, X(t_k)) - f(t_{k-1}, X(t_k))]$$
$$+ [f(t_{k-1}, X(t_k)) - f(t_{k-1}, X(t_{k-1}))]$$
$$= f_t(\tau_k, X(t_k))(t_k - t_{k-1}) + f_x(t_{k-1}, X(t_{k-1}))(X(t_k) - X(t_{k-1}))$$
$$+ \tfrac{1}{2} f_{xx}(t_{k-1}, \eta_k)(X(t_k) - X(t_{k-1}))^2$$

with η_k as in step 2, $t_{k-1} \leq \tau_k \leq t_k$. □

The multi-dimensional Itô formula immediately yields the following important corollary.

Corollary 2.53 (Product rule or partial integration). *Let X_t, Y_t be one-dimensional Itô processes with*

$$X_t = X_0 + \int_0^t K_s \, ds + \int_0^t H_s \, dW_s,$$
$$Y_t = Y_0 + \int_0^t \mu_s \, ds + \int_0^t \sigma_s \, dW_s.$$

Then we have

$$X_t \cdot Y_t = X_0 \cdot Y_0 + \int_0^t X_s \, dY_s + \int_0^t Y_s \, dX_s + \int_0^t d\langle X, Y \rangle_s$$
$$= X_0 \cdot Y_0 + \int_0^t (X_s \mu_s + Y_s K_s + H_s \sigma_s) \, ds + \int_0^t (X_s \sigma_s + Y_s H_s) \, dW_s.$$

(For a proof see Exercise (8).)

Excursion 3: The Itô Formula

The stock price equation. We now consider a simple continuous-time market model with a bond and one stock, where the stock price is only influenced by a one-dimensional Brownian motion. This means we have $d = m = 1$. As before, we model the price of the stock at time t by

$$P(t) = p \cdot \exp\left(\left(b - \tfrac{1}{2}\sigma^2\right)t + \sigma W_t\right).$$

To demonstrate an interesting application of the Itô formula we choose

$$X_t = 0 + \int_0^t \left(b - \tfrac{1}{2}\sigma^2\right) s \, ds + \int_0^t \sigma \, dW_s,$$

$$f(x) = p \cdot e^x.$$

Then the Itô formula implies

$$f(X_t) = p + \int_0^t \left[f(X_s)\left(b - \tfrac{1}{2}\sigma^2\right) + \tfrac{1}{2}f(X_s)\cdot\sigma^2\right] ds + \int_0^t f(X_s) \cdot \sigma \, dW_s,$$

hence

> (2.10) $$P(t) = p + \int_0^t P(s) \cdot b \, ds + \int_0^t P(s) \cdot \sigma \, dW_s$$
>
> The Stock Price Equation

This equation is also valid for time-dependent b and σ if we choose

$$X_t = \int_0^t \left(b(s) - \tfrac{1}{2}\sigma^2(s)\right) ds + \int_0^t \sigma(s) \, dW_s.$$

Note that the functions b and σ have to satisfy suitable requirements such that X_t is an Itô process. Written in differential form, the stock price equation is given by

> (2.10) $$dP(t) = P(t)\left(b \, dt + \sigma \, dW_t\right)$$
> $$P(0) = p$$
>
> The Stock Price Equation

We also say that $P(t)$ is a solution of the stochastic differential equation (2.10). Below, we shall give conditions for existence and uniqueness of solutions of stochastic differential equations of a similar linear form. However, uniqueness for equation (2.10) can be proved in an elementary way:

Let $Y(t)$ be a second solution of the stochastic differential equation (2.10). Then define for $t \geq 0$
$$Z(t) := \frac{1}{P(t)}.$$
By Itô's formula we obtain
$$dZ(t) = Z(t)\left((\sigma^2 - b)\, dt - \sigma\, dW_t\right).$$
Then, the product rule yields
$$d(Z(t) \cdot Y(t)) = Z(t)Y(t)\left(b - b + \sigma^2\right) dt$$
$$+ Z(t)Y(t)(\sigma - \sigma)\, dW_t - Z(t)Y(t)\sigma^2\, dt = 0,$$
hence
$$Y(t) = const \cdot P(t).$$
Consequently the solution of equation (2.10) is uniquely determined by the initial condition $Z(0) \cdot Y(0) = 1$.

The following theorem is a generalization of the foregoing example

Theorem 2.54 (Variation of constants). *Let $\{(W(t), \mathcal{F}_t)\}_{t \in [0,\infty)}$ be an m-dimensional Brownian motion. Let $x \in \mathbb{R}$ and A, a, S_j, σ_j be progressively measurable, real-valued processes with*
$$\int_0^t (|A(s)| + |a(s)|)\, ds < \infty \text{ for all } t \geq 0 \text{ a.s. } P,$$
$$\int_0^t \left(S_j^2(s) + \sigma_j^2(s)\right) ds < \infty \text{ for all } t \geq 0 \text{ a.s. } P.$$
Then the stochastic differential equation

$$(2.11)$$
$$dX(t) = (A(t) \cdot X(t) + a(t))\, dt + \sum_{j=1}^{m} (S_j(t) X(t) + \sigma_j(t))\, dW_j(t)$$
$$X(0) = x$$

possesses the unique solution $\{(X(t), \mathcal{F}_t)\}_{t \in [0,\infty)}$ with respect to $\lambda \otimes P$ given by

$$(2.12) \quad X(t) = Z(t) \cdot \left(x + \int_0^t \frac{1}{Z(u)}\left(a(u) - \sum_{j=1}^{m} S_j(u)\sigma_j(u)\right) du\right.$$
$$\left. + \sum_{j=1}^{m} \int_0^t \frac{\sigma_j(u)}{Z(u)}\, dW_j(u)\right)$$

where

$$(2.13) \quad Z(t) = \exp\left(\int_0^t \left(A(u) - \tfrac{1}{2} \cdot \|S(u)\|^2\right) du + \int_0^t S(u)\, dW(u)\right)$$

is the unique solution of the homogeneous equation

$$(2.14) \quad dZ(t) = Z(t)\left(A(t)\, dt + S(t)'\, dW(t)\right),$$
$$Z(0) = 1.$$

Remark. The process $\{(X(t), \mathcal{F}_t)\}_{t \in [0,\infty)}$ solves the stochastic differential equation (2.11) in the sense that $X(t)$ satisfies

$$X(t) = x + \int_0^t \left(A(s) \cdot X(s) + a(s)\right) ds$$
$$+ \sum_{j=1}^m \int_0^t \left(S_j(s) X(s) + \sigma_j(s)\right) dW_j(s)$$

for all $t \geq 0$ P-almost surely. In particular, equation (2.11) (and other corresponding stochastic differential equations) always has to be understood in this integral form!

Proof of Theorem 2.54. i) Similarly to the example "the stock price equation" it can be shown that $Z(t)$ solves the homogeneous stochastic differential equation (2.14). Further, $Y(t) = y \cdot Z(t)$ solves the homogeneous equation with initial condition $Y(0) = y$. As before, we can show uniqueness of this solution.

ii) We now show that $X(t)$ given by (2.12) solves the inhomogeneous linear stochastic differential equation (2.11). Let therefore $Z(t)$ be given by (2.13) and let

$$Y(t) := x + \int_0^t \frac{1}{Z(u)}\left(a(u) - \sum_{j=1}^m S_j(u)\sigma_j(u)\right) du$$
$$+ \sum_{j=1}^m \int_0^t \frac{\sigma_j(u)}{Z(u)}\, dW_j(u).$$

Application of the product rule results in:

$$dX(t) = d(Z(t) \cdot Y(t)) = Z(t) \cdot dY(t) + Y(t) \cdot dZ(t) + d\langle Y, Z\rangle_t$$

$$= Z(t) \cdot \left(\frac{1}{Z(t)}\left(a(t) - \sum_{j=1}^{m} S_j(t) \cdot \sigma_j(t)\right) dt\right.$$

$$\left. + \frac{1}{Z(t)} \sum_{j=1}^{m} \sigma_j(t) \, dW_j(t)\right)$$

$$+ Y(t) \cdot Z(t) \left(A(t) \, dt + S(t)' \, dW(t)\right) + S(t)' \cdot Z(t) \cdot \frac{1}{Z(t)} \sigma(t) \, dt$$

$$= (a(t) + A(t) \cdot X(t)) \, dt + (X(t) \cdot S(t)' + \sigma(t)') \, dW(t).$$

Hence, $X(t)$ solves the stochastic differential equation (2.11).

iii) Let $\tilde{X}(t)$, $X(t)$ be two solutions of the stochastic differential equation. Then

$$\hat{X}(t) := \tilde{X}(t) - X(t)$$

solves the homogeneous equation

$$d\hat{X}(t) = \hat{X}(t)\left(A(t)\,dt + \sum_{j=1}^{m} S_j(t)\,dW_j(t)\right),$$

$$\hat{X}(0) = 0.$$

But by i) we then have $\hat{X}(t) = 0$ for all $t \geq 0$ P-almost surely.

□

2.2. Trading Strategy and Wealth Process

Now, after the introduction of Itô calculus we are able to model stock prices with time dependent, random rates of return and volatilities. This will be the basis of all following continuous-time market models.

2.2. Trading Strategy and Wealth Process

General assumptions:
Let $(\Omega, \mathcal{F}, P)$ be a complete probability space. We assume that there is an m-dimensional Brownian motion $\{(W(t), \mathcal{F}_t)\}_{t \in [0, \infty)}$ defined on that space. The dynamics of the bond and stock prices will be modeled according to

$$P_0(t) = p_0 \cdot \exp\left(\int_0^t r(s)\, ds\right) \qquad \text{"bond"}$$

$$P_i(t) = p_i \cdot \exp\left(\int_0^t \left(b_i(s) - \tfrac{1}{2} \sum_{j=1}^m \sigma_{ij}^2(s)\right) ds \right.$$
$$\left. + \sum_{j=1}^m \int_0^t \sigma_{ij}(s)\, dW_j(s)\right) \qquad \text{"stock"}$$

for $t \in [0, T]$, $T > 0$, $i = 1, ..., d$. The functions $r(t)$, $b(t) = (b_1(t), ..., b_d(t))'$, $\sigma(t) = (\sigma_{ij}(t))_{ij}$ should all be progressively measurable processes with respect to $\{\mathcal{F}_t\}_t$ which are component-wise uniformly bounded in (t, ω). Further, we assume $\sigma(t)\sigma(t)'$ to be uniformly positive definite (i.e. there is a positive constant $K > 0$ with $x'\sigma(t)\sigma(t)'x \geq K x'x$ for all $x \in \mathbb{R}^d$ and all $t \in [0, T]$ P-a.s.).

By Theorem 2.54, variation of constants, these prices are the unique solutions of the following stochastic differential equations (note that the above boundedness assumptions on $r(t)$, $b(t)$, $\sigma(t)$ ensure the applicability of Theorem 2.54):

$$dP_0(t) = P_0(t) \cdot r(t)\, dt$$
$$P_0(0) = p_0 \qquad \text{"bond"}$$

$$dP_i(t) = P_i(t)\left(b_i(t)\, dt + \sum_{j=1}^m \sigma_{ij}(t)\, dW_j(t)\right), \qquad i = 1, ..., d$$
$$P_i(0) = p_i \qquad \text{"stock"}$$

In particular, these equations give us the representations of the prices as Itô processes.

Remark. Note that in the above general assumptions we have not required a deterministic rate of return $r(t)$ of the bond. This rate $r(t)$ is allowed to be a stochastic process. Thus, the bond is no longer riskless. However, by the boundedness assumption on $r(t)$, the risk involved in the bond price is much smaller than that of the stock prices which are driven by Brownian motions.

Possible actions of the investors. After having modeled the prices we shall now model the actions of the market participants. Here, we assume that the investor has the following possibilities of actions:

(1) He can rebalance his holdings, i.e. he can sell some securities and invest the money in other securities. This action will be modeled by the *portfolio process* or by the *trading strategy*.

(2) He is also allowed to consume parts of his wealth which will be incorporated in our setting by the *consumption process*.

2.2.1. Requirements on a market model. We now collect some requirements that should be valid in a realistic market model:

(1) The investor should not be able to foresee events; especially, he is not allowed to have knowledge of future prices.

(2) The actions of a single investor should not have any impact on the stock prices; this is the so-called *small investor hypothesis*.

(3) The investor is endowed with a fixed initial capital at time $t = 0$. Of course, different investors can have different endowments.

(4) Money which is not invested into stocks has to be invested in bonds.

(5) The investors have to act in a self-financing way, i.e. each change in their wealth is due to gains or losses from investment and /or consumption. There is no secret source for new money, but also no secret sink where it can vanish.

We make some further assumptions which will prove to be very convenient for the development of the theory:

(6) The securities are perfectly divisible.

(7) Negative positions in securities are possible. A negative position in the bond will be interpreted as a credit. A negative stock position means that we have sold some stock short, i.e. we have sold shares that we do not possess and thus owe these shares to another investor. Of course, they have to be delivered later.

(8) Rebalancing of the holdings does not lead to transaction costs.

Negative bond positions and credit interest rates. If the interest rate $r(t)$ is constant, then the possibility to have a negative bond position means that it is possible to borrow money for the same rate as we would get for investing in bonds. For some institutions this situation is indeed close to reality. In our market model the interest may depend on the market

2.2. Trading Strategy and Wealth Process

situation (i.e. on $(t,\omega) \in [0,T] \times \Omega$), but not on the fact that we have a positive or a negative bond position.

Mathematical realizations of some requirements. We recapitulate that our market consists of a bond and d stocks. The initial capital of the investor is $x > 0$ (requirement (3)). Now at time $t = 0$ he can buy a selection of securities $\varphi(0) = (\varphi_0(0), \varphi_1(0), ..., \varphi_d(0))'$ where $\varphi_i(0)$ denotes the number of shares of security i held at time $t = 0$. Similarly, the components of the vector $\varphi(t) = (\varphi_0(t), \varphi_1(t), ..., \varphi_d(t))'$ denote the numbers of shares of the different securities held at time t. This vector process $\varphi(t)$ is called a trading strategy. Requirement (1) forces the trading strategies to be progressively measurable with respect to $\{\mathcal{F}_t\}_t$. Decisions on buying and selling always have to be made on the basis of the information available at time t, and this is modeled by $\{\mathcal{F}_t\}_t$. Requirement (5) implies that only self-financing trading strategies should be used. This will be made more precise in the following definitions.

A discrete-time example of a self-financing trading strategy. In the continuous-time model we shall define a self-financing trading strategy by a requirement which at first sight does not seem to be very intuitive. Therefore this requirement will be motivated by the following discrete-time example.

Now consider a market consisting of one stock and a riskless bond. We look at a two-period model given by the time points $t = 0, 1, 2$. The vector $(\varphi_0(t), \varphi_1(t))'$ denotes the numbers of shares of bond and stock held at time t, respectively. As we allow negative positions and perfectly divisible assets, $\varphi_0(t)$ and $\varphi_1(t)$ can attain every arbitrary real number. Let $C(t)$ be the consumption of the investor at time t where we assume $C(0) = 0$. $X(t)$ denotes his wealth at time t, $X(0) = x$ his initial capital. $P_0(t), P_1(t)$ are the bond and stock prices at time t, respectively.

At time $t = 0$ the investor uses his initial capital to buy shares of bond and stock, i.e. we have

$$X(0) = x = \varphi_0(0) \cdot P_0(0) + \varphi_1(0) \cdot P_1(0).$$

At time $t = 1$ the security prices have changed and the investor consumes parts of his wealth. Thus his current wealth is given by

$$X(1) = \varphi_0(0) \cdot P_0(1) + \varphi_1(0) \cdot P_1(1) - C(1).$$

In total we have

$$X(1) = x + \varphi_0(0) \cdot (P_0(1) - P_0(0)) + \varphi_1(0) \cdot (P_1(1) - P_1(0)) - C(1),$$

i.e. his wealth at time $t = 1$ equals his initial wealth plus gains or losses from the price changes of stock and bond minus consumption. Further, at that

time, the investor is allowed to rebalance his remaining holdings. However, we must have
$$X(1) = \varphi_0(1) \cdot P_0(1) + \varphi_1(1) \cdot P_1(1)$$
as the investor is required to invest his whole remaining capital at the market. Similarly, at time $t = 2$, we have

(2.15) $$X(2) = \varphi_0(2) \cdot P_0(2) + \varphi_1(2) \cdot P_1(2),$$

and further

(2.16) $$X(2) = x + \sum_{i=1}^{2} [\varphi_0(i-1) \cdot (P_0(i) - P_0(i-1))$$
$$+ \varphi_1(i-1) \cdot (P_1(i) - P_1(i-1))] - \sum_{i=1}^{2} C(i).$$

In the discrete-time model the condition characterizing a self-financing trading strategy can be formulated as: "wealth before rebalancing minus consumption has to equal wealth after rebalancing", i.e.

(2.17) $$\varphi_0(i) \cdot P_0(i) + \varphi_1(i) \cdot P_1(i)$$
$$= \varphi_0(i-1) \cdot P_0(i) + \varphi_1(i-1) \cdot P_1(i) - C(i).$$

In a continuous-time setting, such a requirement makes no sense as we can trade securities at each time instant. In particular, it is impossible to distinguish between "before" and "after" at the same time instant. Instead of requirement (2.17) we take the approach to define the wealth process corresponding to the strategy $\varphi(t)$, namely $X(t)$, via equation (2.15) (i.e. "wealth = total wealth of the shares held"). Equation (2.16) will then be used to define a self-financing trading and consumption strategy where we shall of course replace all sums by the corresponding integrals. This suggests the requirement

$$X(t) = x + \int_0^t \varphi_0(s) \, dP_0(s) + \int_0^t \varphi_1(s) \, dP_1(s) - \int_0^t c(s) \, ds.$$

Note that the price processes are Itô processes. This leads to natural conditions on the $\varphi_i(s)$ to ensure existence of the integrals (see Definition 2.55).

Our considerations so far will now be made precise from a mathematical point of view.

Definition 2.55. (1) A *trading strategy* φ is an $\mathbb{R}^{d+1}$-valued progressively measurable process with respect to $\{\mathcal{F}_t\}_{t \in [0,T]}$
$$\varphi(t) := (\varphi_0(t), \varphi_1(t), ..., \varphi_d(t))'$$

2.2. Trading Strategy and Wealth Process

satisfying

(2.18) $$\int_0^T |\varphi_0(t)|\, dt < \infty \text{ a.s. } P,$$

(2.19) $$\sum_{j=1}^d \int_0^T (\varphi_i(t) \cdot P_i(t))^2\, dt < \infty \text{ a.s. } P \text{ for } i = 1, ..., d.$$

The value $x := \sum_{i=0}^d \varphi_i(0) \cdot p_i$ is called *initial value* of φ.

(2) Let φ be a trading strategy with initial value $x > 0$. The process

$$X(t) := \sum_{i=0}^d \varphi_i(t) P_i(t)$$

is called *wealth process* corresponding to φ with *initial wealth* x.

(3) A non-negative progressively measurable process $c(t)$ with respect to $\{\mathcal{F}_t\}_{t \in [0,T]}$ with

(2.20) $$\int_0^T c(t)\, dt < \infty \text{ a.s. } P$$

is called a *consumption rate process* (for short: *consumption process*).

Definition 2.56. A pair (φ, c) consisting of a trading strategy φ and a consumption rate process c is called *self-financing* if the corresponding wealth process $X(t)$, $t \in [0, T]$, satisfies:

(2.21) $$X(t) = x + \sum_{i=0}^d \int_0^t \varphi_i(s)\, dP_i(s) - \int_0^t c(s)\, ds \text{ a.s. } P.$$

"current wealth" = "initial wealth" + "gains / losses" − "consumption"

Remark 2.57. We have

$$\int_0^t \varphi_0(s)\, dP_0(s) = \int_0^t \varphi_0(s) P_0(s) r(s)\, ds$$

$$\int_0^t \varphi_i(s)\, dP_i(s) = \int_0^t \varphi_i(s) P_i(s) b_i(s)\, ds$$
$$+ \sum_{j=1}^m \int_0^t \varphi_i(s) P_i(s) \sigma_{ij}(s)\, dW_j(s), \quad i = 1, ..., d.$$

The conditions (2.18), (2.19) and (2.20) in the definitions and the boundedness requirements on r, b and σ thus ensure existence of all the integrals occuring on the right-hand side of equation (2.21).

Definition 2.58. Let (φ, c) be a self-financing pair consisting of a trading strategy and a consumption process with corresponding wealth process $X(t) > 0$ P-a.s. for all $t \in [0, T]$. Then the $\mathbb{R}^d$-valued process

$$\pi(t) := (\pi_1(t), ..., \pi_d(t))', \ t \in [0, T] \text{ with } \pi_i(t) = \frac{\varphi_i(t) \cdot P_i(t)}{X(t)}$$

is called a *self-financing portfolio process corresponding to the pair* (φ, c).

Remark 2.59. (1) The portfolio process denotes the fractions of total wealth invested in the different stocks. Therefore, the fraction of wealth invested in the bond is given by

$$\left(1 - \pi(t)' \underline{1}\right) = \frac{\varphi_0(t) \cdot P_0(t)}{X(t)} \text{ where } \underline{1} := (1, ..., 1)' \in \mathbb{R}^d.$$

(2) Given the knowledge of the wealth $X(t)$ and the prices $P_i(t)$, it is possible for an investor to describe his activities via a self-financing pair (π, c). More precisely, in this case portfolio process and trading strategy are equivalent descriptions of the same action.

The wealth equation. The description of the trading activities by the portfolio process enables us to derive a simple stochastic differential equation for the wealth process. Let therefore (φ, c) be a self-financing pair consisting of a trading strategy and a consumption process. By additionally using Definition 2.58 we have

$$dX(t) = \sum_{i=0}^{d} \varphi_i(t) \, dP_i(t) - c(t) \, dt$$

$$= \varphi_0(t) P_0(t) r(t) \, dt +$$
$$\sum_{i=1}^{d} \varphi_i(t) P_i(t) \left(b_i(t) \, dt + \sum_{j=1}^{m} \sigma_{ij}(t) \, dW_j(t) \right) - c(t) \, dt$$

$$= \left(1 - \pi(t)' \underline{1}\right) X(t) r(t) \, dt$$
$$+ \sum_{i=1}^{d} X(t) \pi_i(t) \left(b_i(t) \, dt + \sum_{j=1}^{m} \sigma_{ij}(t) \, dW_j(t) \right) - c(t) \, dt$$

$$= \left(1 - \pi(t)' \underline{1}\right) X(t) r(t) \, dt$$
$$+ X(t) \pi(t)' b(t) \, dt + X(t) \pi(t)' \sigma(t) \, dW(t) - c(t) \, dt.$$

We thus obtain the *wealth equation*

2.2. Trading Strategy and Wealth Process

$$
\begin{aligned}
(2.22) \quad dX(t) &= [r(t) X(t) - c(t)] \, dt \\
&\quad + X(t) \pi(t)' \left((b(t) - r(t) \underline{1}) \, dt + \sigma(t) \, dW(t) \right) \\
X(0) &= x
\end{aligned}
$$

By Theorem 2.54, the variation of constants formula, this stochastic differential equation has a unique solution given some suitable integrability requirements for $\pi(t)$. As b, r, σ are uniformly bounded and as the consumption process c satisfies requirement (2.20), we only need the condition

$$
(2.23) \qquad \int_0^T \pi_i^2(t) \, dt < \infty \text{ a.s. } P
$$

for $i = 1, ..., d$ to ensure uniqueness and existence of the solution of the stochastic differential equation (2.22).

Now we are able to give an alternative definition of a portfolio process. We describe it as the process of the fractions of wealth invested in the different assets without referring to a trading strategy.

Definition 2.60. The progressively measurable $\mathbb{R}^d$-valued process $\pi(t)$ is called a *self-financing portfolio process* corresponding to the consumption process $c(t)$ if the corresponding wealth equation (2.22) possesses a unique solution $X(t) = X^{\pi,c}(t)$ with

$$
(2.24) \qquad \int_0^T (X(t) \cdot \pi_i(t))^2 \, dt < \infty \text{ a.s. } P \text{ for } i = 1, ..., d.
$$

Remark 2.61. The condition (2.24) on the portfolio process and the wealth process is indeed exactly the integrability condition (2.19) on the trading strategy and the price processes. If the portfolio process satisfies condition (2.23) then continuity of the corresponding wealth process yields that condition (2.24) is satisfied, too. Thus, condition (2.24) is weaker than condition (2.23). Note further that if there is no consumption, then condition (2.23) implies strict positivity of the wealth process. This can be seen by looking at the explicit form of the solution of equation (2.22) under assumption (2.23). However, condition (2.24) allows for portfolio processes that can lead to the ruin of the investor (i.e. it allows $X(t) = 0$ for some $t \in [0, T]$ or even negative values of $X(t)$). This will be of relevance in connection with the replication approach to option pricing.

Definition 2.62. A self-financing pair (φ, c) or (π, c) consisting of a trading strategy φ or a portfolio process π and a consumption process c will be called *admissible for the initial wealth* $x > 0$, if the corresponding wealth process

satisfies
$$X(t) \geq 0 \text{ a.s. } P \text{ for all } t \in [0, T].$$
The set of admissible pairs (π, c) will be denoted by $\mathcal{A}(x)$.

An example. After having presented so many theoretical definitions we now look at a seemingly simple example. Consider a constant portfolio process and a consumption rate that is proportional to the current wealth
$$\pi(t) \equiv \pi \in \mathbb{R}^d \text{ constant}, \ c(t) = \gamma \cdot X(t),$$
with some $\gamma > 0$, $X(t)$ being the wealth process corresponding to (π, c). Hence, the investor rebalances his holdings in such a way that the fractions of wealth invested in the different stocks and in the bond remain constant over time. Further, the velocity of the increase in consumption ("the consumption rate") is always proportional to the current wealth of the investor. Please note that although $\pi(t)$ remains constant over time, the investor has to trade at each time instant as the stock prices change at each time instant and of course each in a different way. The wealth equation corresponding to this example has the form
$$dX(t) = (r(t) - \gamma) X(t) \ dt + X(t) \pi' ((b(t) - r(t) \underline{1}) \ dt + \sigma(t) \ dW(t))$$
$$X(0) = 0.$$
By Theorem 2.54, "variation of constants", this results in a wealth process of
$$X(t) = x \cdot \exp\left(\int_0^t \left[r(s) - \gamma + \pi' (b(s) - r(s) \cdot \underline{1}) - \tfrac{1}{2} \|\pi' \sigma(s)\|^2 \right] ds \right.$$
$$\left. + \int_0^t \pi' \sigma(s) \ dW(s) \right).$$
In particular, $X(t)$ is strictly positive and we have $(\pi, c) \in \mathcal{A}(x)$. So if the investor wants to avoid bankruptcy such a strategy is a good one. It will also prove to be optimal from other viewpoints (see Chapter 5).

2.3. Properties of the Continuous-Time Market Model

In this section, we shall concentrate on the special case of $d = m$. Hence, the dimension of the underlying Brownian motion equals the number of stocks. We shall restrict ourselves to the case that past and present prices are the only sources of information for our investors. Mathematically, we

2.3. Properties of the Continuous-Time Market Model

shall model this by choosing the Brownian filtration as $\{\mathcal{F}_t\}_{t\in[0,T]}$. We are particularly interested in the set of all final wealths $X(T)$ that we can attain when starting with an initial capital of x. The surprising result will be that every final wealth $X(T)$ can be generated given a sufficient initial capital of x.

> **General assumption for this section:**
> $$d = m$$

First we need some notation:

> **Notation:**
> $\gamma(t) := \exp\left(-\int_0^t r(s)\, ds\right)$
> $\theta(t) := \sigma^{-1}(t)(b(t) - r(t)\underline{1})$
> $Z(t) := \exp\left(-\int_0^t \theta(s)'\, dW(s) - \frac{1}{2}\int_0^t \|\theta(s)\|^2\, ds\right)$
> $H(t) := \gamma(t) \cdot Z(t)$

Please note that the uniform boundedness of b and r together with the uniform positive definiteness of $\sigma\sigma'$ imply the uniform boundedness of $\|\theta(t)\|^2$. $\theta(t)$ might be interpreted as a kind of relative risk premium for stock investment. The process $H(t)$ will play a crucial role in connection with option pricing. Note that $H(t)$ is positive, continuous, and progressively measurable with respect to $\{\mathcal{F}_t\}_{t\in[0,T]}$. Further, it is the unique solution of the stochastic differential equation

(2.25) $$dH(t) = -H(t)\left(r(t)\, dt + \theta(t)'\, dW(t)\right),$$
$$H(0) = 1.$$

Note that (2.25) is the Itô process representation of $H(t)$.

The following theorem can be regarded as one of the main theorems presented in this book. It shows a remarkable property of the market model in the case $d = m$.

Theorem 2.63 (Completeness of the market). (1) *Let the self-financing pair (π, c) consisting of a portfolio process π and a consumption process c be admissible for an initial wealth of $x \geq 0$, i.e. we have $(\pi, c) \in \mathcal{A}(x)$. Then the corresponding wealth process $X(t)$*

satisfies

$$E\left(H(t)X(t) + \int_0^t H(s)c(s)\,ds\right) \leq x \text{ for all } t \in [0,T].$$

(2) Let $B \geq 0$ be an $\mathcal{F}_T$-measurable random variable and $c(t)$, $t \in [0,T]$, a consumption process satisfying

$$x := E\left(H(T)B + \int_0^T H(s)c(s)\,ds\right) < \infty.$$

Then there exists a portfolio process $\pi(t)$, $t \in [0,T]$, with $(\pi,c) \in \mathcal{A}(x)$ and the corresponding wealth process $X(t)$ satisfies

$$X(T) = B \text{ a.s. } P.$$

Implications of Theorem 2.63. In view of part (1) the process $H(t)$ can be regarded as the appropriate discounting process that determines the initial wealth at time $t=0$

$$E\left(\int_0^T H(s) \cdot c(s)\,ds\right) + E(H(T) \cdot B)$$

which is necessary to be able to attain future aims (such as living according to a given consumption process or obtaining a wealth B at time $t=T$). Thus, part (1) puts bounds on the desires of an investor given his initial capital $x \geq 0$. Part (2) proves that future aims which are feasible in the sense of part (1) can indeed be realized. Part (2) thus says that each desired final wealth in $t=T$ can be attained exactly via trading according to an appropriate self-financing pair (π,c) if one possesses sufficient initial capital. This property of our model will be called *completeness* and we shall talk of a *complete market*.

Proof of Theorem 2.63.
(1) Let $(\pi,c) \in \mathcal{A}(x)$. Application of the product rule, Corollary 2.53, to $H(t) \cdot X(t)$ yields (note the explicit forms of the wealth equation (2.22) for $X(t)$ and the stochastic differential equation (2.25) for $H(t)$):

$$(2.26) \quad H(t) \cdot X(t) + \int_0^t H(s)c(s)\,ds$$

$$= x + \int_0^t H(s)\,dX_s + \int_0^t X(s)\,dH(s) + \langle X, H\rangle_t + \int_0^t H(s)c(s)\,ds$$

2.3. Properties of the Continuous-Time Market Model

$$= x + \int_0^t H(s)X(s)\left[r(s) + \pi(s)'(b(s) - r(s) \cdot \underline{1}) - r(s)\right.$$

$$\left. - \pi(s)'\sigma(s)\theta(s)\right] ds + \int_0^t H(s)X(s)\left[\pi(s)'\sigma(s) - \theta(s)'\right] dW(s)$$

$$= x + \int_0^t H(s)X(s)\left[\pi(s)'\sigma(s) - \theta(s)'\right] dW(s).$$

Due to $(\pi, c) \in \mathcal{A}(x)$ the left-hand side of equation (2.26) is non-negative. Hence, by Theorem 2.22 the local martingale which forms the right-hand side of the equation is a super-martingale. Thus:

$$E\left(H(t)X(t) + \int_0^t H(s)c(s)\,ds\right)$$

$$= E\left(x + \int_0^t H(s)X(s)\left(\pi(s)'\sigma(s) - \theta(s)'\right) dW(s)\right) \leq x.$$

(2) Define

$$X(t) := \frac{1}{H(t)} \cdot E\left(\int_t^T H(s)c(s)\,ds + H(T) \cdot B \mid \mathcal{F}_t\right).$$

Thus, $X(t)$ is $\mathcal{F}_t$-measurable and we have $X(T) = B$ P-a.s., $X(t) \geq 0$. As $\{\mathcal{F}_t\}_t$ is the Brownian filtration, the conditional expectation of a random variable given $\mathcal{F}_0$ is P-a.s. constant and so it coincides with its unconditional expectation. This yields $X(0) = x$ P-almost surely. Now define

$$M(t) := X(t) \cdot H(t) + \int_0^t H(s)c(s)\,ds$$

$$= E\left(\int_0^T H(s)c(s)\,ds + H(T)B \mid \mathcal{F}_t\right).$$

This process is an $\{\mathcal{F}_t\}_t$-martingale with $M(0) = x$ P-almost surely. By Corollary 2.70 (see the next section on the martingale representation theorem), M can be represented as an Itô integral

$$M(t) = x + \int_0^t \Psi(s)' \, dW(s) \text{ a.s. } P \text{ for all } t \in [0, T],$$

where $\Psi(t)$ is an $\{\mathcal{F}_t\}_t$-progressively measurable, $\mathbb{R}^d$-valued process satisfying

$$\int_0^T \|\Psi(t)\|^2 \, dt < \infty \text{ a.s. } P.$$

In total, we arrive at

(2.27) $\quad X(t)H(t) + \int_0^t H(s)c(s)\,ds = x + \int_0^t \Psi(s)'\,dW(s)$ a.s. P.

In particular $X(t)$ can be chosen such that it possesses continuous paths (note that $H(t)$, $\int H(s)c(s)ds$, and the Itô integral are continuous with respect to t and that $H(t)$ is strictly positive). By the following Lemmas 2.64 and 2.65, comparison of the representations (2.26) and (2.27) yields the fact that $X(t)$ defined as above is the wealth process corresponding to the pair $(\pi, c) \in \mathcal{A}(x)$ with:

$$\pi(t) = \begin{cases} (\sigma(t)^{-1})' \left(\dfrac{\Psi(t)}{H(t)X(t)} + \theta(t) \right) & \text{if } X(t) > 0, \\ 0 & \text{otherwise.} \end{cases}$$

□

Lemma 2.64. $X(t)$ and $\pi(t)$ as in the proof of part (2) of Theorem 2.63 satisfy

$$\int_0^T (\pi_i(t)X(t))^2 \, dt < \infty \text{ a.s. } P, \ i = 1, ..., d.$$

Proof. We have

$$\|\pi(t)X(t)\| \leq \left\| (\sigma(t)^{-1})' \frac{\Psi(t)}{H(t)} + (\sigma(t)^{-1})' \theta(t) X(t) \right\|$$

$$\leq \underbrace{\left\| (\sigma(t)^{-1})' \frac{\Psi(t)}{H(t)} \right\|}_{\alpha(t)} + \underbrace{\left\| (\sigma(t)^{-1})' \theta(t) X(t) \right\|}_{\beta(t)}.$$

i) As $\sigma(t)\sigma(t)'$ is uniformly positive definite, we have

$$\alpha^2(t) \leq \frac{1}{K} \cdot \frac{\|\Psi(t)\|^2}{|H(t)|^2}.$$

2.3. Properties of the Continuous-Time Market Model

Continuity and strict positivity of $H(t)$ on $[0,T]$ implies
$$|H(t)| \geq \min_{s \in [0,T]} H(s) = H(s^*) > 0$$
for P-almost all $\omega \in \Omega$ with $s^* = s^*(\omega)$. As the integral $\int_0^T \|\Psi(t)\|^2 dt$ is finite for P-almost all $\omega \in \Omega$, we have
$$\int_0^T \alpha^2(t) \, dt \leq \frac{1}{K} \int_0^T \frac{\|\Psi(t)\|^2}{\left(\min_{s \in [0,T]} H(s)\right)^2} ds < \infty$$
for P-almost all $\omega \in \Omega$.

ii) $\beta(t)$ satisfies
$$\beta^2(t) = X^2(t) \cdot (b(t) - r(t) \cdot \underline{1})' \cdot \left(\sigma^{-1}(t)'\sigma^{-1}(t)\right)'$$
$$\cdot \left(\sigma^{-1}(t)'\sigma^{-1}(t)\right) \cdot (b(t) - r(t)\underline{1}).$$

As $\sigma(t)\sigma(t)'$ is uniformly positive definite, we have
$$\beta^2(t) \leq X^2(t) \cdot \frac{1}{K^2} \|b(t) - r(t) \cdot \underline{1}\|^2.$$

As b and r are uniformly bounded and $X(t)$ is continuous on $[0,T]$, this yields
$$\int_0^T \beta^2(t) \, dt \leq \frac{1}{K^2} \int_0^T X^2(t) \|b(t) - r(t) \cdot \underline{1}\|^2 dt$$
$$\leq \frac{1}{K^2} \left(\max_{t \in [0,T]} X(t)\right)^2 \cdot \int_0^T \|b(t) - r(t) \cdot \underline{1}\|^2 dt < \infty$$
for P-almost all $\omega \in \Omega$.

iii) Due to i), ii), and the relation $(a^2 + b^2)/2 \geq 2ab$, we arrive at
$$\int_0^T \|\pi(t) X(t)\|^2 dt \leq 2 \left(\int_0^T \alpha^2(t) \, dt + \int_0^T \beta^2(t) \, dt\right) < \infty$$
for P-almost all $\omega \in \Omega$. $\square$

Lemma 2.65. *Let $\pi(t)$, $X(t)$, $c(t)$ be as in the proof of part (2) of Theorem 2.63. If $X(t)$ solves the stochastic differential equation*
$$d(H(t)X(t)) = H(t)X(t)\left(\pi(t)'\sigma(t) - \theta(t)'\right) dW(t) - H(t)c(t) \, dt$$
$$X(0) = x,$$
then $X(t)$ is the wealth process corresponding to (π, c) with $X(0) = x$.

Proof. Let $\tilde{X}(t) := X(t)H(t)$. First assume that we have $X(t) > 0$ for all $t \in [0, T]$ P-almost surely. Together with our assumptions we have

$$d\tilde{X}(t) = H(t)\left[X(t)\left(\pi(t)'\sigma(t) - \theta(t)'\right) dW(t) - c(t) dt\right]$$
$$= H(t)\left(\frac{\Psi(t)'}{H(t)} dW(t) - c(t) dt\right)$$
$$= \Psi(t)' dW(t) - H(t)c(t) dt.$$

Application of the Itô formula, Theorem 2.49, yields

$$d\left(\frac{1}{H(t)}\right) = \frac{1}{H(t)}\left[\left(r(t) + \|\theta(t)\|^2\right) dt + \theta(t)' dW(t)\right],$$

and by the product rule, Corollary 2.53, we have

$$dX(t) = d\left(\frac{\tilde{X}(t)}{H(t)}\right) = \tilde{X}(t) \, d\left(\frac{1}{H(t)}\right) + \frac{1}{H(t)} d\tilde{X}(t) + d\left\langle\tilde{X}, \frac{1}{H}\right\rangle_t$$
$$= \left(\frac{\tilde{X}(t)}{H(t)}\left(r(t) + \|\theta(t)\|^2\right) - c(t) + \frac{\theta(t)'\Psi(t)}{H(t)}\right) dt$$
$$+ \left(\frac{\tilde{X}(t)}{H(t)}\theta(t)' + \frac{\Psi(t)'}{H(t)}\right) dW(t)$$
$$= \left(X(t)\left(r(t) + \theta(t)'\left(\theta(t) + \frac{\Psi(t)}{H(t)X(t)}\right)\right) - c(t)\right) dt$$
$$+ X(t)\left(\theta(t) + \frac{\Psi(t)}{H(t)X(t)}\right)' dW(t)$$
$$= \left(X(t)\left[r(t) + \pi(t)'(b(t) - r(t)\cdot\underline{1})\right] - c(t)\right) dt$$
$$+ X(t)\pi(t)'\sigma(t) dW(t).$$

Hence, $X(t)$ solves the wealth equation corresponding to (π, c). Due to $X(t) \geq 0$ and Lemma 2.64, we also have $(\pi, c) \in \mathcal{A}(x)$.

If we now assume that $X(t)$ attains the value of zero for some $(t_0, \omega_0) \in [0, T] \times \Omega$, then due to $H(t) > 0$ for all $t \in [0, T]$, $c(t) \geq 0$ for all $t \in [0, T]$ and $B \geq 0$, we must have

$$c(t, \omega_0) = 0 \text{ for all } t \geq t_0,$$
$$B(\omega_0) = 0.$$

Consequently $X(t, \omega_0)$ retains the value of zero on $[t_0, T]$. This implies

$$\Psi(t, \omega_0) = 0, \ \pi(t, \omega_0) = 0 \text{ for all } t \in [t_0, T].$$

In this case, we have $dX(t) = 0$ for all $t \geq t_0$. Due to $X(t) = 0$, $\pi(t) = 0$, $c(t) = 0$ this then also coincides with the right-hand side of the wealth equation. □

Remark 2.66. (1) Note that $1/H(t)$ is the wealth process corresponding to the pair
$$(\pi(t), c(t)) = \left(\sigma^{-1}(t)'\theta(t), 0\right)$$
with an initial wealth of $x := 1/H(0) = 1$ and a final wealth of $B := 1/H(T)$ (compare Exercise (10)).

(2) Further it can be shown that the portfolio process π constructed in the proof of part (2) of Theorem 2.63 is the unique (up to indistinguishability with respect to P) portfolio process with $(\pi, c) \in \mathcal{A}(x)$ and $X(T) = B$ P-a.s. (compare also with Remark 2.69).

Excursion 4: The Martingale Representation Theorem

General assumptions for this section:
Let $(\Omega, \mathcal{F}, P)$ be a complete probability space. On this space we have an m-dimensional Brownian motion $\{(W_t, \mathcal{F}_t)\}_{t \in [0,\infty)}$ with $\{\mathcal{F}_t\}_t$ being the Brownian filtration.

Definition 2.67. A real-valued martingale $\{(M_t, \mathcal{F}_t)\}_{t \in [0,T]}$ with respect to the Brownian filtration $\{\mathcal{F}_t\}_t$ is called a *Brownian martingale*.

Theorem 2.68 (Martingale representation theorem)**.** Let $\{(M_t, \mathcal{F}_t)\}_{t \in [0,T]}$ be a Brownian martingale with
$$EM_t^2 < \infty \text{ for all } t \in [0,T],$$
i.e. a square-integrable Brownian martingale. Then there exists a progressively measurable $\mathbb{R}^m$-valued process $\Psi(t)$, $t \in [0,T]$, with
$$E\left(\int_0^T \|\Psi(t)\|^2 dt\right) < \infty$$
and
$$M_t = M_0 + \int_0^t \Psi(s)' dW(s) \text{ a.s. } P.$$

Proof. As M_0 is $\mathcal{F}_0$-measurable it must be constant P-almost surely. Thus, we can w.l.o.g. assume $M_0 = 0$. As M_t is a martingale, this also yields

$E(M_t) = 0$ for all $t \in [0,T]$. Further, M_t is closed as a martingale on $[0,T]$, i.e. it has the form

(2.28) $$M_t = E(M_T \mid F_t) \text{ a.s. } P.$$

Corresponding to the Brownian filtration we now look at the vector space $L^{2,m}[0,T]$ defined by

$$L^{2,m}[0,T] := \big\{(X(t), \mathcal{F}_t)_{t \in [0,T]} \quad \mathbb{R}^m\text{-valued, progressively measurable} \\ \text{process} \mid X_i \in L^2[0,T], i = 1, ..., m\big\}.$$

Then $L^{2,m}[0,T]$ is a Hilbert space with inner product

$$\left(H, \tilde{H}\right) := E\left(\int_0^T H(s) \cdot \tilde{H}(s)\, ds\right).$$

Let $L^{2,0}(\Omega, \mathcal{F}_T, P)$ be the space of all square-integrable, $\mathcal{F}_T$-measurable random variables Z with $E(Z) = 0$. We assume $L^{2,0}(\Omega, \mathcal{F}_T, P)$ to be equipped with the usual inner product

$$\left(I, \tilde{I}\right) := E\left(I \cdot \tilde{I}\right).$$

As the mapping

$$I : L^{2,m}[0,T] \to L^{2,0}(\Omega, \mathcal{F}_T, P)$$
$$X \mapsto I_T(X) := \int_0^T X(s)\, dW(s)$$

is an isometry, the space

$$V := \big\{I_T(X) \mid X \in L^{2,m}[0,T]\big\}$$

must be a complete subspace of $L^{2,0}(\Omega, \mathcal{F}_T, P)$. If we can now prove the equality $V = L^{2,0}(\Omega, \mathcal{F}_T, P)$, then we obtain that each square integrable random variable with zero expectation can be represented as a stochastic integral with a suitable integrand $\Psi \in L^{2,m}[0,T]$. In particular, this will then be valid for the random variable M_T which implies

$$M_T = \int_0^T \Psi(s)\, dW(s).$$

Then the representation (2.28) and the martingale property of stochastic integrals with integrands in $L^{2,m}[0,T]$ yield the assertion of the theorem

$$M_t = E\left(\int_0^T \Psi(s)\, dW(s) \mid \mathcal{F}_t\right) = \int_0^t \Psi(s)\, dW(s).$$

<u>Next aim:</u> Show that V and $L^{2,0}(\Omega, \mathcal{F}_T, P)$ coincide.

Excursion 4: The Martingale Representation Theorem

Let $Z \in L^{2,0}(\Omega, \mathcal{F}_T, P) \cap V^\perp$, i.e. we have $E(Z \cdot N) = 0$ for all $N \in V$. Then the assertion $V = L^{2,0}(\Omega, \mathcal{F}_T, P)$ is equivalent to $Z \equiv 0$ P-almost surely.

(1) For $t \in [0, T]$ we define a martingale with $Z(0) = E(Z) = 0$ by

$$Z(t) := E(Z | \mathcal{F}_t) \text{ a.s. } P.$$

As the filtration $\{\mathcal{F}_t\}_t$ satisfies the usual conditions, we can assume $Z(t)$ to be right-continuous by Lemma 2.41. For $H \in L^{2,m}[0, T]$ set

$$N(T) := I_T(H), \quad N(t) := E(N(T) | \mathcal{F}_t) = I_t(H).$$

As $N(t)$ is a continuous martingale, Theorem 2.17, optional sampling, implies

$$N(\tau) = E(N(T) | \mathcal{F}_\tau) = I_\tau(H) = \int_0^T H(s) \cdot 1_{[0,\tau]}(s)\, ds \in V$$

for all stopping times $\tau \leq T$ and thus also

$$0 = E(Z \cdot N(\tau)) = E(E(Z \cdot N(\tau) | \mathcal{F}_\tau))$$
$$= E(N(\tau) E(Z | \mathcal{F}_\tau)) = E(Z(\tau) N(\tau)).$$

Hence, by the characterization of a martingale given in Theorem 2.19, $Z(t) \cdot N(t)$ is indeed a martingale.

(2) For arbitrary but fixed $\theta \in \mathbb{R}^m$ let

$$f(x, t) := \exp\left(i\theta' x + \tfrac{1}{2} \|\theta\|^2 t\right)$$

$$= \underbrace{\exp\left(\tfrac{1}{2} \|\theta\|^2 t\right) \cdot \cos(\theta' x)}_{f_1(x,t)} + i \cdot \underbrace{\left[\exp\left(\tfrac{1}{2} \|\theta\|^2 t\right) \cdot \sin(\theta' x)\right]}_{f_2(x,t)},$$

$$M^\theta(t) := f(W(t), t),$$

for $t \in [0, T]$. Then we have

$$\left|M^\theta(t)\right| = \exp\left(\tfrac{1}{2} \|\theta\|^2 t\right).$$

Application of the multi-dimensional Itô formula, Theorem 2.52, to the real and imaginary parts of f yields

$$M^\theta(t) = f_1(W(t), t) + i \cdot f_2(W(t), t)$$

$$= 1 + \sum_{j=1}^m i \cdot \int_0^t \theta_j \cdot f(W(s), s) \, dW_j(s)$$

$$+ \int_0^t \left(\tfrac{1}{2} \|\theta\|^2 - \tfrac{1}{2} \sum_{j=1}^m \theta_j^2 \right) f(W(s), s) \, ds$$

$$= 1 + \sum_{j=1}^m i \cdot \int_0^t \theta_j M^\theta(s) \, dW_j(s).$$

As $|M^\theta(t)|$ is bounded on $[0, T]$ for fixed $\theta \in \mathbb{R}^m$, the stochastic integrals after the last equality sign are indeed martingales. In particular, $M^\theta(t)$ is thus a Brownian martingale.

(3) By parts (1) and (2) of the proof $Z(t) \cdot M^\theta(t)$ is a martingale. Hence, we have

$$E\left(Z(t) \cdot M^\theta(t) | \mathcal{F}_s\right) = Z(s) \cdot M^\theta(s)$$

$$= Z(s) \cdot \exp\left(i\theta' W(s) + \tfrac{1}{2}\|\theta\|^2 s\right).$$

and thus

$$E\left(Z(t) \cdot \exp\left(i\theta' [W(t) - W(s)]\right) | \mathcal{F}_s\right) = Z(s) \cdot \exp\left(-\tfrac{1}{2}\|\theta\|^2 (t-s)\right)$$

for $0 \leq s \leq t \leq T$. With $0 = t_0 < t_1 < t_2 < \ldots < t_n \leq T$, $\Delta_k := W(t_k) - W(t_{k-1})$, $\theta_j \in \mathbb{R}^m$, $j = 1, \ldots, n$, we obtain

$$E\left(Z(T) \cdot \exp\left(i \sum_{j=1}^n \theta'_j \Delta_j\right)\right)$$

$$= E\left(E\left(Z(T) \cdot \exp\left(i \sum_{j=1}^n \theta'_j \Delta_j\right) \Big| \mathcal{F}_{t_{n-1}}\right)\right)$$

$$= \exp\left(-\tfrac{1}{2}\|\theta_n\|^2 (t_n - t_{n-1})\right) \cdot E\left(Z(t_{n-1}) \cdot \exp\left(i \sum_{j=1}^{n-1} \theta'_j \Delta_j\right)\right)$$

$$= \cdots = \exp\left(-\tfrac{1}{2} \sum_{j=1}^n \|\theta_j\|^2 (t_j - t_{j-1})\right) \cdot E(Z(0)) = 0,$$

due to $Z(0) = 0$. Thus, we have

$$Z(T) \perp \exp\left(i\sum_{j=1}^{n} \theta_j' \Delta_j\right) \text{ for all } \theta_j \in \mathbb{R}^m, \, j = 1, ..., n.$$

As $Z(T) = Z$ is $\mathcal{F}_T$-measurable we can define the following measure $\tilde{P}$ on $\mathcal{F}_T$ via

$$d\tilde{P} = Z \cdot dP.$$

By (3), for an arbitrary $\theta_j \in \mathbb{R}^m$ we have

$$0 = E\left(Z \cdot \exp\left(i\sum_{j=1}^{n} \theta_j' \Delta_j\right)\right) = \tilde{E}\left(\exp\left(i\sum_{j=1}^{n} \theta_j' \Delta_j\right)\right).$$

Uniqueness of the Fourier transform then implies

$$\tilde{P}\Big|_{\sigma(W(t_1),...W(t_n))} = 0.$$

As the σ-field $\mathcal{F}_T$ is generated by the finite-dimensional vectors $(W(t_1), ..., W(t_n))$ we even have

$$\tilde{P}\Big|_{\mathcal{F}_T} = 0,$$

which leads to $Z = 0$ P-almost surely.

$\square$

Remark 2.69. The integrand Ψ of the martingale representation theorem is unique with respect to $P \otimes \lambda$. This also implies the uniqueness of the portfolio process π constructed in Theorem 2.63. To see the uniqueness note the following chain of implications. From

$$M(T) = M(0) + \int_0^T \Psi(s)' dW(s) = M(0) + \int_0^T \tilde{\Psi}(s)' dW(s)$$

we obtain

$$0 = \int_0^T \left(\Psi(s) - \tilde{\Psi}(s)\right)' dW(s)$$

which results in

$$0 = E\left(\int_0^T \left(\Psi(s) - \tilde{\Psi}(s)\right)' dW(s)\right)^2 = E\left(\int_0^T \left\|\Psi(s) - \tilde{\Psi}(s)\right\|^2 ds\right)$$

and finally implies $P \otimes \lambda$-uniqueness.

By suitable localization we can deduce the following corollary from Theorem 2.68 (see Exercise (12)).

Corollary 2.70. *Let $\{(M_t, \mathcal{F}_t)\}_{t \in [0,T]}$ be a local martingale with respect to the Brownian filtration $\{\mathcal{F}_t\}_t$. Then there exists a progressively measurable $\mathbb{R}^m$-valued process $\Psi(t)$, $t \in [0,T]$, with*

$$\int_0^T \|\Psi(t)\|^2\, dt < \infty$$

and

$$M_t = M_0 + \int_0^t \Psi(s)'\, dW(s) \quad a.s.\ P.$$

Remark 2.71. By Corollary 2.70 each local martingale with respect to the Brownian filtration can be represented as an Itô process. Hence, this is also the case for each (not necessarily square-integrable) Brownian martingale. In particular, for all these processes the quadratic variation and quadratic covariation are defined.

Exercises

(1) Prove: If Y is a modification of the stochastic process X and if X and Y both have continuous paths then they are indistinguishable.

(2) Let τ be a stopping time and $\{(X_t, \mathcal{F}_t)\}_{t \geq 0}$ a right-continuous (sub-)martingale. Show that under these assumptions the stopped process $\{(X_{t \wedge \tau}, \mathcal{F}_t)\}_{t \geq 0}$ is again a (sub-)martingale.

(3) Let the process $\{P(t)\}_{t \geq 0}$ be defined by

$$P(t) = p \cdot e^{\left(b - \frac{1}{2}\sigma^2\right)t + \sigma W(t)},$$

where $W(t)$ is a one-dimensional Brownian motion, $p, b, \sigma \in \mathbb{R}$ are real constants with $\sigma \neq 0$.
Show:
 (a) $\operatorname{Var}(P(t)) = p^2 e^{2bt}\left(e^{\sigma^2 t} - 1\right)$.
 (b) $P(t) \xrightarrow{t \to \infty} \begin{cases} \infty & \text{a.s. } P \text{ if } b > \frac{1}{2}\sigma^2 \\ 0 & \text{a.s. } P \text{ if } b < \frac{1}{2}\sigma^2 \end{cases}$.
 (c) Compare the result of (b) with the limiting behavior of $E(P(t))$, $\operatorname{Var}(P(t))$ for $t \to \infty$.

(4) Let $\{(X(t), \mathcal{F}_t)\}_{t \geq 0}$ be a stochastic process with a filtration $\{\mathcal{F}_t\}_t$ satisfying the usual conditions.
Show that for all $n \in \mathbb{N}$ the random variable $\tau(\omega) := \inf\{t \geq 0 \mid X(t, \omega) \geq n\}$ is a stopping time.

Exercises

(5) Let $\{(X(t), \mathcal{F}_t)\}_{t \geq 0}$ be a one-dimensional Itô process. Prove that its representation

$$X(t) = X(0) + \int_0^t K(s)\,ds + \int_0^t H(t)\,dW(s)$$

is uniquely determined. More precisely, if

$$X(t) = Y(0) + \int_0^t \mu(s)\,ds + \int_0^t \sigma(t)\,dW(s)$$

is another representation, then we have
- $X(0) = Y(0)$ a.s. P
- $K(s)$ and $\mu(s)$ as well as $H(s)$ and $\sigma(s)$ are equivalent with respect to $\lambda \otimes P$.

Hint:
   (a) Show that a continuous martingale $\{(M(t), \mathcal{F}_t)\}_{t \in [0,T]}$ of the form

$$M(t) = \int_0^t v(s)\,ds \text{ with } \int_0^T |v(s)|\,ds \leq C < \infty$$

satisfies:

$$\lim_{n \to \infty} E\left(\sum_{i=1}^n \left(M\left(\tfrac{iT}{n}\right) - M\left(\tfrac{(i-1)T}{n}\right)\right)^2\right) = 0,$$

$$E\left(\sum_{i=1}^n \left(M\left(\tfrac{iT}{n}\right) - M\left(\tfrac{(i-1)T}{n}\right)\right)^2\right) = E\left(M(T)^2 - M(0)^2\right).$$

In particular, due to $M(0) = 0$ these two equalities imply $M(t) = 0$ for all $t \in [0, T]$ P-almost surely.
   (b) By suitably stopping (and taking the limit $n \to \infty$) show that the assertion of (a) is also valid under the assumption of $\int_0^T |v(s)|\,ds < \infty$ a.s. P.
   (c) Apply the result of part (b) to the continuous (local) martingale $M(t) := \int_0^t (H(s) - \sigma(s))\,dW(s) = \int_0^t (\mu(s) - K(s))\,ds$.

(6) Show that the processes M_t and H_t occuring in the proof of Itô's formula satisfy

$$E\left(\sum_{k=1}^m \left((M_{t_k} - M_{t_{k-1}})^2 - \int_{t_{k-1}}^{t_k} H_s^2\,ds\right)\right)^2$$

$$= E\left(\sum_{k=1}^m \left((M_{t_k} - M_{t_{k-1}})^2 - \int_{t_{k-1}}^{t_k} H_s^2\,ds\right)^2\right)$$

under the assumptions made there.

(7) Let $\{(X(t), \mathcal{F}_t)\}_{t \geq 0}$ be an Itô process. Let τ be a stopping time. Prove that for suitable f we have:
$$\int_0^s f(X(t \wedge \tau))\, dX(t \wedge \tau) = \int_0^{s \wedge \tau} f(X(t))\, dX(t).$$

(8) Prove the product rule, Corollary 2.53.

(9) Let $\{(W(t), \mathcal{F}_t)\}_{t \geq 0}$ be a one-dimensional Brownian motion. Show that the following processes are martingales with respect to $\{\mathcal{F}_t\}_t$:
   (a) $X(t) = \exp\left(\frac{t}{2}\right) \cdot \cos(W(t))$;
   (b) $X(t) = \exp\left(\frac{t}{2}\right) \cdot \sin(W(t))$;
   (c) $X(t) = (W(t) + t) \cdot \exp\left(-W(t) - \frac{t}{2}\right)$.

   Hint: Itô formula.

(10) Let $H(t)$ be defined as in Section 2.3, p. 65.
   (a) Show that $1/H(t)$ is the wealth process corresponding to the pair
   $$(\pi(t), c(t)) = \left(\sigma^{-1}(t)' \sigma^{-1}(t)(b(t) - r(t) \cdot \underline{1}), 0\right)$$
   and an initial wealth of $x = 1/H(0) = 1$.
   (b) Let $(\pi, c) \in \mathcal{A}(1)$ with $c \equiv 0$ and
   $$E\left(\int_0^T \pi(t)' \sigma(t)\, dW(t)\right) = 0, \quad \int_0^T \left\|\pi(t)^2\right\| dt < \infty.$$
   Show that if for the wealth process X(t) corresponding to $(\pi, 0)$ the expected value $E(\ln(X(T)))$ exists then we have
   $$E(\ln(X(T))) \leq E\left(\ln\left(\frac{1}{H(T)}\right)\right).$$
   (Remark: The portfolio process corresponding to $1/H(t)$ is therefore called *growth optimum portfolio*.)

(11) Let $B \geq -K$ be an $\mathcal{F}_T$-measurable random variable with $K > 0$ and $T > 0$ fixed. Show that under suitable assumptions there exist an initial wealth of $x \geq -K$ and a trading strategy φ such that the corresponding wealth process $X(t)$ satisfies
$$X(t) \geq -K \text{ for all } t \in [0, T],$$
$$X(T) = B \text{ a.s. } P.$$

(12) By suitable localization deduce Corollary 2.70 from the martingale representation theorem.

Chapter 3

Option Pricing

3.1. Introduction

The most important application of the Itô calculus in financial mathematics is that of option pricing. In this area, the most famous result is the Black-Scholes formula for pricing European put and call options. As a tribute to the importance of the formula for both theory and practical applications, Robert Merton and Myron Scholes were awarded the Nobel Prize for Economics in 1997 to honour their contributions to option pricing. Sadly, Fischer Black had passed away two years before.

Options are so-called derivative securities, i.e. securities which are derived from underlying assets. Options have been traded for centuries, but it was in this century that they finally gained economic importance. They became especially popular since 1973, when they were traded in an organized way on The Chicago Board Options Exchange.

In general, a *call option* (for short: *call*) is a contract that gives the holder the right (but not the obligation!) to buy a fixed amount of an asset at a specified time in future for an already agreed price, the *strike price* or *exercise price*, from the seller, also called *writer* of the option. The opposite option is a *put option* (for short: *put*). By buying it the holder receives the right to sell a fixed amount of an asset to the writer of the option for the strike price. Here the writer of the put option is obliged to buy the asset while the holder can decide on selling or not. We usually distinguish between so-called *American options* and *European options*. With an American option the holder of the option is free to sell or to buy the asset during the whole timespan of the contract, in contrast to a European option where the holder can only exercise his option at maturity of the contract. The day when the contract ceases to exist is called *expiry* or *expiration date*.

Today there exist options on equities, bonds, goods such as oil, metals, corn, pork bellies, currencies, or even on options. They are traded in enormous volumes on stock exchanges all over the world. Also, the explicit form of the option contracts can be very different from the above described *plain vanilla* puts and calls. We will present some examples of these *exotic options* in Chapter 4.

Example: European call. A European call on one share of a stock offers the buyer of the option the right to buy this share at time $t = T$ (at *maturity*) for the strike price $K \geq 0$ which was fixed at time $t = 0$. So if the share price $P_1(t)$ at $t = T$ exceeds K then the holder of the option is able to buy the share at a price of K. He can then sell the share immediately at the market for the price of $P_1(T)$. Thus, he makes a gain of $P_1(T) - K$ (of course ignoring transaction costs). If, however, we have $P_1(T) < K$ then the holder of the option does not make use of his right to buy that share at the price K. If he would be interested in buying that share, he could get it cheaper in the market! Thus, in this case, the gain from holding the option is zero. Putting the two cases together we see that holding a European call option leads to a payment of

$$(P_1(T) - K)^+ \text{ at } t = T.$$

Example: European put. A European put gives the holder of the option the right to sell one share at time $t = T$ for the price $K > 0$. Thus, by similar considerations as for the European call, he makes a gain of

$$(K - P_1(T))^+ \text{ at } t = T.$$

Payoff diagrams. Practitioners often describe options - or more precisely their value at expiry - by so-called *payoff diagrams*. This is simply the graph of the final gain through this option as a function of the stock price $P_1(T)$ at time T. Of course, this is only possible if the final payment can be represented as a function of $P_1(T)$. Figure 3.1 shows the payoff diagram for the European call and Figure 3.2 shows the payoff diagram for the European put.

It is common to combine these two types of diagrams to generate different types of payoff profiles (which corresponds to holding a certain combination of puts and calls; see also Exercise (1)).

A short history of option trading. The first intensive use of options occured at the beginning of the 17th century in the Netherlands. Then, during the "tulip mania", the tulip growers wanted some insurance against

3.1. Introduction

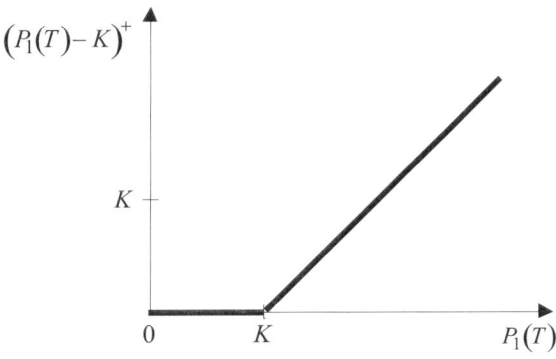

Figure 3.1. Payoff diagram of a call

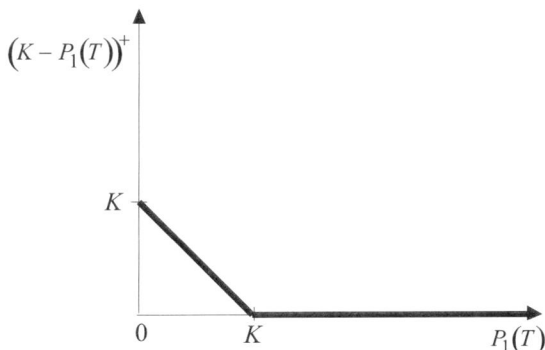

Figure 3.2. Payoff diagram of a put

fluctuations in prices. Therefore, they bought contracts giving them the right to sell tulips for a fixed price to the sellers of these contracts if the market price of tulips would decline. Obviously this was some kind of a put option. The sellers of these contracts were hoping for a price increase so that the tulip growers would not make use of the contracts and they could get away with the gain out of the contract deal. But then, in 1637, the Dutch tulip market crashed and the option sellers were not able to keep their part of the agreements. The consequence was a serious economic crisis in the Netherlands. Moreover, options and option-type contracts received a bad reputation in Europe, which lasted for some time.

The organized trading of options started in London in the 18th century. Due to the absence of strict laws for option trading, there often occured irregularities such as put option writers who were unable to pay or call option writers who were unable to deliver the stocks. This was put to an end when in 1930 option trading was put into a framework of law.

But it was in the beginning of the 1970s that trading in options gained the economic importance it still has today. One key event responsible for this evolution was the opening of the Chicago Board Options Exchange in 1973. Since then, organized option trading has spread all over the world.

Why are options traded at all? The main reason to buy an option is the possibility to hedge against non-favourable price fluctuations of the underlying asset (just remember the intention of the Dutch tulip growers). Of course, it depends on the type of option against which risk (price increase or price decrease) the holder of the option is hedged. With the help of option contracts risks of future cash flows can be eliminated or bounded. A typical application is the following: Assume that a European company trading worldwide has to make a payment of 10 million dollars next spring. By buying a call option on dollars with a strike price of 1.14 Euro for 1 dollar with maturity next spring, the company is insured against an increase of the exchange rate for dollars. If however the exchange rate would be lower the company could buy the dollars at the market.

Of course, options are also traded by speculators who hope for an overproportional increase of the option value compared to the price of the underlying asset. For example, it is obvious that the price of an option increases less then one dollar if the price of the underlying stock increases by one dollar. However, the relative price increase of the option will typically be higher than that of the stock in this case. This is the so-called *leverage effect* (see Exercise (14)). Further, options are attractive for speculators as they are much cheaper than the underlying asset itself and so with little capital it is possible to make relatively large gains. But it should not be forgotten that with options speculators also suffer big losses; in fact, it is not unusual to lose everything.

A short history of option pricing. The theory of option pricing in its contemporary form has its origin in the dissertation "Théorie de la Spéculation" of L. Bachelier in 1900 [**BACH 00**]. In this work one can also find the first mathematical description of Brownian motion as a stochastic process (but not under the name Brownian motion). It was Bachelier's aim to model stock prices as a Brownian motion with drift. He then wanted to derive theoretical prices for options on these stocks and wanted to compare them with the actual market prices. His suggestion for an option price was the use of the expected value of the discounted payments caused by an option. The main drawback of Bachelier's modeling was the possibility of negative prices in his setting.

Bachelier's work was then forgotten for a long time. After the introduction of geometric Brownian motion in the sixties, Fischer Black and Myron Scholes obtained the decisive breakthrough in 1973 [**BL/SC 73**]. The method of Black and Scholes for deriving the Black-Scholes formula will be presented in Section 3.3. We shall first describe the more modern approach of option pricing via the replication principle in Section 3.2. It is a natural application of martingale theory and in particular the martingale representation theorem. The work of J. M. Harrison and S. R. Pliska [**HA/PL 81**] can be viewed as the starting point for this approach in a continuous-time setting.

3.2. Option Pricing via the Replication Principle

We face the problem of finding a reasonable price $\hat{p}$ for an option, as for example for a European call. We know that a fixed deterministic payment of B at the future time T has a value of

$$e^{-rT} \cdot B$$

if we assume a constant bond interest rate of r. This is called the *present value* or the *discounted value* of the amount B paid at time T. It equals exactly the sum that has to be invested in the bond at time $t = 0$ to obtain an amount of B at time T as a consequence of this bond investment. If the interest rate $r(t)$ is a random variable and also time dependent we would then consider the expected value

$$E\left(e^{-\int_0^T r(s)\,ds} \cdot B\right).$$

By investing this amount of money in the bond at time $t = 0$, we would receive an expected payment of B at time T. It is now a natural choice to identify today's option price as the expected value of the option's terminal payment discounted by the bond price at time t. So for a European call this would lead to the suggestion of

$$\hat{p} = E\left(e^{-\int_0^T r(s)\,ds} \cdot (P_1(T) - K)^+\right).$$

In the following we shall demonstrate that in general this leads to a *wrong price*! Note therefore that discounting the final payment by the bond price was an arbitrary choice which ignored the possibility to invest money in other securities.

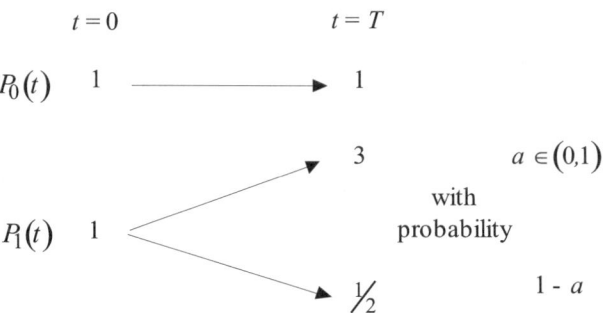

Figure 3.3. Price diagram in a discrete-time setting

A discrete-time example of option pricing. To demonstrate the method of the replication principle we first take a look at a simple discrete-time setting. We consider a market where a bond with price $P_0(t)$ and a stock with price $P_1(t)$ are traded. For simplicity we assume an interest rate of $r = 0$ and look at a European call with strike $K = 1$. The possible price movements are given by the diagram in Figure 3.3.

Hence, we have

$$E\left((P_1(T) - K)^+\right) = (3 - 1) \cdot a + 0 \cdot (1 - a) = 2 \cdot a.$$

This price would depend on the personal view toward the probability of success a. Note that a is unknown! In the following we shall see that this critical parameter does not enter the "true" option price. The main reason for this is that the option is a redundant security. Its final payment can also be obtained by following a suitably self-financing trading strategy in stock and bond. This principle of synthetically constructing the option is called the *replication principle*. For this we have to determine $(\varphi_0(0), \varphi_1(0))$ such that we obtain

(3.1) $\qquad X(T) = \varphi_0(0) P_0(T) + \varphi_1(0) P_1(T) = (P_1(T) - K)^+.$

Then, as the option price we set

$$\hat{p} = \varphi_0(0) P_0(0) + \varphi_1(0) P_1(0).$$

Hence, the option price equals the initial capital needed in $t = 0$ to buy the replication strategy $(\varphi_0(0), \varphi_1(0))$. This will prove to be the only reasonable price of the option as for all other choices there exist possibilities of riskless gains without initial capital, so-called *arbitrage opportunities*.

To see this, assume first that the option price $\tilde{p}$ would be smaller than $\hat{p}$. Then we could buy the option for $\tilde{p}$ and sell $(\varphi_0(0), \varphi_1(0))$ for $\hat{p}$ (i.e. we hold the position $(-\varphi_0(0), -\varphi_1(0))$. At time $t = T$ the payments obtained from possession of the option and from holding the position $(-\varphi_0(0), -\varphi_1(0))$

3.2. Option Pricing via the Replication Principle

neutralize each other. Hence, we would have realized a gain of $(\hat{p} - \tilde{p})$ at time $t = 0$ without the use of our own capital.

As existing arbitrage opportunities would be realized by all market participants they can only exist for a very short time. Then the market situation would lead to price adjustments wiping out the arbitrage opportunity. It is therefore reasonable to assume the absence of arbitrage in a good market model.

If the call price $\tilde{p}$ would be greater than $\hat{p}$ then we would sell the call and hold the position $(\varphi_0(0), \varphi_1(0))$ which only costs $\hat{p}$. As above we would have realized a riskless gain of $(\tilde{p} - \hat{p})$ at $t = 0$.

In our example requirement (3.1) yields the system of equations

$$\varphi_0(0) \cdot 1 + \varphi_2(0) \cdot 3 = 2$$
$$\varphi_0(0) \cdot 1 + \varphi_2(0) \cdot \tfrac{1}{2} = 0$$

with the unique solution

$$(\varphi_0(0), \varphi_1(0)) = \left(-\tfrac{2}{5}, \tfrac{4}{5}\right).$$

Hence, the only reasonable option price must be given by

$$\hat{p} = -\tfrac{2}{5} \cdot 1 + \tfrac{4}{5} \cdot 1 = \tfrac{2}{5}.$$

This price now is independent of the unknown probability a. As this solution is unique, the market consisting of stock, bond, and call option does not contain any arbitrage opportunity. Note further that the above calculated call price coincides with the expected value of the discounted terminal payment of the call if and only if we have $a = 1/5$. In this case, $P_1(t)$ is even a martingale. This is no coincidence as we will later see.

General assumptions:
Here we shall make the same assumptions as in Chapter 2, Section 2, p. 57, and use the notation of Section 3, p. 65. Specifically, we assume that the self-financing pair (π, c) is admissible for an initial capital of $x \geq 0$, i.e. we assume $(\pi, c) \in \mathcal{A}(x)$. Thus in particular the assumptions of Theorem 2.63 (complete markets) are satisfied.

We first have to define the notion of an arbitrage opportunity:

Definition 3.1. A self-financing and admissible pair (φ, c), consisting of a trading strategy φ and a consumption process c is called an *arbitrage opportunity* if the corresponding wealth process satisfies:

$$X(0) = 0, \ X(T) \geq 0 \text{ a.s. } P,$$

$$P(X(T) > 0) > 0 \text{ or } P\left(\int_0^T c(t)\, dt > 0\right) > 0.$$

Corollary 3.2. *In the complete continuous-time market model there is no arbitrage opportunity.*

Proof. This is a direct consequence of Theorem 2.63:

Let (φ, c) be an arbitrage opportunity. Then, as $H(t)$ is strictly positive, we have:

$$E\left(H(T)X(T) + \int_0^T H(s)c(s)\, ds\right) > 0 = X(0) = x.$$

But this is a contradiction to Theorem 2.63 (1). Hence, there is no arbitrage opportunity. □

To enable us to price various kinds of options in the following, we generalize the concept behind put and call options in the following definition:

Definition 3.3. A *contingent claim* (g, B) consists of an $\{\mathcal{F}_t\}_t$-progressively measurable payout rate process $g(t)$, $t \in [0, T]$, $g(t) \geq 0$, and an $\mathcal{F}_T$-measurable terminal payment $B \geq 0$ at time $t = T$ with

(3.2) $$E\left(\left(\int_0^T g(t)\, dt + B\right)^\mu\right) < \infty \text{ for some } \mu > 1.$$

Remark 3.4. (1) In the sequel we shall use the name option as a synonym for contingent claim although this might be a slight misuse.

(2) The above definition of a contingent claim only generalizes options of European type where the time of the terminal payment is fixed. It does not contain options of American type where the time of the final payment can be chosen freely.

Examples of contingent claims.

(1) European call: $g \equiv 0$, $B = (P_1(T) - K)^+$.

(2) European put: $g \equiv 0$, $B = (K - P_1(T))^+$.

(3) Continuous dividend payment: $g(t) \equiv \delta P_1(t)$ for all $t \in [0, T]$ with some $\delta > 0$, $B \equiv 0$.

In analogy to the discrete-time example, the fair price of the contingent claim (g, B) will be defined as the minimal initial value which is needed to set up a replication strategy for (g, B).

3.2. Option Pricing via the Replication Principle

Definition 3.5. (1) (π, c) is called a *replication strategy* for the contingent claim (g, B) if we have

$$g(t) = c(t) \text{ a.s. } P \text{ for all } t \in [0, T],$$
$$X(T) = B \text{ a.s. } P,$$

where $X(t)$ is the wealth process corresponding to (π, c).

(2) The *set of replication strategies of price* x is the set

$$\mathcal{D}(x) := \mathcal{D}(x; (g, B)) := \{(\pi, c) \in \mathcal{A}(x) \mid$$
$$(\pi, c) \text{ replication strategy for } (g, B)\}.$$

(3) The *fair price* of the contingent claim (g, B) is defined as

$$\hat{p} := \inf \{p \mid \mathcal{D}(p) \neq \emptyset\}.$$

Remark 3.6. The uniform boundedness of $r(t)$, $b(t)$, $\sigma(t)$, the uniformly positive definiteness of $\sigma(t)\sigma(t)'$, assumption (3.2) and Hölder's inequality altogether imply:

$$\tilde{x} := E\left(H(T)B + \int_0^T H(t)g(t) \, dt\right) < \infty.$$

Hence, by the theorem on complete markets, Theorem 2.63, there exists a portfolio process π corresponding to B and g such that we have $(\pi, g) \in \mathcal{A}(x) \cap \mathcal{D}(\tilde{x})$. In particular, this yields

$$\hat{p} \leq \tilde{x}.$$

We now show that we even have equality.

Theorem 3.7 (Fair price of a contingent claim). *The fair price of the contingent claim (g, B) is given by*

$$\hat{p} = E\left(H(T)B + \int_0^T H(t)g(t) \, dt\right) < \infty,$$

and there exists a unique (with respect to $P \otimes \lambda$) replication strategy $(\hat{\pi}, \hat{c}) \in \mathcal{D}(\hat{p})$. Its wealth process $\hat{X}(t)$ (also called valuation process *of (g, B)) is given by*

$$\hat{X}(t) = \frac{1}{H(t)} E\left(H(T)B + \int_t^T H(s)g(s) \, ds \mid \mathcal{F}_t\right).$$

Remark 3.8. Theorem 3.7 also gives us the fair price of the contingent claim (g, B) at time t as this price $\hat{p}(t)$ has to coincide with $\hat{X}(t)$. Otherwise, there would be arbitrage opportunities in the market consisting of stock, bond, and contingent claim.

Proof of Theorem 3.7. In Remark 3.6 we have already shown $\hat{p} \leq \tilde{x}$ ($\tilde{x}$ defined as above). So we only have to prove $\hat{p} \geq \tilde{x}$. Let therefore $(\pi, c) \in \mathcal{D}(x)$ be a replication strategy for (g, B) with wealth process $X(t)$ and price $x = X(0)$. Then by Theorem 2.63 (1) and the replication property of (π, c) we have

$$x \geq E\left(H(T) X(T) + \int_0^T H(s) c(s) \, ds\right)$$

$$= E\left(H(T) B + \int_0^T H(s) g(s) \, ds\right) = \tilde{x}.$$

This implies

$$\hat{p} = \inf\{x \mid \mathcal{D}(x) \neq \emptyset\} \geq \tilde{x},$$

and all remaining claims of the theorem follow from the proof of Theorem 2.63. □

Significance of the process $H(t)$. Let $g \equiv 0$. The equality

$$\hat{p} = E(H(T) B) = \int_\Omega H(T, \omega) B(\omega) \, P(d\omega)$$

shows that the price of the option is indeed given as an expected value of a "discounted" terminal payment in $t = T$ but with the special discount factor $H(T)$ instead of $1/P_0(T)$. $H(T, \omega)$ gives us today's value of one unit of money paid at time $t = T$ if the state of economy is $\omega \in \Omega$. Thus, $H(T)$ can be regarded as a state dependent discount factor. In particular, all basic securities which are available in our market come into consideration in the factor $H(T)$.

As a first application of Theorem 3.7 we can now deduce the famous Black-Scholes formula for the prices of European calls and puts:

Corollary 3.9 (Black-Scholes formula). *Consider a market model consisting of one stock and a bond with constant market coefficients, i.e.*

$$d = m = 1,$$

$$r(t) \equiv r, \quad b(t) \equiv b, \quad \sigma(t) \equiv \sigma > 0$$

for all $t \in [0, T]$, $T > 0$, $r, b, \sigma \in \mathbb{R}$.
(1) The price $X_C(t)$ at time t of a European call option with strike price $K > 0$ and maturity T is given by

3.2. Option Pricing via the Replication Principle

$$X_C(t) = P_1(t) \cdot \Phi(d_1(t)) - K \cdot e^{-r(T-t)} \Phi(d_2(t))$$

$$d_1(t) = \frac{\ln\left(\frac{P_1(t)}{K}\right) + \left(r + \frac{1}{2}\sigma^2\right)(T-t)}{\sigma\sqrt{T-t}} \quad \text{"Call"}$$

$$d_2(t) = \frac{\ln\left(\frac{P_1(t)}{K}\right) + \left(r - \frac{1}{2}\sigma^2\right)(T-t)}{\sigma\sqrt{T-t}} = d_1(t) - \sigma\sqrt{T-t}$$

where Φ is the distribution function of the standard normal distribution.

(2) The price $X_P(t)$ of a European put option with strike price $K > 0$ and maturity T is given by

$$X_P(t) = K \cdot e^{-r(T-t)} \cdot \Phi(-d_2(t)) - P_1(t) \Phi(-d_1(t)) \quad \text{"Put"}$$

where $d_i(t)$ are defined as in part (1).

Proof.
(1) For ease of notation we only prove the assertion for $t = 0$. By Theorem 3.7 we have

$$X_C(0) = E\left(H(T)(P_1(T) - K)^+\right)$$
$$= E\big(\exp\left(-\left[r + \tfrac{1}{2}\theta^2\right]T - \theta \cdot W(T)\right)$$
$$\cdot \left(p_1 \cdot \exp\left(\left[b - \tfrac{1}{2}\sigma^2\right]T + \sigma W(T)\right) - K\right)^+\big)$$

with $\theta = (b-r)/\sigma$. Here the positive part $(\ldots)^+$ is strictly positive if and only if we have

$$W(T) > \frac{1}{\sigma}\left(\ln\left(\frac{K}{p_1}\right) - \left(b - \tfrac{1}{2}\sigma^2\right)T\right) =: \hat{K}.$$

As $W(T)$ is normally distributed with expected value 0 and variance T, we obtain

$$X_C(0) = \int_{\hat{K}}^{\infty} e^{-\left(r+\frac{1}{2}\theta^2\right)T - \theta x}\left(p_1 \cdot e^{\left(b-\frac{1}{2}\sigma^2\right)T + \sigma x} - K\right) \cdot \frac{1}{\sqrt{2\pi T}} \cdot e^{-\frac{x^2}{2T}}\, dx$$

$$= p_1 \cdot \int_{\hat{K}}^{\infty} \frac{1}{\sqrt{2\pi T}} \cdot \exp\left(\left(b - \tfrac{1}{2}\sigma^2 - r - \tfrac{1}{2}\theta^2\right)T + (\sigma - \theta)x - \frac{x^2}{2T}\right) dx$$

$$- K \cdot \int_{\hat{K}}^{\infty} \exp(-rT) \cdot \frac{1}{\sqrt{2\pi T}} \exp\left(-\tfrac{1}{2}\theta^2 T - \theta x - \frac{x^2}{2T}\right) dx.$$

A suitable grouping in the exponents yields

$$X_C(0) = p_1 \int_{\hat{K}}^{\infty} \frac{1}{\sqrt{2\pi T}} \cdot \exp\left(\frac{(x-(\sigma-\theta)T)^2}{2T}\right) dx$$

$$- K \cdot \exp(-rT) \cdot \int_{\hat{K}}^{\infty} \frac{1}{\sqrt{2\pi T}} \cdot \exp\left(\frac{(x+\theta T)^2}{2T}\right) dx$$

$$= p_1 \cdot \left(1 - \Phi\left(\frac{\hat{K}-(\sigma-\theta)T}{\sqrt{T}}\right)\right) - K \cdot e^{-rT} \cdot \left(1 - \Phi\left(\frac{\hat{K}+\theta T}{\sqrt{T}}\right)\right)$$

$$= p_1 \cdot \Phi\left(\frac{\ln\left(\frac{p_1}{K}\right) + \left(r + \frac{1}{2}\sigma^2\right)T}{\sigma\sqrt{T}}\right) - K \cdot e^{-rT} \cdot \Phi\left(\frac{\ln\left(\frac{p_1}{K}\right) + \left(r - \frac{1}{2}\sigma^2\right)T}{\sigma\sqrt{T}}\right).$$

(2) is proved similar to (1). $\square$

Remark 3.10. (1) The Black-Scholes formula for the European call and the European put does not depend on the drift coefficient b ("the mean rate of return") of the stock price. This most surprising result is possibly the main reason for the acceptance of the formula in practice as b seems to be that parameter which depends the most on the subjective view of an investor toward the future behavior of the stock price. As b does not enter the Black-Scholes formula we speak of a *preference free valuation*.

(2) We can show by suitable differentation: $X_C(t)$ decreases in t and increases in r, $P_1(t)$ and σ (for $\sigma > 0$). To show this the following identities prove to be useful:

$$d_2(t) = d_1(t) - \sigma\sqrt{T-t},$$

$$P_1(t)\varphi(d_1(t)) = Ke^{-r(T-t)}\varphi(d_2(t)),$$

where $\varphi(.)$ is the probability density function of the standard normal distribution (see also Exercise (2)).

(3) To give the proof of the Black-Scholes formula for general $t \in [0,T]$ instead of $t = 0$, please note that we have

$$P_1(T) = P_1(t) \cdot \exp\left(\left(b - \tfrac{1}{2}\sigma^2\right)(T-t) + \sigma(W(T) - W(t))\right)$$

and that the increment $W(T) - W(t)$ of the Brownian motion is independent of $\mathcal{F}_s$, $s \leq t$ and $\mathcal{N}(0, T-t)$-distributed. This yields

$$X_C(t) = E\left(\frac{H(T)}{H(t)}(P_1(T)-K)^+ \mid F_t\right)$$
$$= E\left(\frac{H(T)}{H(t)}(P_1(T)-K)^+ \mid W(t)\right).$$

But as in our setting of constant market coefficients, the value of $W(t)$ is uniquely determined by $P_1(t)$ and vice versa, so we also write

$$X_C(t) = E^{t,P_1(t)}\left(\frac{H(T)}{H(t)}(P_1(T)-K)^+\right)$$
$$:= E\left(\frac{H(T)}{H(t)}(P_1(T)-K)^+ \mid P_1(t)\right).$$

This sole dependence on the current stock price (and not on past stock prices) of the future price evolution of the option is called the Markov property. As long as the stock price process is given by a geometric Brownian motion the Markov property is a direct consequence of the independence of the increments of the Brownian motion. For more general stock price processes it will be implied by the Markov property of solutions to stochastic differential equations. This fact will play an important role in the next section where we shall look at the connection between option prices and partial differential equations. It will then be presented in more detail.

Notation: The Greeks. In practice, some derivatives of the option price $X(t)$ with respect to various parameters are calculated to judge the sensitivity of the option price with respect to fluctuations of these parameters. The importance of these derivatives is underlined by the fact that they even have special names ("the Greeks"). So the following are called

$$\frac{\partial}{\partial t}X(t) \quad \Theta \quad \text{"Theta"}$$
$$\frac{\partial}{\partial P_1(t)}X(t) \quad \Delta \quad \text{"Delta"}$$
$$\frac{\partial^2}{\partial P_1(t)^2}X(t) \quad \Gamma \quad \text{"Gamma"}$$
$$\frac{\partial}{\partial \sigma}X(t) \quad \quad \text{"Vega"}$$
$$\frac{\partial}{\partial r}X(t) \quad P \quad \text{"Rho"}$$

of an option. Here, $X(t)$ can also represent the price of a portfolio of options. To make a portfolio of options neutral against changes in these parameters, certain hedging methods are widely used in practice. They more or less consist of setting up linear portfolios in different types of options to obtain vanishing partial derivatives with respect to the desired parameters (see also Exercise (13)).

The Black-Scholes trading strategy. By looking at the Black-Scholes formula for the European call we can easily guess the trading strategy φ corresponding to the replication strategy $(\pi, 0)$. The immediate candidate is (w.l.o.g. let $P_0(0) = 1$):

$$\varphi_0(t) = -Ke^{-rT}\Phi(d_2(t)),$$
$$\varphi_1(t) = \Phi(d_1(t)).$$

We only have to check that this strategy is self-financing. This can be done (in a tedious way!) by verifying the equation

$$dX_C(t) = \varphi_0(t)\, dP_0(t) + \varphi_1(t)\, dP_1(t)$$

with the help of the Itô formula. However, we shall do this via a simple method later on (see Proposition 3.16). Note in particular that we have

$$0 \leq \varphi_1(t) \leq 1 \text{ for all } t \in [0, T],$$
$$-Ke^{-rT} \leq \varphi_0(t) \leq 0 \text{ for all } t \in [0, T].$$

Hence, the stock position of the Black-Scholes strategy is always (!) partly financed via a credit. The stock position itself is always positive and bounded above by holding one share.

Black-Scholes formula and change of measure. By introducing the notation

$$W^Q(t) := W(t) + \theta \cdot t$$

we obtain

$$\hat{p} = X_C(0) = E\left(\exp\left(-\left(r + \tfrac{1}{2}\theta^2\right)T - \theta W(T)\right)\right.$$
$$\left.\left(p_1 \exp\left[\left(b - \tfrac{1}{2}\sigma^2\right)T + \sigma W(T)\right] - K\right)^+\right)$$
$$= E\left(\exp(-rT) \cdot \left(p_1 \exp\left[\left(r - \tfrac{1}{2}\sigma^2\right)T + \sigma W^Q(T)\right] - K\right)^+\right.$$
$$\left.\cdot \exp\left(-\tfrac{1}{2}\theta^2 T - \theta W(T)\right)\right)$$
$$= E_Q\left(e^{-rT} \cdot (P_1(T) - K)^+\right)$$

where $E_Q(.)$ denotes the expected value with respect to the measure Q which is given by the Radon-Nikodym derivative

$$\frac{dQ}{dP} = \exp\left(-\tfrac{1}{2}\theta^2 T - \theta W(T)\right).$$

If we could now show that

(*) Q is a probability measure which is equivalent to P if restricted to $\mathcal{F}_T$ and $\{(W^Q(t), \mathcal{F}_t)\}_{t \in [0,T]}$ is a Brownian motion under Q,

then we would obtain:

(1) The discounted stock price

$$\frac{P_1(t)}{P_0(t)} = \frac{p_1}{p_0} \cdot \exp\left(\sigma W^Q(t) - \tfrac{1}{2}\sigma^2 t\right)$$

is a Q-martingale (Q is therefore called an equivalent martingale measure) and we have

$$dP_1(t) = P_1(t)\left(r\,dt + \sigma\,dW^Q(t)\right).$$

(2) The option price equals the expectation with respect to Q of the option payment discounted back to today. Hence, it equals its "natural price" in the so-called "risk neutral market" where all normalized security prices $P_i(t)/P_i(0)$ have the same expectation.

The proof of assertion(*) is the main aim of the following excursion.

Excursion 5: Girsanov's Theorem

General assumptions for this section:
Let $\{(X(t), \mathcal{F}_t)\}_{t \geq 0}$ be an m-dimensional progressively measurable process where $\{\mathcal{F}_t\}$ is the Brownian filtration with

$$\int_0^t X_i^2(s)\,ds < \infty \text{ a.s. } P \text{ for all } t \geq 0,\ i = 1,...,m.$$

Let further

$$Z(t, X) := \exp\left(-\sum_{i=1}^m \int_0^t X_i(s)\,dW_i(s) - \tfrac{1}{2}\int_0^t \|X(s)\|^2\,ds\right).$$

As the argument in $Z(t,X)$ is an Itô process, the Itô formula, Theorem 2.49, implies

$$Z(t,X) = 1 - \sum_{i=1}^{m} \int_0^t Z(s,X) X_i(s) \, dW_i(s).$$

Thus, $Z(t,X)$ is a continuous local martingale with $Z(0,X) = 1$. As $Z(t,X)$ is also positive, it is a super-martingale by Theorem 2.22. If $Z(t,X)$ is even a martingale then we have $E(Z(t,X)) = 1$ for all $t \geq 0$. Then, for all $T \geq 0$ we can define a probability measure Q_T on $\mathcal{F}_T$ via

(3.3) $$Q_T(A) := E(1_A \cdot Z(T,X)) \text{ for } A \in \mathcal{F}_T.$$

Hence, $Z(T,X)$ is the Radon-Nikodym density of Q_T with respect to P. The so-defined family of probability measures has the following consistency property

$$Q_T(A) = Q_t(A)$$

for all $A \in \mathcal{F}_t$, $t \in [0,T]$, because we have

$$Q_T(A) = E(1_A \cdot Z(T,X)) = E(E(1_A \cdot Z(T,X) \,|\, \mathcal{F}_t))$$
$$= E(1_A \cdot E(Z(T,X) \,|\, \mathcal{F}_t)) = E(1_A \cdot Z(t,X)) = Q_t(A).$$

In particular, for bounded stopping times $0 \leq \tau \leq T$ and $A \in \mathcal{F}_\tau$ the optional sampling theorem, Theorem 2.17, yields

$$Q_T(A) = E(1_A \cdot Z(T,X)) = E(E(1_A \cdot Z(T,X) \,|\, \mathcal{F}_\tau))$$
$$= E(1_A \cdot E(Z(T,X) \,|\, \mathcal{F}_\tau)) = E(1_A \cdot Z(\tau,X)) = Q_\tau(A).$$

The following theorem now demonstrates the way a Q_T-Brownian motion $W^{Q_T}(t)$ can be constructed from a P-Brownian motion $W(t)$ via a change of measure from P to Q_T.

Theorem 3.11 (Girsanov's theorem). *Let the process $Z(t,X)$ be a martingale and define the process $\{(W^Q(t), \mathcal{F}_t)\}_{t \geq 0}$ by*

$$W_i^Q(t) := W_i(t) + \int_0^t X_i(s) \, ds, \quad 1 \leq i \leq m, \quad t \geq 0.$$

Then, for each fixed $T \in [0,\infty)$ the process $\{(W^Q(t), \mathcal{F}_t)\}_{t \in [0,T]}$ is an m-dimensional Brownian motion on $(\Omega, \mathcal{F}_T, Q_T)$ where the probability measure Q_T is defined in (3.3).

Proof.
i) We first prove the following identity:

$$(3.4) \qquad E_{Q,T}(Y \mid \mathcal{F}_s) = \frac{1}{Z(S,X)} E(Y \cdot Z(R,X) \mid \mathcal{F}_s)$$

for all stopping times S, R with $0 \leq S \leq R \leq T$ and $\mathcal{F}_R$-measurable Y with $E_{Q,T}(|Y|) < \infty$. Here, $E_{Q,t}$ denotes the expectation with respect to Q_t, $t \in [0,T]$. Now let $A \in \mathcal{F}_S$. Then by the consistency property of the Q-measure we obtain

$$E_{Q,T}\left(1_A \cdot \frac{1}{Z(S,X)} \cdot E(Y \cdot Z(R,X) \mid \mathcal{F}_s)\right)$$

$$= E_{Q,S}\left(1_A \cdot \frac{1}{Z(S,X)} \cdot E(Y \cdot Z(R,X) \mid \mathcal{F}_s)\right)$$

$$= E(1_A \cdot E(Y \cdot Z(R,X) \mid \mathcal{F}_s)) = E(1_A \cdot Y \cdot Z(R,X))$$

$$= E_{Q,R}(1_A \cdot Y) = E_{Q,T}(1_A \cdot Y).$$

By the definition of conditional expectation, this implies relation (3.4). Note that in particular the right-hand side of (3.4) is $\mathcal{F}_S$-measurable.

ii) Let $\theta \in \mathbb{R}^m$ be arbitrary but fixed. Then define on $\mathbb{R}^m \times [0,\infty)$ (compare with the proof of the martingale representation theorem!):

$$f(x,t) := \exp\left(i\theta' x + \tfrac{1}{2} \|\theta\|^2 t\right),$$

$$M^\theta(t) := f(W^Q(t), t) := \exp\left(i\theta' W^Q(t) + \tfrac{1}{2}\|\theta\|^2 t\right)$$

$$= \exp\left(i\theta'\left(W(t) + \int_0^t X(s)\,ds\right) + \tfrac{1}{2}\|\theta\|^2 t\right).$$

By applying the multi-dimensional Itô formula, Theorem 2.52, to the real and to the imaginary part of f we get

$$M^\theta(t) = 1 + \sum_{j=1}^m \int_0^t f_{x_j}(W^Q(s), s)\, dW_j^Q(s) + \int_0^t f_t(W^Q(s), s)\, ds$$

$$+ \tfrac{1}{2} \sum_{j,k=1}^m \int_0^t f_{x_j x_k}(W^Q(s), s)\, d\left\langle W_j^Q, W_k^Q \right\rangle_s.$$

Note that we have $\left\langle W_j^Q, W_k^Q \right\rangle_s = \delta_{jk} \cdot s$ and thus

$$M^\theta(t) = 1 + \sum_{j=1}^{m} i \cdot \int_0^t \theta_j \cdot f\left(W^Q(s), s\right) \left[dW_j(s) + X_j(s)\, ds\right]$$

$$+ \int_0^t \left(\tfrac{1}{2}\|\theta\|^2 - \tfrac{1}{2}\sum_{j=1}^m \theta_j^2\right) f\left(W^Q(s), s\right)\, ds$$

$$= 1 + \sum_{j=1}^{m} i \cdot \int_0^t \theta_j f\left(W^Q(s), s\right)\, dW_j(s)$$

$$+ \sum_{j=1}^{m} i \cdot \int_0^t \theta_j X_j(s) f\left(W^Q(s), s\right)\, ds.$$

Hence, we have now obtained the representation of $M^\theta(t)$ as an Itô process.

iii) Compute $Z(t, X) \cdot M^\theta(t)$:

With the help of the product rule, Corollary 2.53, we obtain

$$Z(t, X) \cdot M^\theta(t) = 1 + \int_0^t Z(s, X)\, dM^\theta(s)$$

$$+ \int_0^t M^\theta(s)\, dZ(s, X) + \int_0^t d\left\langle M^\theta, Z(\cdot, X)\right\rangle_s$$

$$= 1 + \sum_{j=1}^{m} i \left[\int_0^t Z(s, X) \cdot \theta_j \cdot f\left(W^Q(s), s\right) dW_j(s) \right.$$

$$\left. + \int_0^t Z(s, X) \cdot \theta_j \cdot f\left(W^Q(s), s\right) X_j(s)\, ds \right]$$

$$- \sum_{j=1}^{m} \int_0^t f\left(W^Q(s), s\right) \cdot Z(s, X) \cdot X_j(s)\, dW_j(s)$$

$$- \sum_{j=1}^{m} i \cdot \int_0^t \theta_j \cdot f\left(W^Q(s), s\right) \cdot Z(s, X) \cdot X_j(s)\, ds$$

$$= 1 + \sum_{j=1}^{m} i \cdot \int_0^t Z(s, X) \cdot M^\theta(s) \cdot (\theta_j + i \cdot X_j(s)) \, dW_j(s).$$

Thus, $Z(t, X) \cdot M^\theta(t)$ is a local martingale under P.

iv) Now we show that $\{M^\theta(t)\}_{t \in [0,T]}$ is a Q_T-martingale:

Let τ_n be a suitable stopping time for the (P-)local martingale $Z(t, X) \cdot M^\theta(t)$ such that the stopped process is a (P-)martingale. By using relation (3.4) we then have for $0 \leq s \leq t \leq T$

$$E_{Q,T}\left(M^\theta(t \wedge \tau_n) \mid \mathcal{F}_{s \wedge \tau_n}\right)$$
$$= E\left(Z(t \wedge \tau_n, X) M^\theta(t \wedge \tau_n) \mid \mathcal{F}_{s \wedge \tau_n}\right) \cdot \frac{1}{Z(s \wedge \tau_n, X)}$$
$$= M^\theta(s \wedge \tau_n) \cdot \frac{Z(s \wedge \tau_n, X)}{Z(s \wedge \tau_n, X)} = M^\theta(s \wedge \tau_n).$$

Consequently $M^\theta(t)$ is a local martingale under Q_T. As $|M^\theta(t)|$ is bounded on $[0, T]$, $M^\theta(t)$ is even a Q_T-martingale. To see this, take the limit $n \to \infty$ in the above relation for $M^\theta(t)$ and use the theorem on dominated convergence.

v) Prove that $W^Q(t)$ is a (Q_T-)Brownian motion:

The fact that $M^\theta(t)$ is a Q_T-martingale implies

$$1 = E_{Q,T}\left(\frac{M^\theta(t)}{M^\theta(s)} \mid \mathcal{F}_s\right)$$
$$= E_{Q,T}\left(\exp\left(i\theta'\left(W^Q(t) - W^Q(s)\right) + \tfrac{1}{2}\|\theta\|^2(t-s)\right) \mid \mathcal{F}_s\right)$$

for $0 \leq s \leq t \leq T$. This is correct if and only if we have

$$E_{Q,T}\left(\exp\left(i \cdot \theta'\left(W^Q(t) - W^Q(s)\right)\right) \mid \mathcal{F}_s\right) = \exp\left(-\tfrac{1}{2}\|\theta\|^2(t-s)\right).$$

As this expression coincides with the Fourier transform of a $\mathcal{N}(0, (t-s) \cdot I)$-distributed random variable under Q_T (where I denotes the identity matrix), this implies that the increments $W^Q(t) - W^Q(s)$ are $\mathcal{N}(0, (t-s) \cdot I)$-distributed under Q_T. This equality further implies that the increments $W^Q(t) - W^Q(s)$ are independent of $\mathcal{F}_S$ under Q_T. As moreover $W^Q(t)$ has continuous paths, we have thus shown that $W^Q(t)$ is a Brownian motion under Q_T. □

The Novikov condition. To apply Girsanov's theorem, we need to have a criterion to check if $Z(t, X)$ is a martingale. A sufficient condition for this is the so-called *Novikov condition*:

$$E\left(\exp\left(\tfrac{1}{2}\int_0^t \|X(s)\|^2 \, ds\right)\right) < \infty.$$

A proof of this fact can be found in [**KA/SH 91**], Section 3.5.D. We shall only prove a weaker version of it that is sufficient for our applications (see also Corollary 37.11 in [**RO/WI 87**]):

Proposition 3.12. *If we have $\int_0^T \|X(s)\|^2 \, ds < K$ for some constant $K > 0$, then $Z(t, X)$ is a martingale.*

Proof. (only for $m = 1$, the case of $m > 1$ is similar)
i) Let
$$M_t := -\int_0^t X(s) \, dW(s).$$

Then for $y > 0$ we have

(3.5) $$P\left(\max_{0 \le s \le t} M_s \ge y\right) \le \exp\left(-\frac{y^2}{2K}\right).$$

To see this, note that for $y > 0$, $\theta > 0$, application of Theorem 2.24 to the non-negative, continuous super-martingale $Z(t, \theta X)$ with $Z(0, X) = 1$ yields:

$$P\left(\max_{0 \le s \le t} M_s \ge y\right)$$
$$\le P\left(\max_{0 \le s \le t} \exp\left(\theta \cdot M_s - \tfrac{1}{2}\theta^2 \int_0^s X^2(u) \, du\right) \ge \exp\left(\theta y - \tfrac{1}{2}\theta^2 K\right)\right)$$
$$\le \exp\left(-\theta y + \tfrac{1}{2}\theta^2 K\right).$$

The choice of $\theta := y/K$ now proves assertion (3.5).

ii) Let $\xi(t) := \max_{0 \le s \le t} M(s)$ and let F^ξ be the distribution function of $\xi(t)$ under P. Then using partial integration and relation (3.5) for $\theta > 0$ leads to

(3.6) $$E\left(e^{\theta \cdot \xi(t)}\right) = \int_0^\infty e^{\theta y} dF^\xi(y) = 1 + \theta \cdot \int_0^\infty e^{\theta y} P(\xi(t) \ge y) \, dy$$
$$\le 1 + \theta \int_0^\infty e^{\theta y} e^{-y^2/2K} \, dy < \infty.$$

iii) As $Z(t, X)$ is a local martingale there exists a localizing sequence $\tau_n \xrightarrow{n \to \infty} \infty$ with

(3.7) $$E(Z(t \wedge \tau_n, X) \mid \mathcal{F}_s) = Z(s \wedge \tau_n, X).$$

As both $Z(t \wedge \tau_n, X)$ and $Z(s \wedge \tau_n, X)$ are dominated by $\exp(\xi(t))$ and as relation (3.6) is valid, passing to the limit $n \to \infty$ in relation (3.7) yields the martingale property of $Z(t, X)$. □

3.2. Continuation: Option Pricing via the Replication Principle

Girsanov's theorem and option pricing. Due to the uniform boundedness of r, b and the positive definiteness of $\sigma\sigma'$, the assumptions of Proposition 3.12 are satisfied if we choose

$$X(t) := \theta(t).$$

Then, $Z(t,\theta)$ takes the role of $Z(t)$ in the notation of p. 65. Application of Girsanov's theorem, Theorem 3.11, implies that $W^Q(t)$ defined as

$$W_i^Q(t) := W(t) + \int_0^t \theta_i(s)\,ds,\ t \in [0,T],\ i = 1, ..., d,$$

is a Q_T-Brownian motion with respect to the filtration $\{\mathcal{F}_t\}_{t \in [0,T]}$. Here, Q_T is given by

$$Q_T(A) = E(1_A \cdot Z(T)),\ A \in \mathcal{F}_T.$$

Hence, we have the following Radon-Nikodym derivative

$$\frac{dQ_T}{dP} = Z(T,\theta).$$

In particular, $Z(T,\theta)$ is strictly positive. Consequently, P and Q_T are equivalent probability measures, i.e. they possess the same zero sets. Moreover, the discounted price processes

$$\frac{P_i(t)}{P_0(t)},\ i = 0,...,d,$$

are martingales with respect to Q_T (this can be seen with the help of the Novikov condition or by Proposition 3.12). Therefore, Q_T is called an *equivalent martingale measure*. In the following, we shall show that the so-defined probability measure Q_T is the unique equivalent martingale measure in our market model. To do so, we need a lemma characterizing the form of probability measures which are equivalent to P on $\mathcal{F}_T$.

Lemma 3.13. *Let Q be a probability measure which is equivalent to P restricted on $\mathcal{F}_T$. Then the density process $\{D_t\}_{t \in [0,T]}$ defined by*

$$D_t := \frac{dQ}{dP}|_{\mathcal{F}_t},\ t \in [0,T],$$

satisfies: $\{(D_t, \mathcal{F}_t)\}_{t \in [0,T]}$ is a positive Brownian martingale with respect to P satisfying

$$D_t = 1 + \int_0^t \Psi(s)'\,dW(s)$$

for a progressively measurable d-dimensional process Ψ with

$$\int_0^T \|\Psi(s)\|^2 \, ds < \infty \text{ a.s. } P.$$

Proof. As Q and P are equivalent on $\mathcal{F}_T$, Q and P are also equivalent when they are restricted to $\mathcal{F}_t$, $t \in [0, T]$. By the definition of conditional expectation, we obtain for all $A \in \mathcal{F}_t$:

$$\int_A D_T dP = \int_A \tfrac{dQ}{dP}|_{\mathcal{F}_T} \, dP = \int_A \tfrac{dQ}{dP}|_{\mathcal{F}_t} \, dP = \int_A D_t dP,$$

and hence

$$D_t = E(D_T | \mathcal{F}_t),$$

which implies the martingale property of D_t. As Q and P are equivalent, D_t has to be strictly positive almost surely. Finally, the martingale property of D_t implies all the assertions on the form of the representation of D_t via $\Psi(s)$, $s \in [0, T]$, by Corollary 2.70 to the martingale representation theorem. □

Now we are in the position to prove the already announced theorem on uniqueness of the equivalent martingale measure.

Theorem 3.14 (Uniqueness of the equivalent martingale measure). *In our complete market model Q_T is the unique equivalent martingale measure on $\{\mathcal{F}_t\}_{t \in [0,T]}$ for the price processes $P_i(t)$, $i = 0, 1, ..., d$.*

Proof. Let

$$Y_i(t) := \frac{P_i(t)}{P_0(t)}, \quad i = 1, ..., d.$$

Then we have

$$dY_i(t) = Y_i(t) \left[(b_i(t) - r(t)) \, dt + \sum_{j=1}^d \sigma_{ij}(t) \, dW_j(t) \right]$$

$$= Y_i(t) \left[\sum_{j=1}^d \sigma_{ij}(t) \theta_j(t) \, dt + \sum_{j=1}^d \sigma_{ij}(t) \, dW_j(t) \right]$$

$$= Y_i(t) \sum_{j=1}^d \sigma_{ij}(t) \, dW_j^Q(t).$$

By Proposition 3.12, each $Y_i(t)$ is a martingale as the components σ_{ij} are uniformly bounded (see also the explicit form of the solution of the above equation for $Y_i(t)$). Let now Q be another equivalent martingale measure

3.2. Continuation: Option Pricing via the Replication Principle

with density $\{D_t\}_{t\in[0,T]}$ as in Lemma 3.13. Then Lemma 3.13 and the product rule, Corollary 2.53, imply

$$(3.8) \quad D_t \cdot Y_i(t) =$$

$$p_i + \int_0^t D_s \, dY_i(s) + \int_0^t Y_i(s) \, dD_s + \langle D, Y_i \rangle_t$$

$$= p_i + \int_0^t \left[D_s \cdot Y_i(s) \cdot \sum_{j=1}^d \sigma_{ij}(s) \cdot \theta_j(s) + Y_i(s) \cdot \sum_{j=1}^d \Psi_j(s) \cdot \sigma_{ij}(s) \right] ds$$

$$+ \sum_{j=1}^d \int_0^t \left[D_s Y_i(s) \sigma_{ij}(s) + Y_i(s) \Psi_j(s) \right] dW_j(s).$$

For $Y_i(t)$ to be a Q-martingale it is necessary that $D_t \cdot Y_i(t)$ is a P-martingale. In particular, this requires a vanishing ds-term on the right-hand side of (3.8). Consequently, we must have

$$\Psi(s) = -D_s \cdot \theta(s)$$

(up to $P \otimes \lambda$-equivalence). Thus, D_s has the representation

$$D_t = 1 - \int_0^t D_s \cdot \theta(s)' \, dW(s).$$

However, this stochastic differential equation possesses the density process $Z(t)$ corresponding to Q_T as its unique solution. Consequently, Q and Q_T have to coincide on $\mathcal{F}_T$. □

Remark. In Section 3.6 we shall show the more general result that the existence of an equivalent martingale measure implies absence of arbitrage opportunities in our market. In the other direction, absence of arbitrage (under some technical conditions) implies the existence of an equivalent martingale measure (see Section 3.6).

Corollary 3.15 (Option pricing using the equivalent martingale measure). Let (g, B) be a contingent claim such that $g(s)$ is uniformly bounded on

$[0, T]$. Then its price process $\hat{X}(t)$ satisfies

$$\hat{X}(t) = E_Q \left(\exp\left(-\int_t^T r(s)\, ds\right) \cdot B \right.$$
$$\left. + \int_t^T \exp\left(-\int_t^s r(u)\, du\right) \cdot g(s)\, ds \,\Big|\, \mathcal{F}_t \right)$$

for $0 \leq t \leq T$ with $E_Q = E_{Q,T}$.

Proof. Note

$$H(t) = \exp\left(-\int_0^t r(s)\, ds\right) \cdot Z(t) = \gamma(t) \cdot Z(t).$$

Further $Z(t)$ obeys the stochastic differential equation

$$dZ(t) = -\theta(t) \cdot Z(t)\, dW(t).$$

Let $t \in [0, T]$ be fixed. Then, the product rule, Corollary 2.53, implies

$$\frac{Z(T)}{Z(t)} \cdot \int_t^T \frac{\gamma(s)}{\gamma(t)} \cdot g(s)\, ds$$
$$= \int_t^T \frac{Z(s)}{Z(t)} \cdot \frac{\gamma(s)}{\gamma(t)} \cdot g(s)\, ds + \int_t^T \left(\int_t^s \frac{\gamma(u)}{\gamma(t)} \cdot g(u)\, du\right) \cdot \frac{1}{Z(t)}\, dZ(s)$$

$$= \int_t^T \frac{H(s)}{H(t)} g(s)\, ds + \int_t^T \underbrace{\left(\int_t^s \frac{\gamma(u)}{\gamma(t)} \cdot g(u)\, du\right) \cdot (-\theta(s)) \cdot \frac{Z(s)}{Z(t)}}_{f(s)}\, dW(s).$$

As $g(s)$ is uniformly bounded on $[0,T]$ and as $\theta(s)$ satisfies the assumptions of Proposition 3.12 (which also implies square integrability of $Z(s)/Z(t)$), the process

$$\int_0^u f(s)\, dW(s),\ u \geq 0,$$

3.2. Continuation: Option Pricing via the Replication Principle

is a P-martingale with zero expectation. This in particular implies

$$E\left(\int_t^T f(s)\,dW(s)\,|\,\mathcal{F}_t\right)$$

$$= E\left(\int_0^T f(s)\,dW(s) - \int_0^t f(s)\,dW(s)\,|\,\mathcal{F}_t\right) = 0.$$

Then, Theorem 3.7 together with identity (3.4) imply

$$\hat{X}(t) = E\left(\frac{H(T)}{H(t)} \cdot B + \int_t^T \frac{H(s)}{H(t)} g(s)\,ds\,|\,\mathcal{F}_t\right)$$

$$= E\left(\frac{Z(T)}{Z(t)} \cdot \left[\exp\left(-\int_t^T r(s)\,ds\right) \cdot B\right.\right.$$

$$\left.\left. + \int_t^T \exp\left(-\int_t^s r(u)\,du\right) \cdot g(s)\,ds\right] - \int_t^T f(s)\,dW(s)\,|\,F_t\right)$$

$$= E_Q\left(\exp\left(-\int_t^T r(s)\,ds\right) \cdot B + \int_t^T \exp\left(-\int_t^s r(u)\,du\right) \cdot g(s)\,ds\,|\,\mathcal{F}_t\right).$$

$\square$

Independence of the option price of b. Corollary 3.15 in particular says that in case of $g \equiv 0$ we have

$$\hat{p} = E_Q\left(\exp\left(-\int_0^T r(s)\,ds\right) \cdot B\right).$$

Thus, $\hat{p}$ equals the *natural price* with respect to a new probability measure Q. However, this measure cannot be chosen freely. It is uniquely determined. By interpreting the choice of $b(t)$ as the choice of the probability measure P, it becomes clear why P is often called the *subjective measure* while Q is referred to as the *objective measure*. Further, in $(\Omega, \mathcal{F}_T, Q)$ we have

$$dP_i(t) = P_i(t) \cdot \left(r(t)\,dt + \sum_{j=1}^d \sigma_{ij}(t)\,dW_j^Q(t)\right), \quad i = 0, 1, ..., d,$$

i.e. all security prices - including the bond price - have the same mean rate of return $r(t)$. Therefore we talk of a *risk-neutral market* and call $Q = Q_T$ a *risk-neutral measure*. As in the risk-neutral market the role of $b(t)$ is taken over by $r(t) \cdot \underline{1}$, the stock price drift indeed enters the option price. However, due to its form of $r(t) \cdot \underline{1}$ its origin as stock price drift cannot be recognized. Especially in the Black-Scholes formula it cannot be distinguished from the riskless interest rate.

Practical calculation of the option price. Typically the option price can be calculated more easily with the help of Corollary 3.15 than with Theorem 3.7. To get a feeling for this we recommend the reader to derive the Black-Scholes formula with the help of Corollary 3.15. We highlight the advantages of this method via the following example.

3.2.1. Example: European digital call. The somewhat strange-looking European digital call is in fact widely used in practice. Here, if the stock price $P_1(t)$ exceeds a certain boundary K at the time $t = T$, the owner of the call is paid an amount of B^* units of money; otherwise, he gets nothing. Therefore, the European digital call is also called "cash-or-nothing-call". Here we choose $B^* = 1$ and thus obtain a final payment of

$$B = 1_{\{P_1(T) \geq K\}}.$$

In the Black-Scholes model, i.e. in the case of $d = m = 1$, b, r, σ constant, $\sigma > 0$, we have by Corollary 3.15

$$\hat{X}(t) = E_Q\left(e^{-r(T-t)} \cdot 1_{\{P_1(T) \geq K\}} \mid \mathcal{F}_t\right)$$
$$= e^{-r(T-t)} \cdot Q\left(P_1(T) \geq K \mid P_1(t)\right).$$

Let t be fixed. Then, we have $P_1(T) \geq K$ if and only if we have

$$W^Q(T) - W^Q(t) \geq \frac{1}{\sigma}\left(\ln\left(\frac{K}{P_1(t)}\right) - \left(r - \tfrac{1}{2}\sigma^2\right)(T - t)\right) =: \hat{K}.$$

As $W^Q(T) - W^Q(t)$ is normally distributed with expectation 0 and variance $(T - t)$, we obtain

$$\hat{X}(t) = e^{-r(T-t)} \int_{\hat{K}}^{\infty} \frac{1}{\sqrt{2\pi(T-t)}} \exp\left(-\frac{x^2}{2(T-t)}\right) dx$$
$$= e^{-r(T-t)} \Phi\left(\frac{\ln\left(\frac{P_1(t)}{K}\right) + \left(r - \tfrac{1}{2}\sigma^2\right)(T-t)}{\sigma\sqrt{T-t}}\right).$$

3.3. Option Pricing by the Partial Differential Approach

In their famous work of 1973, Black and Scholes indeed do not use the replication approach to price options. Instead, their method consists of transforming the option pricing problem into the task of solving a parabolic partial differential equation with a final condition. The connection between this task – a so-called Cauchy problem – and the computation of the expected value of a functional of a solution to a stochastic differential equation is covered by the Feynman-Kac representation theorem. It will be presented in detail in Excursion 6. As the computation of option prices via the replication method as given in Theorem 3.7 actually consists of the computation of an expectation of a functional of the underlying stock prices, the Feynman-Kac representation theorem also gives the connection between the replication approach and the partial differential equation approach to option pricing.

Besides the use of partial differential equations as a technical tool, the main conceptual idea of Black and Scholes lies in the construction of a riskless portfolio consisting of positions in bond, option, and the underlying stock.

> **General assumptions for this section:**
> We consider a Black-Scholes model, i.e. we have $d = m = 1$, b, r, σ are constants with $\sigma > 0$.

Construction of a riskless portfolio and a Cauchy problem. In their article [**BL/SC 73**], Black and Scholes consider a portfolio consisting of variable positions in bond and stock and exactly one sold option. For simplicity, we now restrict ourselves to the case of a European call with strike price K. Black and Scholes assume that the call price at time t can be represented as a function $C(t, P_1(t))$ of time t and the current stock price $P_1(t)$ (note that such an assumption is not needed in the replication approach!). Having sold the call corresponds to a wealth position of $-C(t, P_1(t))$ as by selling the call we enter the obligation to pay $(P_1(T) - K)^+$ at time T. $C(t, P_1(t))$ is just the amount of money we have to pay at time t to get rid of this obligation by closing out the position (i.e. by buying the same call). Of course, the option price at maturity T is given by

$$C(T, P_1(T)) = (P_1(T) - K)^+.$$

The main idea of Black and Scholes is to follow a self-financing trading strategy $(\varphi_0(t), \varphi_1(t))$ in stock and bond such that the wealth process including exactly one sold call option

$$Y(t) := \varphi_0(t) P_0(t) + \varphi_1(t) P_1(t) - C(t, P_1(t))$$

possesses no random fluctuations. This is regarded as a *riskless portfolio*. If then the option price $C(t, P_1(t))$ satisfies the assumptions needed for the application of the multi-dimensional Itô formula, Theorem 2.52 (i.e. if $C(t, p)$ is sufficiently smooth), then we obtain (note that $(\varphi_0(t), \varphi_1(t))$ are assumed to be self-financing!):

$$\begin{aligned} dY(t) &= \varphi_0(t)\, dP_0(t) + \varphi_1(t)\, dP_1(t) - dC(t, P_1(t)) \\ &= \Big[\varphi_0(t) \cdot P_0(t) \cdot r + \varphi_1(t) \cdot P_1(t) \cdot b \\ &\quad - \big(C_t + C_p \cdot P_1(t) \cdot b + \tfrac{1}{2} C_{pp} \cdot P_1^2(t) \cdot \sigma^2 \big) \Big] dt \\ &\quad + \big(\varphi_1(t) \cdot P_1(t) \cdot \sigma - C_p \cdot P_1(t) \cdot \sigma \big) dW(t). \end{aligned}$$

For $Y(t)$ to be the wealth process corresponding to a riskless portfolio the diffusion coefficient has to vanish. Hence, we must have

$$\varphi_1(t) = C_p(t, P_1(t)).$$

For arbitrage reasons, the wealth process $Y(t)$ must behave as a multiple of the bond price. We thus require

$$dY(t) = r \cdot Y(t)\, dt.$$

If we now substitute $\varphi_1(t)$ by $C_p(t, P_1(t))$, then the above requirement on the drift coefficient yields

$$\begin{aligned} r \cdot Y(t) &\stackrel{!}{=} r \cdot \varphi_0(t) \cdot P_0(t) + b \cdot C_p \cdot P_1(t) \\ &\quad - \big(C_t + C_p \cdot P_1(t) \cdot b + \tfrac{1}{2} C_{pp} \cdot P_1^2(t) \cdot \sigma^2 \big) \\ &= r \cdot \Big(\varphi_0(t) \cdot P_0(t) + \varphi_1(t) \cdot P_1(t) - C(t, P_1(t)) \Big) + r \cdot C(t, P_1(t)) \\ &\quad + (b - r) \cdot C_p \cdot P_1(t) - \big(C_t + b \cdot C_p \cdot P_1(t) + \tfrac{1}{2} C_{pp} \cdot \sigma^2 \cdot P_1^2(t) \big) \\ &= r \cdot Y(t) + \underbrace{\big(r \cdot C - r \cdot C_p \cdot P_1(t) - C_t - \tfrac{1}{2} C_{pp} \cdot \sigma^2 \cdot P_1(t) \big)}_{\stackrel{!}{=} 0}. \end{aligned}$$

Together with the final condition in $t = T$ and some suitable smoothness assumptions, we thus obtain that the call price $C(t, P_1(t))$ solves the following Cauchy problem

3.3. Option Pricing by the Partial Differential Approach

> (3.9) $\frac{1}{2}\sigma^2 p^2 C_{pp} + r \cdot p \cdot C_p + C_t - r \cdot C = 0$, $(t,p) \in [0,T] \times (0,\infty)$
>
> $$C(T,p) = (p-K)^+, \; p \in (0,\infty)$$
>
> with
>
> $$C \in C\left([0,T] \times (0,\infty)\right) \cap C^{1,2}\left([0,T] \times (0,\infty)\right).$$

As for arbitrage reasons we further have

$$0 \leq C(t, P_1(t)) \leq P_1(t);$$

the call price is uniquely determined by the problem (3.9) if this problem possesses a unique solution which grows at most polynomially and if there exists a self-financing trading strategy $(\varphi_0(t), \varphi_1(t))$ which corresponds to $Y(t)$ and possesses all the properties needed for the derivation of problem (3.9).

Now we are able to formulate the following proposition:

Proposition 3.16. (1) *The Cauchy problem (3.9) possesses a unique solution $C(t,p)$ which grows at most polynomially. It is given by*

$$C(t, P_1(t)) = P_1(t)\Phi(d_1(t)) - Ke^{-r(T-t)}\Phi(d_2(t))$$

with $d_1(t)$ and $d_2(t)$ as in Corollary 3.9 – the Black-Scholes formula.

(2) $(\varphi_0(t), \varphi_1(t))$ *with*

$$\varphi_0(t) = \frac{(C(t, P_1(t)) - C_p(t, P_1(t)) \cdot P_1(t))}{P_0(t)},$$

$$\varphi_1(t) = C_p(t, P_1(t)),$$

constitutes a self-financing trading strategy with wealth process $C(t, P_1(t))$. In particular, $(\varphi_0(t), \varphi_1(t))$ is a replication strategy for the European call and $C(t, P_1(t))$ is the price of the European call at time t.

Proof. (1) The Feynman-Kac Theorem 3.26, which will be the main topic in the following excursion, implies the uniqueness of a solution of the Cauchy problem which grows at most polynomially. One can verify (in a tedious way) that the Black-Scholes price is a solution of the Cauchy problem (see also Remark 3.10 (2)). Obviously, it grows only polynomially in p and therefore coincides with the desired solution.

(2) As $C(t, P_1(t))$ solves the Cauchy problem (3.9) the assumptions which are necessary to apply the Itô formula are given. By using

part (1) we then obtain

$$dC(t, P_1(t))$$
$$= (C_t(t, P_1(t)) + C_p(t, P_1(t)) \cdot P_1(t) \cdot b$$
$$+ \tfrac{1}{2} C_{pp}(t, P_1(t)) \cdot P_1^2(t) \cdot \sigma^2) dt + C_p(t, P_1(t)) \cdot P_1(t) \cdot \sigma \, dW(t)$$

$$= \Big(C_p(t, P_1(t)) \cdot P_1(t) \cdot b + r \cdot [C(t, P_1(t))$$
$$- C_p(t, P_1(t)) \cdot P_1(t)] \Big) dt + C_p(t, P_1(t)) \cdot P_1(t) \cdot \sigma \, dW(t).$$

On the other hand, a self-financing trading strategy (φ_0, φ_1) with wealth process $C(t, P_1(t))$ has to satisfy the equation

$$dC(t, P_1(t)) = [\varphi_0(t) \cdot P_0(t) \cdot r + \varphi_1(t) \cdot P_1(t) \cdot b] \, dt$$
$$+ \varphi_1(t) \cdot P_1(t) \cdot \sigma \, dW(t).$$

Comparison of the two representations for $dC(t, P_1(T))$ leads to the form of (φ_0, φ_1) which is given in part (2). On one hand this implies

$$C(t, P_1(t)) = \varphi_0(t) \cdot P_0(t) + \varphi_1(t) \cdot P_1(t)$$

(i.e. $C(t, P_1(t))$ is indeed the wealth process corresponding to (φ_0, φ_1)). On the other hand, all the assertions of part (2) which correspond to (φ_0, φ_1) are thus verified. In particular, (φ_0, φ_1) satisfies all the requirements on a trading strategy. Moreover, it can immediately be verified that the self-financing strategy $(\underline{\varphi_0}, \underline{\varphi_1})$ corresponding to $Y(t)$ and needed for the derivation of problem (3.9) is given by

$$\underline{\varphi_0}(t) := \varphi_0(t) + y \text{ with } y := Y(0)$$
$$\underline{\varphi_1}(t) := \varphi_1(t).$$

This implies that $C(t, P_1(t))$ is indeed the price of the call.

$\square$

Remark 3.17. (1) By Proposition 3.16 the stock position in the trading strategy $\varphi_1(t)$ is given by the "Delta" $C_p(t, p)$ of the option price.

(2) The convexity of the final payment $(p - K)^+$ is preserved by $C(t, p)$ for $t \in [0, T)$. Therefore, $\varphi_0(t)$ of part (2) in Proposition 3.16 is negative (note therefore: f convex, $f(0) = 0 \Rightarrow f(x) - f'(x) \cdot x < 0$).

(3) It is remarkable that for the existence of the replicating trading strategy the martingale representation theorem was not needed in the above method. Even more, instead of only an existence result

3.3. Option Pricing by the Partial Differential Approach

for the replicating strategy (as in the replication approach) the above proposition even gives its explicit form! Moreover, we did not need to prove separately that (φ_0, φ_1) is self-financing, as it is by construction!

Remark 3.18 (Solving the Black-Scholes equation (3.9)). Of course, Black and Scholes did not solve the Cauchy problem (3.9) by guessing the solution and then verifying it! Their method consisted of transforming (3.9) into the form of the heat equation which is well-known in physics. Then the heat equation was solved. We sketch this method following Section 5.4. of **[W/D/H 95]**:

By making the substitutions
$$x = \ln(p/K), \qquad \tau = \tfrac{1}{2}\sigma^2(T-t),$$
$$C(t,p) = Kv(\tau, x), \qquad \rho = \frac{2v}{\sigma^2},$$
we obtain the following problem which is equivalent to (3.9):

(3.10)
$$v_\tau = v_{xx} + (\rho - 1) v_x - \rho v, \quad \tau > 0, \ x \in \mathbb{R},$$
$$v(0, x) = (e^x - 1)^+, \ x \in \mathbb{R}.$$

With the ansatz
$$v(\tau, x) = e^{\alpha x + \beta \tau} u(\tau, x)$$
for suitable real constants α, β, we obtain the partial differential equation
$$\beta u + u_\tau = \alpha^2 u + 2\alpha u_x + u_{xx} + (\rho - 1)(\alpha u + u_x) - \rho u.$$

With the choices of
$$\alpha = -\tfrac{1}{2}(\rho - 1), \qquad \beta = -\tfrac{1}{4}(\rho + 1)^2$$
it gets the form

(3.11)
$$u_\tau = u_{xx}, \ \tau > 0, \ x \in \mathbb{R},$$
with initial condition

(3.12)
$$u(0, x) = g(x) := \left(e^{\frac{1}{2}(\rho+1)x} - e^{\frac{1}{2}(\rho-1)x} \right)^+, \ x \in \mathbb{R}.$$

From the theory of the heat equation it is well-known that (3.11), (3.12) will be solved by
$$u(\tau, x) = \frac{1}{2\pi} \int_{-\infty}^{\infty} g(x) \cdot \exp\left(-\frac{(x-y)^2}{4\tau}\right) dy$$

(see also Exercise (4)). The computation of this integral is now similar to the computations of the proof of Corollary 3.9. We therefore leave the explicit computations and the back substitution up to the complete form of the Black-Scholes formula to the reader.

We now look at a d-dimensional Black-Scholes model with d stocks. Under suitable requirements on the final payment, the method of Proposition 3.16 can be generalized.

Proposition 3.19. *Let there exist a polynomially bounded solution $f : [0,T] \times (0,\infty)^d \to \mathbb{R}$, i.e.*

$$\max_{0 \leq t \leq T} |f(t,p)| \leq M\left(1 + \|p\|^k\right) \text{ for a fixed } M > 0, \ k \in \mathbb{N}, \ p \in (0,\infty)^d,$$

of the Cauchy problem

$$f_t + \tfrac{1}{2}\sum_{i,j=1}^d a_{ij} p_i p_j f_{p_i p_j} + \sum_{i=1}^d r p_i f_{p_i} - rf = 0 \text{ on } [0,T) \times \mathbb{R}^d,$$

$$f(T, p_1, ..., p_d) = g(p_1, ..., p_d) \text{ for } p \in \mathbb{R}^d,$$

such that f is continuous and $f \in C^{1,2}([0,T) \times (0,\infty)^d)$. Further, let

$$E_Q\left(g(P_1(T), ..., P_d(T))\right) < \infty,$$

where $E_Q = E_{Q,T}$ is defined as in Excursion 5. Then the price $X_B(t)$ of the contingent claim $B = g(P_1(T), ..., P_d(T))$ in the d-dimensional Black-Scholes model is given by

$$X_B(t) = f(t, P_1(t), ..., P_d(t)).$$

Further,

$$\Psi_i(t) = f_{p_i}(t, P_1(t), ..., P_d(t)), \ i = 1, ..., d,$$

$$\Psi_0(t) = \frac{f(t, P_1(t), ..., P_d(t)) - \sum_{i=1}^d \Psi_i(t) \cdot P_i(t)}{P_0(t)}$$

is a replication strategy for B.

Proof. Due to the special form of the final payment B and the independence of the increments of the d-dimensional Brownian motion $W(t)$, Corollary 3.15 implies

$$X_B(t) = E\left(e^{-r(T-t)} g(P_1(T), ..., P_d(T)) \mid \mathcal{F}_t\right)$$

$$= E^{t, P_1(t), ..., P_d(t)}\left(e^{-r(T-t)} g(P_1(T), ..., P_d(T))\right)$$

(for the last notation see Remark 3.10). Under the above existence assumptions for a solution of the Cauchy problem, the Feynman-Kac theorem yields

$$f(t, P_1(t), ..., P_d(t)) = X_B(t).$$

By imitating the relevant parts of the proof of Proposition 3.16 we obtain the assertion on the replication strategy $\Psi(t) = (\Psi_0(t), ..., \Psi_d(t))$. □

Summary: Derivation of the Black-Scholes formula. The price $C(t, P_1(T))$ of a European call was on one hand given as a conditional expectation

$$C(t, P_1(t)) = E_Q^{t,P_1(t)} \left(e^{-r(T-t)} (P_1(T) - K)^+ \right)$$

where we have

$$dP_1(s) = P_1(s) \left(r\, ds + \sigma\, dW^Q(s) \right), \ s \in [t, T],$$

and on the other hand as a solution of the Cauchy problem

$$C_t + \tfrac{1}{2}\sigma^2 p^2 C_{pp} + r \cdot p \cdot C_p - r \cdot C = 0, \quad (t,p) \in [0,T) \times (0, \infty),$$

$$C(T, p) = (p - K)^+, \ p \in (0, \infty).$$

In the following excursion we shall show that this connection is not just a random coincidence. It is a special case of a deep connection between solutions of partial differential equations and stochastic differential equations.

Excursion 6: The Feynman-Kac Representation

> **General assumptions for this section:**
> We still make the assumptions of Chapter 2, Section 2.2, p. 57. However, we do not necessarily assume $m = d$ (where m is the dimension of the Brownian motion).

Definition 3.20. If on $(\Omega, \mathcal{F}, P)$ there exists a d-dimensional continuous process $\{(X(t), \mathcal{F}_t)\}_{t \geq 0}$ with

$$X(0) = x, \ x \in \mathbb{R}^d \text{ fixed,}$$

$$X_i(t) = x_i + \int_0^t b_i(s, X(s))\, ds + \sum_{j=0}^m \int_0^t \sigma_{ij}(s, X(s))\, dW_j(s)$$

P-a.s. for all $t \geq 0$, $i \in \{1, ..., d\}$, satisfying

$$\int_0^t \left(|b_i(s, X(s))| + \sum_{j=1}^m \sigma_{ij}^2(s, X(s)) \right) ds < \infty$$

P-a.s. for all $t \geq 0$, $i \in \{1, ..., d\}$, then $X(t)$ is called a *strong solution of the stochastic differential equation*

(3.13)
$$dX(t) = b(t, X(t))\, dt + \sigma(t, X(t))\, dW(t)$$
$$X(0) = x$$

where
$$b : [0, \infty) \times \mathbb{R}^d \to \mathbb{R}^d, \quad \sigma : [0, \infty) \times \mathbb{R}^d \to \mathbb{R}^{d,m}$$
are given functions.

Remark 3.21. (1) By Theorem 2.54, "variation of constants", we already know that stochastic differential equations of the form
$$dX(t) = (b(t) \cdot X(t) + a(t))\, dt + (\sigma(t) \cdot X(t) + \nu(t))\, dW(t)$$
possess a unique, explicitly given strong solution (given some requirements on b, a, σ, and ν).

(2) Here we do not present the notion of a weak solution, therefore we refer the interested reader to Chapter 5.3 in [**KA/SH 91**].

The following theorem is an analogy to the existence and uniqueness result of Picard and Lindelöf in the deterministic case:

Theorem 3.22 (Existence and uniqueness of solutions of stochastic differential equations). *Let the coefficients $b(t,x)$, $\sigma(t,x)$ of the stochastic differential equation (3.13) be continuous functions with*

(3.14) $$\|b(t,x) - b(t,y)\| + \|\sigma(t,x) - \sigma(t,y)\| \leq K \|x - y\|$$

(3.15) $$\|b(t,x)\|^2 + \|\sigma(t,x)\|^2 \leq K^2 \left(1 + \|x\|^2\right)$$

for all $t \geq 0$, $x, y \in \mathbb{R}^d$ and a constant $K > 0$ (where $\|.\|$ denotes the Euclidean norm of suitable dimension). Then there exists a continuous, strong solution $\{(X(t), \mathcal{F}_t)\}_{t \geq 0}$ of (3.13) with

(3.16) $$E\left(\|X(t)\|^2\right) \leq C \cdot \left(1 + \|x\|^2\right) \cdot e^{C \cdot T} \text{ for all } t \in [0, T]$$

for some constant $C = C(K, T)$ and $T > 0$. Further, $X(t)$ is unique up to indistinguishability.

Proof.
Step 1: Uniqueness
Let X and $\tilde{X}$ be two solutions of (3.13). For $n \in \mathbb{N}$ we define the stopping times
$$\tau_n := \inf\{t \geq 0 \mid \|X(t)\| \geq n\}, \quad \tilde{\tau}_n := \inf\{t \geq 0 \mid \|\tilde{X}(t)\| \geq n\},$$
$$s_n := \tau_n \wedge \tilde{\tau}_n.$$

Continuity of both X and $\tilde{X}$ yield
$$\lim_{n\to\infty} s_n = +\infty \text{ a.s. } P.$$
Due to $\|v_1 + ... + v_n\|^2 \leq n^2 \left(\|v_1\|^2 + ... + \|v_n\|^2\right)$ for $v_i \in \mathbb{R}^d$, $i = 1, ..., n$, $n \in \mathbb{N}$, Hölder's inequality, the Itô isometry and assumption (3.14), we have

(3.17)
$$E\left(\left\|X(t \wedge s_n) - \tilde{X}(t \wedge s_n)\right\|^2\right)$$

$$= E\left(\left\|\int_0^{t \wedge s_n} \left(b(u, X(u)) - b\left(u, \tilde{X}(u)\right)\right) du \right.\right.$$

$$\left.\left. + \int_0^{t \wedge s_n} \left(\sigma(u, X(u)) - \sigma\left(u, \tilde{X}(u)\right)\right) dW(u)\right\|^2\right)$$

$$\leq 4t \cdot E\left(\int_0^{t \wedge s_n} \left\|\left(b(u, X(u)) - b\left(u, \tilde{X}(u)\right)\right)\right\|^2 du\right)$$

$$+ 4 \cdot E\left(\int_0^{t \wedge s_n} \left\|\left(\sigma(u, X(u)) - \sigma\left(u, \tilde{X}(u)\right)\right)\right\|^2 du\right)$$

$$\leq 4(T+1) \cdot K^2 \cdot E\left(\int_0^t \left\|\left(X(u \wedge s_n) - \tilde{X}(u \wedge s_n)\right)\right\|^2 du\right)$$

$$= 4(T+1) \cdot K^2 \cdot \int_0^t E\left(\left\|\left(X(u \wedge s_n) - \tilde{X}(u \wedge s_n)\right)\right\|^2\right) du.$$

Application of Grønwall's inequality to the continuous function
$$g(t) := E\left(\left\|X(t \wedge s_n) - \tilde{X}(t \wedge s_n)\right\|^2\right)$$
yields $g(t) \equiv 0$ due to (3.17). Hence $\{X(t \wedge s_n)\}_{t \geq 0}$ and $\{\tilde{X}(t \wedge s_n)\}_{t \geq 0}$ are modifications of each other. As they both have continuous paths they are then even indistinguishable. We obtain the same result for X and $\tilde{X}$ by taking the limit $n \to \infty$.

Step 2: Existence - some estimates
As in the deterministic case, the existence of a solution will be proved via the construction of an iterative sequence:

(3.18)
$$X^{(0)}(t) \equiv x$$

$$X^{(k+1)}(t) := x + \int_0^t b\left(s, X^{(k)}(s)\right) ds + \int_0^t \sigma\left(s, X^{(k)}(s)\right) dW(s)$$

for $t \in [0, T]$, $k = 0, 1, 2, \ldots$. $X^{(k)}(t)$ is obviously $\mathcal{F}_t$-measurable and has continuous paths. Further, due to (3.15) and an inequality similar to (3.17), we obtain the following inequality

(3.19) $\quad E\left(\left\|X^{(k+1)}(t)\right\|^2\right)$

$$\leq 9\|x\|^2 + 9(t+1)K^2 \int_0^t \left(1 + E\left(\left\|X^{(k)}(s)\right\|^2\right)\right) ds$$

for all $t \in [0, T]$. Here, existence of the expectations on the right-hand side follows by induction from the initial condition $X^{(0)} = x$ and thus by

$$E\left(\left\|X^{(1)}(t)\right\|^2\right) \leq E\left(\left\|x + \int_0^t b(s, x)\, ds + \int_0^t \sigma(s, x)\, dW(s)\right\|^2\right).$$

In particular, by (3.19) and (3.15) we have

$$\sup_{0 \leq t \leq T} E\left(\left\|X^{(k)}(t)\right\|^2\right) < \infty,$$

which implies that all the integrals appearing on the right-hand side of (3.18) exist. With the notation of

$$C := C(T, K) := 9(T+1)K^2$$

relation (3.19) implies the inequality

$$E\left(\left\|X^{(k+1)}(t)\right\|^2\right) \leq C\left(1 + \|x\|^2\right) + C \int_0^t E\left(\left\|X^{(k)}(s)\right\|^2\right) ds.$$

By induction, repeated application of this inequality to the integrand on the right-hand side yields

(3.20) $\quad E\left(\left\|X^{(k+1)}(t)\right\|^2\right)$

$$\leq C\left(1 + \|x\|^2\right)\left(1 + Ct + \frac{(Ct)^2}{2} + \ldots + \frac{(Ct)^{k+1}}{(k+1)!}\right)$$

$$\leq C\left(1 + \|x\|^2\right) e^{Ct}.$$

Step 3: Existence - convergence of the iteration
Due to (3.15) and (3.20), the process

$$M(t) := \int_0^t \left(\sigma\left(s, X^{(k)}(s)\right) - \sigma\left(s, X^{(k-1)}(s)\right) \right) dW(s)$$

is a d-dimensional, square-integrable martingale. Due to (3.15) component-wise application of Doob's inequality thus results in

$$(3.21) \quad E\left(\sup_{0 \leq s \leq t} \|M(s)\|^2 \right)$$

$$\leq 4 \cdot E \int_0^t \left\| \sigma\left(s, X^{(k)}(s)\right) - \sigma\left(s, X^{(k-1)}(s)\right) \right\|^2 ds$$

$$\leq 4 \cdot K^2 \cdot E \int_0^t \left\| X^{(k)}(s) - X^{(k-1)}(s) \right\|^2 ds.$$

Again, due to (3.15) for

$$B(t) := \int_0^t \left(b\left(s, X^{(k)}(s)\right) - b\left(s, X^{(k-1)}(s)\right) \right) ds$$

we obtain the relation

$$(3.22) \quad E(\|B(t)\|)^2 \leq K^2 \cdot t \cdot \int_0^t E\left(\left\| X^{(k)}(s) - X^{(k-1)}(s) \right\|^2 \right) ds.$$

Hence, due to $X^{(k+1)}(t) - X^{(k)}(t) = B(t) + M(t)$, relations (3.21) and (3.22) imply

$$(3.23) \quad E\left(\sup_{0 \leq s \leq t} \left\| X^{(k+1)}(s) - X^{(k)}(s) \right\|^2 \right)$$

$$\leq K^2 \cdot (4 + T) \cdot \int_0^t E\left(\left\| X^{(k)}(s) - X^{(k-1)}(s) \right\|^2 \right) ds.$$

Repeated application of (3.23) to the integrand on the right-hand side of this inequality and using the notations

$$D := K^2(4 + T), \quad D^* := \sup_{0 \leq t \leq T} E\left(\left\| X^{(1)}(t) - x \right\|^2 \right)$$

yield the following estimate

$$(3.24) \quad E\left(\sup_{0 \leq s \leq t} \left\|X^{(k+1)}(s) - X^{(k)}(s)\right\|^2\right) \leq D^* \frac{(Dt)^k}{k!}.$$

Note that due to (3.20) D^* is finite. In a similar way as in the extension theorem for stochastic integrals, Theorem 2.42, we now show that the sequence $X^{(k)}$ of continuous processes converges uniformly:
Equation (3.24) and Chebyshev's inequality yield

$$(3.25) \quad P\left(\max_{0 \leq t \leq T} \left\|X^{(k+1)}(t) - X^{(k)}(t)\right\| \geq \frac{1}{2^{k+1}}\right) \leq 4D^* \frac{(4DT)^k}{k!}.$$

With the choice of

$$A_k := \left\{\max_{0 \leq t \leq T} \left\|X^{(k+1)}(t) - X^{(k)}(t)\right\| \geq \frac{1}{2^{k+1}}\right\},$$

application of the Borel-Cantelli lemma to the sequence A_k, $k \in \mathbb{N}$, implies the uniform convergence of the sequence of the paths of $X^{(k)}(t)$, $k \in \mathbb{N}$, due to (3.25). Consequently, there exists a continuous process $X(t)$ with

$$X(t) = \lim_{k \to \infty} X^{(k)}(t) \text{ a.s. } P, \text{ for all } t \in [0, T].$$

As T was chosen arbitrarily, we have the convergence on $[0, \infty)$. Further, this, (3.20), and Fatou's lemma imply inequality (3.16).

Step 4: Solution property
To prove that $X(t)$ is indeed a solution of the stochastic differential equation, we still have to show the convergence of the integrals on the right-hand side of (3.18). The uniform convergence of $X^{(k)}(t)$ against $X(t)$ on $[0, T]$ yields

$$(3.26) \quad \max_{0 \leq t \leq T} \left\|X(t, \omega) - X^{(k)}(t, \omega)\right\| \leq 2^{-k}$$

for all $k \geq N(\omega)$ for some suitable $N(\omega) \in \mathbb{N}$. Hence, with (3.14) and (3.26) we obtain

$$(3.27) \quad \left\|\int_0^t b(s, X(s))\, ds - \int_0^t b\left(s, X^{(k)}(s)\right) ds\right\|^2$$

$$\leq K^2 \cdot T \cdot \int_0^T \left\|X(s) - X^{(k)}(s)\right\|^2 ds \xrightarrow{k \to \infty} 0.$$

To see the convergence of the stochastic integrals, note that for fixed $t \in [0, T]$ the sequence $\{X^{(k)}(t)\}_{k \in \mathbb{N}}$ is a Cauchy sequence in $L^2(\Omega, \mathcal{F}, P)$ (due to (3.24)), and thus due to

$$X^{(k)}(t) \xrightarrow{k \to \infty} X(t) \text{ a.s. } P,$$

we also have
$$E\left(\left\|X^{(k)}(t) - X(t)\right\|^2\right) \xrightarrow{k \to \infty} 0.$$
Hence, by the Itô isometry, (3.16) and (3.14), we get

$$(3.28) \quad E\left\|\int_0^t \left(\sigma\left(s, X^{(k)}(s)\right) - \sigma(s, X(s))\right) dW(s)\right\|^2$$

$$= E\int_0^t \left\|\sigma\left(s, X^{(k)}(s)\right) - \sigma(s, X(s))\right\|^2 ds$$

$$\leq K^2 \cdot \int_0^t E\left(\left\|X^{(k)}(t) - X(t)\right\|^2\right) ds \xrightarrow{k \to \infty} 0 \text{ for all } t \in [0, T],$$

where the theorem on dominated convergence can be applied due to the uniform convergence of $X^{(k)}(t)$ against $X(t)$ on $[0, T]$. Inequalities (3.27) and (3.28) imply the desired convergence of the integrals on the right-hand side of (3.18) for fixed $t \in [0, T]$. Here we can restrict to a suitable subsequence to get the almost sure convergence of the stochastic integral. The continuity of both the right- and left-hand side of the stochastic differential equation now yields convergence of the integrals for arbitrary $t \geq 0$ by the usual arguments. □

Application of the relation
$$|x_1|^p + ... + |x_n|^p \leq n(|x_1| + ... + |x_n|)^p \leq n^{p+1}(|x_1|^p + ... + |x_n|^p)$$
for arbitrary $x \in \mathbb{R}^n$, $p > 1$, and similar estimates as in the first three steps of the preceding proof (see [**KA/SH 91**], p. 303, 389) imply the following useful lemma.

Lemma 3.23. *Under the assumptions of Theorem 3.22 the solution X of the stochastic differential equation satisfies for $m \geq 1$ and fixed $T > 0$*
$$E\left(\max_{0 \leq s \leq t} \|X(s)\|^{2m}\right) \leq C\left(1 + \|x\|^{2m}\right) e^{Ct}$$
for all $t \in [0, T]$ and a suitable constant $C = C(T, K, m, d)$.

Notation. The solution of the stochastic differential equation (3.13) with initial condition $X(t) = x$ will especially be denoted by
$$X^{t,x}(s).$$
For simplicity, we often omit the upper indices in the following, but mark corresponding expectations with this upper index instead:
$$E\left(...X^{t,x}(s)...\right) = E^{t,x}\left(...X(s)...\right).$$

Remark 3.24. (1) The foregoing results can be generalized to the case of a random initial condition

$$X(0) = Z$$

if Z is a square-integrable random variable (of course, for Lemma 3.23 we need the condition $E(\|Z\|^{2m}) < \infty$) which is independent of the Brownian filtration $\{\mathcal{F}_t\}_{t\geq 0}$. Then, $X(t)$ is adapted to the P-augmentation $\{\mathcal{G}_t\}_{t\geq 0}$ of

$$\mathcal{G}_t^* := \sigma(Z, W(s); 0 \leq s \leq T)$$

(i.e. $X(t)$ is $\mathcal{G}_t$-measurable).

(2) It can be shown that the solution $\{(X(t), \mathcal{F}_t)\}_t$ of (3.13) is a Markov process, i.e. for all Borel measurable, bounded functions f we have

(3.29) $\quad E(f(X(s)) \mid \mathcal{F}_t) = E(f(X(s)) \mid X(t)) = g(X(t))$

for fixed $t \leq s$ with $g(x) := E(f(X^{t,x}(s)))$ (see e.g. [**RO/WI 87**], Section V.4). We shall therefore use the above notation $E^{t,x}(f(X(s)))$ in this sense. However, as in our applications the Markov property is typically a direct consequence of the independence of the increments of Brownian motion, so we abandon a presentation of a proof of the Markov property of X.

Definition 3.25. Let $X(t)$ be the unique solution of the stochastic differential equation (3.13) under the conditions (3.14) and (3.15). For $f : \mathbb{R}^d \to \mathbb{R}$, $f \in C^2(\mathbb{R}^d)$, the operator A_t, defined by

$$(A_t f)(x) := \frac{1}{2} \sum_{i=1}^d \sum_{k=1}^d a_{ik}(t, x) \cdot \frac{\partial^2 f}{\partial x_i \partial x_k}(x) + \sum_{i=1}^d b_i(t, x) \cdot \frac{\partial f}{\partial x_i}(x)$$

with

$$a_{ik}(t, x) := \sum_{j=1}^m \sigma_{ij}(t, x) \cdot \sigma_{kj}(t, x)$$

is called the *characteristic operator* corresponding to $X(t)$.

Examples.

(1) $X(t) = W(t)$ solves the stochastic differential equation $dX(t) = dW(t)$, $X(0) = 0$. Hence,

$$\tfrac{1}{2}\Delta = \tfrac{1}{2} \sum_{i=1}^d \frac{\partial^2}{\partial x_i^2}$$

is the characteristic operator of the d-dimensional Brownian motion.

(2) The stock price process

$$X(t) = x \cdot e^{\left(b - \frac{1}{2}\sigma^2\right)t + \sigma W(t)}$$

solves the stochastic differential equation

$$dX(t) = X(t)(b\,dt + \sigma\,dW(t))$$
$$X(0) = x$$

and thus has the characteristic operator A_t given by

$$(A_t f)(x) = \tfrac{1}{2}\sigma^2 x^2 f''(x) + b\,x\,f'(x).$$

Description of the Cauchy problem corresponding to A_t. Let $T > 0$ be fixed. We now consider the following *Cauchy problem* corresponding to the operator A_t.

Find a function $v(t,x) : [0,T] \times \mathbb{R}^d \to \mathbb{R}$ with

(3.30) $\qquad -v_t + kv = A_t v + g \quad \text{on } [0,T) \times \mathbb{R}^d$
$\qquad\qquad v(T,x) = f(x) \quad \text{for } x \in \mathbb{R}^d$

where

$$f : \mathbb{R}^d \to \mathbb{R},\ g : [0,T] \times \mathbb{R}^d \to \mathbb{R},\ k : [0,T] \times \mathbb{R}^d \to [0,\infty).$$

To ensure the uniqueness of a solution of (3.30) we additionally require that v obeys a polynomial growth condition:

(3.31) $\qquad \max_{0 \le t \le T} |v(t,x)| \le M\left(1 + \|x\|^{2\mu}\right)$ with $M > 0$, $\mu \ge 1$.

Usually, we assume that for suitable constants L, λ, the functions f, g, k satisfy

---

f, g, k continuous with

(3.32) $\qquad |f(x)| \le L\left(1 + \|x\|^{2\lambda}\right), \quad L > 0,\ \lambda \ge 1 \text{ or } f(x) \ge 0,$

(3.33) $\qquad |g(t,x)| \le L\left(1 + \|x\|^{2\lambda}\right), \quad L > 0,\ \lambda \ge 1 \text{ or } g(t,x) \ge 0.$

Theorem 3.26 (The Feynman-Kac representation). *Let the assumptions (3.32) and (3.33) be satisfied. Let further $v(t,x) : [0,T] \times \mathbb{R}^d \to \mathbb{R}$ be a continuous solution of the Cauchy problem (3.30) with $v \in C^{1,2}([0,T) \times \mathbb{R}^d)$. Denote by A_t in (3.30) the characteristic operator corresponding to the unique solution $X(t)$ of the stochastic differential equation (3.13) with* *continuous coefficients b, σ satisfying (3.14) and*

$$b_i(t,x),\ \sigma_{ij}(t,x): [0,\infty) \times \mathbb{R}^d \to \mathbb{R}\ \text{for}\ i=1,...,d,\ j=1,...,m.$$

If $v(t,x)$ satisfies the polynomial growth condition (3.31) we then have the representation

$$v(t,x) = E^{t,x}\left(f(X(T)) \cdot \exp\left(-\int_t^T k(\theta, X(\theta))\,d\theta\right)\right.$$
$$\left. + \int_t^T g(s, X(s)) \cdot \exp\left(-\int_t^s k(\theta, X(\theta))\,d\theta\right) ds\right).$$

In particular, $v(t,x)$ is the unique solution of (3.30) which satisfies (3.31).

Remark 3.27. So if we can show that (3.30) possesses some solution satisfying (3.31) then it is given by the above expectation as a function of the initial parameters of (3.13). However, in general we do not have the opposite direction. More precisely, the above expectation need not necessarily be the solution of (3.30) as it may not be smooth enough. If on the other side we can calculate this expectation then we can check if it possibly solves the Cauchy problem. If this is indeed the case then it is the unique solution of (3.30) satisfying (3.31). We highlight these relations by the following example.

Example. Solve the following Cauchy problem

$$\tfrac{1}{2} v_{xx} = -v_t,$$
$$v(T,x) = x^2.$$

Here we have $k, g \equiv 0$ and $f(x) = x^2$. We know that $1/2 \cdot v_{xx}$ is the characteristic operator of the Brownian motion (see the example above). So by Theorem 3.26 and Remark 3.27, we have a natural candidate for the solution of our Cauchy problem

$$\tilde{v}(t,x) = E^{t,x}\left(W^2(T)\right) = x^2 + (T-t).$$

It is easy to verify that $\tilde{v}$ indeed solves the above Cauchy problem. It is thus also the unique solution of (3.30) satisfying (3.31).

Proof of Theorem 3.26. For simplicity we assume $m = d = 1$ and $k(\theta, X(\theta)) \equiv k$. The proof of the general case is similar.

Excursion 6: The Feynman-Kac Representation

Let $0 \leq t \leq s \leq T$. Then the multi-dimensional Itô formula, Theorem 2.52, and Corollary 2.53 yield

$$v(s, X(s)) \cdot e^{-k(s-t)}$$
$$= v(t,x) \cdot 1 + \int_t^s e^{-k(u-t)} d\left(\nu(u, X(u))\right) + \int_t^s v(u, X(u)) \, d\left(e^{-k(u-t)}\right)$$

$$= v(t,x) + \int_t^s e^{-k(u-t)} \left(v_t + v_x \cdot b(u, X(u))\right.$$
$$\left. + \tfrac{1}{2} v_{xx} \cdot \sigma^2(u, X(u)) - k \cdot v\right) du$$
$$+ \int_t^s e^{-k(u-t)} \left(v_x \cdot \sigma(u, X(u))\right) dW(u).$$

As we have $A_t v = \tfrac{1}{2} v_{xx} \cdot \sigma^2(t, X(t)) + v_x \cdot b(t, X(t))$ and as $v(t,x)$ solves (3.30), we further have

(3.34) $\quad v(s, X(s)) \cdot e^{-k(s-t)} = v(t,x) - \int_t^s e^{-k(u-t)} \cdot g(u, X(u)) \, du$
$$+ \int_t^s e^{-k(u-t)} \left(v_x \cdot \sigma(u, X(u))\right) dW(u).$$

Define the stopping time

$$\tau_n := \inf\{s \geq t : \|X(s)\| \geq n\}.$$

We then choose $s = T \wedge \tau_n$ in (3.34) and take the expectation. As the integrand of the stochastic integral is bounded (note the definition of the stopping time!), the expectation of the stochastic integral is zero. We thus obtain

$$v(t,x) = \underbrace{E^{t,x}\left(v(\tau_n, X(\tau_n)) \cdot e^{-k(\tau_n - t)} \cdot 1_{\{\tau_n \leq T\}}\right)}_{B}$$
$$+ \underbrace{E^{t,x}\left(f(X(T)) \cdot e^{-k(T-t)} \cdot 1_{\{\tau_n > T\}}\right)}_{D}$$
$$+ \underbrace{E^{t,x}\left(\int_t^{T \wedge \tau_n} e^{-k(u-t)} \cdot g(u, X(u)) \, du\right)}_{G}.$$

We now have the following facts:

(1) By the theorem on dominated convergence (respectively monotonous convergence), (3.33) and the inequality

(3.35) $$E^{t,x}\left(\max_{t\leq\theta\leq s}\|X(\theta)\|^{2r}\right) \leq C\left(1+\|x\|^{2r}\right)\cdot e^{C(s-t)}$$

for all $r \geq 1$ and a constant $C = C(K, r, T, d) > 0$ (see Lemma 3.23), imply the convergence

$$G \xrightarrow{n\to\infty} E^{t,x}\left(\int_t^T e^{-k(u-t)}\cdot g(u, X(u))\, du\right).$$

(2) The polynomial growth condition (3.31) yields
$$E^{t,x}\left(|v(\tau_n, X(\tau_n))|\cdot 1_{\{\tau_n\leq T\}}\right) \leq M\cdot\left(1+n^{2\mu}\right)\cdot P^{t,x}(\tau_n \leq T).$$
Due to Chebyshev's inequality and (3.35), we get

$$P^{t,x}(\tau_n \leq T) = P^{t,x}\left(\max_{t\leq\theta\leq T}\|X(\theta)\| \geq n\right)$$
$$\leq n^{-2r} E^{t,x}\left(\max_{t\leq\theta\leq T}\|X(\theta)\|^{2r}\right) \leq n^{-2r} C\left(1+\|x\|^{2r}\right) e^{CT}.$$

Using these two relations and choosing $r > \mu$ results in
$$B \xrightarrow{n\to\infty} 0.$$

(3) With (3.32) we can apply the theorem on dominated convergence (respectively monotonous convergence) which yields
$$D \xrightarrow{n\to\infty} E^{t,x}\left(f(X(T))\cdot e^{-k(T-t)}\right).$$

In total, by the facts (1)-(3) we get the asserted form of $v(t, x)$. □

3.4. Arbitrage Bounds for American and European Options

The aim of this section is not the determination of exact option pricing formulae, but that of upper and lower bounds for their prices. These bounds will be derived solely by the principle of no-arbitrage independent of the modeling of the underlying stock prices. So the only tool we can use is the principle that we do not fix an option price which permits arbitrage opportunities. We therefore speak of *arbitrage bounds*. The justification of these bounds lies in the fact that in the presence of the possibility to make gains without initial capital, all investors that are faced with such a possibility will try to realize it. This would result in an immediate adjustment of prices by the market such that this arbitrage opportunity would disappear. In the

3.4. Arbitrage Bounds for American and European Options

following we shall therefore assume that the stock prices do not permit such a possibility. Thus, for the validity of the arbitrage bounds derived below we always have to check if the assumed market model is free of arbitrage.

In contrast to the exact price determination in the Black-Scholes case the determination of arbitrage bounds for American options is much easier than for options of European type (see Section 3.5 for the valuation of American options in the Black-Scholes case). The method to prove all given bounds typically consists of constructing an arbitrage strategy for option prices above the upper or below the lower bound.

Obvious bounds for prices of American and European puts and calls are

$$C_E(t, P_1(t)) \geq 0, \; P_E(t, P_1(t)) \geq 0, \; C_A(t, P_1(t)) \geq 0, \; P_A(t, P_1(t)) \geq 0,$$

where C_E, C_A denote the prices of European and American calls, P_E, P_A those of European and American puts. Here, $P_1(t)$ is the current price of the underlying stock. For a "proof" of the above relations note that in the case of negative prices even the strategy

- "Buy the corresponding option and let it expire without exercising it"

is an arbitrage strategy, as at $t = 0$ the investor receives an amount of money (namely the "option price") and does not have to make any future payments resulting from this strategy.

General assumptions for this section:
To prove the following bounds we assume it to be possible to invest or to borrow money at the riskless rate r at each time instant t. We do not need any further requirement on the market model or the price behavior of the stocks in this section.

Proposition 3.28. (1) The price $C_A(t, P_1(t))$ of an American call with strike $K \geq 0$ satisfies

$$(3.36) \qquad (P_1(t) - K)^+ \leq C_A(t, P_1(t)) \leq P_1(t).$$

(2) The price $P_A(t, P_1(t))$ of an American put with strike $K \geq 0$ satisfies

$$(3.37) \qquad (K - P_1(t))^+ \leq P_A(t, P_1(t)) \leq K.$$

Proof. (1) In the case $(P_1(t) - K)^+ > C_A(t, P_1(t))$ the strategy
- "Buy the option and exercise it immediately"

is an arbitrage strategy. Note that in t it yields the payment

$$P_1(t) - K - C_A(t, P_1(t)) > 0$$

and there will be no further payment. We thus would have a riskless gain without initial capital. In the case $P_1(t) < C_A(t, P_1(t))$ an arbitrage strategy can be constructed as follows:

- "Sell the call for $C_A(t, P_1(t))$, buy the stock for $P_1(t)$, invest the positive rest $C_A(t, P_1(t)) - P_1(t)$ at the riskless rate r".

If then the buyer of the option exercises it at some time he receives the stock and pays an amount of K to the option seller. If, however, the option is never exercised then the option seller retains the stock. In both cases, to follow this strategy no initial capital is required, but it results in a strictly positive final wealth of (at least)

$$(C_A(t, P_1(t)) - P_1(t)) \cdot e^{r(T-t)}.$$

This shows that the so-constructed strategy is an arbitrage strategy. In particular, we have proved inequality (3.36).

(2) The analogous proof is left to the reader. $\square$

As an American option additionally contains the possibility of a free choice of the exercise time (compared to a European one), we must have the following relations for European and American options with the same strike price and the same time to maturity:

(3.38) $\qquad C_A(t, P_1(t)) \geq C_E(t, P_1(t)), \quad P_A(t, P_1(t)) \geq P_E(t, P_1(t)).$

These relations will be needed for the proof of the following proposition:

Proposition 3.29. (1) For the price $C_E(t, P_1(t))$ of a European call with strike price $K \geq 0$ and exercise date T, we have

(3.39) $\qquad \left(P_1(t) - e^{-r(T-t)}K\right)^+ \leq C_E(t, P_1(t)) \leq P_1(t),$

if there will be no dividend payments on the stock in $[0, T]$.

(2) For the price $P_E(t, P_1(t))$ of a European put with strike price $K \geq 0$ and exercise date T, we have

(3.40) $\qquad \left(e^{-r(T-t)}K - P_1(t)\right)^+ \leq P_E(t, P_1(t)) \leq K,$

if there will be no dividend payments on the stock in $[0, T]$.

Proof. (1) Due to the inequalities (3.36) and (3.38) we obviously have $C_E(t, P_1(t)) \leq P_1(t)$. Let us now assume

(3.41) $\qquad C_E(t, P_1(t)) < \left(P_1(t) - e^{-r(T-t)}K\right)^+$

where due to the non-negativity of the call price this automatically implies the strict positivity of the expression on the right-hand side of (3.41). But then the following strategy constitutes an arbitrage strategy:

- "Buy the call for $C_E(t, P_1(t))$ and sell one unit of stock short (i.e. sell without possessing it now, but deliver later). Invest the positive rest $P_1(t) - C_E(t, P_1(t))$ at the riskless rate r".

By (3.41) this riskless investment leads to a capital of

$$(P_1(t) - C_E(t, P_1(t))) \cdot e^{r(T-t)} > K$$

at $t = T$. At $t = T$ we can have the following two cases:

1. $P_1(T) > K$:
In this case, the option buyer exercises the call, thus buys the stock at a price of K and closes out the short selling of the stock at time t. In total the option buyer can realize a gain of

$$(P_1(t) - C_E(t, P_1(t))) \cdot e^{r(T-t)} - K > 0$$

at time $t = T$.

2. $P_1(T) \leq K$:
Here, the option will not be exercised. To close out the short position in the stock, the option buyer purchases one share at the market for a price of $P_1(t) \leq K$. He thus makes a gain of

$$(P_1(t) - C_E(t, P_1(t))) \cdot e^{r(T-t)} - P_1(T) > K - K = 0.$$

In both cases a strictly positive terminal wealth can be attained without any initial capital which shows the arbitrage property of the strategy.

(2) The similar proof will be left to the reader. $\square$

Remark 3.30. Due to (3.36) and (3.38), inequality (3.39)

$$\left(P_1(t) - e^{-r(T-t)}K\right)^+ \leq C_A(t, P_1(t)) \leq P_1(t),$$

is also valid for American calls.

Further examples for arbitrage bounds for options having payoff profiles different from the standard puts and calls can be constructed easily. It is important to note that we often obtain tighter bounds for a portfolio of options than we would obtain by simply adding up all the bounds corresponding to every single option. Sometimes it is even possible to determine the price of the portfolio from pure arbitrage considerations independent of the stock price model. By far the most well-known example is:

Theorem 3.31 (Put-call parity for European options). *For the prices $P_E(t, P_1(t))$, $C_E(t, P_1(t))$ of European put and call options with the same* *maturity time T and the same strike price K, we have*

(3.42) $$C_E(t, P_1(t)) + Ke^{-r(T-t)} = P_E(t, P_1(t)) + P_1(t)$$

if the underlying stock pays no dividends on $[0, T]$.

Proof. The left-hand side of equation (3.42) corresponds to the strategy to buy a call and to invest $Ke^{-r(T-t)}$ units of money into the bond. It leads to a terminal wealth of

(3.43) $$X_C(T) = (P_1(T) - K)^+ + K = K \cdot 1_{\{P_1(T)<K\}} + P_1(T) \cdot 1_{\{P_1(T) \geq K\}}.$$

The strategy corresponding to the right-hand side of (3.42), buying one put and one share of the stock leads to a final wealth of
(3.44)
$$X_P(T) = (K - P_1(T))^+ + P_1(T) = K \cdot 1_{\{P_1(T)<K\}} + P_1(T) \cdot 1_{\{P_1(T) \geq K\}}.$$

As both strategies lead to the same final wealth (and cause no other payments before T), their values at time $t = T$ have to coincide. This implies the validity of (3.42) at $t = T$. If (3.42) would not hold for some $t < T$ then we could construct an arbitrage strategy by buying the strategy corresponding to the "cheap side" of (3.42) and selling the "expensive one" (i.e. by holding the corresponding negative positions). This would lead to a positive payment at time t which could be invested at the riskless rate. As due to (3.43) and (3.44) the payments of the two strategies neutralize each other at maturity, we would thus have realized a positive final wealth without initial capital. Hence equation (3.42) has to hold for all $t \in [0, T]$. □

Remark 3.32. (1) If we transform the put-call parity (3.42) into

(3.45) $$C_E(t, P_1(t)) - P_E(t, P_1(t)) = P_1(t) - Ke^{-r(T-t)},$$

then this equality is even trivial in $t = T$ due to

$$C_E(T, P_1(T)) - P_E(T, P_1(T)) = (P_1(T) - K)^+ - (K - P_1(T))^+ \\ = P_1(T) - K.$$

(2) A further simple proof of equation (3.42) can be obtained with the help of (3.45) by graphical subtraction of the payoff diagrams of the call (see Figure 3.1) and the put (see Figure 3.2) which obviously leads to the payoff diagram of $P_1(T) - K$; see Figure 3.4.

3.4. Arbitrage Bounds for American and European Options

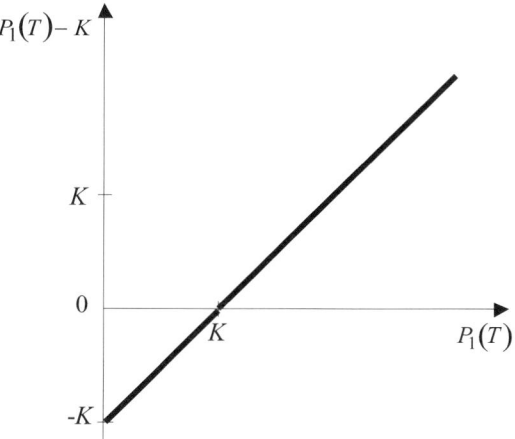

Figure 3.4. Payoff diagram of the combined option "call–put"

(3) The put-call parity also gives us a simple way of proving the Black-Scholes formula for a European put in case the price for the corresponding call is already known (see Corollary 3.9):

$$\begin{aligned} P_E(t, P_1(t)) &= C_E(t, P_1(t)) - P_1(t) - Ke^{-r(T-t)} \\ &= P_1(t) \cdot \Phi(d_1(t)) - Ke^{-r(T-t)}\Phi(d_2(t)) - P_1(t) - Ke^{-r(T-t)} \\ &= -P_1(t) \cdot (1 - \Phi(d_1(t))) + Ke^{-r(T-t)}(1 - \Phi(d_2(t))) \\ &= -P_1(t) \cdot (\Phi(-d_1(t))) + Ke^{-r(T-t)}(\Phi(-d_2(t))). \end{aligned}$$

In the case of American options, the put-call parity is in general not valid. All the given proofs of (3.42) required the same exercise time for both put and call. This need not necessarily be true for American puts and calls. Even more, for American puts and calls with the same maturity and the same strike price it can never be profitable to exercise both at the same time! Before proving a related variant of (3.42) in the case of American options we continue with a result that – at first glance – might be quite surprising.

Proposition 3.33. *Consider a stock that pays no dividends on $[0, T]$. Assume that the riskless rate r is strictly positive. Then, the prices of a European and an American call on the stock with the same maturity T and strike price K coincide, i.e. we have*

(3.46) $$C_A(t, P_1(t)) = C_E(t, P_1(t)) \text{ for all } t \in [0, T],$$

and it is never favorable to exercise the American call early (i.e. before maturity T).

Proof. Due to (3.38) and (3.39) we have

$$(3.47) \qquad C_A(t, P_1(t)) \geq C_E(t, P_1(t)) \geq \left(P_1(t) - e^{-r(T-t)}K\right)^+.$$

Of course, it might be reasonable to exercise an American call at time $t < T$ if we have $P_1(t) > K$. But in this case, due to $r > 0$ and inequality (3.47), we obtain

$$(3.48) \quad C_A(t, P_1(t)) \geq \left(P_1(t) - e^{-r(T-t)}K\right)^+ > (P_1(t) - K)^+ = P_1(t) - K,$$

i.e. the price of an American call before maturity T is always strictly larger than its intrinsic value $P_1(t) - K$, the gain we would make by immediate exercise of the call. Hence, exercising an American call in our situation can only be favorable at time T. Thus the payments resulting from possessing a European and an American call coincide. The assumption of absence of arbitrage then yields assertion (3.46). □

Remark 3.34. (1) Of course, the owner of an American option which is deeply in the money (i.e. the corresponding stock price is far above the strike price) has the desire to make use of this favourable situation. As due to Proposition 3.33 exercising the call early is not profitable, the only action to benefit from this situation is to sell the call. Due to inequality (3.48) this yields a higher gain than immediate exercise of the call.

(2) Even under the aspect of only holding the call to ensure the right to buy the stock, it is not favourable to exercise the call early. Even if the stock price increases further the already agreed exercise price will still be K. On the other hand, if the holder of the option would exercise it early and the stock price would fall below K during the remaining time before maturity, then a lower price for obtaining the stock would have been possible. As long as the potential stock buyer has not exercised the option he is insured against price fluctuations of the stock. In the worst case he lets the option expire without exercising it, but then as a substitute he buys the stock at the market price which is below K at time T. Further, by exercising the option early he would lose the riskless interest payments on the money that he set aside to buy the stock.

As a final arbitrage relation we present the analogue to (3.42) for American puts and calls.

Theorem 3.35 (Put-call relation for American options). *Under the assumptions of Proposition 3.33 we have*

$$(3.49) \qquad P_1(t) - K \leq C_A(t, P_1(t)) - P_A(t, P_1(t)) \leq P_1(t) - Ke^{-r(T-t)}.$$

Proof. (1) The right-hand inequality in (3.49) is implied by the put-call parity for European options and the relations

$$C_A(t, P_1(t)) = C_E(t, P_1(t)), \ P_A(t, P_1(t)) \geq P_E(t, P_1(t)).$$

(2) To prove the left-hand inequality in (3.49) we assume that for some pair $(t, P_1(t))$ we have the opposite relation. Then the strategy
- "Buy the call, sell the put, sell the stock short for $P_1(t)$, and invest K units of money at the riskless rate r"

is an arbitrage strategy. To see this, note:
- Due to the above assumption the costs of this strategy equal $C_A(t, P_1(t)) - P_A(t, P_1(t)) + P_1(t) - K < 0$. We have thus realized a gain at time t.
- If the put will be exercised before T then the holder of the above strategy is forced to buy the stock for the price of K. He immediately uses the purchased stock to close out his initially made short sale of the stock (at time t). He then still possesses the call and that part of the money he has invested at the riskless rate which was not needed for purchasing the stock. So the wealth of his holdings are not negative. Also, remind yourself of the fact that he has already realized a positive gain at time t.
- If the put is not exercised before T then one of the following two cases can occur:
  $P_1(T) \geq K$: The holder of the above strategy uses the call to buy the stock for a price of K and closes out his short position in the stock. In addition to the initial gain, he then still possesses that part of the money invested at the riskless rate which was not needed to buy the stock.
  $P_1(T) < K$: In this case the put will be exercised. Thus, the investor is forced to buy the stock at price K. He then uses the stock for closing out his short position. Again, in addition to the initial gain, he still possesses that part of the money invested at the riskless rate which was not needed to buy the stock.

□

3.5. Pricing of American Options

The surprising result of the last section consisted of the fact that solely by arbitrage considerations we could show that a European call and its corresponding American variant have the same price. This result was surprising due to the fact that therefore the possibility to choose the exercise date has no value at all! However, as this is not the case for general American options, explicit determination of the price of an American option is much more difficult than in the European case.

> **General assumptions for this section:**
> We consider a Black-Scholes model, i.e. we have $d = m = 1$, b, r, σ are constants with $\sigma > 0$.

First we give a definition of an American contingent claim. For simplicity, we do not include the possibility of a payout rate process here.

Definition 3.36. An *American contingent claim* consists of a progressively measurable stochastic process $B = \{(B(t), \mathcal{F}_t)\}_{t \in [0,T]}$ with $B(t) \geq 0$ and a final payment $B(\tau)$ at the exercise time $\tau \in [0,T]$ chosen by the holder of the contingent claim. Here, we assume that:

- τ is a stopping time;
- $E\left(\sup_{0 \leq s \leq T} (B(s))^\mu\right) < \infty$ for some $\mu > 1$; $\quad(*)$
- $\{(B(t), \mathcal{F}_t)\}_{t \in [0,T]}$ possesses continuous paths.

Examples. The most important American contingent claims are the American call on a stock with strike price K, i.e.
$$B(t) = (P_1(t) - K)^+$$
and the corresponding American put
$$B(t) = (K - P_1(t))^+.$$
Here the strike price can even be chosen as some continuous function in time t.

Definition 3.37. (1) An admissible pair $(\pi, c) \in \mathcal{A}(x)$ consisting of a portfolio process and a consumption process with corresponding wealth process $X^\pi(t) \geq B(t)$ for all $t \in [0,T]$ is called a *hedging strategy* for the American contingent claim B with price $x > 0$.

(2) Let $\mathcal{H}(x)$ be the set of hedging strategies for the American contingent claim B with price $x > 0$.

(3) $\hat{p} = \inf\{x > 0 \mid \mathcal{H}(x) \neq \emptyset\}$ is called the *fair price* of the American contingent claim.

Remark 3.38. (1) At a first look it might be surprising that we have not required $X^\pi(t) = B(t)$ for all $t \in [0,T]$. However, such a requirement can only be satisfied in degenerate cases. Even more, existence of such a strategy would very often imply the existence of an arbitrage possibility. To see this, note that for a call with $P_1(0) < K$ (i.e. $B(0) = 0$) we would thus have $X^\pi(0) = 0$ but at the exercise time τ we would have $X(\tau) \geq 0$ and strict positivity with a positive probability (exactly then when we have $P_1(\tau) > K$). On the other hand, the requirement of $X^\pi(t) \geq (P_1(t) - K)^+$ can be satisfied by the Black-Scholes strategy (at least for the case of $r \geq 0$). This follows from the equality of the prices of the European and American calls.

(2) Due to assumption (*) in Definition 3.36 and the optional sampling theorem, Theorem 2.17, the assertions of the theorem on complete markets, Theorem 2.63, are still valid if there the time instants t and T are replaced by a stopping time τ with values in $[0, T]$. Thus the assertions of the main result on option pricing in complete markets, Theorem 3.7, stay valid with τ in place of T. So if the stopping time τ corresponding to an American claim would have been already fixed, then we would obtain the price of an American contingent claim given by

$$E(H(\tau) B(\tau)) = E_Q\left(\frac{1}{P_0(\tau)} B(\tau)\right),$$

as a corollary to Theorem 3.7. Here, Q is the unique equivalent martingale measure in our market. However, as the buyer of an option is interested in choosing an optimal exercising strategy, a plausible guess for the price of an American contingent claim B is

$$\hat{p} = \sup_{\tau \in \Sigma_{0,T}} E(H(\tau) B(\tau))$$

where $\Sigma_{0,T}$ denotes the set of all stopping times with respect to $\{\mathcal{F}_t\}_t$ attaining values in $[0, T]$. Indeed, we have the following theorem.

Theorem 3.39. *The fair price $\hat{p}$ of an American contingent claim B is given by*

$$\hat{p} = \sup_{\tau \in \Sigma_{0,T}} E(H(\tau) B(\tau)) = \sup_{\tau \in \Sigma_{0,T}} E_Q\left(e^{-r\tau} B(\tau)\right),$$

and there exists a stopping time τ^* such that the supremum will be attained for the hedging strategy $(\pi^*, 0)$ corresponding to τ^*.

Remarks on the proof. The proof follows e.g. from Theorem 2.5.3 in [**KA/SH 98**]. However, it requires technical tools such as the Snell envelope or the Doob-Meyer decomposition, which will not be presented in this book.

The main difficulty of the proof is to show that

$$X(t) = \operatorname*{ess\,sup}_{\tau \in \sum_{t,T}} E_Q\left(e^{-r(T-\tau)} B(\tau) \mid \mathcal{F}_t\right)$$

is a wealth process corresponding to a suitable portfolio process. Here, "ess sup" denotes the essential supremum. Again $X(t)$ will be called the valuation process of B. The possibility to choose the exercise time of an American contingent claim creates an asymmetry between the situations of the holder and the writer of the claim. In spite of this, we shall show by simple arbitrage arguments that $\hat{p}$ suggested above is the only price that permits no arbitrage possibility.

Theorem 3.40. *The fair price $\hat{p}$ of the American contingent claim B given by*

$$\hat{p} = \sup_{\tau \in \sum_{0,T}} E(H(\tau) B(\tau))$$

is the only price which does not create an arbitrage opportunity.

Proof.
i) We first show $\hat{p} \geq x$:
If at $t = 0$ the price x of B would satisfy the inequality $\hat{p} < x$ then the following would constitute an arbitrage strategy:

- sell the contingent claim for x,
- in the interval $[0, \rho] \subset [0, T]$ follow the hedging strategy $(\pi^*, 0)$ of Theorem 3.39, thereby needing an initial capital of $\hat{p} < x$. Here ρ denotes an arbitrary stopping time chosen by the buyer of the contingent claim,
- invest the remaining money $x - \hat{p}$ into the bond,
- at time ρ pay the owner of the contingent claim the amount of $B(\rho)$,
- from $t = \rho$ on invest the remaining wealth into the bond.

Note that no initial capital is needed in $t = 0$ to follow the just described strategy. Due to the hedging property, at time ρ the wealth $X(\rho)$ corresponding to the optimal hedging strategy satisfies

$$X(\rho) \geq B(\rho).$$

In addition, the difference $x - \hat{p}$ invested in the bond has then grown to $(x - \hat{p})e^{r\rho} > 0$ (in fact it can also decrease if we have $r < 0$). Thus, in total, following the above strategy leads to a positive final wealth, and we have therefore shown the existence of an arbitrage opportunity.

ii) We show $\hat{p} \leq x$:
If we would have $\hat{p} > x$ then buying the contingent claim B for the price

3.5. Pricing of American Options

of $x < \hat{p}$ and selling the optimal hedging strategy of Theorem 3.39 short is an arbitrage strategy. To see this, note that exercising the claim at the optimal time τ^* exactly offsets the negative position in the hedging strategy. Further, there still remains the initial positive difference which now has a value of $(\hat{p} - x)e^{r\tau^*}$ (given it was invested in the bond at time $t = 0$). □

Due to the two preceding theorems it is now also clear that the optimal strategy must look like:

Corollary 3.41. *Let*
$$X(t) = \operatorname*{ess\,sup}_{\tau \in \sum_{t,T}} E_Q\left(e^{-r(\tau-t)} B(\tau) \mid \mathcal{F}_t\right).$$

Then
$$\tau^* = \inf\{s \geq t \mid X(s) = B(s)\}$$
is an optimal exercise time.

Remark. This corollary says that the intrinsic value of the option (i.e. the amount of money we would receive by exercising the option immediately) coincides with the option price at the optimal exercise time.

The main problem in pricing American contingent claims is the fact that in general neither $X(t)$ nor τ^* have explicit representations. Even in the simplest case of an American put, numerical methods are needed for their computation. For further results we refer to [**MYNE 92**].

By Theorem 3.39 the computation of the fair price $\hat{p}$ consists of the solution of an optimal stopping problem. The evolution of the optimal expected payment of such a problem as a function of the initial parameters $(t, P_1(t))$ possesses a characterization similar to that of the Cauchy problem in the partial differential equation approach for pricing European options. We shall present it here only for the special case of an American put option and refer the reader to [**J/L/L 90**] for the theoretical background.

Theorem 3.42. *The following variational inequality*
$$u_t(t,x) + \tfrac{1}{2}\sigma^2 \cdot u_{xx}(t,x) + \left(r - \tfrac{1}{2}\sigma^2\right) u_x(t,x) - ru(t,x) \leq 0$$
$$u(t,x) \geq (K - e^x)^+$$
$$\left(u(t,x) - (K - e^x)^+\right) \cdot \left(u_t(t,x) + \tfrac{1}{2}\sigma^2 u_{xx}(t,x) + \left(r - \tfrac{1}{2}\sigma^2\right) u_x(t,x) - ru(t,x)\right) = 0$$
$$u(T,x) = (K - e^x)^+$$
for $x \in \mathbb{R}$, $(t,x) \in [0,T] \times \mathbb{R}$,
possesses a unique continuous solution $u(t,x)$ such that its derivatives u_x,

u_t, u_{xx} (which exist in the sense of distributions) are locally bounded. This solution satisfies

$$u(t, \ln(x)) = \operatorname*{ess\,sup}_{\tau \in \Sigma_{t,T}} E_Q^{t,x} \left(e^{-r(\tau-t)} \right.$$
$$\left. \cdot \left(K - x \cdot \exp((r - \tfrac{1}{2}\sigma^2)(\tau - T) + \sigma(W(\tau) - W(t))) \right)^+ \right),$$

i.e. it coincides with the price of an American put with maturity T and strike price K.

3.6. Arbitrage, Equivalent Martingale Measures and Option Pricing

In the previous sections, completeness of the market was the essential property which - together with arbitrage arguments - justified the replication approach of option pricing. In addition, many explicit computations were only possible due to the special form of the security prices. In this section, we shall make more general remarks on the relations between arbitrage, equivalent martingale measures, complete markets and option pricing in incomplete markets. Very often, these remarks are valid for much more general security price models than the ones we shall assume in the following.

> **General assumptions for this section:**
> We consider a market where $d+1$ securities with strictly positive prices $P_0(t), ..., P_d(t)$ are traded. Here the prices are assumed to be Itô processes with respect to an m-dimensional Brownian motion $\{(W_t, \mathcal{F}_t)\}_{t \in [0,\infty)}$ with $m \geq d$ where $\{\mathcal{F}_t\}_{t \in [0,\infty)}$ is the Brownian filtration.

Notations.
As a trading strategy $\varphi(t) = (\varphi_0(t), ..., \varphi_d(t))'$, $t \geq 0$, we define a $(d+1)$-dimensional progressively measurable process such that the stochastic integrals

$$\int_0^T \varphi_i(s) dP_i(s), \quad \int_0^T \varphi_i(s) d\hat{P}_i(s), \ i = 0, 1, ..., d,$$

exist for all $T \geq 0$ where

$$\hat{P}_i(t) := \frac{P_i(t)}{P_0(t)}$$

denotes the discounted price processes (by $P_0(t)$). By the multi-dimensional version of Itô's formula, Theorem 2.52, $\hat{P}_i(t)$ is again an Itô process. The

3.6. Arbitrage, Equivalent Martingale Measures and Option Pricing

wealth process $X(t)$ corresponding to the trading strategy $\varphi(t)$ and the self-financing condition are defined as usual by the equations

$$X(t) = \sum_{i=0}^{d} \varphi_i(t) P_i(t) = x + \sum_{i=0}^{d} \int_0^t \varphi_i(s) dP_i(s) \text{ a.s. } P, \text{ for all } t \geq 0.$$

Note that for simplicity we do not consider the possibility of consumption in this section. Again, a self-financing strategy will be called admissible if the corresponding wealth process is non-negative. In the literature the discount process $P_0(t)$ is often called a *numeraire*. It can be a bond price, a stock price, or even the value of a portfolio of securities as long as it is ensured that it stays positive during the trading interval $[0, T]$.

Arbitrage and equivalent martingale measures. We shall first look at the connection between the existence of an equivalent martingale measure and the absence of an arbitrage strategy in our market model. As the definition of an arbitrage opportunity is exactly the same as in Section 3.1 (and will thus not be repeated here), we only give an explicit definition of an equivalent martingale measure.

Definition 3.43. A probability measure Q defined on $(\Omega, \mathcal{F}_T)$ which is equivalent to P (i.e. P and Q have the same zero sets) is called an *equivalent martingale measure* for $P_0(t), ..., P_d(t)$ if the discounted prices

$$\hat{P}_i(t) = \frac{P_i(t)}{P_0(t)}, \ i = 1, ..., d, \ t \in [0, T]$$

are martingales with respect to Q.

Proposition 3.44. *All martingale measures Q for $P_0(t), ..., P_d(t)$ which are equivalent to P can be obtained from P by a Girsanov transformation with an m-dimensional progressively measurable stochastic process $\{(\theta(t), \mathcal{F}_t)\}_{t \geq 0}$ where for all $t \geq 0$ we have*

$$\int_0^t \theta_i^2(s) \, ds < \infty \text{ a.s. } P, \text{ for } i = 1, ..., m,$$

and where $Z(t, \theta)$, defined as in Excursion 5, p. 93, is a martingale with respect to P. In particular, Q is given as

$$Q(A) := Q_T(A) := E(1_A \cdot Z(T, \theta)) \text{ for all } A \in \mathcal{F}_T.$$

Proof. With the help of a suitable variant of Lemma 3.13 and a modification of the proof of Theorem 3.14 (see Exercise (7)). $\square$

We are now going to demonstrate that the existence of an equivalent martingale measure implies the absence of an arbitrage opportunity.

Theorem 3.45 (Equivalent martingale measure $\Rightarrow$ no arbitrage). *If there exists an equivalent martingale measure then the market given by the price processes $P_0(t), ..., P_d(t)$ contains no arbitrage opportunity.*

Proof. i) Let
$$\hat{X}(t) := \frac{X(t)}{P_0(t)}$$
be the discounted wealth process corresponding to the trading strategy $\varphi(t)$. By applying the Itô formula to the above quotient we can show (see Exercise (8)):

$\varphi(t)$ is self-financing $\Leftrightarrow$

$$\hat{X}(t) = \frac{x}{p_0} + \sum_{i=1}^{d} \int_0^t \varphi_i(s) \, d\hat{P}_i(s) \text{ a.s. } P, \text{ for all } t \in [0,T],$$

$$x := X(0), \quad p_0 := P_0(0).$$

Therefore, note in particular that all equivalent (to P) martingale measures Q can be represented by a Girsanov transformation due to Proposition 3.44. Thus, all discounted prices $\hat{P}_i(t)$ can be represented as Itô integrals with respect to $W^Q(t)$ due to Corollary 2.70 to the martingale representation theorem (where $W^Q(t)$ is a Q-Brownian motion). If $\varphi(t)$ is even admissible (i.e. we have $X(t) \geq 0$), then $\hat{X}(t)$ is a non-negative local martingale with respect to Q, and thus by Theorem 2.22, it is also a Q-super-martingale.

ii) Now let $\varphi(t)$ be admissible and assume that it is an arbitrage strategy with corresponding wealth process $X(t)$. Due to i) we then have

(3.50) $$0 = \hat{X}(0) \geq E_Q\left(\hat{X}(T)\right),$$

where E_Q denotes the expected value with respect to Q. As $\varphi(t)$ is admissible, $\hat{X}(t)$ is non-negative. Together with relation (3.50) this leads to

$$Q\left(\hat{X}(T) > 0\right) = 0.$$

But due to the equivalence of P and Q we then also have

$$P\left(\hat{X}(T) > 0\right) = 0$$

which contradicts the assumption that $\varphi(t)$ is an arbitrage strategy. Thus, the market must be free of arbitrage. $\square$

The opposite direction to the above theorem "absence of arbitrage implies the existence of an equivalent martingale measure" is only valid under some additional requirements on the trading strategy. The proof of this assertion is beyond the scope of this book. We therefore refer the reader

3.6. Arbitrage, Equivalent Martingale Measures and Option Pricing

to [**D/SCH 94**] and the references cited therein. The equivalence relation between the existence of equivalent martingale measures and the absence of (certain types of) arbitrage opportunities which is proved in that paper is called the "fundamental theorem of asset pricing".

Equivalent martingale measures and completeness of the market. In the complete market model of the preceding sections, there existed exactly one equivalent martingale measure. This is no coincidence but a special case of a deeper relation. To be able to examine the pricing of contingent claims in the following we need slightly stronger integrability requirements as in the complete market models of the previous sections.

Definition 3.46. (1) A *contingent claim* B is a non-negative $\mathcal{F}_T$-measurable random variable with

$$E_Q\left(\frac{1}{P_0(T)} \cdot B\right) < \infty$$

for all equivalent martingale measures Q.

(2) The contingent claim B is called *attainable* if there exists an admissible trading strategy $\varphi(t)$ with corresponding wealth process $X(t)$ and

$$B = X(T) \text{ a.s. } P,$$

such that $\hat{X}(t) = X(t)/P_0(t)$ is a martingale with respect to some equivalent martingale measure Q.

Note that in part (2) of the above definition we implicitly require the existence of an equivalent martingale measure Q. The proof of the following theorem requires a number of technical tools that we shall not present in this book. They can be found in [**HA/PL 81**] and [**HA/PL 83**].

Theorem 3.47. *The security market under examination is complete (i.e. each contingent claim is attainable) if and only if there exists a unique equivalent martingale measure Q.*

Option pricing in incomplete markets. A market in which not every contingent claim is attainable is called *incomplete*. Possible reasons for incompleteness of a market can be

- trading constraints such as the prohibition to invest into a particular stock,
- additional random fluctuations in the market coefficients such as stochastic volatility (i.e. the volatility $\sigma(t)$ might be an Itô process which is not measurable with respect to the filtration generated by the security prices).

In an incomplete market, typically the σ-algebra $\mathcal{F}_T$ is bigger than the one generated by the final wealths which were produced by admissible trading strategies

$$X(T) = x + \sum_{i=0}^{d} \int_0^T \varphi_i(s)\,dP_i(s).$$

In such an incomplete market the replication argument of Section 3.2 has only limited relevance.

Theorem 3.48 (Prices of attainable contingent claims). *The unique price process $X^*(t)$ of an attainable contingent claim B is given by*

$$X^*(t) = E_Q\left(\frac{P_0(t)}{P_0(T)} B \mid \mathcal{F}_t\right) \quad \text{for } t \in [0, T],$$

where Q is an equivalent martingale measure as in Definition 3.46 (2).

Proof. Let $\varphi(t)$ be a replication strategy for B. Then the corresponding wealth process $X(t)$ satisfies

(3.51) $$X(T) = B \text{ a.s. } P.$$

As due to Theorem 3.45 our market contains no arbitrage opportunity, therefore we must also have

(3.52) $$X^*(t) = X(t) \text{ a.s. } P, \ t \in [0, T],$$

where $X^*(t)$ is the price process of the claim B. As $\hat{X}(t)$ is a Q-martingale due to the definition of the attainability of B, equations (3.51) and (3.52) imply

$$X^*(t) = X(t) = P_0(t)\hat{X}(t) = P_0(t)E_Q\left(\hat{X}(T) \mid \mathcal{F}_t\right) = E_Q\left(\frac{P_0(t)}{P_0(T)} B \mid \mathcal{F}_t\right).$$

$\square$

For non-attainable claims, the foregoing theorem has no meaning at all. To demonstrate this we shall give a simple example of a non-attainable contingent claim in an incomplete market.

Example: A non-attainable contingent claim. We consider a Black-Scholes market with constant coefficients and $d = m = 2$. We assume that it is forbidden for our investor to have a non-zero position in the second stock. This constraint can also be interpreted as the second stock being a non-traded good such as a market index. So, in fact, our investor is in a Black-Scholes market with $d = 1$ and $m = 2$. However, he is allowed to trade in certain options on the non-traded asset. In particular, we look at the following option with final payment

$$B = 1_{\{P_1(T) \geq P_2(T)\}}.$$

3.6. Arbitrage, Equivalent Martingale Measures and Option Pricing

With the help of Corollary 3.15 and Proposition 3.19 (see Exercise (9)), it is easy to calculate the unique price $X_B(t)$ and the unique replication strategy $(\varphi_0(t), \varphi_1(t), \varphi_2(t))$ in the (for our investor, fictitious) complete market with $d = m = 2$ as

$$X_B(t) = e^{-r(T-t)} \Phi(d(t)),$$

$$\varphi_1(t) = e^{-r(T-t)} \frac{1}{\sqrt{((\sigma_{11}-\sigma_{21})^2 + (\sigma_{12}-\sigma_{22})^2)(T-t)}} \frac{1}{P_1(t)} \varphi(d(t)),$$

$$\varphi_2(t) = e^{-r(T-t)} \frac{1}{\sqrt{((\sigma_{11}-\sigma_{21})^2 + (\sigma_{12}-\sigma_{22})^2)(T-t)}} \frac{1}{P_2(t)} \varphi(d(t)),$$

$$\varphi_0(t) = (X_B(t) - \varphi_1(t) P_1(t) - \varphi_2(t) P_2(t)) \frac{1}{P_0(t)},$$

with

$$d(t) := \frac{\ln\left(\frac{P_1(t)}{P_2(t)}\right) - \frac{1}{2}\left(\sigma_{11}^2 + \sigma_{12}^2 - \sigma_{21}^2 - \sigma_{22}^2\right)(T-t)}{\sqrt{\left((\sigma_{11}-\sigma_{21})^2 + (\sigma_{12}-\sigma_{22})^2\right)(T-t)}},$$

where $\varphi(x)$ is the density function of the standard normal distribution. In particular, the second non-tradable asset is needed for the replication of B. Consequently, as the replication strategy for B is unique (see Theorem 2.63), B is thus not attainable for our investor. He is therefore faced with an incomplete market.

In the sequel we shall show that even in such incomplete markets we can determine arbitrage-free option prices with the help of equivalent martingale measures. However, due to the missing replication possibility in the case of non-attainable options, we do not obtain a unique price.

Theorem 3.49 (Option price and equivalent martingale measures). *Let Q be an equivalent martingale measure (to P). Let B be an arbitrary (not necessarily attainable) contingent claim. If we choose*

$$X_B^Q(t) := E_Q\left(\frac{P_0(t)}{P_0(T)} B \mid \mathcal{F}_t\right)$$

as the price of this contingent claim then the extended security market consisting of the original $d+1$ securities and the contingent claim contains no arbitrage opportunity.

Proof. Due to Proposition 3.44 all martingale measures Q equivalent to P can be obtained from P via a Girsanov transformation. Thus,

$$Y_Q(t) := \frac{X_B^Q(t)}{P_0(t)}$$

is a Brownian martingale with respect to Q. Corollary 2.70 to the martingale representation theorem then in particular implies that $Y_Q(t)$ is an Itô process with respect to Q. Inversion of the Girsanov transformation shows that $Y_Q(t)$ is also an Itô process with respect to P. Thus, the extended market as in the above assertion has the form of our general market model if we identify the contingent claim as our $(d+1)$-th stock. As Q then also is an equivalent martingale measure in this market (to see this note that the price of the contingent claim is defined in the appropriate way!), Theorem 3.45 gives us the absence of arbitrage for the extended market. $\square$

A non-attainable contingent claim (continuation). For our investor in the above Black-Scholes market with $d=1$, $m=2$, there exists a whole family of equivalent martingale measures. Obviously, by introducing the processes

$$W_1^a(t) := W_1(t) + a\frac{b_1 - r}{\sigma_{11}}t, \quad W_2^a(t) := W_2(t) + (1-a)\frac{b_1 - r}{\sigma_{12}}t,$$

the process

(3.53) $\quad Y(t) := \dfrac{P_1(t)}{P_0(t)}$

$\qquad = \dfrac{P_1(0)}{P_0(0)} \cdot \exp\Big(\big(b_1 - r - \tfrac{1}{2}(\sigma_{11}^2 + \sigma_{12}^2)\big)t + \sigma_{11}W_1(t) + \sigma_{12}W_2(t)\Big)$

can be rewritten as

(3.54) $\quad Y(t) = \dfrac{P_1(0)}{P_0(0)} \cdot \exp\left(-\tfrac{1}{2}\big(\sigma_{11}^2 + \sigma_{12}^2\big)t + \sigma_{11}W_1^a(t) + \sigma_{12}W_2^a(t)\right).$

Here, $\{(W_i^a(t), \mathcal{F}_t)\}_t$, $i = 1, 2$, are Brownian motions with respect to a suitable probability measure Q^a. Further, w.l.o.g. we assume $\sigma_{11} \neq 0 \neq \sigma_{12}$ (if for example we were to have $\sigma_{12} = 0$, then choosing $a = 1$ and an arbitrary Girsanov transformation with respect to $W_2(t)$ would yield an equivalent martingale measure). We further assume $P_0(0) = 1$. Obviously, for all real numbers a the probability measure Q^a, associated to the Brownian motions $W_i^a(t)$ by the Girsanov theorem, is an equivalent martingale measure for $P_0(t)$, $P_1(t)$. If on the other hand we apply the product rule to $Z(t) \cdot Y(t)$ (where $Z(t)$ is the density process with respect to P of some arbitrary probability measure which is equivalent to P), then similar to the proof of Lemma 3.13 we can show that all equivalent martingale measures for $P_0(t)$, $P_1(t)$ must have the form of Q^a for some real number a. By Theorem 3.49 an arbitrage free price for B is obtained by setting

$$X_B^a(0) = E_{Q^a}\left(\frac{1}{P_0(T)}B \mid \mathcal{F}_0\right) = e^{-rT}\Phi(d^a(t))$$

3.6. Arbitrage, Equivalent Martingale Measures and Option Pricing

with

$$d^a(t) := \frac{\ln\left(\frac{p_1}{p_2}\right) + \left(r - b_2 - \left(a\frac{\sigma_{21}}{\sigma_{11}} + (1-a)\frac{\sigma_{22}}{\sigma_{12}}\right)(b_1 - r)\right)T}{\sqrt{\left((\sigma_{11} - \sigma_{21})^2 + (\sigma_{12} - \sigma_{22})^2\right)T}}$$

$$- \frac{\frac{1}{2}\left(\sigma_{11}^2 + \sigma_{12}^2 - \sigma_{21}^2 - \sigma_{22}^2\right)T}{\sqrt{\left((\sigma_{11} - \sigma_{21})^2 + (\sigma_{12} - \sigma_{22})^2\right)T}}$$

for an arbitrary but fixed real number a, $p_1 = P_1(t)$, $p_2 = P_2(t)$. We further assume $b_1 > r$. Due to $\sigma_{11} \neq 0 \neq \sigma_{22}$ and $\det(\sigma) \neq 0$, the above representation of the option price directly implies

$$\frac{\sigma_{21}\sigma_{12} - \sigma_{22}\sigma_{11}}{\sigma_{11}\sigma_{12}} > 0 \Rightarrow \lim_{a \to \infty} X_B^a(0) = 0 \text{ and } \lim_{a \to -\infty} X_B^a(0) = e^{-rT},$$

$$\frac{\sigma_{21}\sigma_{12} - \sigma_{22}\sigma_{11}}{\sigma_{11}\sigma_{12}} < 0 \Rightarrow \lim_{a \to \infty} X_B^a(0) = e^{-rT} \text{ and } \lim_{a \to -\infty} X_B^a(0) = 0.$$

In particular, all possible values in $(0, e^{-rT})$ can be attained as an option price via suitable choices of the equivalent martingale measures. Note also that we could have obtained this "price domain" $(0, e^{-rT})$ by simple arbitrage considerations as we have $0 \leq B \leq 1$.

The situation of the above example is typical for incomplete markets. Of course, the set of arbitrage free prices can be bounded by arbitrage considerations. But typically there remains an interval with non-empty interior as the set of possible prices. This can be seen as the basis for price negotiations between the buyer and seller of an option. Surveys on criteria for selecting a particular equivalent martingale measure (which would then uniquely determine the option price!) such as the minimal martingale measure, the Esscher measure, or the variance optimal measure can be found in [**BI/KI 98**] or [**GRUN 98**].

The so-called minimal martingale measure plays a special role under all equivalent martingale measures. It has been introduced by Föllmer and Schweizer in [**F/SCH 91**]. Since that time it has been studied intensively in different areas of option pricing. In our general market it is identical to the so-called value preserving measure (see [**KORN 98**]). For an introduction to the theory of value preserving portfolio strategies we refer the interested reader to [**HELLW 87**], [**WIES 95**], or [**KORN 97**].

Hedging of options in incomplete markets. In incomplete markets, by definition, non-attainable contingent claims cannot be replicated. So at least an investor wants to insure himself as well as possible against the risk with which he is faced by selling or buying such a non-attainable claim.

This action of insuring against risk is called *hedging* and the corresponding trading strategy is called a *hedging strategy* or a *hedge* for short. If a replication strategy for a claim exists, then the risk caused by buying or selling the claim can be completely eliminated by following the replication strategy. We shall therefore call such a strategy a *perfect hedge*.

As already stated, the typical reason for incompleteness in the type of market models we consider here is that the dimension of the Brownian motion is bigger than d. Therefore, we observe a similar situation as in (linear) regression problems. The space of $\mathcal{F}_T$-measurable, non-negative square integrable random variables is of a higher dimension than the space of all final wealths that can be generated by following admissible trading strategies. Similar to the usual method in linear regression ("least squares"), a non-attainable contingent claim can be projected on the space of attainable contingent claims. In [**SCHW 92**] (and in a series of papers of Schweizer) this will be done by Hilbert space projection techniques with the help of the Föllmer-Schweizer decomposition and the minimal martingale measure. An alternative to this method is the approach of risk minimization pioneered by Föllmer and Sondermann in [**F/SON 86**]. In this approach it is assumed that the security prices are martingales (which of course is a strong restriction) and non-self-financing replication strategies are considered. More precisely, we look at trading strategies φ such that the difference

$$C_\varphi(t) := \sum_{i=0}^{d} \varphi_i(t) P_i(t) - \left(x + \sum_{i=0}^{d} \int_0^t \varphi_i(s) \, dP_i(s) \right)$$

is a martingale with $E(C_\varphi(t)) = 0$ and the replication property

(3.55) $$B = \sum_{i=0}^{d} \varphi_i(T) \cdot P_i(T)$$

is valid.

In a complete market it is possible to generate a "cost process" $C_\varphi(t) \equiv 0$ by following a replication strategy for the claim B. However, for a non-attainable claim, requirement (3.55) can only be satisfied with a non-vanishing cost process C_φ. Föllmer and Sondermann propose to use a mean-self-financing strategy which minimizes the "remaining risk" of future costs

$$R_\varphi(t) := E\left((C_\varphi(T) - C_\varphi(t))^2 \mid \mathcal{F}_t \right)$$

for all $t \in [0,T]$. A corresponding trading strategy is then called a risk minimizing strategy. In the general case where the security prices are no longer martingales, Föllmer and Schweizer (see [**F/SCH 91**]) had to give a suitable modification of the notion of a risk minimizing strategy. In such a situation there only exist locally risk minimizing strategies. Again, for solving the corresponding problem, both the Föllmer-Schweizer decomposition and the minimal martingale measure are the main technical tools (see [**F/SCH 91**]).

3.7. Market Numeraire and Numeraire Invariance

In Section 3.2 we have demonstrated that the price of an option in the complete market is always given as the expected value of the final payment B discounted by the bond price $P_0(T)$ where the underlying probability measure is the unique equivalent martingale measure Q (for simplicity we shall not consider a payout rate process $g(t)$ here). In Theorem 3.49, we could show that in incomplete markets the computation of this discounted expectation with respect to an arbitrary equivalent martingale measure leads to an arbitrage free option price which is no longer unique. Now the usual investor thinking in deterministic terms might find it natural to compare a riskless payment (as given by holding a long bond position) with a risky one if he is faced with the problem to value exactly the risky payment. On the other hand such a comparison is a very arbitrary one. There are other investments which could also serve as a comparison: the stock(s) or any admissible combination of stocks and bond having a strictly positive corresponding wealth process. Even more generally, we can choose any strictly positive Itô process $\{(Y(t), \mathcal{F}_t)\}_{t \in [0,T]}$ as a discount process. We shall call such a discount process a *numeraire*. Some natural questions arising in this connection are:

- Does a change of numeraire (i.e. the choice of a numeraire different from $P_0(t)$) affect the option price or its calculation?

- Does there exist a numeraire such that the option price is given as the expected value of the final payment B with respect to the original measure P when discounted by this numeraire?

In the following we shall answer these questions mainly in the complete market model of Sections 3.2.-5.

> **General assumptions for this section:**
> We look at the complete market model of Section 2.3 with $d = m$.

As we have first introduced the replication principle for pricing options without using the term equivalent martingale measure, Theorem 3.7 offers a natural candidate for answering the second of the above questions:

$$\frac{1}{H(t)} = \exp\left(\int_0^t \left(r(s) + \tfrac{1}{2}\|\theta(s)\|^2\right) ds + \int_0^t \theta(s)' dW(s)\right).$$

By using the product rule, Corollary 2.53, and the stochastic differential equations of the stock prices, we can immediately verify that $H(t) \cdot P_i(t)$ are P-martingales for i=0,...,d. Even more, $1/H(t)$ forms the wealth process corresponding to the admissible pair $(\pi, c) = (\sigma(t)^{-1}(b(t) - r(t) \cdot \underline{1}), 0) \in \mathcal{A}(1)$ (see Exercise (10)). This means that this numeraire can be replicated at the market by trading in a suitable way. It is therefore also called a *market numeraire* or a *numeraire portfolio* (see [**LONG 90**]). Summing up we obtain:

Theorem 3.50. *In the complete market setting of Section 2.3, $1/H(t)$ is the unique numeraire such that the corresponding discounted price processes $H(t) \cdot P_i(t)$, $i = 0, 1, ..., d$, are martingales with respect to P.*

Proof. Taking into account all the remarks preceding the theorem we only have to show the uniqueness assertion. As a numeraire is a strictly positive Itô process with respect to $\{\mathcal{F}_t\}_t$, it admits the representation

$$dY(t) = Y(t)\left(\mu_Y(t) dt + \sigma_Y(t)' dW(t)\right)$$

for a suitable real-valued process $\mu_Y(t)$ and a suitable $\mathbb{R}^d$-valued process $\sigma_Y(t)$ (of course, both satisfying suitable integrability requirements). Application of the product rule 2.53 yields

$$(3.56) \quad d\left(\frac{P_0(t)}{Y(t)}\right) = \frac{P_0(t)}{Y(t)} \cdot \left(\left(r(t) - \mu_Y(t) + \sigma_Y(t)'\sigma_Y(t)\right) dt - \sigma_Y(t)' dW(t)\right),$$

$$(3.57) \quad d\left(\frac{P_i(t)}{Y(t)}\right) = \frac{P_i(t)}{Y(t)}\left(\left(b_i(t) - \mu_Y(t) + \sigma_Y(t)'\sigma_Y(t)\right.\right.$$
$$\left.\left. - \sigma_{i\cdot}(t)\sigma_Y(t)\right) dt + \left(\sigma_{i\cdot}(t) - \sigma_Y(t)'\right) dW(t)\right), i = 1, ..., d,$$

where $\sigma_{i\cdot}(t)$ denotes the i-th row of the volatility matrix $\sigma(t)$. For the quotients $P_i(t)/Y(t)$ to be P-martingales, it is necessary that all the drift coefficients in (3.56) and (3.57) vanish. Therefore, (3.56) implies

$$(3.58) \qquad \mu_Y(t) = r(t) + \sigma_Y(t)'\sigma_Y(t).$$

Inserting this into the drift coefficients in (3.57) for $i = 1, ..., d$ leads to the system of equations

$$b(t) - r(t) = \sigma(t)\sigma_Y(t)$$

3.7. Market Numeraire and Numeraire Invariance

which yields
$$\sigma_Y(t) = \sigma(t)^{-1}(b(t) - r(t)) = \theta(t)$$
and
$$\mu_Y(t) = r(t) + \theta(t)'\theta(t).$$
Hence, $Y(t)$ obeys the same linear stochastic differential equation as $1/H(t)$. Thus the uniqueness assertion is implied by the uniqueness assertion of the variation of constants formula, Theorem 2.54. □

Remark. In the general case, a numeraire portfolio is defined as a self-financing portfolio process with a corresponding strictly positive wealth process $X(t)$ (with X(0)=1) such that the price processes discounted by $X(t)$, $P_i(t)/X(t)$, are martingales with respect to the "original" (or "physical") measure P. Even in general market models it is possible to show that a numeraire portfolio is unique if it exists at all (see [**BECH 98**]).

Let us make the first of the two questions above more precise. To do this, remember that the option price $E(H(T)B)$ computed in the complete market setting had nothing to do with a question on numeraires at all! The numeraire $P_0(t)$ was brought into the game later in an artificial way. The reason for its appearance was the introduction of the martingale measure Q which itself helped us to interpret the option price. Therefore in the complete market the first question can be reformulated in the following way:

- For a given numeraire $Y(t)$ in the complete market setting, does there exist a martingale measure Q_Y which is equivalent to P and satisfies

(3.59) $$E_{Q_Y}\left(\frac{Y(t)}{Y(T)}B \mid \mathcal{F}_t\right) = E\left(\frac{H(T)}{H(t)}B \mid \mathcal{F}_t\right)$$

  for all contingent claims B, $t \in [0, T]$?

The answer follows more or less directly from the equality of the above expectations. For such an equivalent martingale measure Q_Y the strictly positive Radon-Nikodym derivative of Q_Y with respect to P
$$Z_Y(T) = \frac{dQ_Y}{dP},$$
has to satisfy

(3.60) $$Z_Y(t) = H(t) \cdot Y(t) \text{ a.s. } P, \text{ for all } t \in [0,T]$$

due to (3.59) and the equivalence of Q_Y and P on $\mathcal{F}_T$. As $Y(t)$ is a strictly positive Itô process it can be represented as
$$dY(t) = Y(t)\left(\mu_Y(t)\ dt + \sigma_Y(t)'\ dW(t)\right).$$

Applying the product rule, Corollary 2.53, to equation (3.60) yields that the process $Z_Y(t)$ has to obey the stochastic differential equation

$$(3.61) \quad dZ_Y(t) = Z_Y(t) \Big(\big(\mu_Y(t) - r(t) - \theta(t)' \sigma_Y(t)\big) \, dt + \big(\sigma_Y(t)' - \theta(t)'\big) \, dW(t) \Big).$$

By Proposition 3.44 all equivalent (to P) martingale measures can be obtained via a suitable Girsanov transformation with a density process $Z_Y(t)$. This density process has to be a P-martingale. A necessary (but not sufficient) condition for the P-martingale property of $Z_Y(t)$ is a vanishing drift term in equation (3.61). Hence, we have

$$(3.62) \quad \mu_Y(t) - r(t) = \theta(t)' \sigma_Y(t).$$

If now $Y(t)$ is a wealth process corresponding to an admissible pair $(\pi, c) \in \mathcal{A}(y)$ for some $y > 0$, then the explicit form of the wealth equation (2.22) implies equality in (3.62), too. Such a $Y(t) = Y^\pi(t)$ with a corresponding portfolio process $\pi(t)$ satisfies

$$\mu_Y(t) = r(t) + \pi'(t) \big(b(t) - r(t) \cdot \underline{1}\big),$$
$$\sigma_Y(t)' = \pi(t)' \sigma(t),$$
$$dZ_Y(t) = Z_Y(t) \underbrace{\big(\pi(t)' \sigma(t) - (b(t) - r(t)) \sigma^{-1}(t)'\big)}_{=:\theta_\pi(t)'} \, dW(t)$$
$$= Z_Y(t) \theta_\pi(t)' \, dW(t).$$

If $Z_Y(t)$ is indeed a P-martingale (which is e.g. the case if the process $\theta_\pi(t)$ is bounded), then by Girsanov's theorem the process

$$W_Y(t) := W(t) - \int_0^t \theta_\pi(s) \, ds$$

is a Brownian motion with respect to Q_Y. Applying Itô's formula to the quotient $P_i(t)/Y(t)$ and using the definitions of $W_Y(t)$, $\mu_Y(t)$, $\sigma_Y(t)$, and $\theta_\pi(t)$ yields

$$d\left(\frac{P_0(t)}{Y(t)}\right) = -\frac{P_0(t)}{Y(t)} \sigma_Y(t)' \, dW_Y(t),$$
$$d\left(\frac{P_i(t)}{Y(t)}\right) = \frac{P_i(t)}{Y(t)} \big(\sigma_{i.}(t) - \sigma_Y(t)'\big) \, dW_Y(t),$$

i.e. the quotients are Q_Y-local martingales. Under stronger requirements on the market coefficients (such as the market coefficients being constant) and for a constant portfolio process, Novikov's condition or Proposition 3.12 even implies the Q_Y martingale property. Of course there is a much

3.7. Market Numeraire and Numeraire Invariance

larger class of portfolio processes and there exist weaker requirements on the market coefficients such that the process $Z_Y(t)$ is a P-martingale and such that the quotients $P_i(t)/Y(t)$ are Q_Y-martingales. We shall leave the task of formulating more general sufficient conditions to the reader. Instead of this we give the following theorem which follows directly from our preceding discussion.

Theorem 3.51 (Numeraire invariance in the complete market)**.** *We consider the complete market model of Section 2.3 with constant market coefficients $r(t) \equiv r$, $b(t) \equiv b$, $\sigma(t) \equiv \sigma > 0$. Then we have*

(1) *For all constant portfolio processes $\pi(t) \equiv \pi$ the process $Z_Y(t)$ given by*

$$Z_Y(t) = H(t) \cdot Y^\pi(t)$$

is a P-martingale, where $Y^\pi(t)$ is the wealth process corresponding to π. The corresponding probability measure Q_Y with

$$Z_Y(T) = \frac{dQ_Y}{dP}$$

is the unique equivalent martingale measure for the price processes discounted by $Y^\pi(t)$.

(2) *The fair price $\hat{p}$ of a contingent claim B with $E(B^\mu) < \infty$ for some $\mu > 1$ is given as*

$$\hat{p} = E(H(T)B) = E_{Q_Y}\left(\frac{1}{Y_\pi(T)}B\right),$$

if $Y^\pi(t)$ is the numeraire of part (1).

Remark 3.52. (1) As could be guessed from the remarks at the beginning of this section, the price of a contingent claim is not affected by a (sufficiently harmless) change of numeraire, but only gets a different representation. However, a change of numeraire can lead to significant simplifications in carrying out the calculations of prices of particular options. A specific example is the calculation of the price of an indexed option described in the next chapter.

(2) In general in incomplete markets the situation is much more complex than the above treated complete model. As mostly in incomplete markets the price of a non-attainable contingent claim is not unique, for each numeraire there exists a whole family of equivalent martingale measures. A survey over the typical results in this situation is given e.g. in [**MU/RU 97**].

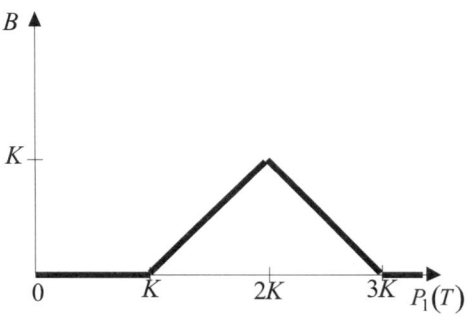

Figure 3.5. Butterfly spread

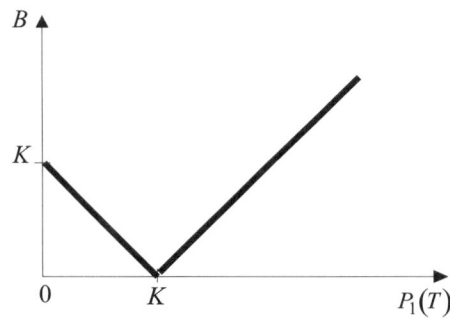

Figure 3.6. Straddle

Exercises

(1) Under the assumptions of the Black-Scholes model determine the fair prices of the following options given by their payoff diagrams.
   Hint: Try to interpret the payoff profiles as linear combinations of suitable puts and calls.
   (a) Butterfly spread with mean basis price $2K$: see Figure 3.5
   (b) Straddle with basis price K: see Figure 3.6
   (c) Strangle with basis prices $K_1 < K_2$: see Figure 3.7
   (d) Bull spread with basis prices $K_1 < K_2$: see Figure 3.8

(2) Show that in the Black-Scholes setting the price $X_C(t)$ of a European call satisfies:
   (a) $X_C(t)$ decreases in t
   (b) $X_C(t)$ increases in r
   (c) $X_C(t)$ increases in $P_1(t)$
   (d) $X_C(t)$ increases in σ for $\sigma > 0$

Exercises

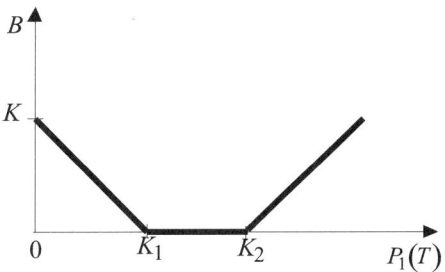

Figure 3.7. Strangle

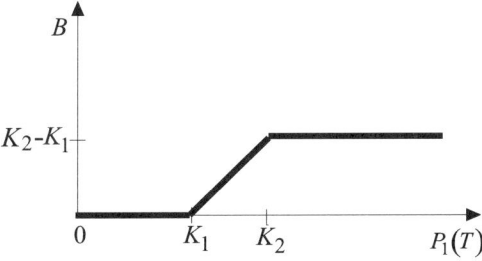

Figure 3.8. Bull spread

(3) Compute the price of a European call with the help of the equivalent martingale measure in:
   (a) a Black-Scholes model
   (b) a market model with $d = 2$, $\sigma = \begin{pmatrix} \sigma_{11} & \sigma_{12} \\ \sigma_{21} & \sigma_{22} \end{pmatrix}$, where the call is a call on the first stock, i.e. the final payment B is given by $B = (P_1(T) - K)^+$.

(4) Let
$$\varphi(t, x) = \frac{1}{\sqrt{2\pi t}} \exp\left(-\frac{x^2}{2t}\right).$$
   (a) Show that $\varphi(t, x)$ is a solution of the partial differential equation
$$u_t = \tfrac{1}{2} u_{xx}.$$
   (b) Show that the problem
$$u_t(t, x) = u_{xx}(t, x), \quad (t, x) \in [0, \infty) \times \mathbb{R},$$
$$u(0, x) = g(x), \quad x \in \mathbb{R},$$
   with a bounded function g is solved by
$$u(t, x) = E\left(g\left(\sqrt{2t} \cdot Y + x\right)\right)$$
   for some random variable $Y \sim \mathcal{N}(0, 1)$.

(5) Prove Proposition 3.28, part (2).

(6) Prove Proposition 3.29, part (2).

(7) Prove Proposition 3.44.

(8) Show: With the notations and assumptions of Section 3.6 we have the following equivalence for a trading strategy $\varphi(t)$:

$\varphi(t)$ is self-financing $\Leftrightarrow$

$$\hat{X}(t) = \frac{x}{p_0} + \sum_{i=1}^{d} \int_0^t \varphi_i(s) \, d\hat{P}_i(s) \text{ a.s. } P \text{ for all } t \in [0,T]$$

(compare to the proof of Theorem 3.45).

(9) In the case of a two-dimensional Black-Scholes model compute the fair price of the contingent claim with the final payment

$$B = 1_{\{P_1(T) \geq P_2(T)\}}.$$

(10) *Black-Scholes formula with dividend rates*

If a stock pays a dividend rate $\delta P_1(t)$ for some $\delta > 0$ per unit of time then its price in the Black-Scholes model is modelled as the solution of

$$dP_1(t) = P_1(t)\left((b-\delta)\,dt + \sigma\,dW(t)\right),$$
$$P_1(0) = p.$$

Show that the price $C(t, P_1(t))$ of a European call on this stock with strike K is given by:

$$C(t, P_1(t)) = e^{-\delta(T-t)} P_1(t) \Phi(\delta_1(t)) - e^{-r(T-t)} K \Phi(\delta_2(t)),$$

with

$$\delta_1(t) = \frac{\ln\left(\frac{P_1(t)}{K}\right) + \left(r - \delta + \frac{1}{2}\sigma^2\right)(T-t)}{\sigma\sqrt{T-t}},$$

$$\delta_2(t) = \delta_1(t) - \sigma\sqrt{T-t}.$$

Hint: One way to show this would be to imitate the method of Section 3.2. Note therefore that following the strategy $\varphi_1(t)$ would lead to a dividend payment of

$$\int_0^T \delta P_1(t) \, dt \text{ on } [0,T].$$

Another approach would be to imitate the method of Section 3.3 to derive the Cauchy problem

$$C_t + \tfrac{1}{2}\sigma^2 p^2 C_{pp} + (r-\delta) p C_p - rC = 0,$$
$$C(t,p) = (p-K)^+$$

and to show that $C(t,p)$ as given above is its solution.

(11) *Garman-Kohlhagen model for currency options*

In the Garman-Kohlhagen model the exchange rate $S(t)$ between the domestic and a foreign currency (e.g. Euro/Dollar) in units of the domestic currency is given as the solution of

$$dS(t) = \mu\, dt + \sigma\, dW(t), \quad S(0) = s \text{ for } \mu, \sigma \in \mathbb{R}.$$

Let r_d denote the riskless domestic rate, r_f the foreign riskless rate. Show that under these assumptions the price of a call option with time to maturity $T - t$ and strike K on one unit of the foreign currency is given by

$$C(t, S(t)) = \exp(-r_f(T-t))\, S(t)\, \Phi(\gamma_1(t))$$
$$- K \exp(-r_d(T-t))\, \Phi(\gamma_2(t))$$

with

$$\gamma_1(t) = \frac{\ln\left(\frac{S(t)}{K}\right) + \left(r_d - r_f + \frac{1}{2}\sigma^2\right)(T-t)}{\sigma\sqrt{T-t}},$$
$$\gamma_2(t) = \gamma_1(t) - \sigma\sqrt{T-t},$$

in units of the domestic currency.

Hint: Interpret the evolution of the price of one unit of the foreign currency (measured in units of the domestic currency) as that of a stock with a suitable dividend rate and use the result of Exercise 10.

(12) Compute the price of the "asset or nothing" option which is given by

$$B = P_1(T) \cdot 1_{\{P_1(T) \geq K\}}$$

in the one-dimensional Black-Scholes model.

(13) (a) In the one-dimensional Black-Scholes model compute both the gamma and the delta of a European call and a European put with maturity T and strike K.

(b) Assume that an investor holds one European call with strike K_1 and maturity T_1. Further, he can trade in European puts with maturities T_2, T_3 and strikes of K_2, K_3. In the Black-Scholes model, determine the numbers $\varphi_1(t)$, $\varphi_2(t)$ of the two different puts the investor has to hold such that the portfolio - consisting of the call and the put position - is both delta- and gamma-neutral at time t.

(14) In a Black-Scholes market show that the absolute price change of a European call as a function of the price of the underlying stock is smaller than the absolute price change of the underlying itself.

Hint: Compare C_p and the quotient $p \cdot C_p/C$ where C denotes the call price and C_p its partial derivative with respect to p.

Chapter 4

Pricing of Exotic Options and Numerical Algorithms

In this chapter we shall introduce some types of options differing from the simple – "plain vanilla" – puts and calls. We subsume them all under the term *exotic options* which will subsequently be subdivided. Very often the valuation process for such options cannot be obtained explicitly neither by calculating the expectation of Theorem 3.7 nor via solving the corresponding Cauchy problem analytically. To get the prices of those options, suitable numerical methods have to be developed. Therefore, we subdivide this chapter into the treatment of exotic options with explicit price formulae and into the presentation of some popular numerical methods for obtaining prices of exotic options which admit no known explicit pricing formula. To prove convergence of those algorithms we shall need some basics on the theory of weak convergence of stochastic processes. This will be provided in a separate excursion in this chapter.

> **General assumptions for this chapter:**
> Unless otherwise stated, we consider a Black-Scholes model with $d = m$ (mostly $d = 1$) and constant coefficients b, r, σ with $\sigma > 0$ (or σ regular if $d > 1$). We further make the assumptions of Chapter 2, Section 2, p. 57. All options are assumed to be of European type.

Examples of exotic options. This short survey is not intended to be complete or in any way systematic. Its only purpose is to give a short impression of the variety of different types of options. For example, there exist options on the minimum or maximum of a stock price such as the European call on the maximum which is given by the terminal payment

$$B = \left(\max_{0 \leq t \leq T} P_1(t) - K\right)^+.$$

So-called barrier options occur in numerous variations at option markets. Such types of options have a zero value (are "knocked out") if the stock price exceeds a certain barrier or can only have a positive payment at maturity if a certain barrier is reached (they are "knocked in"). Some possible examples are:

$$B = (P_1(T) - K_1)^+ \cdot 1_{\left\{\min_{0 \leq t \leq T} P_1(t) > K_2\right\}} \quad \text{"Down-and-out call"}$$

$$B = (P_1(T) - K_1)^+ \cdot 1_{\left\{\min_{0 \leq t \leq T} P_1(t) \leq K_2\right\}} \quad \text{"Down-and-in call"}$$

$$B = (P_1(T) - K_1)^+ \cdot 1_{\left\{\min_{0 \leq t \leq T} P_1(t) > K_2, \max_{0 \leq t \leq T} P_1(t) < K_3\right\}}$$
$$\text{"Double-barrier call"}$$

with $K_2 < K_1 < K_3$. For average options either the strike price is a geometric or arithmetic mean or the underlying price process is given as an average stock price. Typical examples are:

$$B = \left(P_1(T) - \frac{1}{T}\int_0^T P_1(s)\, ds\right)^+ \quad \text{"Asian option"}$$

$$B = \left(\frac{1}{T}\int_0^T P_1(s)\, ds - K\right)^+ \quad \text{"Fixed-strike-average"}$$

$$B = \frac{1}{T}\left(\int_0^T (P_1(T) - K)^+\, dt\right)$$

Use of the equivalent martingale measure. Due to Corollary 3.15, the price of a European option with final payment B is always given by

$$\hat{p} = E_Q\left(e^{-rT} B\right),$$

where Q is the unique equivalent (to P) martingale measure, and E_Q denotes the expectation with respect to Q. As we are only interested in expectations, we can therefore w.l.o.g. always assume that the subjective measure

P already coincides with the equivalent martingale measure. Thus, we assume that the stock prices are given as solutions of the stochastic differential equations

$$(4.1) \qquad dP_i(t) = P_i(t) \left(r\, dt + \sum_{i=1}^{d} \sigma_{ij}\, dW_j(t) \right), \ i = 1, ..., d.$$

In the sequel this will allow us to calculate all option prices with respect to P and to assume the form of the stock prices given by (4.1).

4.1. Exotic Options with Explicit Pricing Formulae

In this section we introduce some exotic options where the prices can be computed explicitly. For further examples of exotic options and their prices we refer to [**ZHANG 97**].

a) Path independent options on one stock

Digital or binary option. The terminal payments in $t = T$ of a binary call or a binary put with bound K are given by

$$B_d^{Call} = 1_{\{P_1(T) > K\}},$$
$$B_d^{Put} = 1_{\{P_1(T) < K\}},$$

i.e. if the final price $P_1(T)$ exceeds K (in the case of a call) or is smaller than K (in the case of a put), the owner of the corresponding binary option receives one unit of money at time T. For the prices of these options we obtain (see also Chapter 3.2, p. 104):

$$X_d^{Call}(t) = e^{-r(T-t)} \Phi(d_2(t)), \qquad \text{"Digital call"}$$
$$X_d^{Put}(t) = e^{-r(T-t)} \Phi(-d_2(t)), \qquad \text{"Digital put"}$$

with

$$d_2(t) = \frac{\ln\left(\frac{P_1(t)}{K}\right) + \left(r - \frac{1}{2}\sigma^2\right)(T-t)}{\sigma\sqrt{T-t}},$$

where Φ is the distribution function of the standard normal distribution. Some authors also refer to options with a jump in the final payoff as digital options. In this sense some of the types of options described below also fall under this class.

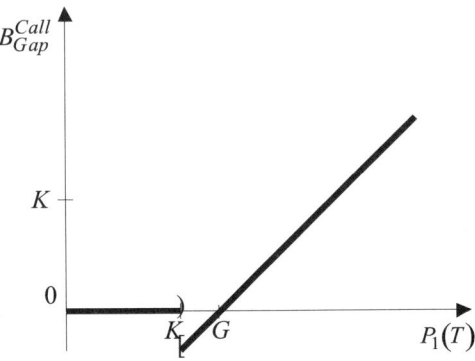

Figure 4.1. Gap call with $G > K$

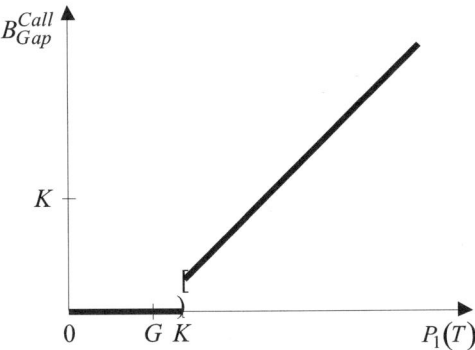

Figure 4.2. Gap call with $G < K$

Gap options. The final payments of gap-options are given by

$$B_{Gap}^{Call} = (P_1(T) - G) \cdot 1_{\{P_1(T) \geq K\}},$$
$$B_{Gap}^{Put} = (G - P_1(T)) \cdot 1_{\{P_1(T) \leq K\}},$$

where in general we have $G \neq K$ with $G, K \geq 0$. In the case of a gap call the difference between $P_1(T)$ and G will be paid in the end if $P_1(T)$ exceeds K. Note that the final payoff can be negative if $G > K$, i.e. the buyer of the option can end up with having to pay money at both the purchasing time and at maturity. Although – in contrast to Definition 3.3 – gap options can lead to a negative final payment, all theorems on option pricing given so far are still applicable as the payments are bounded from below. For illustrational purposes we give some payoff diagrams for the gap call; see Figure 4.1 and Figure 4.2. We distinguish between the cases of $G > K$ and $G < K$.

a) Path independent options on one stock

If we look at the following decompositions of the final payments of the gap options

$$B_{Gap}^{Call} = B^{Call} - (G - K) \cdot B_d^{Call} \text{ with } B^{Call} = (P_1(T) - K)^+,$$
$$B_{Gap}^{Put} = B^{Put} - (K - G) \cdot B_d^{Put} \text{ with } B^{Put} = (K - P_1(T))^+,$$

where all the calls, puts, and digitals appearing above correspond to the strike (or the bound) K, and use the pricing formulae for calls, puts, and digitals (see Corollary 3.9), we obtain

$$X_{Gap}^{Call}(t) = X^{Call}(t) - (G - K) \cdot X_d^{Call}(t)$$
$$= P_1(t) \Phi(d_1(t)) - G \cdot e^{-r(T-t)} \cdot \Phi(d_2(t)),$$

$$X_{Gap}^{Put}(t) = X^{Put}(t) - (K - G) \cdot X_d^{Put}(t)$$
$$= -P_1(t) \Phi(-d_1(t)) + G \cdot e^{-r(T-t)} \cdot \Phi(-d_2(t)),$$

with

$$d_1(t) = \frac{\ln\left(\frac{P_1(t)}{K}\right) + \left(r + \frac{1}{2}\sigma^2\right)(T - t)}{\sigma\sqrt{T - t}},$$

$$d_2(t) = d_1(t) - \sigma\sqrt{T - t}.$$

Paylater options. Paylater options are closely related to gap options. Their final payoffs are given by

$$B_{PL}^{Call} = \left(P_1(T) - \left(K + D^{Call}\right)\right) \cdot 1_{\{P_1(T) \geq K\}},$$
$$B_{PL}^{Put} = \left((K - D^{Put}) - P_1(T)\right) \cdot 1_{\{P_1(T) \leq K\}},$$

where D^{Call}, D^{Put} have to be determined in such a way that the prices of the paylater options equal zero in $t = 0$. By interpreting D^{Call}, D^{Put} as premiums for the options then they have to be paid at maturity (therefore the name "paylater options") and even then only if the underlying stock exceeds K (in the case of a call) or stays below K (in the case of a put). Similar as in the case of gap options, the final payoffs can be decomposed as follows:

(4.2) $$B_{PL}^{Call} = B^{Call} - D^{Call} \cdot B_d^{Call},$$
(4.3) $$B_{PL}^{Put} = B^{Put} - D^{Put} \cdot B_d^{Put}.$$

As we require

$$X_{PL}^{Call}(0) = 0, \quad X_{PL}^{Put}(0) = 0,$$

and as we already know the pricing formulae for B^{Call}, B_d^{Call}, B^{Put}, B_d^{Put}, this yields the values for D^{Call}, D^{Put} as

$$D^{Call} = \frac{X^{Call}(0)}{X_d^{Call}(0)}, \quad D^{Put} = \frac{X^{Put}(0)}{X_d^{Put}(0)}.$$

Inserting these values into equations (4.2) and (4.3) results in prices of paylater calls and puts given by

$$X_{PL}^{Call}(t) = P_1(t) \cdot \Phi(d_1(t)) - \frac{p_1 \cdot \Phi(d_1(0))}{\Phi(d_2(0))} \Phi(d_2(t)) \cdot e^{rt},$$

$$X_{PL}^{Put}(t) = -P_1(t) \cdot \Phi(-d_1(t)) + \frac{p_1 \cdot \Phi(-d_1(0))}{\Phi(-d_2(0))} \cdot \Phi(-d_2(t)) \cdot e^{rt}.$$

Note that although buying paylater options in $t = 0$ does not require a positive payment to the seller, there are no arbitrage opportunities as their final payment can be negative. Therefore, the prices of paylater options can even become negative before maturity.

Compound Options. By purchasing a compound option we receive the right to buy (or sell) at time T another option with maturity $T_1 \geq T$ for an already agreed price of K. We have to distinguish between the following four cases

$$B_{com}^{CC} = \left(X^{Call}(T) - K\right)^+ \quad \text{``Call on a call''}$$

$$B_{com}^{CP} = \left(X^{Put}(T) - K\right)^+ \quad \text{``Call on a put''}$$

$$B_{com}^{PC} = \left(K - X^{Call}(T)\right)^+ \quad \text{``Put on a call''}$$

$$B_{com}^{PP} = \left(K - X^{Put}(T)\right)^+ \quad \text{``Put on a put''}$$

where the puts and calls appearing inside typically have a strike price of K_1 different from K. Here, we concentrate on the determination of the price of a call on a call. The remaining cases can be treated similarly. We first give the following proposition.

Proposition 4.1. (1) *For a given $K > 0$ and given maturity T_1 of a European call with strike K_1, there exists a uniquely determined $p^* > 0$ for $T \leq T_1$ such that for $P_1(T) = p^*$ we have*

$$X^{Call}(T) = X^{Call}(T, p^*) = K.$$

(2) *With the notations*

$$g_1(t) = \frac{\ln\left(\frac{P_1(t)}{p^*}\right) + \left(r + \frac{1}{2}\sigma^2\right)(T-t)}{\sigma\sqrt{T-t}}, \quad g_2(t) = g_1(t) - \sigma\sqrt{T-t},$$

a) Path independent options on one stock

$$h_1(t) = \frac{\ln\left(\frac{P_1(t)}{K_1}\right) + \left(r + \frac{1}{2}\sigma^2\right)(T_1 - t)}{\sigma\sqrt{T_1 - t}}, \quad h_2(t) = h_1(t) - \sigma\sqrt{T_1 - t},$$

the price of a call on a call satisfies

$$X_{com}^{CC}(t) = P_1(t)\Phi^{(\rho_1)}(g_1(t), h_1(t))$$
$$- K_1 e^{-r(T_1-t)}\Phi^{(\rho_1)}(g_2(t), h_2(t)) - K e^{-r(T-t)}\Phi(g_2(t))$$

for $t \in [0, T]$, where $\Phi^{(\rho)}(x, y)$ is the distribution function of a bivariate standard normal distribution with correlation coefficient ρ and where

$$\rho_1 := \sqrt{\frac{T-t}{T_1-t}}, \quad e.g. \quad \begin{pmatrix} X \\ Y \end{pmatrix} \sim \mathcal{N}\left(\begin{pmatrix} 0 \\ 0 \end{pmatrix}, \begin{pmatrix} 1 & \rho_1 \\ \rho_1 & 1 \end{pmatrix}\right).$$

Proof. (1) From the explicit form of the Black-Scholes formula we obtain

(4.4) $$\lim_{P_1(T)\downarrow 0} X^{Call}(T, P_1(T)) = 0,$$

(4.5) $$\lim_{P_1(T)\uparrow+\infty} X^{Call}(T, P_1(T)) = +\infty$$

for $T \leq T_1$. Here, the first limit assertion is a consequence of the trivial bounds 0 and $P_1(T)$ for $X^{Call}(T, P_1(T))$. For the second limit assertion note that

$$\frac{d}{dp}X^{Call}(T, p) = \Phi(d_1(T))$$

is positive and even increases in p. Now from (4.4) and (4.5) together with the intermediate value theorem we get the existence of p^* of assertion (1).

(2) For $t \leq T$ we have

$$X_{com}^{CC}(t) = E^{t,P_1(t)}\left(e^{-r(T-t)}B_{com}^{CC}\right) = \frac{1}{\sqrt{2\pi(T-t)}}\int_{\tilde{w}}^{\infty}e^{-\frac{x^2}{2(T-t)}}$$
$$\cdot e^{-r(T-t)}\left(X^{Call}\left(T, P_1(t) \cdot e^{\left(r-\frac{1}{2}\sigma^2\right)(T-t)+\sigma x}\right) - K\right)dx$$

with

$$\tilde{w} = \frac{1}{\sigma}\cdot\left(\ln\left(\frac{p*}{P_1(T)}\right) - \left(r - \frac{1}{2}\sigma^2\right)(T-t)\right).$$

With the help of the explicit form of $X^{Call}(T, p)$ we obtain

$$X_{com}^{CC}(t) = I_1 - I_2 - I_3$$

with

$$I_1 = P_1(t) \int_{\tilde{w}}^{\infty} \frac{1}{\sqrt{2\pi(T-t)}} e^{-\frac{x^2}{2(T-t)}} e^{\sigma x - \frac{1}{2}\sigma^2(T-t)} \Phi(a) \, dx,$$

$$I_2 = \int_{\tilde{w}}^{\infty} \frac{1}{\sqrt{2\pi(T-t)}} e^{-\frac{x^2}{2(T-t)}} e^{-r(T_1-t)} K_1 \Phi(b) \, dx,$$

$$I_3 = \int_{\tilde{w}}^{\infty} \frac{1}{\sqrt{2\pi(T-t)}} e^{-\frac{x^2}{2(T-t)}} e^{-r(T-t)} K \, dx,$$

where we have

$$a = \frac{\sigma x + \ln\left(\frac{P_1(t)}{K_1}\right) + \left(r + \frac{1}{2}\sigma^2\right)(T_1 - t) + \left(r - \frac{1}{2}\sigma^2\right)(T - t)}{\sigma\sqrt{T_1 - T}},$$

$$b = \frac{\sigma x + \ln\left(\frac{P_1(t)}{K_1}\right) + \left(r - \frac{1}{2}\sigma^2\right)(T_1 - t)}{\sigma\sqrt{T_1 - T}}.$$

In analogy to the calculations leading to the Black-Scholes formula we immediately obtain

$$I_3 = K e^{-r(T-t)} \Phi\left(\frac{\ln\left(\frac{P_1(t)}{p*}\right) + \left(r - \frac{1}{2}\sigma^2\right)(T - t)}{\sigma\sqrt{T - t}}\right).$$

The following Lemma 4.2 is useful for the determination of I_1 and I_2. With its help we get

$$I_1 = P_1(t) \Phi^{(\rho_1)}(g_1(t), h_1(t)).$$

Taking $K_1 e^{-r(T_1-t)}$ out of I_2 and applying Lemma 4.2 once more leads to

$$I_2 = K_1 e^{-r(T_1-t)} \cdot \Phi^{(\rho_1)}(g_2(t), h_2(t)).$$

The tedious but locally simple steps leading to this result will be left to the reader (see Exercise (1)).

□

Lemma 4.2. *If X and Y are independent random variables with*

$$X \sim \mathcal{N}(\mu, \sigma^2), \quad Y \sim \mathcal{N}(0, 1),$$

a) Path independent options on one stock

then for $\tilde{x}, \alpha, \beta \in \mathbb{R}$, $\alpha > 0$, we have

$$\int_{\tilde{x}}^{\infty} \varphi_{\mu,\sigma^2}(x) \cdot \Phi(\alpha x + \beta)\, dx = P(X \geq \tilde{x}, Y \leq \alpha X + \beta)$$

$$= P(X \geq \tilde{x}, Z \leq \beta),$$

where

$$(X, Z) \sim \mathcal{N}\left(\begin{pmatrix} \mu \\ -\alpha\mu \end{pmatrix}, \begin{pmatrix} \sigma^2 & -\alpha\sigma^2 \\ -\alpha\sigma^2 & 1 + \alpha^2\sigma^2 \end{pmatrix}\right).$$

Here φ_{μ,σ^2} is the density function of the normal distribution with mean μ and variance σ^2.

Remark 4.3. (1) Similarly we obtain the price of a put on a call as

$$X_{com}^{PC}(t) = -P_1(t)\,\Phi^{(\rho_2)}\left(-g_1(t), h_1(t)\right)$$
$$+ K_1 e^{-r(T_1-t)}\Phi^{(\rho_2)}\left(-g_2(t), h_2(t)\right) + Ke^{-r(T-t)}\Phi\left(-g_2(t)\right)$$

for $t \in [0, T]$ with

$$\rho_2 := -\sqrt{\frac{T-t}{T_1-t}}.$$

(2) If for a put with strike K_1 and maturity T_1 the value p^* defined by

$$X^{Put}(T, p^*) = K$$

is given for a fixed K, then we can obtain the pricing formulae for a call on this put or a put on this put in the same way as above. If we assume a strike of K and maturity $T \leq T_1$ for the compound options then we obtain their prices at time $t \in [0, T]$ as

$$X_{com}^{CP}(t) = -P_1(t)\,\Phi^{(\rho_1)}\left(-g_1(t), -h_1(t)\right)$$
$$+ K_1 e^{-r(T_1-t)}\Phi^{(\rho_1)}\left(-g_2(t), -h_2(t)\right) - Ke^{-r(T-t)}\Phi\left(-g_2(t)\right),$$

$$X_{com}^{PP}(t) = P_1(t)\,\Phi^{(\rho_2)}\left(g_1(t), -h_1(t)\right)$$
$$+ K_1 e^{-r(T_1-t)}\Phi^{(\rho_2)}\left(g_2(t), -h_2(t)\right) + Ke^{-r(T-t)}\Phi\left(g_2(t)\right).$$

Chooser options. The characteristic feature of this kind of option is that at time T the holder can choose between either receiving a European call (on the underlying stock) with strike $K_1 \geq 0$ and maturity $T_1 \geq T$ or a European put (on the underlying stock) with strike $K_2 \geq 0$ and maturity $T_2 \geq T$. From the Black-Scholes formula the values of both these European options are known as functions of $(T, P_1(T))$, so we can deduce the explicit form of the payoff of the chooser option as

$$B_{Ch} = \max\left(X_{T_1,K_1}^{Call}(T, P_1(T)), X_{T_2,K_2}^{Put}(T, P_1(T))\right),$$

where the lower indices denote the maturity dates and the strike prices of the European options. Note that the price of the call at time T is strictly increasing in $P_1(T)$ and satisfies (4.4) and (4.5). Further, the price of the put at time T strictly decreases in $P_1(T)$. Thus, there exists exactly one value $p^* \geq 0$ with

$$X_{T_1,K_1}^{Call}(T,p^*) = X_{T_2,K_2}^{Put}(T,p^*).$$

For larger values of $P_1(T)$ the maximum in B_{Ch} will be attained by the call price, and for smaller values of $P_1(T)$, it will be attained by the put price. So this results in the following representation of B_{Ch}.

$$B_{Ch} = X_{T_1,K_1}^{Call}(T) \cdot 1_{\{P_1(T) \geq p^*\}} + X_{T_2,K_2}^{Put}(T) \cdot 1_{\{P_1(T) < p^*\}}.$$

With the help of this decomposition the price of a chooser option can be calculated similar to the price of a compound option, and for $t < T$ we obtain

$$X_{Ch}(t) = P_1(t) \cdot \Phi^{(\rho_1)}(g_1(t), h_1(t)) - K_1 e^{-r(T-t)} \Phi^{(\rho_1)}(g_2(t), h_2(t))$$
$$- P_1(t) \cdot \Phi^{(\lambda_1)}(-g_1(t), -h_3(t)) + K_2 e^{-r(T_2-t)} \Phi^{(\lambda_1)}(-g_2(t), -h_4(t)),$$

where the notation of $\Phi^{(\rho)}, g_1, g_2, h_1, h_2, \rho_1$ is defined as in Proposition 4.1. As an extra notation we have to introduce

$$h_3(t) = \frac{\ln\left(\frac{P_1(t)}{K_2}\right) + \left(r + \frac{1}{2}\sigma^2\right)(T_2 - t)}{\sigma\sqrt{T_2 - t}}, \quad \lambda_1 := \sqrt{\frac{T - t}{T_2 - t}},$$

$$h_4(t) = h_3(t) - \sigma\sqrt{T_2 - t}.$$

b) Options on more than one underlying stock

Indexed options. Here, we consider a two-dimensional Black-Scholes model with stock prices given by

$$dP_1(t) = P_1(t) \cdot (b_1\,dt + \sigma_{11}\,dW_1(t) + \sigma_{12}\,dW_2(t)), \quad P_1(0) = p_1,$$

$$dP_2(t) = P_2(t) \cdot (b_2\,dt + \sigma_{21}\,dW_1(t) + \sigma_{22}\,dW_2(t)), \quad P_2(0) = p_2.$$

Let $a_1, a_2 \in (0, \infty)$. An indexed option with parameters a_1, a_2 is then given by the final payment

(4.6) $$B_{ind} = (a_1 P_1(T) - a_2 P_2(T))^+.$$

The name "indexed option" has its origin in the fact that in practice $P_2(t)$ is often used to model a market index such as the Dow Jones index (which is of course a crude simplification). If in addition we choose

$$a_1 = \frac{1}{P_1(0)}, \quad a_2 = \frac{1}{P_2(0)},$$

b) Options on more than one underlying stock

then the payoff of an indexed option is the difference between the relative price increase of the first stock and the relative price increase of the second stock (typically a market index) if that difference is positive. So the evolution of the stock price is compared with the evolution of the index (it is "indexed"). We set

$$s_1 := a_1 \cdot p_1, \quad s_2 := a_2 \cdot p_2,$$

and introduce the following notation

(4.7) $$A := \left\{ \omega \;\middle|\; \frac{a_1 P_1(T)}{a_2 P_2(T)} \geq 1 \right\}.$$

To determine the fair price of the indexed option we shall use the technique of change of numeraire as introduced in Section 3.7. Therefore let Q, Q_1, Q_2 be the equivalent martingale measures corresponding to the choices of numeraire $P_0(T)$, $P_1(T)/p_1$, and $P_2(T)/p_2$, respectively. By Corollary 3.15 and Theorem 3.51 and the use of (4.7), the fair price $X_{ind}(0)$ of the indexed call is given by

(4.8) $$\begin{aligned} X_{ind}(0) &= E_Q\left(e^{-rT}(a_1 P_1(T) - a_2 P_2(T))^+\right) \\ &= a_1 \cdot E_Q\left(e^{-rT} P_1(T) \cdot 1_A\right) - a_2 \cdot E_Q\left(e^{-rT} P_2(T) \cdot 1_A\right) \\ &= a_1 \cdot E_{Q_1}\left(\frac{p_1}{P_1(T)} P_1(T) \cdot 1_A\right) - a_2 \cdot E_{Q_2}\left(\frac{p_2}{P_2(T)} P_2(T) \cdot 1_A\right) \\ &= s_1 \cdot Q_1(A) - s_2 \cdot Q_2(A). \end{aligned}$$

It only remains to calculate the probabilities of A under the two different probability measures Q_1, Q_2. For this, note that the Q_1-Brownian motion $W^{(1)}(t)$ and the Q_2-Brownian motion $W^{(2)}(t)$ are given by (see Exercise (4)):

$$W^{(i)}(t) = W(t) + \begin{pmatrix} \frac{(b_1-r)\sigma_{22}-(b_2-r)\sigma_{12}}{\sigma_{11}\sigma_{22}-\sigma_{12}\sigma_{21}} - \sigma_{i1} \\ \frac{(b_2-r)\sigma_{11}-(b_1-r)\sigma_{21}}{\sigma_{11}\sigma_{22}-\sigma_{12}\sigma_{21}} - \sigma_{i2} \end{pmatrix} \cdot T, \quad i = 1, 2.$$

This results in

$$\frac{P_1(T)}{P_2(T)} = \frac{p_1}{p_2} \exp\left((\sigma_{11} - \sigma_{21}) W_1^{(i)}(T) + (\sigma_{12} - \sigma_{22}) W_2^{(i)}(T)\right.$$
$$\left. - (-1)^i \tfrac{1}{2}\left((\sigma_{11} - \sigma_{21})^2 + (\sigma_{12} - \sigma_{22})^2\right) T\right), \quad i = 1, 2,$$

and thus in

$$
\begin{aligned}
(4.9)\quad Q_i(A) &= Q_i\left(\exp\left((\sigma_{11}-\sigma_{21})W_1^{(i)}(T)+(\sigma_{12}-\sigma_{22})W_2^{(i)}(T)\right) \geq \right.\\
&\qquad\left. \frac{s_2}{s_1}\exp\left((-1)^i \cdot \tfrac{1}{2}\left[(\sigma_{11}-\sigma_{21})^2+(\sigma_{12}-\sigma_{22})^2\right]\cdot T\right)\right)\\
&= Q_i\left(Z \geq \frac{\ln\left(\frac{s_2}{s_1}\right)+(-1)^i\cdot \tfrac{1}{2}\left[(\sigma_{11}-\sigma_{21})^2+(\sigma_{12}-\sigma_{22})^2\right]T}{\sqrt{\left[(\sigma_{11}-\sigma_{21})^2+(\sigma_{12}-\sigma_{22})^2\right]T}}\right)\\
&= \Phi\left(\frac{\ln\left(\frac{s_1}{s_2}\right)+(-1)^{i+1}\cdot\tfrac{1}{2}\left[(\sigma_{11}-\sigma_{21})^2+(\sigma_{12}-\sigma_{22})^2\right]T}{\sqrt{\left[(\sigma_{11}-\sigma_{21})^2+(\sigma_{12}-\sigma_{22})^2\right]T}}\right),
\end{aligned}
$$

where Z obeys a standard normal distribution. With the notations of

$$(4.10)\qquad \tilde{\sigma}_1^2 := \sigma_{11}^2+\sigma_{12}^2,\ \tilde{\sigma}_2^2 := \sigma_{21}^2+\sigma_{22}^2$$

$$(4.11)\qquad \rho := \frac{\sigma_{11}\sigma_{21}+\sigma_{12}\sigma_{22}}{\tilde{\sigma}_1\cdot\tilde{\sigma}_2}$$

we finally obtain the following formula from (4.8) and (4.9)

$$
\begin{aligned}
X_{ind}(0) &= s_1\cdot\Phi\left(\frac{\ln\left(s_1/s_2\right)+\tfrac{1}{2}\left(\tilde{\sigma}_1^2+\tilde{\sigma}_2^2-2\rho\tilde{\sigma}_1\tilde{\sigma}_2\right)T}{\sqrt{\left(\tilde{\sigma}_1^2+\tilde{\sigma}_2^2-2\rho\tilde{\sigma}_1\tilde{\sigma}_2\right)T}}\right)\\
&\quad - s_2\cdot\Phi\left(\frac{\ln\left(s_1/s_2\right)-\tfrac{1}{2}\left(\tilde{\sigma}_1^2+\tilde{\sigma}_2^2-2\rho\tilde{\sigma}_1\tilde{\sigma}_2\right)T}{\sqrt{\left(\tilde{\sigma}_1^2+\tilde{\sigma}_2^2-2\rho\tilde{\sigma}_1\tilde{\sigma}_2\right)T}}\right).
\end{aligned}
$$

Options on the minimum / maximum of two stocks. We now look at options on the minimum or maximum of two stock prices. They are given by the following payoffs

$$
\begin{aligned}
B_{\min}^{Call} &= (\min(P_1(T),P_2(T))-K)^+ &\text{"Call on minimum"}\\
B_{\max}^{Call} &= (\max(P_1(T),P_2(T))-K)^+ &\text{"Call on maximum"}\\
B_{\min}^{Put} &= (K-\min(P_1(T),P_2(T)))^+ &\text{"Put on minimum"}\\
B_{\max}^{Put} &= (K-\max(P_1(T),P_2(T)))^+ &\text{"Put on maximum"}
\end{aligned}
$$

b) Options on more than one underlying stock

As underlying stock price model we consider the two-dimensional Black-Scholes model described in (4.1). We first compute

$$X_{\min}^{Call}(0) = E\left(e^{-rT}\left(\min\left(P_1(T), P_2(T)\right) - K\right)^+\right)$$
$$= E\left(e^{-rT} P_1(T) \cdot 1_{\{K \leq P_1(T) \leq P_2(T)\}}\right) + E\left(e^{-rT} P_2(T) \cdot 1_{\{K \leq P_2(T) \leq P_1(T)\}}\right)$$
$$- K e^{-rT} \cdot P\left(\min\left(P_1(T), P_2(T)\right) \geq K\right).$$

Let

$$\tilde{Y} := \sigma_{11} W_1(T) + \sigma_{12} W_2(T), \quad \tilde{Z} := \sigma_{21} W_1(T) + \sigma_{22} W_2(T),$$

$$Y := \frac{\tilde{Y}}{\tilde{\sigma}_1 \sqrt{T}}, \quad Z := \frac{\tilde{Z}}{\tilde{\sigma}_2 \sqrt{T}}.$$

W.l.o.g. let $\tilde{\sigma}_i > 0$, i=1,2, $\tilde{\sigma}_i, \rho$ as in (4.10) and (4.11). Then we have

$$\begin{pmatrix} Y \\ Z \end{pmatrix} \sim \mathcal{N}\left(\begin{pmatrix} 0 \\ 0 \end{pmatrix}, \begin{pmatrix} 1 & \rho \\ \rho & 1 \end{pmatrix}\right).$$

Thus, (Y, Z) have the joint density function given by

$$\varphi^{(\rho)}(y, z) = \frac{1}{2\pi\sqrt{1-\rho^2}} e^{-\frac{1}{2(1-\rho^2)}\left(y^2 - 2\rho yz + z^2\right)}.$$

This yields

$$A := E\left(e^{-rT} P_1(T) \cdot 1_{\{K \leq P_1(T) \leq P_2(T)\}}\right)$$
$$= \int_a^\infty \int_b^\infty p_1 \exp\left(-\tfrac{1}{2}\tilde{\sigma}_1^2 T + \tilde{\sigma}_1\sqrt{T} y\right)$$
$$\cdot \frac{1}{2\pi\sqrt{1-\rho^2}} \exp\left(-\frac{1}{2(1-\rho^2)}\left(y^2 - 2\rho yz + z^2\right)\right) dz\, dy$$

with

$$a := \frac{\ln\left(\frac{K}{p_1}\right) - \left(r - \tfrac{1}{2}\tilde{\sigma}_1^2\right) T}{\tilde{\sigma}_1 \sqrt{T}},$$

$$b := \frac{\ln\left(\frac{p_1}{p_2}\right) - \tfrac{1}{2}\left(\tilde{\sigma}_1^2 - \tilde{\sigma}_2^2\right) T + \tilde{\sigma}_1\sqrt{T} y}{\tilde{\sigma}_2 \sqrt{T}}.$$

Integrating with respect to z in A (do a suitable completion of the square!) leads to

$$A = p_1 \cdot \int_a^\infty \frac{1}{\sqrt{2\pi}} \exp\left(-\frac{\left(y - \tilde{\sigma}_1\sqrt{T}\right)^2}{2}\right) \cdot \Phi(d + k \cdot y)\, dy$$

with
$$d := \frac{\ln\left(\frac{p_2}{p_1}\right) + \frac{1}{2}\left(\tilde{\sigma}_1^2 - \tilde{\sigma}_2^2\right)T}{\tilde{\sigma}_2\sqrt{(1-\rho^2)T}},$$
$$k := \frac{\rho\tilde{\sigma}_2 - \tilde{\sigma}_1}{\tilde{\sigma}_2\sqrt{(1-\rho^2)}}.$$

By Lemma 4.2 we then have
$$A = p_1 \cdot P\left(Z_1 \geq a, Z_2 \leq d\right) = p_1 \cdot P\left(\tilde{Z}_1 \leq \tilde{a}, \tilde{Z}_2 \leq \tilde{b}\right)$$
with
$$\begin{pmatrix} Z_1 \\ Z_2 \end{pmatrix} \sim \mathcal{N}\left(\begin{pmatrix} \tilde{\sigma}_1\sqrt{T} \\ -K\tilde{\sigma}_1\sqrt{T} \end{pmatrix}, \begin{pmatrix} 1 & -K \\ -K & 1+K^2 \end{pmatrix}\right),$$
$$\tilde{Z}_1 := \tilde{\sigma}_1 \cdot \sqrt{T} - Z_1, \quad \tilde{Z}_2 := \frac{\tilde{\sigma}_2\sqrt{1-\rho^2}\left(Z_2 + k\tilde{\sigma}_1\sqrt{T}\right)}{\sigma},$$

(4.12)
$$\sigma^2 := \tilde{\sigma}_1^2 + \tilde{\sigma}_2^2 - 2\rho\tilde{\sigma}_1\tilde{\sigma}_2,$$
$$\tilde{a} := \frac{\ln\left(\frac{p_1}{K}\right) + \left(r - \frac{1}{2}\tilde{\sigma}_1^2\right)T}{\tilde{\sigma}_1\sqrt{T}}, \quad \tilde{b} := \frac{\ln\left(\frac{p_2}{p_1}\right) - \frac{1}{2}\sigma^2 T}{\sigma \cdot \sqrt{T}}.$$

As by Lemma 4.2 $\left(\tilde{Z}_1, \tilde{Z}_2\right)$ are distributed according to $\mathcal{N}\left(\begin{pmatrix} 0 \\ 0 \end{pmatrix}, \begin{pmatrix} 1 & \tilde{\rho} \\ \tilde{\rho} & 1 \end{pmatrix}\right)$ with

(4.13)
$$\tilde{\rho} := \frac{\rho\tilde{\sigma}_2 - \tilde{\sigma}_1}{\sigma}, \quad \tilde{\tilde{\rho}} := \frac{\rho\tilde{\sigma}_1 - \tilde{\sigma}_2}{\sigma},$$

and by introducing the following abbreviations

(4.14)
$$d_1 := \frac{\ln\left(\frac{p_1}{K}\right) + \left(r + \frac{1}{2}\tilde{\sigma}_1^2\right)T}{\tilde{\sigma}_1\sqrt{T}}, \quad d_2 := \frac{\ln\left(\frac{p_2}{K}\right) + \left(r + \frac{1}{2}\tilde{\sigma}_2^2\right)T}{\tilde{\sigma}_2\sqrt{T}},$$

(4.15)
$$d_3 := \frac{\ln\left(\frac{p_2}{p_1}\right) - \frac{1}{2}\sigma^2 T}{\sigma\sqrt{T}}, \quad d_4 := \frac{\ln\left(\frac{p_1}{p_2}\right) - \frac{1}{2}\sigma^2 T}{\sigma\sqrt{T}},$$

we obtain
$$A = E\left(e^{-rT} P_1(T) \cdot 1_{\{K \leq P_1(T) \leq P_2(T)\}}\right) = p_1 \cdot \Phi^{(\tilde{\rho})}(d_1, d_3).$$

By interchanging $P_1(T)$ and $P_2(T)$ we get
$$E\left(e^{-rT} P_2(T) \cdot 1_{\{K \leq P_2(T) \leq P_1(T)\}}\right) = p_1 \cdot \Phi^{(\tilde{\tilde{\rho}})}(d_2, d_4),$$

and a similar calculation yields
$$P\left(\min\left(P_1(T), P_2(T)\right) \geq K\right) = \Phi^{(\rho)}\left(d_1 - \tilde{\sigma}_1\sqrt{T}, d_2 - \tilde{\sigma}_2\sqrt{T}\right).$$

Hence the price of the minimum call is determined. If we now take the usual relations between put and call and between minimum and maximum, we obtain (see Exercise (5)):

Proposition 4.4. *With the notation of (4.10)-(4.15), the prices of the minimum / maximum options are given by*

$$X_{\min}^{Call}(0) = p_1 \cdot \Phi^{(\tilde{\rho})}(d_1, d_3) + p_2 \Phi^{(\tilde{\tilde{\rho}})}(d_2, d_4)$$
$$- Ke^{-rT}\Phi^{(\rho)}\left(d_1 - \tilde{\sigma}_1\sqrt{T}, d_2 - \tilde{\sigma}_2\sqrt{T}\right),$$
$$X_{\min}^{Put}(0) = X_{\min}^{Call}(0) + Ke^{-rT} - p_1\Phi(d_3) - p_2\Phi(d_4),$$
$$X_{\max}^{Call}(0) = X_{(1)}^{Call}(0) + X_{(2)}^{Call}(0) - X_{\min}^{Call}(0),$$
$$X_{\max}^{Put}(0) = X_{(1)}^{Put}(0) + X_{(2)}^{Put}(0) - X_{\min}^{Put}(0),$$

where $X_{(i)}^{Call}$, $X_{(i)}^{Put}$ *denote the prices of the ordinary European calls and puts on stock i with strike K, $i = 1, 2$.*

c) Path dependent options

One-sided barrier options. The owner of a one-sided barrier option receives the final payoff of a European call (or put) if the stock price does not exceed (or does exceed) a given barrier before time T. We shall look in detail at the following different types of one-sided barrier options:

$B_{do}^{Call} = (P_1(T) - K)^+ \cdot 1_{\{P_1(t) > b \text{ for all } t \in [0,T]\}}$ "Down-and-out call"

$B_{do}^{Put} = (K - P_1(T))^+ \cdot 1_{\{P_1(t) > b \text{ for all } t \in [0,T]\}}$ "Down-and-out put"

$B_{uo}^{Call} = (P_1(T) - K)^+ \cdot 1_{\{P_1(t) < b \text{ for all } t \in [0,T]\}}$ "Up-and-out call"

$B_{uo}^{Put} = (K - P_1(T))^+ \cdot 1_{\{P_1(t) < b \text{ for all } t \in [0,T]\}}$ "Up-and-out put"

and the corresponding *in*-versions

$$B_{di}^{Call} = (P_1(T) - K)^+ \cdot 1_{\{\text{there exists a } t \in [0,T] \text{ with } P_1(t) \leq b\}}$$
"Down-and-in call"

$$B_{di}^{Put} = (K - P_1(T))^+ \cdot 1_{\{\text{there exists a } t \in [0,T] \text{ with } P_1(t) \leq b\}}$$
"Down-and-in put"

$$B_{ui}^{Call} = (P_1(T) - K)^+ \cdot 1_{\{\text{there exists a } t \in [0,T] \text{ with } P_1(t) \geq b\}}$$
"Up-and-in call"

$$B_{ui}^{Put} = (K - P_1(T))^+ \cdot 1_{\{\text{there exists a } t \in [0,T] \text{ with } P_1(t) \geq b\}}$$
"Up-and-in put".

If we however know the prices for the *out*-versions then we immediately obtain those of the corresponding *in*-versions. This is due to the following relations called *in-out-parity*:

$$X_{ui}^{Call}(0) = X^{Call}(0) - X_{uo}^{Call}(0),$$
$$X_{ui}^{Put}(0) = X^{Put}(0) - X_{uo}^{Put}(0),$$
$$X_{di}^{Call}(0) = X^{Call}(0) - X_{do}^{Call}(0),$$
$$X_{di}^{Put}(0) = X^{Put}(0) - X_{do}^{Put}(0).$$

For example, the third relationship results from the decomposition

$$(P_1(T) - K)^+ = (P_1(T) - K)^+ \cdot 1_{\{P_1(t) > b \text{ for all } t \in [0,T]\}}$$
$$+ (P_1(T) - K)^+ \cdot 1_{\{\text{ there exists a } t \in [0,T] \text{ with } P_1(t) \leq b\}}.$$

Here, we shall restrict ourselves to the computation of the price of a down-and-out call. To do so, we need the following lemma on the joint distribution of the final value and the running maximum of a one-dimensional Brownian motion with drift:

Lemma 4.5. *Let* $M(t) := \max_{0 \leq s \leq t} W(s)$ *be the running maximum of a one-dimensional Brownian motion* $W(t)$. *Then for* $x \geq 0$, $x \geq w$, *we have*

(1) $P(W(t) \leq w, M(t) < x) = \Phi\left(\dfrac{w}{\sqrt{t}}\right) - 1 + \Phi\left(\dfrac{2x - w}{\sqrt{t}}\right).$

(2) *For* $\mu \in \mathbb{R}$ *let* $\tilde{W}(t) := W(t) + \mu \cdot t$ *and* $\tilde{M}(t) := \max_{0 \leq s \leq t} \tilde{W}(s)$. *Then the following relation is valid:*

$$P\left(\tilde{W}(t) \leq w, \tilde{M}(t) < x\right) = \Phi\left(\dfrac{w - \mu t}{\sqrt{t}}\right) - e^{2\mu x}\Phi\left(\dfrac{w - 2x - \mu t}{\sqrt{t}}\right).$$

Proof. Assertion (1) is a consequence of Proposition 2.8.1 in [**KA/SH 91**] which itself is a consequence of the reflection principle of D. André (see e.g. Section 2.6.A in [**KA/SH 91**]). Part (2) follows from (1) by using Girsanov's Theorem 3.11 (see Exercise (12)). □

For the calculation of the price of a down-and-out call, we first assume that for an initial value of $p_1 = P_1(0)$, barrier b, strike K, we have the relations

$$b < p_1, \quad K < b.$$

I.e. if the down-and-out call is not "knocked out" before T it will automatically be in the money. With the help of the choice

$$\mu = \frac{r - \frac{1}{2}\sigma^2}{\sigma},$$

c) Path dependent options

the relation $\min\{-(W(t) + \mu \cdot t)\} = -\max\{W(t) + \mu \cdot t\}$ and some explicit calculations (from Lemma 4.5 we obtain the density of

$$\left(W(T) + \mu \cdot T, \min_{0 \leq t \leq T}(W(t) + \mu \cdot t)\right)),$$

we obtain

$$X_{do}^{Call}(0) = p_1 \Phi(d_1) - be^{-rT}\Phi\left(d_1 - \sigma\sqrt{T}\right)$$
$$+ e^{-rT}(b-K)\Phi\left(d_1 - \sigma\sqrt{T}\right) - p_1\left(\frac{b}{p_1}\right)^{2\frac{r}{\sigma^2}+1}\Phi(d_2)$$
$$+ e^{-rT}K\left(\frac{b}{p_1}\right)^{2\frac{r}{\sigma^2}-1}\Phi\left(d_2 - \sigma\sqrt{T}\right)$$

with

$$d_1 = \frac{\ln\left(\frac{p_1}{b}\right) + \left(r + \frac{1}{2}\sigma^2\right)T}{\sigma\sqrt{T}}, \quad d_2 = \frac{\ln\left(\frac{b}{p_1}\right) + \left(r + \frac{1}{2}\sigma^2\right)T}{\sigma\sqrt{T}}.$$

A similar formula can be obtained for the case of $b \leq K$, i.e.

$$X_{do}^{Call}(0) = p_1\Phi(d_3) - Ke^{-rT}\Phi\left(d_3 - \sigma\sqrt{T}\right)$$
$$- p_1\left(\frac{b}{p_1}\right)^{2\frac{r}{\sigma^2}+1}\Phi(d_4) + e^{-rT}K\left(\frac{b}{p_1}\right)^{2\frac{r}{\sigma^2}-1}\Phi\left(d_4 - \sigma\sqrt{T}\right),$$

where we get d_3 out of d_1 by substituting b by K and d_2 out of d_4 by substituting b by b^2/K. We get similar results for the other types of barrier options. Here, we do not go into further details.

Options on the minimum / maximum of the stock price ("lookback options"). Typically a lookback option is given by a payoff in which the minimum or the maximum of the stock price on $[0, T]$ appear. Thus a lookback option is a path-dependent one. Typical forms of it are

$$B_{\max LB}^{Call} = \left(\max_{t \in [0,T]} P_1(t) - K\right)^+, \quad K \geq p_1 = P_1(0),$$

$$B_{LB}^{Call} = \left(P_1(T) - \min_{t \in [0,T]} P_1(t)\right).$$

Again, we can apply Lemma 4.5 to obtain

$$X_{LB}^{Call}(0) = p_1 \cdot \left(\Phi(d_1) - e^{-rT}\Phi(d_1 - \sigma\sqrt{T})\right)$$
$$+ p_1 \frac{\sigma^2}{2r} e^{-rT}\left(\Phi(-d_1 + 2\frac{r}{\sigma}\sqrt{T}) - e^{rT}\Phi(-d_1)\right),$$

$$X_{\max LB}^{Call}(0) = p_1 \Phi(d_2) - Ke^{-rT}\Phi\left(d_2 - \sigma\sqrt{T}\right)$$
$$+ p_1 \frac{\sigma^2}{2r}\left(\Phi(d_2) - e^{-rT}\left(\frac{K}{p_1}\right)^{2\frac{r}{\sigma^2}} \Phi\left(d_2 - 2\frac{r}{\sigma}\right)\sqrt{T}\right),$$

with

$$d_1 = \frac{\left(r + \frac{1}{2}\sigma^2\right)T}{\sigma\sqrt{T}}, \quad d_2 = \frac{\ln\left(\frac{p_1}{K}\right) + \left(r + \frac{1}{2}\sigma^2\right)T}{\sigma\sqrt{T}}.$$

Excursion 7: Weak Convergence of Stochastic Processes

In all the cases of exotic options that do not admit an explicit pricing formula we have to use a suitable numerical algorithm to compute the price at least approximately. Very often the basis of such a numerical algorithm lies in a discretization of the stock price process. Typically, it is then easy to calculate the expected discounted payoff of the option in the discretized model. For this value to be seen as a reasonable approximation of the (unknown) option price in the Black-Scholes model it has to be proved that the sequence of expectations calculated in the discretized models converges to the Black-Scholes price if the discretization gets finer and finer. The suitable framework to prove this convergence is the concept of weak convergence of stochastic processes. We shall look at some of its basics. For our purposes, it is enough if we restrict ourselves to stochastic processes $\{X(t)\}_{t \in [0,1]}$ with continuous paths on $[0,1]$.

> **General assumptions for this section:**
> We consider the special probability space
> $$(\Omega, \mathcal{F}, P) = (C[0,1], \mathcal{B}(C[0,1]), P),$$
> i.e. the space of continuous, real-valued functions on $[0,1]$ equipped with the corresponding Borel σ-field and a probability measure P.

In this setting, the *function valued random variable* X on $(\Omega, \mathcal{F}, P)$ given by

(4.16) $$X(\omega) := \omega, \quad \omega \in C[0,1],$$

defines a real-valued stochastic process with distribution P. The value of this process at time $t \in [0,1]$ can be obtained via projection on the "t-th coordinate" of ω,

$$X(t, \omega) := \pi_t \circ X(\omega) := \omega(t).$$

Now, we could define the convergence of stochastic processes X_n via the usual weak convergence of random variables,
$$X_n(t) \xrightarrow{n \to \infty} X(t) \quad \text{for all } t \in [0,1] \text{ in distribution}.$$
But this notion of convergence would be too weak. Instead, we have to consider the weak convergence of probability measures on metric spaces (see [**BILL 68**]).

Definition 4.6. Let $(S, \mathcal{B}(S))$ be a metric space with metric ρ. Again $\mathcal{B}(S)$ denotes the Borel-σ-field over S. Let further $P, P_n, n \in \mathbb{N}$, be probability measures on $(S, \mathcal{B}(S))$. Then we say that the sequence P_n *converges weakly* to P (or: *converges in distribution*) if for every continuous and bounded real valued function f on S we have
$$\int_S f \, dP_n \xrightarrow{n \to \infty} \int_S f \, dP.$$

From this we obtain as a special case the weak convergence of stochastic processes with continuous paths by noting that $(C[0,1], \mathcal{B}(C[0,1]))$ is a metric space endowed with the following metric:
$$\rho(x, y) = \sup_{0 \leq t \leq 1} |x(t) - y(t)|.$$

Definition 4.7. The sequence of continuous stochastic processes $\{X_n(t)\}_{t \in [0,1]}$ is said to *converge weakly* (or *in distribution*) to X if for all $f \in C(C[0,1], \mathbb{R})$ we have
$$(4.17) \qquad Ef(X_n) \xrightarrow{n \to \infty} Ef(X).$$
Here, $C(C[0,1], \mathbb{R})$ is the space of the uniformly continuous, bounded functionals on $C[0,1]$.

The convergence in (4.17) has to be understood in the following sense: The stochastic process X_n is defined on the probability space $(C[0,1], \mathcal{B}(C[0,1]), P_n)$ according to (4.16), the process X is defined on $(C[0,1], \mathcal{B}(C[0,1]), P)$. Here, P, P_n are probability measures on $(C[0,1], \mathcal{B}(C[0,1]))$. By (4.16) we can rewrite (4.17) as
$$Ef(X_n) = \int f(X_n) \, dP = \int f \, dP_n$$
$$\xrightarrow{n \to \infty} \int f \, dP = \int f(X) \, dP = Ef(X).$$

Thus, the weak convergence of stochastic processes is represented as the weak convergence of the probability measures $P_n \to P$. Weak convergence is preserved under continuous mappings as we have the following theorem (which is a special case of Theorem 5.1 of [**BILL 68**]).

Theorem 4.8. *Let P, P_n, $n \in \mathbb{N}$, be probability measures on the metric space $(S, \mathcal{B}(S))$ endowed with the metric ρ. Further, let $h : S \to S'$ be a measurable mapping into a metric space S' with metric ρ' and Borel-σ-field $\mathcal{B}(S')$. If for the set D_h of points of discontinuity of h we have*

$$P(D_h) = 0,$$

then we get

$$P_n \xrightarrow{n \to \infty} P \text{ in distribution} \Rightarrow P_n \cdot h^{-1} \xrightarrow{n \to \infty} P \cdot h^{-1} \text{ in distribution.}$$

As $(\mathbb{R}^k, \mathcal{B}(\mathbb{R}^k))$ is also a metric space, Theorem 4.8 implies:

Corollary 4.9. *If the sequence X_n of continuous stochastic processes converges weakly to the continuous process X, then for every fixed $t \in [0, 1]$ the random variables $X_n(t)$ converge in distribution to $X(t)$.*

We even have a stronger result than given in the corollary. Let therefore the projections

$$\pi_{t_1, \ldots, t_k} : C[0, 1] \to \mathbb{R}^k$$

be defined as

$$\pi_{t_1, \ldots, t_k}(\omega) = (\omega(t_1), \ldots, \omega(t_k))$$

for fixed $0 \leq t_1 < \ldots < t_k \leq 1$. Then, from Theorem 4.8 we also get the implication

$$X_n \xrightarrow{n \to \infty} X \text{ in distribution}$$
$$\Rightarrow (X_n(t_1), \ldots, X_n(t_k)) \xrightarrow{n \to \infty} (X(t_1), \ldots, X(t_k)) \text{ in distribution.}$$

Hence, weak convergence of the stochastic processes also implies convergence of the finite-dimensional distributions. However, in general, the converse is not true. Convergence of all finite-dimensional distributions

$$P_n \cdot \pi^{-1}_{t_1, \ldots, t_k}$$

does not in general imply convergence of the distributions P_n of the corresponding processes.

If, however, the sequence of the P_n is relatively compact (i.e. each subsequence contains a weakly convergent subsequence), then we can easily show that convergence of the finite-dimensional subsequences implies weak convergence of the P_n (see [**BILL 68**]).

Now, if we want to approximate (in the sense of weak convergence) the one-dimensional Brownian motion $W(t)$, the central limit theorem (for sums of real valued random variables) suggests the following algorithm:

Excursion 7: Weak Convergence of Stochastic Processes   173

(1) Choose a sequence $\{\xi_n\}_{n\in\mathbb{N}}$ of i.i.d. random variables of a simple form with $E(\xi_i) = 0$, $Var(\xi_i) = \sigma^2 < \infty$ and set

$$S_0 := 0, \quad S_n = \sum_{i=1}^n \xi_i.$$

For example, we could choose $\xi_i = Y_i - q$ with $Y_i \sim B(1,q)$.

(2) By means of linear interpolation construct a stochastic process $X_n(t)$ with continuous paths out of that sequence

(4.18) $$X_n(t,\omega) = \frac{1}{\sigma\sqrt{n}} S_{[nt]}(\omega) + (nt - [nt]) \frac{1}{\sigma\sqrt{n}} \xi_{[nt]+1}(\omega),$$

for $t \in [0,1]$, $n \in \mathbb{N}$. I.e. we have $X_n\left(\frac{k}{n}, \omega\right) = \frac{1}{\sigma\sqrt{n}} S_k(\omega)$, and for $t \in \left(\frac{k}{n}, \frac{k+1}{n}\right)$ we obtain $X_n(t)$ by linear interpolation.

(3) The finite-dimensional distributions of X_n converge in distribution to that of a Brownian motion. To see this, note

- From $\frac{[ns]}{n} \xrightarrow{n\to\infty} s$ and the central limit theorem, we obtain

(4.19) $$\frac{1}{\sigma\sqrt{n}} S_{[ns]} \xrightarrow{n\to\infty} W(s) \text{ in distribution.}$$

- Chebyshev's inequality yields

$$\left| X_n(s) - \frac{1}{\sigma\sqrt{n}} S_{[ns]} \right| \leq \frac{1}{\sigma\sqrt{n}} \left| \xi_{[ns]+1} \right| \xrightarrow{n\to\infty} 0 \text{ in probability.}$$

Hence, (4.19) implies

(4.20) $$X_n(s) \xrightarrow{n\to\infty} W(s) \text{ in distribution.}$$

- Due to the independence of the ξ_i, (4.19), and the theorem of Slutsky this results in

$$\left(\frac{1}{\sigma\sqrt{n}} S_{[ns]}, \frac{1}{\sigma\sqrt{n}} \left(S_{[nt]} - S_{[ns]} \right) \right) \xrightarrow{n\to\infty} (W_s, W_t - W_s)$$

for $s < t$. From this we get

$$(X_n(s), X_n(t) - X_n(s)) \xrightarrow{n\to\infty} (W_s, W_t - W_s) \text{ in distribution}$$

in a similar way as in (4.20). Again, Slutsky's theorem implies

$$(X_n(s), X_n(t)) \xrightarrow{n\to\infty} (W_s, W_t) \text{ in distribution.}$$

Analogously we prove the desired convergence of finite tuples of $X_n(t_i)$-components.

(4) Show that the sequence of the distributions P_n on $(C[0,1], \mathcal{B}(C[0,1]))$ corresponding to X_n is relatively compact.

So, for a given choice of the ξ_i it only remains to show the relative compactness of the sequence of distributions corresponding to X_n. This is the major part of the work in the proof of the following theorem (see [**BILL 68**]).

Theorem 4.10 (Donsker's theorem). *Let $\{\xi_n\}_{n\in\mathbb{N}}$, be an i.i.d. sequence with $E(\xi_i) = 0$, $0 < Var(\xi_i) = \sigma^2 < \infty$. Then the sequence X_n of stochastic processes defined by (4.18) converges weakly to the one-dimensional Brownian motion $W(t)$, $t \in [0, 1]$.*

Remark 4.11. The convergence assertion and the limiting distribution in Theorem 4.10 are independent of the exact choice of ξ_i. Therefore, the theorem is often called *Donsker's invariance principle*. The theorem can be viewed as a "process version" of the central limit theorem. W.l.o.g. it can be assumed valid for arbitrary intervals $[0, T]$.

For practical applications in the coming sections the following variant of Donsker's theorem is very useful (see [**BILL 68**]).

Theorem 4.12 (Donsker's theorem for triangular schemes). *The random variables $\xi_{n_1}, ..., \xi_{n_{k_n}}$, $n \in \mathbb{N}$, $k_n \in \mathbb{N}$, are assumed to be i.i.d. with*

$$E(\xi_{n_1}) = 0, \quad 0 < Var(\xi_{n_1}) = \sigma_{n_1}^2 \leq c,$$

where $c > 0$ is a suitable constant. Let

$$S_{n_i} := \xi_{n_1} + ... + \xi_{n_i}, \ 1 \leq i \leq k_n,$$
$$s_{n_i}^2 := \sigma_{n_1}^2 + ... + \sigma_{n_i}^2 = i \cdot \sigma_{n_1}^2,$$
$$s_n^2 := s_{n_{k_n}}^2 = k_n \cdot \sigma_{n_1}^2.$$

Define the process $X_n(t)$, $t \in [0,1]$, by

$$X_n(0) := 0,$$

$$X_n\left(s_{n_i}^2 / s_n^2\right) := S_{n_i} / s_n, \ i = 1, ..., k_n,$$

and via linear interpolation on the intervals $\left[s_{n_{i-1}}^2 / s_n^2, s_{n_i}^2 / s_n^2\right]$. If we have $k_n \to \infty$ and $s_n \to \infty$ for $n \to \infty$, then X_n converges weakly to the Brownian motion W.

With the results shown so far we have

$$E(h(X_n)) \xrightarrow{n \to \infty} E(h(X))$$

for continuous and bounded functionals $h : C[0,T] \to \mathbb{R}$. But this is in general not sufficient for our practical applications. In particular, if in the

Black-Scholes model we approximate the Brownian motion by a sequence of processes X_n as above, Donsker's theorem would not directly imply

$$E\left(e^{b\cdot T + \sigma \cdot X_n(T)}\right) \xrightarrow{n \to \infty} E\left(e^{b\cdot T + \sigma \cdot W(T)}\right)$$

as the exponential functional is not bounded. Additionally, we need the uniform integrability of the sequence $\exp(\sigma X_n(T))$ due to the following theorem.

Theorem 4.13. *Let the sequence of random variables $\{X_n\}_{n \in \mathbb{N}}$ be uniformly integrable. Assume further that we have*

$$X_n \xrightarrow{n \to \infty} X \text{ in distribution.}$$

Then this implies

$$E(X_n) \xrightarrow{n \to \infty} E(X).$$

4.2. Monte-Carlo Simulation

Description of the basic idea. The basis of Monte-Carlo simulation is the strong law of large numbers stating that the arithmetic mean of independent, identically distributed random variables converges towards their mean almost surely. As by Corollary 3.15 computing an option price is nothing else than computing the discounted expectation (with respect to the equivalent martingale measure) of the payoff B, this suggests the following approach:

Algorithm: *Determine the option price via Monte-Carlo simulation.*

(1) Simulate n independent realizations B_i of the final payoff B.

(2) Choose $\left(\frac{1}{n} \sum_{i=1}^{n} B_i\right) \cdot e^{-rT}$ as an approximation for the option price $E_Q\left(e^{-rT} B\right)$.

Here, the arithmetic mean computed in the second step constitutes an unbiased and - due to the strong law of large numbers - strongly consistent estimator for the option price. The second step above should cause no problems. However, the first step consisting of generating the realizations of B can only be done approximately.

Simulation of the payoff B. We assume that the payment $B = B(P_1(t), t \in [0,T])$ is a functional of the price process $P_1(t)$, $t \in [0,T]$. Thus, to simulate B, we first have to simulate a path $P_1(t)$, $t \in [0,T]$, of the stock price process with respect to the equivalent martingale measure Q. As such a path is given by infinitely many (i.e. uncountably many) values, it can only be simulated approximately. To do this, use the following procedure:

(1) Divide the interval $[0, T]$ into $N \gg 1$ equidistant parts.
(2) Generate N independent random numbers Y_i which are $\mathcal{N}(0,1)$-distributed.
(3) From those, simulate an (approximate) path $W(t)$ of the Brownian motion on $[0, T]$:
$$W(0) = 0,$$
$$W\left(j \cdot \tfrac{T}{N}\right) = W\left((j-1) \cdot \tfrac{T}{N}\right) + \sqrt{\tfrac{T}{N}} \cdot Y_j, \quad j = 1, ..., N,$$
$$W(t) = W\left((j-1)\tfrac{T}{N}\right) + \left(t - (j-1)\tfrac{T}{N}\right) \cdot \tfrac{N}{T} \cdot \left[W\left(j\tfrac{T}{N}\right) - W\left((j-1)\tfrac{T}{N}\right)\right]$$
$$\text{for } t \in \left[(j-1)\tfrac{T}{N}, j\tfrac{T}{N}\right].$$
(4) Use this to generate an (approximate) path of the price process $P_1(t)$:
$$P_1(t) = p_1 \cdot e^{\left(r - \tfrac{1}{2}\sigma^2\right)t} \cdot e^{\sigma \cdot W(t)}, \quad t \in [0, T].$$
(5) With this simulated path of the price process compute an estimate for the payoff B. For example in the case of a European call:
$$B_i = (P_1(T) - K)^+.$$

Remark 4.14. For the practical realization of the computation of B_i in step 5 above it often proves to be more convenient to do the interpolation in step 4 and not in step 3:
$$P_1(0) = p_1,$$
$$P_1\left(j \cdot \tfrac{T}{N}\right) = P_1\left((j-1) \cdot \tfrac{T}{N}\right) \cdot e^{\left(r - \tfrac{1}{2}\sigma^2\right)\tfrac{T}{N}} \cdot e^{\sigma\sqrt{\tfrac{T}{N}} \cdot Y_j}, \quad j = 1, ..., N,$$
$$P_1(t) = P_1\left((j-1)\tfrac{T}{N}\right) + \left(t - (j-1)\tfrac{T}{N}\right) \cdot \tfrac{N}{T} \cdot \left[P_1\left(j\tfrac{T}{N}\right) - P_1\left((j-1)\tfrac{T}{N}\right)\right]$$
$$\text{for } t \in \left[(j-1)\tfrac{T}{N}, j\tfrac{T}{N}\right].$$
For large N the differences between both methods are negligible.

Convergence of the method. Let $P_1^{(N)}(t), t \in [0, T]$, be the approximate price process generated as above. If now B is a continuous and bounded functional on $C([0,T])$ then by Donsker's Theorem 4.10 and by Theorem 4.8, we also have the convergence of
$$E_Q\left(B\left(P_1^{(N)}(t), t \in [0, T]\right)\right) \xrightarrow{N \to \infty} E_Q\left(B\left(P_1(t), t \in [0, T]\right)\right)$$
by the definition of weak convergence. If B is a continuous functional on $C([0, T])$, then convergence to the option price is guaranteed if the family
$$\left\{B\left(P_1^{(N)}(t), t \in [0, T]\right) \mid N \in \mathbb{N}\right\}$$

is uniformly integrable. Showing this uniform integrability can be quite tricky for specific choices of B. Then for a given N the expected value

$$E_Q\left(B\left(P_1^{(N)}(t), t \in [0,T]\right)\right)$$

will be approximated by the arithmetic mean

$$\frac{1}{n}\sum_{i=1}^{n} B\left(P_{1,i}^{(N)}(t),\ t \in [0,T]\right),$$

by means of the strong law of large numbers. Here $P_{1,i}^{(N)}(t)$, $t \in [0,T]$, $i = 1,...,n$ are different paths which have been generated according to the above procedure.

Advantages. The Monte-Carlo method for estimating an option price is very easy to implement. Nowadays, reasonable random number generators for generating pseudo-random numbers can be found in every programming language. Further, every arbitrary exotic option can be approximated by the Monte-Carlo simulation.

Of course, there are a lot of refinements of the above, crude Monte-Carlo algorithm to obtain faster convergence (see e.g. [**RUBI 81**]).

Disadvantages. Even in times of high speed computers the method is time consuming as both n and N have to be very large to yield good estimates for the option prices. Frequently the values of n and N have to be so large that the whole reservoir of pseudo-random numbers is used and an already used sequence of pseudo-random numbers has to be reused. Thus, the independence assumption of the different simulations is no longer true. In fact, there is a strong dependence of the method on the quality of the random number generator used.

4.3. Approximation via Binomial Trees

Description of the basic idea. While the Monte-Carlo simulation for option pricing relies on the strong law of large numbers, the approximation method via binomial trees can be motivated by the central limit theorem.

To explain the method we look at the following stock price process $P_1^{(n)}(i)$, $i = 0, 1, ..., n$, in discrete time with possible paths given by the binomial tree in Figure 4.3. This binomial tree represents a price process which starts in p at time $t = 0$. In each node of the tree the price $P_1^{(n)}(i)$ can increase by the factor u with probability q or by the factor d with probability $(1-q)$ (where we have $d < u$). Such a stock price model is also called a Cox-Ross-Rubinstein model (see [**C/R/R 79**]). Note in particular

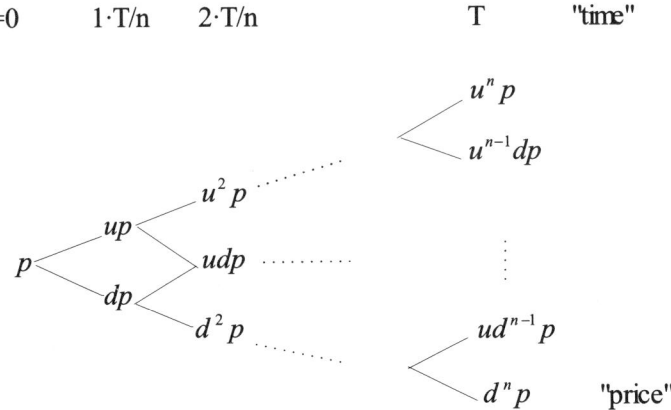

Figure 4.3. Binomial tree

that both the probability of a price increase by the factor u and the possible values of the relative price change

$$\frac{P_1^{(n)}(i)}{P_1^{(n)}(i-1)}$$

should be the same in each node. For arbitrage reasons the factors u, d have to satisfy

$$d < e^{r\Delta t} < u \text{ with } \Delta t := \frac{T}{n}.$$

Otherwise there would be the possibility of riskless gains. More precisely, in the case of $d \geq e^{r\Delta t}$ financing a stock investment via a credit is such an opportunity. In the case of $u \leq e^{r\Delta t}$ selling stock short and investing the profit in the bond constitutes an arbitrage gain. If X_n denotes the number of "up-moves" of $P_1^{(n)}(n)$, then we have

$$X_n \sim B(n, q),$$

$$P_1^{(n)}(n) = p \cdot u^{X_n} \cdot d^{n-X_n} = p \cdot e^{X_n \cdot \ln(u/d) + n \cdot \ln(d)}.$$

In particular, for $q = 1/2$, $\tilde{b} \in \mathbb{R}$ and the choice of

$$u = e^{\tilde{b}\Delta t + \sigma\sqrt{\Delta t}}, \quad d = e^{\tilde{b}\Delta t - \sigma\sqrt{\Delta t}}$$

together with the notations

$$\tilde{b} = \tfrac{1}{2}\frac{\ln(u) + \ln(d)}{\Delta t}, \quad \sigma = \tfrac{1}{2}\frac{\ln(u) - \ln(d)}{\sqrt{\Delta t}},$$

4.3. Approximation via Binomial Trees

we have the convergence of

$$P_1^{(n)}(n) = p \cdot \exp\left(\tilde{b} \cdot T + \sigma\sqrt{T}\left(\frac{2X_n - n}{\sqrt{n}}\right)\right)$$
$$\xrightarrow{n \to \infty} p \cdot \exp\left(\tilde{b} \cdot T + \sigma \cdot W(T)\right) = P_1(T) \text{ in distribution}$$

due to the central limit theorem. Note that

$$\frac{(2X_n - n)}{\sqrt{n}}$$

has zero mean and variance 1 and that $2X_n$ is the sum of n independent, double Bernoulli variables. A generalization of this convergence relation (more precisely: the convergence of the discrete to the continuous price process) represents one building block of the binomial approach. The other part of the method is based on the fact that the discounted expected payoff of the option in the discrete model can be computed easily. With increasing degree of fineness of the time discretization, the discounted expected final payment in the discrete-time model will converge to that of the continuous-time model if the family

$$B_n := B\left(P_1^{(n)}(i), \ i = 0, 1, ..., n\right)$$

is uniformly integrable. To prove this can be really complicated for some choices of B, B_n. Summing up all the above remarks, we arrive at the following algorithm:

<u>Algorithm:</u> *Approximation via binomial trees:*

(1) For $n \gg 1$ set up a suitable binomial tree for the price process $P_1^{(n)}(i)$ in discrete time.

(2) Compute the discounted expected payoff $E^{(n)}(e^{-rt}B_n)$ in the discrete-time model as an approximation for $E_Q(e^{-rt}B)$.

Of course, the choice of n (i.e. the fineness of the (space and) time discretization) is the essential factor for the accuracy of the approximation for the option price computed in the second step and for the computational complexity. Therefore, the above algorithm is performed iteratively for different (increasing) values of n and will be stopped if the sequence of approximations for the option price converges.

Choice of the parameters in the binomial tree. As the increments

$$\frac{P_1^{(n)}(i)}{P_1^{(n)}(i-1)}$$

in the binomial tree are all independent and identically distributed, Donsker's theorem for triangular schemes, Theorem 4.12, and Theorem 4.8 imply weak convergence of $\{P_1^{(n)}(i),\ i = 0, 1, ..., n\}$ to $\{P_1(t), t \in [0, T]\}$, if the first two moments of the logarithm of the increments

$$\ln\left(\frac{P_1^{(n)}(i)}{P_1^{(n)}(i-1)}\right) \quad \text{and} \quad \ln\left(\frac{P_1(i \cdot \frac{T}{n})}{P_1((i-1) \cdot \frac{T}{n})}\right)$$

of both the discrete and continuous price processes coincide at times $i \cdot T/n$. More precisely: if we define a continuous process $P_1^{(s,n)}(t)$ via linear interpolation between $\ln(P_1^{(n)}(i-1))$ and $\ln(P_1^{(n)}(i))$, i.e.

$$\ln\left(P_1^{(s,n)}(t)\right) = \ln\left(P_1^{(n)}(i-1)\right) + \left(t - (i-1)\frac{T}{n}\right) \cdot \frac{n}{T}$$
$$\cdot \left[\ln\left(P_1^{(s,n)}(i)\right) - \ln\left(P_1^{(n)}(i-1)\right)\right] \quad \text{for } t \in \left[(i-1)\frac{T}{n}, i\frac{T}{n}\right],$$

then this continuous process converges weakly to the stochastic price process $P_1(t)$ if the above mentioned moment conditions hold.

As due to Corollary 3.15 we can consider the price process with respect to the equivalent martingale measure Q, w.l.o.g. we can assume that

$$\frac{P_1(t)}{P_0(t)}$$

is a martingale. Let now $Q^{(n)}$ be the binomial measure with respect to the time discretization n, let $E^{(n)}$ be the expectation with respect to that measure and let further $\{\mathcal{F}_i^{(n)}\}_{i \in \{0,1,...,n\}}$ be the filtration generated by the price process $\{P_1^{(n)}(i)\}_{i \in \{0,1,...,n\}}$. Then, the above moment conditions have the form

$$(4.21) \quad \left(r - \tfrac{1}{2}\sigma^2\right) \Delta t = E_Q\left(\ln\left(\frac{P_1(\Delta t)}{P_1(0)}\right)\right) = E^{(n)}\left(\ln\left(\frac{P_1^{(n)}(1)}{P_1^{(n)}(0)}\right)\right)$$
$$= \ln(u) \cdot q + \ln(d) \cdot (1-q),$$

$$(4.22) \quad \left(r - \tfrac{1}{2}\sigma^2\right)^2 (\Delta t)^2 + \sigma^2 \Delta t$$
$$= E_Q\left(\ln\left(\frac{P_1(\Delta t)}{P_1(0)}\right)^2\right) = E^{(n)}\left(\ln\left(\frac{P_1^{(n)}(1)}{P_1^{(n)}(0)}\right)^2\right)$$
$$= \ln(u)^2 \cdot q + \ln(d)^2 \cdot (1-q).$$

Here, due to the assumptions on the distributions of the increments, we can restrict ourselves to the one of the first time step. Then note that the equations (4.21) and (4.22) contain three unknown parameters

u, d "incremental factors", q "probability of an upwards movement".

4.3. Approximation via Binomial Trees

The two conditions (4.21) and (4.22) thus allow a free choice of one of the parameters if we ensure $u, d > 0$ and $q \in (0, 1)$. In practice, popular choices are

$$u = \frac{1}{d}, \; d < 1 \quad \text{or} \quad q = \tfrac{1}{2}.$$

We now concentrate on the case given by $q = 1/2$ (for the situation of the choice $u = 1/d$ and in particular the choice of u, d by Cox, Ross, Rubinstein see Exercise (13)). From (4.21) and (4.22) we have the equations

(4.23) $$\ln(u \cdot d) = 2\left(r - \tfrac{1}{2}\sigma^2\right)\Delta t,$$

(4.24) $$\ln(u)^2 + \ln(d)^2 = 2\left(r - \tfrac{1}{2}\sigma^2\right)^2 (\Delta t)^2 + 2\sigma^2 \Delta t,$$

which are obviously symmetric in u and d. Therefore, we make the ansatz

(4.25) $$u = e^{B+C}, \; d = e^{B-C},$$

which together with (4.23) and (4.24) leads to

$$B = \left(r - \tfrac{1}{2}\sigma^2\right)\Delta t, \; C = |\sigma| \cdot \sqrt{\Delta t}.$$

With (4.25) we obtain

(4.26) $$u = e^{\left(r - \tfrac{1}{2}\sigma^2\right)\Delta t + |\sigma|\sqrt{\Delta t}}, \; d = e^{\left(r - \tfrac{1}{2}\sigma^2\right)\Delta t - |\sigma|\sqrt{\Delta t}}.$$

Thus the two requirements on the moments are satisfied and for $r > 0$ we also have

$$0 < d < u \; \text{and} \; d < e^{r\Delta t}.$$

To obtain the relation $e^{r\Delta t} < u$ which we need for arbitrage reasons, we must have

(4.27) $$|\sigma| \cdot \sqrt{\Delta t} - \tfrac{1}{2}\sigma^2 \Delta t > 0.$$

But this yields the requirement that the time discretization must be sufficiently fine, i.e. we must have

(4.28) $$n > \frac{T \cdot \sigma^2}{4}.$$

The option price in the binomial model. It is easy to show that the stock price model given by the binomial tree together with the possibility of a bond investment at times $i \cdot T/n$ (with a bond price $P_0(t) = e^{rt}$) constitute a complete market. Of course, there the price of an option is given as the discounted expectation of the payoff B in $t = T$ with respect to the unique equivalent martingale measure Q_n (see Exercise (8)). Q_n itself is given by the "upwards probability" $q = q_n$. For a given u and d with

$$0 < d < e^{r\Delta t} < u$$

we obtain q from the martingale requirement

$$(4.29) \quad 0 = E_{Q_n}\left(\frac{P_1^{(n)}(i)}{P_0\left(i \cdot \frac{T}{n}\right)} - \frac{P_1^{(n)}(i-1)}{P_0\left((i-1) \cdot \frac{T}{n}\right)} \,\Big|\, F_{i-1}^{(n)}\right)$$

$$= \frac{P_1^{(n)}(i-1)}{P_0\left((i-1) \cdot \frac{T}{n}\right)} \cdot \left((q \cdot u + (1-q) \cdot d) e^{-r\frac{T}{n}} - 1\right)$$

as

$$q = \frac{e^{r \cdot \frac{T}{n}} - d}{u - d}.$$

Typically, for the choice of u, d as in (4.26) this q differs from $1/2$. Thus, the value $E^{(n)}(e^{-rT}B_n)$ that we compute as an approximation for the option price $E_Q(e^{-rT}B)$ in the continuous model will in general *not* coincide with the option price $E_{Q_n}(e^{-rT}B_n)$ in the binomial model. Of course, there should be a comment on this.

The use of binomial trees serves us only as a method of numerical approximation of the expectation $E_Q(e^{-rT}B)$. The fact that this expectation is an option price has no meaning for our numerical method. Therefore, there is also no reason why the approximating sequence for this expectation should be option prices in some discretized models.

Another method of approximation of $E_Q(e^{-rT}B)$ is to determine q, u, d via requiring the equality of the first two moments of the increments of the discrete- and the continuous-time price processes. Equality of the first moment of the increments together with the independence and identical distribution of all increments in the binomial model imply the martingale condition (4.29). We could then choose u, d in such a way that the second moment of the increments of both price models coincide. So we always compute the option price in the binomial model given by n, q, u, d as an approximation for the option price in the continuous model. Although this concept ("approximate the option price in the continuous model by the discrete-time model option price") seems to be appealing, it cannot be justified by weak convergence arguments.

Computation of the expected discounted payoff in the binomial tree. The possibility of an efficient calculation of the expectation $E^{(n)}(e^{-rT}B_n)$ depends heavily on the type of functional B (respectively its discretized variant B_n). We shall illustrate this with two examples for the case of $n = 2$, a European call and a double-barrier knockout call.

Let us choose $q = 1/2$ and as example we choose the market parameters $r = 0$, $\sigma = 0.5$, $T = 2$, $p = 1$. Then we obtain the binomial tree given in Figure 4.4 for $P_1^{(2)}(i)$.

4.3. Approximation via Binomial Trees

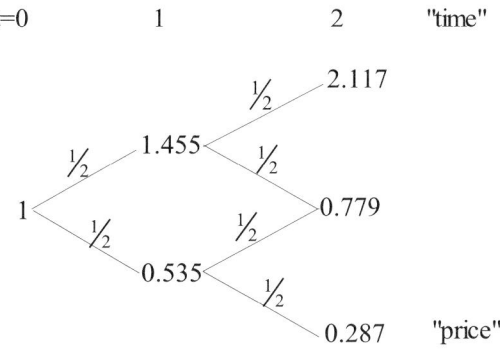

Figure 4.4. Binomial tree

Our aim is to value a European option with a payoff of the form

$$B = f(P_1(T)).$$

We approximate its value by using the above two-period binomial tree and the discretized variant of the payoff

$$B_2 = f\left(P_1^{(2)}(2)\right).$$

The corresponding discounted expected payoff in the discretized model can easily be calculated via backwards induction as

$$E^{(2)}(B_2) = \tfrac{1}{2}\left(\tfrac{1}{2}\left[f(2.117) + f(0.779)\right]\right) + \tfrac{1}{2}\left(\tfrac{1}{2}\left[f(0.779) + f(0.287)\right]\right).$$

More precisely, we first compute the expected discounted payments in the two states $P_1^{(2)}(1) = 1.455$ and $P_1^{(2)}(1) = 0.535$ at time $t = 1$. Then the expected discounted value at time $t = 0$ can be obtained as the arithmetic mean of the two expected values just computed.

For a European call option with strike $K = 0.5$ we would thus get an approximate value of

$$E^{(2)}(B_2) = \tfrac{1}{4} \cdot 1.617 + \tfrac{1}{2} \cdot 0.279 = 0.54375.$$

(compare this with the Black-Scholes value of 0.5416)

This simple backwards induction principle is generally valid for options with a payoff of the form:

$$B = f(P_1(T)).$$

To formulate it let $B_n = f(P_1^{(n)}(n))$ and

$$V^{(n)}\left(i \cdot \tfrac{T}{n}, P_1^{(n)}(i)\right) := E^{(n)}\left(e^{-r\left(T - i \cdot \tfrac{T}{n}\right)} \cdot B_n \,\Big|\, P_1^{(n)}(i)\right)$$

be the expected payoff in $t = T$ discounted back to $t = i \cdot T/n$, if the stock price in the binomial model at time $i \cdot T/n$ attains the value $P_1^{(n)}(i)$. Then, the expected discounted payoff of the option in the binomial model can be obtained according to the following recursion

$$V^{(n)}\left(T, P_1^{(n)}(n)\right) = f\left(P_1^{(n)}(n)\right),$$

$$V^{(n)}\left(i \cdot \tfrac{T}{n}, P_1^{(n)}(i)\right) =$$
$$\tfrac{1}{2}\left[V^{(n)}\left((i+1)\tfrac{T}{n}, uP_1^{(n)}(i)\right) + V^{(n)}\left((i+1)\tfrac{T}{n}, dP_1^{(n)}(i)\right)\right] \cdot e^{-r\tfrac{T}{n}}$$
$$\text{for } i = n-1, ..., 0,$$

$$E^{(n)}\left(e^{-rT} B_n\right) = V^{(n)}(0, p).$$

However, if we would implement the algorithm we would not discount at each step, but only in the end to save the time consuming evaluation of the exponential function. The big advantage of calculating the above mean according to the backwards induction scheme lies in the fact that we only have to compute an arithmetic mean of two numbers in each node of the tree. More precisely, we only have to calculate $n \cdot (n-1)/2$ arithmetic means although the stock price can follow 2^n different paths in the binomial tree. The main reason for that is that the binomial tree constitutes a recombining tree, i.e. adjacent paths can recombine at the next time step. In particular, paths having the same number of upwards and downwards movements lead to the same node in the tree and thus consequently to the same final payment.

In the case of path-dependent options the simple backward induction recursion has to be slightly modified to take into account the path dependency. We shall explain this in the case of a double barrier knockout call with payoff

$$B_{DB}^{Call} = (P_1(T) - 0.5)^+ \cdot 1_{\{P_1(t) \in [0.4, 1.4] \text{ for all } t \in [0,T]\}}$$

and its discrete variant

$$\left(B_{DB}^{Call}\right)_2 = \left(P_1^{(2)}(2) - 0.5\right)^+ \cdot 1_{\left\{P_1^{(2)}(i) \in [0.4, 1.4],\, i=0,1,2\right\}}$$
$$= 0.279 \cdot 1_{\left\{P_1^{(2)}(2)=0.779,\, P_1^{(2)}(1)=0.535\right\}}.$$

The discrete-time approximation of the double-barrier knockout call price is then given as

$$E^{(2)}(B_2) = \tfrac{1}{4} \cdot 0.279 = 0.06975.$$

In contrast to the option given by $f(P_1(T))$, the final payoff $(B_{DB}^{Call})_2$ of the double-barrier knockout call at $T = 2$ in the state of $P_1^{(2)}(2) = 0.779$ can attain the two possible values 0 and 0.279. This is typical for the behavior of path-dependent options. The path-dependent final payoff can in the extreme case lead to a situation that each path of the stock price yields a different final payment. The maximum number of different values of final payments

4.3. Approximation via Binomial Trees

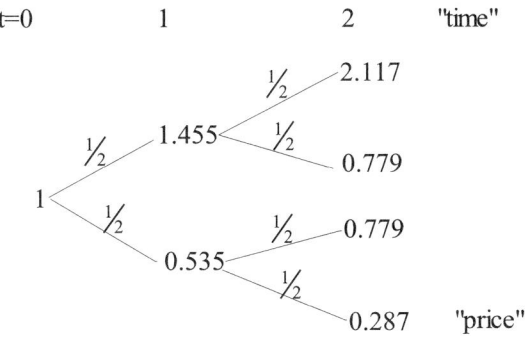

Figure 4.5. Non-recombining binomial tree

is thus 2^n, which can lead to an enormous complexity of both computations and storage for big values of n.

In the case of the double-barrier knockout call, these remarks are valid, but we can make some simplifications to keep the backward induction algorithm efficient. Note first that the binomial tree which corresponds to the above computation of $E^{(2)}(B_{DB}^{Call})_2$ formally has the usual recombining form of a binomial tree. However, the option prices in the node $P_1^{(2)}(2) = 0.779$ are not unique. Here, the payoff depends on the path reaching this node. Thus, we could indeed talk of a non-recombining tree as indicated in Figure 4.5.

The principle of backward induction stays valid, but for a general path-dependent option we have to calculate up to 2^{i-1} arithmetic means at time i (compare this to just $i+1$ such means in the non-path-dependent case). However, in the double-barrier knockout case, we can circumvent this problem by simply proceeding backwards in the recombining tree, but setting the option price to zero in all such nodes where we realize that the knockout-condition is satisfied. So the computational complexity is comparable to that of a European non-path-dependent option.

In other cases such as an average option with final payment of

$$B_{Av}^{Call} = \left(\frac{1}{T} \int_0^T P_1(t) \, dt - K \right)^+,$$

respectively its discrete variant

$$\left(B_{Av}^{Call} \right)_n = \left(\frac{1}{n+1} \sum_{i=0}^n P_1^{(n)}(i) - K \right)^+,$$

the full non-recombining tree has to be considered for the (approximative) calculation of the option price.

Convergence of the model. By Donsker's Theorem 4.10 and Theorem 4.8 the process $P_1^{(s,n)}(t)$, obtained from $P_1^{(n)}(i)$ by linear interpolation, converges weakly to the process $P_1(t)$ if the moment conditions (4.21) and (4.22) are satisfied. If also the family

$$B_{s,n} := B\left(P_1^{(s,n)}(t),\ t \in [0,T]\right)$$

of functionals of $P_1^{(s,n)}(t)$ is uniformly integrable then we obtain the convergence

(4.30) $$E^{(n)}\left(e^{-rt}B_{s,n}\right) \xrightarrow{n \to \infty} E_Q\left(e^{-rT}B\right).$$

Here, $Q^{(n)}$ is defined on the paths of $P_1^{(s,n)}(t)$ by identifying them with the corresponding paths of $P_1^{(n)}(i)$. From (4.30) we then obtain the desired convergence

$$E^{(n)}\left(e^{-rt}B_n\right) \xrightarrow{n \to \infty} E_Q\left(e^{-rT}B\right),$$

if we have

$$\lim E^{(n)}\left(e^{-rt}(B_{s,n} - B_n)\right) = 0.$$

The latter convergence however has to be proved for each type of option explicitly. It is always satisfied if the difference $(B_{s,n} - B_n)$ converges to zero uniformly. This is true for European lookbacks, barrier and double barrier options, and Asian options.

Advantages of the method. Approximation methods based on binomial trees are usually easy to implement. However, their efficiency with regard to speed and storage can depend strongly on the option type under consideration. Typically, binomial methods converge faster than Monte-Carlo simulation. For very big binomial trees, there is also the possibility of a hybrid method via combination of a binomial tree and the Monte-Carlo method: simulate a sufficiently big number of stock price paths in the binomial method and then use the arithmetic mean over the corresponding B_n as an approximation for the option price.

Disadvantages of the method. In particular for double barrier options we can observe a slow and irregular convergence behavior. The accuracy of the approximation does not necessarily increase with the fineness n. Even more, often we experience a so-called saw tooth effect, i.e. the approximative option price seems to converge with increasing n, then suddenly jumps away from the expected limit, followed again by a period of convergence, then suddenly another jump,.... The main reason for this behavior lies in the fact that we are not allowed to choose the nodes of the tree so that they lie close to the barriers.

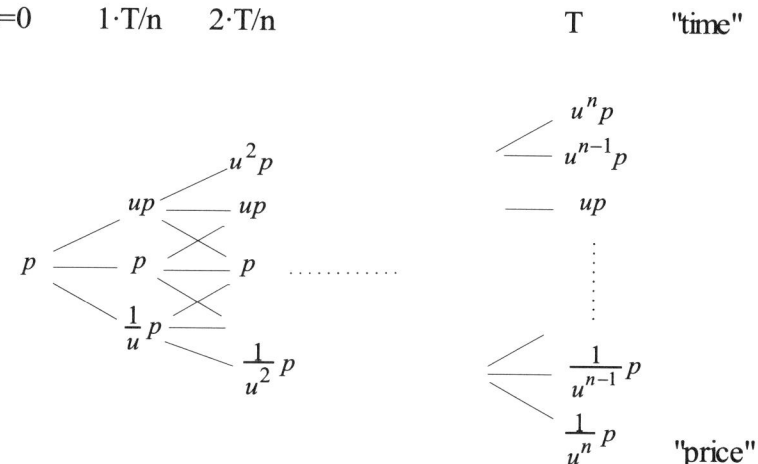

Figure 4.6. Trinomial tree

4.4. Trinomial Trees and Explicit Finite-Difference Methods

As we have already seen in Section 3.3 option prices can be obtained as solutions of corresponding Cauchy problems under certain assumptions. This is in particular the case for options having a final payment of the form

$$B = f(P_1(T))$$

for a suitable f (see Proposition 3.19). If the corresponding Cauchy problem does not admit an explicit analytical solution (or if one is not able to determine it), then there remains the possibility of solving the Cauchy problem numerically. The presentation of such numerical algorithms for solving partial differential equations is beyond the scope of this book. We refer the interested reader to [**W/D/H 93**]. Here we would like to point out that also in the area of numerical methods there is a connection between stochastic methods and partial differential equation methods similar to the Feynman-Kac theorem. We therefore first look at the approximation of the Black-Scholes model by a recombining trinomial tree.

Here we consider a discrete-time stock price process $P_1^{(n)}(i)$, $i = 0, 1, ..., n$, with possible paths in a trinomial tree; see Figure 4.6. For arbitrage reasons we must have

(4.31) $$\frac{1}{u} < e^{r \cdot \frac{T}{n}} < u$$

for a positive u. Further, the probabilities for an upwards movement should equal q_1 in each node of the tree, and those for a downwards movement should equal q_2. Thus, the probability for the stock price to rest at the same level equals $q_3 = 1 - (q_1 + q_2)$. Let

(4.32) $$0 < q_1, q_2 < 1, \quad q_1 + q_2 \leq 1.$$

In the case of $q_1 + q_2 = 1$ we would be in the binomial situation again; therefore we assume $q_1 + q_2 < 1$. Donsker's Theorem 4.12 for triangular schemes again implies weak convergence of $P_1^{(n)}(i)$, $i = 0, 1, ..., n$, (more precisely, convergence of its continuous-time variant) to the stock price process (in the risk-neutral market)

$$P_1(t) = p \cdot \exp\left(\left(r - \tfrac{1}{2}\sigma^2\right) t + \sigma W(t)\right),$$

if the first two moments of the increments of $\ln(P_1(t))$ between $(i-1) \cdot T/n$ and $i \cdot T/n$

$$\ln\left(\frac{P_1(i \cdot \tfrac{T}{n})}{P_1((i-1) \cdot \tfrac{T}{n})}\right),$$

coincide with the corresponding increments of $\ln(P_1^{(n)}(i))$. This leads to the following equations

(4.33) $$\left(r - \tfrac{1}{2}\sigma^2\right) \Delta t = \ln(u) \cdot q_1 + \ln\left(\frac{1}{u}\right) \cdot q_2,$$

(4.34) $$\left(r - \tfrac{1}{2}\sigma^2\right)^2 (\Delta t)^2 + \sigma^2 \Delta t = \ln(u)^2 \cdot q_1 + \ln\left(\frac{1}{u}\right)^2 \cdot q_2.$$

For a given $u > 0$ we can determine q_1, q_2 by solving the above linear system (compare to the binomial model). Here we will not do this; instead we consider the widely-used method of Cox-Ross-Rubinstein. They propose to choose

(4.35) $$u = e^{\lambda \sigma \sqrt{\Delta t}} := e^{\Delta x}$$

for some $\lambda \in [1, \infty)$ and to neglect terms of higher order than Δt in equation (4.34). For small Δt the error will be negligible. Then, from (4.33), (4.34), (4.35), we obtain the equations

(4.36) $$\lambda \sigma \sqrt{\Delta t} (q_1 - q_2) = \left(r - \tfrac{1}{2}\sigma^2\right) \Delta t,$$

(4.37) $$\lambda^2 \sigma^2 \Delta t (q_1 + q_2) = \sigma^2 \Delta t.$$

Their solutions are given as

(4.38) $$q_1 = \tfrac{1}{2}\left(\left(r - \tfrac{1}{2}\sigma^2\right) \frac{1}{\lambda \sigma} \sqrt{\Delta t} + \frac{1}{\lambda^2}\right),$$

(4.39) $$q_2 = \tfrac{1}{2}\left(\frac{1}{\lambda^2} - \left(r - \tfrac{1}{2}\sigma^2\right) \frac{1}{\lambda \sigma} \sqrt{\Delta t}\right).$$

4.4. Trinomial Trees and Explicit Finite-Difference Methods

For sufficiently small Δt (i.e. sufficiently large n), q_1, q_2, q_3 lie in the interval $(0,1)$. Note in particular that the choice of $\lambda = 1$ would yield a binomial model.

As in the binomial model we obtain the following algorithm (where for a fixed n the probability measure $Q^{(n)}$ is given by $q_1, q_2, q_3 = 1 - (q_1 + q_2)$, obtained from (4.38), (4.39), and B_n is defined as in Section 4.3).

Algorithm: *Approximation by trinomial trees*

(1) For $n \gg 1$ set up a suitable trinomial tree for the discrete-time price process $P_1^{(n)}(i)$ (see (4.35), (4.38), (4.39)).

(2) Compute the expected discounted final payment $E^{(n)}(e^{-rT}B_n)$ in the discrete-time model as an approximation for $E_Q(e^{-rT}B)$.

Computation of $E^{(n)}(e^{-rT}B_n)$. Again, we compute $E^{(n)}(e^{-rT}B_n)$ in the trinomial model via backward induction. Let therefore

$$X_1^{(n)}(i) := \ln\left(P_1^{(n)}(i)\right), \ i = 0, 1, ..., n,$$

$$V^{(n)}\left(i \cdot \Delta t, X_1^{(n)}(i)\right) := E^{(n)}\left(e^{-r(T - i \cdot \Delta t)} B_n \,\middle|\, P_1^{(n)}(i)\right).$$

Then, in analogy to the binomial model, compute recursively:

(4.40) $$V^{(n)}\left(T, X_1^{(n)}(n)\right) = f\left(\exp\left(X_1^{(n)}(n)\right)\right),$$

$$V^{(n)}\left(i \cdot \Delta t, X_1^{(n)}(i)\right) = \left[q_1 V^{(n)}\left((i+1)\Delta t, X_1^{(n)}(i) + \Delta x\right)\right.$$
$$\left. + q_3 V^{(n)}\left((i+1)\Delta t, X_1^{(n)}(i)\right) + q_2 V^{(n)}\left((i+1)\Delta t, X_1^{(n)}(i) - \Delta x\right)\right] e^{-r\Delta t},$$
$$i = n-1, ..., 0,$$

$$E^{(n)}\left(e^{-rT} B_n\right) = V^{(n)}(0, p).$$

Convergence of the method follows in a similar way as in the binomial model from Donsker's Theorem 4.10 and the uniform integrability of the B_n which has to be checked separately. For details (also concerning the approximation given by equation (4.36) and (4.37)) see [**C/R/R 79**].

The option price in the trinomial model. In general the final payment of a European call cannot be replicated by a trading strategy in stock and bond in the trinomial model (see Exercise (9)). Also, for this model there exists a whole family of equivalent martingale measures. Hence, the alternative method indicated in the binomial model "compute the option price in an approximating model" cannot be performed without further modifications. Even more: we have not developed a method yet to compute an option price in incomplete markets!

Relations between trinomial trees and explicit finite-difference methods. By Proposition 3.19 the option price solves the following Cauchy problem (given suitable assumptions):

(4.41) $\quad V_t + \frac{1}{2}\sigma^2 p^2 V_{pp} + rpV_p - rV = 0, \ (t,p) \in [0,T] \times (0,\infty),$

$$V(T,p) = f(p), \ p > 0.$$

With the substitution $x = \ln(p)$ and the notations

$$\tilde{V}(t,x) := V(t,p),$$

the problem (4.41) is transformed into the problem

(4.42) $\quad \tilde{V}_t + \frac{1}{2}\sigma^2 \tilde{V}_{xx} + \left(r - \frac{1}{2}\sigma^2\right)\tilde{V}_x - r\tilde{V} = 0, \ (t,x) \in [0,T] \times \mathbb{R},$

$$\tilde{V}(T,x) = f(e^x), \ x \in \mathbb{R}.$$

A popular numerical solution method for solving (4.42) is the so-called explicit finite-difference method. It is based on the method of replacing all partial derivatives appearing in (4.42) by the following difference quotients for a given time discretization $0, \Delta t, 2\Delta t, ..., T$ and space discretization $\ln(p_1)$, $\ln(p_1) \pm \Delta x$, $\ln(p_1) \pm 2\Delta x$, ...:

$$\Delta_t \tilde{V}^{(n)}(t,x) := \frac{\tilde{V}^{(n)}(t+\Delta t, x) - \tilde{V}^{(n)}(t,x)}{\Delta t},$$

$$\Delta_x \tilde{V}^{(n)}(t,x) := \frac{\tilde{V}^{(n)}(t+\Delta t, x+\Delta x) - \tilde{V}^{(n)}(t+\Delta t, x-\Delta x)}{2\Delta x},$$

$$\Delta_{xx} \tilde{V}^{(n)}(t,x) :=$$
$$\frac{\tilde{V}^{(n)}(t+\Delta t, x+\Delta x) - 2\tilde{V}^{(n)}(t+\Delta t, x) + \tilde{V}^{(n)}(t+\Delta t, x-\Delta x)}{(\Delta x)^2}.$$

With the notations of

$$t_i := i \cdot \Delta t, \quad i = 0, 1, ..., n,$$
$$X(j) := \ln(p_1) + j \cdot \Delta x, \quad j \in \mathbb{Z},$$

substituting the differential quotients (= partial derivatives) in (4.42) by "finite differences", and solving for $\tilde{V}^{(n)}(t_i, X(j))$, this leads to

(4.43) $\tilde{V}^{(n)}(t_i, X(j)) =$

$$\frac{1}{1+r\Delta t} \left\{ \left(\frac{1}{2}\sigma^2 \frac{\Delta t}{(\Delta x)^2} + \frac{1}{2}\left(r - \frac{\sigma^2}{2}\right)\frac{\Delta t}{\Delta x}\right) \tilde{V}^{(n)}(t_i + \Delta t, X(j) + \Delta x) \right.$$
$$+ \left(1 - \sigma^2 \frac{\Delta t}{(\Delta x)^2}\right) \tilde{V}^{(n)}(t_i + \Delta t, X(j))$$
$$\left. + \left(\frac{1}{2}\sigma^2 \frac{\Delta t}{(\Delta x)^2} - \frac{1}{2}\left(r - \frac{\sigma^2}{2}\right)\frac{\Delta t}{\Delta x}\right) \tilde{V}^{(n)}(t_i + \Delta t, X(j) - \Delta x) \right\}.$$

As at time T we already know all values of $\tilde{V}^{(n)}(T, x)$ due to the boundary condition, we can obtain $\tilde{V}^{(n)}(T - \Delta t, X(j))$ from the above explicit representation. Via backward induction with step size Δt we reach the starting time $t = 0$ in n steps and in particular obtain $\tilde{V}^{(n)}(0, x)$ as an approximation for the option price $\tilde{V}(0, x)$.

Comparison of (4.35), (4.38), (4.39) with the recursion (4.43) immediately shows that recursion (4.40) in the trinomial tree can be seen as a special finite difference scheme (if we neglect the difference of the two discount factors $e^{-r\Delta T}$ and $(1 + r\Delta t)^{-1}$). We obtain convergence of $\tilde{V}^{(n)}(0, x)$ to $\tilde{V}(0, x)$ if the stability condition

$$0 < \frac{\Delta t}{(\Delta x)^2} \leq \frac{1}{\sigma^2}$$

is satisfied (see Section 8.4 in [**W/D/H 95**]). The proof of this assertion and the presentation of other discretization methods for solving the partial differential equation (4.42) can be found in [**W/D/H 93**].

4.5. The Pathwise Binomial Approach of Rogers and Stapleton

Description of the basic idea. While in the usual binomial method as given in Section 4.3 only the distribution of $P_1(t)$ is approximated by a simpler, discrete distribution, the method of Rogers and Stapleton is based on approximating each single path of $P_1(t)$ by a step function. Here, the approximating step function is only allowed to attain values in a given discrete set and should at most deviate by a given accuracy ϵ from the corresponding path of $P_1(t)$. The decisive idea of Rogers and Stapleton now consists of interpreting the set of all possible paths of such a step function as an infinite binomial tree. Then, they give an algorithm that determines how to compute the (approximate) discounted expected payment of an option in such an infinite tree as an approximation for the option price in the Black-Scholes model.

Algorithm: *Pathwise binomial approach of Rogers and Stapleton*

(1) For a given accuracy Δy and starting point $y := \ln(p_1)$ set up an infinite binomial tree.

(2) Compute the discounted payoff $E^{(\Delta y)}(e^{-rT} B_{\Delta y})$ of the option in the infinite binomial tree as an approximation for $E_Q(e^{-rT} B)$.

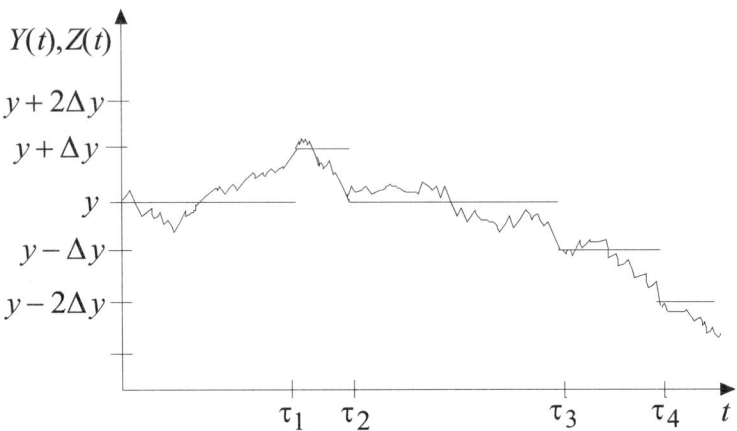

Figure 4.7. Approximation by a step function

Construction of the infinite binomial tree.

i) Approximation

We look at the logarithm $Y(t)$ of the stock price

$$Y(t) = \ln(P_1(t)) = \underbrace{\ln(p_1)}_{=:y} + \sigma \cdot W(t) + \left(r - \tfrac{1}{2}\sigma^2\right) \cdot t.$$

For a given accuracy $\Delta y > 0$ and for each $\omega \in \Omega$, $t \in [0, T]$, we define an approximating step function $Z(t)$ via

$$\tau_0(\omega) := 0,$$
$$\tau_n(\omega) := \inf\{t \in [0,T] \mid t > \tau_{n-1}(\omega),$$
$$|Y(t,\omega) - Y(\tau_{n-1}(\omega),\omega)| > \Delta y\}, \ n = 1, 2, ...,$$
$$\xi_0(\omega) := y,$$
$$\xi_n(\omega) := Y(\tau_n, \omega),$$
$$Z(t,\omega) := \sum_{n=0}^{\infty} \xi_n(\omega) \cdot 1_{[\tau_n, \tau_{n+1})}(t).$$

This means: as soon as $Y(t)$ deviates from the current value of the step function $Z(t)$ by Δy, the step function will be set at exactly this value of $Y(t)$. By construction of $Z(t)$ we then have

$$\sup_{0 \leq t \leq T} |Y(t) - Z(t)| \leq \Delta y.$$

Note that for given y and Δy, $Z(t)$ can only attain values in the set $\{y \pm i\Delta y \mid i \in \mathbb{N}\}$. Further, $Z(t)$ can only jump to the adjacent values $Z(t) \pm \Delta y$; see Figure 4.7. For fixed ω, $Z(t, \omega)$ can only take finitely many values on $[0, T]$. However, there is no a priori upper bound for the number

4.5. The Pathwise Binomial Approach of Rogers and Stapleton

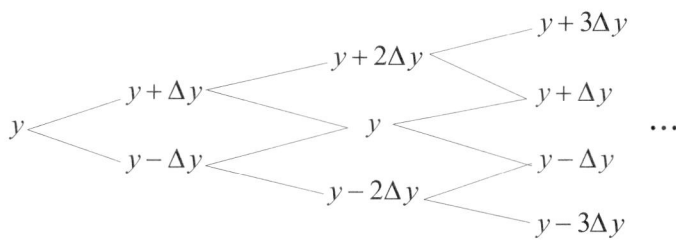

Figure 4.8. Infinite binomial tree

of values that $Z(t,\omega)$ can attain on $[0,T]$. Therefore, we can identify the sequence of values of the step function $Z(t,\omega)$ on $[0,T]$ with a finite path in the infinite binomial tree; see Figure 4.8.

ii) Computation of the transition probabilities

We demonstrate the other basic features of the algorithm by looking at a double barrier knockout call for $Y(t) = \ln(P_1(t))$. Thus, let the final option payment B be given as

$$B = (P_1(T) - K)^+ \cdot 1_{\{\ln(P_1(t)) \in (b_*, b^*) \text{ for all } t \in [0,T]\}}.$$

Here, $K \geq 0$ is the strike price. The real numbers $b_* < y < b^*$ define the interval in which $Y(t)$ has to stay so that the call is still valid in $t = T$. If $Y(t)$ leaves the interval (b_*, b^*) before T then the option runs out worthless. By Corollary 3.15 the price of this call is given by

$$x_B = E_Q\left(e^{-r(T)}(P_1(T) - K)^+ \cdot 1_{\{\ln(P_1(t)) \in (b_*, b^*) \text{ for all } t \in [0,T]\}}\right).$$

We shall calculate this price approximately with the help of the infinite binomial tree. To do this, the infinite tree will be decomposed in finite subtrees. For a fixed $n \in \mathbb{N}$ the possible paths of the step functions $Z(t)$ containing exactly n jumps on $[0,T]$ will be identified with an n-period binomial tree. In this finite tree we are able to calculate the expected discounted payment of the option if the transition probabilities from a node to its successors in the tree are determined. As we have coincidence of the values of $Z(t)$ and $Y(t)$ in both the times τ_{n-1} and τ_n, the transition probabilities in the tree coincide with those of $Y(t)$ to $Y(t) \pm \Delta y$. They can be obtained with the help of Theorem 4.15.

Theorem 4.15. *For a given $\Delta y > 0$ the probability for an upwards movement of $Z(t)$ in τ_n, $n \in \mathbb{N}$, is given by*

$$q = \frac{s(0) - s(-\Delta y)}{s(\Delta y) - s(-\Delta y)}$$

with

$$c := \frac{r - \frac{1}{2}\sigma^2}{\sigma^2} \quad \text{and} \quad s(x) := -e^{-2cx}.$$

The probability for a downwards movement of $Z(t)$ in τ_n, $n \in \mathbb{N}$, is $(1-q)$.

Proof. As the increments $W(t) - W(s)$ of a Brownian motion behave as a Brownian motion $W^*(t-s)$, all the transitions of $Z(t)$ at the jump times τ_n, $n \in \mathbb{N}$, have the same distribution independent of the actual value of $Y(t)$. It therefore suffices to prove the above assertion for the transition of $Z(\tau_0)$ to $Z(\tau_1)$. As we have discussed before, we only have to determine the probability distribution of $Y(t)$ in τ_1 as it coincides with $Z(\tau_1)$ if we have $\tau_1 < T$.

Let $\tau_1^{(n)} := \tau_1 \wedge n$. Then, for a twice continuously differentiable function f, the Itô formula yields

$$f\left(Y\left(\tau_1^{(n)}\right)\right) = f(y) + \int_0^{\tau_1^{(n)}} \left(f'(Y(s))\mu + \tfrac{1}{2}f''(Y(s))\sigma^2\right) ds$$

$$+ \int_0^{\tau_1^{(n)}} f'(Y(s))\sigma\, dW(s)$$

with $\mu := r - \tfrac{1}{2}\sigma^2$. As by the definition of τ_1 we have

$$Y(s) \in [y - \Delta y, y + \Delta y] \text{ for all } s \in [0, \tau_1^{(n)}],$$

$f'(Y(s))$ is bounded on $[0, \tau_1^{(n)}]$ yielding

$$E\left(\int_0^{\tau_1^{(n)}} f'(Y(s))\, dW(s)\right) = 0.$$

This implies

(4.44) $\quad E\left(f\left(Y\left(\tau_1^{(n)}\right)\right)\right)$

$$= f(y) + E\left(\int_0^{\tau_1^{(n)}} \left(f'(Y(s))\mu + \tfrac{1}{2}f''(Y(s))\sigma^2\right) ds\right).$$

Now to determine q we look for an $f \in C^2$ with

(4.45) $\quad \tfrac{1}{2}f''(x)\sigma^2 + f'(x)\mu = 0$ for all $x \in (y - \Delta y, y + \Delta y)$

$$f(y - \Delta y) = 0$$
$$f(y + \Delta y) = 1$$

4.5. The Pathwise Binomial Approach of Rogers and Stapleton

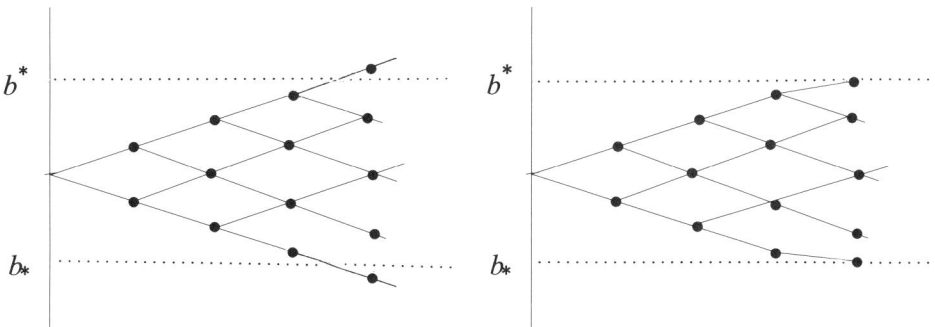

Figure 4.9. Binomial tree   **Figure 4.10.** Modified binomial tree

Due to
$$\lim_{n \to \infty} E\left(f\left(Y\left(\tau_1^{(n)}\right)\right)\right) = E\left(f\left(Y\left(\tau_1\right)\right)\right)$$
and the definition of τ_1 (note that $P(\tau_1 < \infty) = 1$), (4.44) and (4.45) together with
$$E\left(f\left(Y(\tau_1)\right)\right) = q \cdot f(y + \Delta y) + (1 - q) \cdot f(y - \Delta y),$$
we obtain
$$q \cdot 1 = f(y).$$
Explicit solution of the boundary value problem (4.45) via integration, followed by solving the obtained first order linear differential equation by variation of constants and explicit determination of the constants of integration using the boundary condition, leads to

$$f(x) = \frac{1 - \exp\left(-\frac{2\mu}{\sigma^2}(x - (y - \Delta y))\right)}{1 - \exp\left(-\frac{2\mu}{\sigma^2} \cdot 2\Delta y\right)}$$

$$= \frac{\exp\left(\frac{2\mu}{\sigma^2}\Delta y\right) - \exp\left(-\frac{2\mu}{\sigma^2}(x - y)\right)}{\exp\left(\frac{2\mu}{\sigma^2}\Delta y\right) - \exp\left(-\frac{2\mu}{\sigma^2}\Delta y\right)}.$$

Insertion of y into $f(x)$ yields the assertion. □

Continuation: Double-barrier knockout call. For the specific application to the double-barrier knockout call all paths in the tree which exceed b_* by below and b^* by above have zero value; see Figures 4.9 and 4.10. If the process $Z(t)$ differs from b_* or b^* by a value less than Δy then we have to take extra care. To prevent the option being knocked out by the $Y(.)$-process before it is knocked out by the $Z(.)$-process, we have to modify our definition of the $Z(.)$-process. Note that $Y(t)$ can reach the boundary values b_* or b^*, thereby knocking out the option, but it is possible that $Y(t)$

never reaches a value that would cause $Z(t)$ to jump again. To avoid this unpleasant fact, we choose the corresponding node in the tree such that it is exactly b_* or b^*. This ensures a jump of the step function $Z(t)$ exactly when b_* or b^* is reached and not – too late – when $Z(t) - \Delta y$ or $Z(t) + \Delta y$ is reached.

This modification of $Z(t)$ has some remarkable consequences. So $Z(t)$ only attains values in the modified binomial tree. The final payment of the double-barrier knockout call in the modified binomial tree, $B_{\Delta y}$, is given by

$$B_{\Delta y} = \left(e^{Z(T)} - K\right)^+ \cdot 1_{\{Z(t)\in(b_*,b^*) \text{ for all } t\in[0,T]\}}.$$

A further important consequence of the above modification of $Z(t)$ is that $Z(t)$ reaches one of the barriers b_* or b^* if and only if $Y(t)$ reaches the same barrier, i.e. we have

$$1_{\{Z(t)\in(b_*,b^*) \text{ for all } t\in[0,T]\}} = 1_{\{Y(t)\in(b_*,b^*) \text{ for all } t\in[0,T]\}}$$

and the option is knocked out before T in the original model if it is knocked out before T in the modified binomial model. For the pricing of the double-barrier knockout call, it plays no role if we define $Z(t)$ to be constant after reaching b_* or b^* or extend it as it was originally defined. However, it is important for the pricing purpose that the transition probabilities in the modified tree change for $Z(t) \in (b^* - \Delta y, b^*)$ or $Z(t) \in (b_*, b_* + \Delta y)$.

Theorem 4.16. (1) *If we have $Y(\tau_n) = y^*$ with $y^* \in (b^* - \Delta y, b^*)$ then we obtain*

$$q^* = P(Z(\tau_{n+1}) = y^* - \Delta y \mid Z(\tau_n) = y^*) = \frac{s(b^*) - s(y^*)}{s(b^*) - s(y^* - \Delta y)}.$$

With probability $1 - q^*$ $Z(\tau_{n+1})$ reaches the value b^* and the option runs out worthless.

(2) *In case of $Y(\tau_n) = y_*$ with $y_* \in (b_*, b_* + \Delta y)$, we obtain*

$$q_* = P(Z(\tau_{n+1}) = y_* + \Delta y \mid Z(\tau_n) = y_*) = \frac{s(y_*) - s(b_*)}{s(y_* + \Delta y) - s(b_*)}.$$

With probability $1 - q_*$ $Z(\tau_{n+1})$ reaches b_* and the option runs out worthless.

Proof. The proof is similar to that of Theorem 4.15. Only the boundary conditions now have to hold in $y^* - \Delta y$ and b^* (or in b_* and $y_* + \Delta y$). □

Putting together the results of the last two theorems yields a recursion for computing the expected final payment given the number of jumps of $Z(t)$ in $[0,T]$.

4.5. The Pathwise Binomial Approach of Rogers and Stapleton

Proposition 4.17. *Let $\Psi(k,y)$ be the expected final payment of the option in the binomial model for an initial value of $Z(0) = y \in (b_*, b^*)$ and a given number $k \in \mathbb{N} \cup \{0\}$ of upwards and downwards movements of $Z(t)$ on $[0, T]$. Then $\Psi(k, y)$ can be computed inductively according to the following algorithm*

$$\Psi(0, y) = (e^y - K)^+,$$

$$\Psi(n+1, y) = q(y) \cdot \Psi(n, y + \Delta y) + \underline{q}(y) \cdot \Psi(n, y - \Delta y),$$
$$n = 0, 1, 2, \ldots$$

Here the probabilities $q(y)$ for $y \in (b_* + \Delta y, b^* - \Delta y)$ are given by Theorem 4.15. For the same values of y, we have $\underline{q}(y) = 1 - q(y)$. For $y \in (b_*, b_* + \Delta y)$ we have $q(y) = 0$ and $\underline{q}(y)$ is given by q_* in Theorem 4.16 (2). For $y \in (b^* - \Delta y, b^*)$ we have $\underline{q}(y) = 0$ and $q(y)$ is given by q^* in Theorem 4.16 (1).

Proof. Note that setting $q(y)$ and $\underline{q}(y)$ equal to zero on the upper and the lower boundaries of the modified tree yields that paths for which the option runs out worthless do not enter the option price. With this in mind the remaining assertion follows from the preceding two theorems. □

Now for the computation of the discounted expected final payment of the option in the modified binomial tree,

$$E^{(\Delta y)}\left(e^{-rT} B_{\Delta y}\right) = \sum_{n=0}^{\infty} P(v = n) \cdot \Psi(n, y) \cdot e^{-rT},$$

we still need the probability distribution of the sum v of upwards and downwards movements of the stock price in the binomial model. Due to the relation

$$\{\omega \,|\, v(\omega) \geq n\} = \{\omega \,|\, \tau_n(\omega) \leq T\}$$

this distribution can be obtained from that of τ_n as we have

$$P(v = n) = P(v \leq n) - P(v \leq n - 1) = P(\tau_n \geq T) - P(\tau_{n-1} \geq T).$$

Although there is no nice explicit form for this expression, the following theorem helps us to obtain it approximately:

Theorem 4.18. (1) *The random variables $\{\tau_{n+1} - \tau_n\}_{n \in \mathbb{N} \cup \{0\}}$ are independent and identically distributed. Their Laplace transform $\varphi(\lambda)$ is given by*

$$\varphi(\lambda) = E\left(e^{-\lambda \tau_1}\right) = \frac{\cosh\left(\mu \sigma^{-2} \Delta y\right)}{\cosh(\gamma \Delta y)}$$

with $\mu := r - \frac{1}{2}\sigma^2$, $\gamma := \dfrac{\sqrt{\mu^2 + 2\lambda \sigma^2}}{\sigma^2}$, $\lambda > 0$.

(2) $E(\tau_1) = \dfrac{\Delta y}{\mu} \cdot \tanh\left(\dfrac{\mu}{\sigma^2} \cdot \Delta y\right)$ for $\mu \neq 0$,

$$E(\tau_1^2) = 2(E(\tau_1))^2 + \dfrac{\sigma^2 \Delta y}{\mu^3} \cdot \tanh\left(\dfrac{\mu}{\sigma^2}\right) \Delta y - \left(\dfrac{\Delta y}{\mu}\right)^2 \text{ for } \mu \neq 0.$$

(3) $\tau_{n+1} - \tau_n$ is independent of ξ_{n+1}.

Proof. (1) Similarly to the proof of Theorem 4.15 we obtain $\varphi(\lambda)$ as explicit solution of the boundary value problem

(4.46) $\quad \tfrac{1}{2}\sigma^2 g''(z) - \mu g'(z) - \lambda g(z) = 0$ for all $z \in (y - \Delta y, y + \Delta y)$

$$g(y - \Delta y) = 1, \; g(y + \Delta y) = 1$$

To see this we only have to consider $g(Y(\tau_1)) \cdot e^{-\lambda \tau_1}$ instead of $f(Y(\tau_1))$ in the proof of Theorem 4.15.

(2) Suitable differentiation of $\varphi(\lambda)$ to obtain $\varphi'(0)$ and $\varphi''(0)$ yields $E(\tau_1)$ and $E(\tau_1^2)$ (see Exercise (14)).

(3) As in the proof of Theorem 4.15 it is enough to consider the case of $n = 0$. But there we have

$$E\left(e^{-\lambda \tau_1}\right) = q \cdot E\left(e^{-\lambda \tau_1} \,|\, \xi_1 = y + \Delta y\right) + (1-q) \cdot E\left(e^{-\lambda \tau_1} \,|\, \xi_1 = y - \Delta y\right).$$

As in the proof of part (1) (or in the proof of Theorem 4.15) we get

$$g(y) = q \cdot E\left(e^{-\lambda \tau_1} \,|\, \xi_1 = y + \Delta y\right)$$

by solving the boundary value problem (4.46) in part (1) but with the new boundary conditions

$$g(y - \Delta y) = 0, \; g(y + \Delta y) = 1.$$

From the explicit form of $g(y)$, $\varphi(\lambda)$, and q, we get

$$E\left(e^{-\lambda \tau_1}\right) = E\left(e^{-\lambda \tau_1} \,|\, \xi_1 = y + \Delta y\right).$$

Similarly we show

$$E\left(e^{-\lambda \tau_1}\right) = E\left(e^{-\lambda \tau_1} \,|\, \xi_1 = y - \Delta y\right).$$

So the conditional and the unconditional Laplace transform coincide which proves the claimed independence.

$\square$

As we have $\tau_n = \sum_{i=1}^n (\tau_i - \tau_{i-1})$ and as the summands are independent and identically distributed, the central limit theorem yields

$$\dfrac{\tau_n - n \cdot E(\tau_1)}{\sqrt{n \cdot \text{Var}(\tau_1)}} \xrightarrow{n \to \infty} N(0,1) \text{ in distribution.}$$

4.5. The Pathwise Binomial Approach of Rogers and Stapleton

From this we can determine the distribution of τ_n approximately for large n. However, for small n this approximation is not accurate enough. Instead of it, Rogers and Stapleton use the following result given in [**PETR 95**] which we state here without proof.

Theorem 4.19. *We have*

$$P\left(\frac{\tau_n - n \cdot E(\tau_1)}{\sqrt{n \cdot \operatorname{Var}(\tau_1)}} \leq x\right) = \Phi(x) + \frac{\alpha_3 (1 - x^2) e^{-\frac{x^2}{2}}}{\sqrt{72\pi n}} + o\left(n^{-\frac{1}{2}}\right)$$

with

$$\alpha_3 := E\left(\left(\frac{\tau_1 - E(\tau_1)}{\sqrt{\operatorname{Var}(\tau_1)}}\right)^3\right),$$

where Φ is the distribution function of the standard normal distribution.

With the help of the Laplace transform $\varphi(\lambda)$ of Theorem 4.18 we can calculate α_3 (in the case of $\mu \neq 0$) as

$$\alpha_3 = \frac{\Delta y \cdot (A + B - C)}{\left(\frac{\mu}{\sigma^2}\right)^5 \sigma^6 (s(\Delta y) - 1)^3},$$

$$A = 12 \frac{\mu}{\sigma^2} \Delta y \left(s(2\Delta y) + s(\Delta y)\right),$$

$$B = 8 \cdot \left(\frac{\mu}{\sigma^2}\right)^2 (\Delta y)^2 \left(s(\Delta y) - s(2\Delta y)\right),$$

$$C = 3 \cdot (1 + s(\Delta y) - s(2\Delta y) - s(3\Delta y)).$$

Finally, we are able to formulate an algorithm.

Algorithm: *Method of Rogers and Stapleton*

(1) For a given initial value of $y = \ln(P_1(0))$ and a given accuracy of Δy, compute "all" values of

$$\Psi(k, y), \ k \in \mathbb{N} \cup \{0\}$$

according to Proposition 4.17.

(2) Compute $P(\upsilon = n) = P(\tau_n \geq T) - P(\tau_{n-1} \geq T)$ approximately from the distribution of $\{\tau_n\}_n$ with the help of Theorem 4.19 (by neglecting the $o(n^{-1/2})$-terms).

(3) Determine

$$E^{(\Delta y)}\left(e^{-rT} B_{\Delta y}\right) = \sum_{n=0}^{\infty} P(\upsilon = n) \cdot \Psi(n, y) \cdot e^{-rT}$$

as an approximation for $E_Q(e^{-rT} B)$.

Of course, for practical calculations we have to replace "all" and "∞" in the above three steps by a sufficiently large number N.

Convergence of the method. As for fixed $\Delta y > 0$ we have

$$\sup_{0 \leq t \leq T} |Y(t) - Z(t)| < \Delta y$$

we get uniform convergence of $Z(t)$ to $Y(t)$ for $\Delta y \to 0$. With the help of this inequality we can even give estimates for the approximation error. However, these estimates depend on the type of option under consideration. For example in the case of a double-barrier knockout call, where for simplicity we assume $b^* > \ln(K) > b_*$, we get the error estimate

$$\left| B_{DB}^{Call} - B_{\Delta y} \right|$$

$$= \left| \left(e^{Y(T)} - K \right)^+ - \left(e^{Z(T)} - K \right)^+ \right| \cdot 1_{\{Y(t) \in (b_*, b^*) \text{ for all } t \in [0,T]\}}$$

$$\leq \left| \left(e^{Y(T)} - K \right)^+ - \left(e^{Z(T)} - K \right)^+ \right| \cdot 1_{\{Y(T) \in (b_*, b^*)\}}$$

$$\leq \max \left\{ \max_{Y(T) \in [\ln(K), b^*)} \left| \left(e^{Y(T)} - K \right)^+ - \left(e^{Z(T)} - K \right)^+ \right|, \right.$$

$$\left. \max_{Y(T) \in (b_*, \ln(K)]} \left| \left(e^{Y(T)} - K \right)^+ - \left(e^{Z(T)} - K \right)^+ \right| \right\}$$

$$\leq \max \left\{ \left(e^{b^*} - e^{b^* - \Delta y} \right), K \cdot e^{\Delta y} - K \right\}$$

$$= \max \left\{ e^{b^*} \left(1 - e^{-\Delta y} \right), K \left(e^{\Delta y} - 1 \right) \right\},$$

which directly implies convergence of the method for $\Delta y \to 0$.

Advantages of the method. A conceptual advantage of the method lies in the fact that the paths of the approximating process $Z(t)$, $t \in [0, T]$, converge uniformly to the paths $Y(t)$, $t \in [0, T]$, of the logarithm of the price process. The main consequence of this convergence is the above explicit estimate of the approximation error. Another advantage of the method lies in its flexibility, which allows for a choice of the nodes in the binomial tree ensuring that in the double-barrier knockout call case the option runs out worthless in the modified binomial tree if and only if it runs out worthless in the Black-Scholes model. This feature cannot be obtained in the usual binomial model as the moment requirements have to be satisfied there. However, this last advantage of the Rogers-Stapleton algorithm helps to avoid the "saw tooth effect" of the convergence for increasing fineness of the approximation, i.e.

for $\Delta y \to 0$. Numerical examples of the performance of the algorithm and its modifications for other option types are given in [**RO/ST 98**].

Disadvantages of the method. The concept of the method requires a deeper understanding as in the case of the binomial model. It also admits a bigger computational complexity in particular with regard to its implementation. As, however, it yields more accurate results than the conventional binomial method, it is comparable with it regarding the overall efficiency.

Exercises

(1) Show that, with the notation of the proof of Proposition 4.1, we have
$$I_1 = P_1(t)\Phi^{(\rho_1)}(g_1(t), h_1(t))$$
$$I_2 = K_1 e^{-r(T-t)}\Phi^{(\rho_1)}(g_2(t), h_2(t)).$$

(2) Prove Lemma 4.2.

(3) Compute explicitly the price of the chooser option with maturity T and final payment
$$B_{Ch} = \max\left(X_{T_1,K_1}^{Call}(P_1(T),T), X_{T_2,K_2}^{Put}(P_1(T),T)\right).$$

(4) Consider the two-dimensional Black-Scholes model. Let Q_1 be the unique equivalent martingale measure for $P_0(t)$, $P_1(t)$, $P_2(t)$, if $P_1(t)$ is used as the numeraire.
   (a) Determine the Radon-Nikodym density of Q_1 with respect to P.
   (b) Show that
$$W^{(1)}(t) = W(t) + \begin{pmatrix} \left(\frac{(b_1-r)\sigma_{22}-(b_2-r)\sigma_{12}}{\sigma_{11}\sigma_{22}-\sigma_{12}\sigma_{21}} - \sigma_{11}\right)t \\ \left(\frac{(b_2-r)\sigma_{11}-(b_1-r)\sigma_{21}}{\sigma_{11}\sigma_{22}-\sigma_{12}\sigma_{21}} - \sigma_{12}\right)t \end{pmatrix}$$
   is a Q_1-Brownian motion.

(5) Use the notation of Proposition 4.4 and prove the following equalities
   (a) $X_{\min}^{Put}(0) = X_{\min}^{Call}(0) + Ke^{-rT} - p_1\Phi(d_3(0)) - p_2\Phi(d_4(0))$,
   (b) $X_{\max}^{Call}(0) = X_{(1)}^{Call}(0) + X_{(2)}^{Call} - X_{\min}^{Call}$,
   (c) $X_{\max}^{Put}(0) = X_{(1)}^{Put}(0) + X_{(2)}^{Put} - X_{\min}^{Put}$.

   <u>Hints:</u> For a) decompose the payoff of the put into
$$(\min(P_1(T), P_2(T)) - K)^+ + K - \min(P_1(T), P_2(T))$$

and use the already proved formula for a call on the minimum with strike price 0. For b), c) use the well-known relations between minimum and maximum of two real numbers.

(6) Do the explicit calculations needed for the determination of the price $X_{do}^{Call}(0)$ of a European down-and-out call.

(7) Compute the price $X_{do}^{Put}(0)$ of a European down-and-out put.

(8) (a) Show that the binomial model consisting of a stock and a bond is complete. Compute the corresponding equivalent martingale measure Q_n.

(b) Show that the price of an option B in the binomial model is given as $E_{Q_n}(e^{-rT}B)$.

(9) Show by an example that in the trinomial model a European call cannot always be replicated by a trading strategy in bond and stock.

(10) In the one-period trinomial model compute two different equivalent martingale measures.

(11) Give the proof of assertions (1) and (2) in Theorem 4.18.

(12) Derive part (2) of Lemma 4.5 from part (1) with the help of Girsanov's Theorem 3.11.

Hint: Note that $\tilde{W}(t)$ is a Q-Brownian motion, consider $Q(W(t) \leq w, M(t) < x)$, and compute this value explicitly with the help of the density of Q with respect to P.

(13) (a) In the binomial model, determine the parameters u, d, q if additionally to the moment conditions (4.21) and (4.22) we require $u = 1/d$.

(b) Cox, Ross, Rubinstein in [C/R/R 79] suggest the choice of

$$u = e^{\sigma\sqrt{\Delta t}}, \ d = e^{-\sigma\sqrt{\Delta t}}.$$

Show that with this requirement, (4.21) is satisfied but not requirement (4.22). How do we have to choose the left-hand side of (4.22) such that with the above choice of u, d (4.22) is also satisfied? How do we have to interpret this left-hand side?

(14) Let τ_1 be defined as in Section 4.5 (see also Theorem 4.18). Determine $E(\tau_1)$ and $E(\tau_1^2)$.

Chapter 5

Optimal Portfolios

5.1. Introduction and Formulation of the Problem

So far, in the continuous-time market model we were only looking for trading strategies that generate a given payoff profile ("replication") or a lower bound for a payment ("hedging strategy"). The costs of this replication strategy then determined the price of the payoff profile (i.e. the price of the corresponding contingent claim). Now we look at the opposite situation: We are given a fixed initial capital and search for an admissible self-financing pair of portfolio and consumption processes which yields a payment stream as lucrative as possible. We had already considered a similar task in the one-period model at the very beginning of the book. There we looked for a portfolio yielding the biggest possible return for a given bound on its variance. This time we shall look at a more general situation by introducing the so-called portfolio problem.

General formulation of the portfolio problem. For a given initial capital of $x > 0$, the continuous-time *portfolio problem* in our given continuous-time financial market consists of the determination of an optimal consumption and investment strategy. More precisely: The investor has to determine *how many* shares of *which* security he has to hold at *which time instant* and *how much* of his wealth he is allowed to consume to *maximize his utility* from *consumption* during the period $[0, T]$ and / or from the *terminal wealth* at the time horizon $t = T$. Thus, the portfolio problem contains a choice problem ("which" security), a problem of volumes ("how many" shares, "how much"...), and a component which is dynamic with respect to time ("which time"). We shall give the investor the possibility to decide on his actions at each time instant $t \in [0,T]$. The corresponding flow of information which forms the basis of his decisions should be the observation of past and present prices. He should not have any knowledge of future security prices and also he should not have any insider information.

> **General assumptions for this chapter:**
> We make the same assumptions as in Chapter 2, Section 2, p. 57. Further, we always consider a self-financing pair (π, c) consisting of a portfolio process π and a consumption process c to be admissible with initial wealth $x > 0$, for short: $(\pi, c) \in \mathcal{A}(x)$ (see also Definition 2.62).

Solution approaches in the continuous-time market model. Mainly we have to distinguish between two approaches to solve the portfolio problem in the continuous-time market setting of Chapter 2. The (historically) first approach is the stochastic control method which goes back to Robert Merton; see [**MERT 69**], [**MERT 90**]. Merton's main idea consists of interpreting the portfolio problem as a stochastic control problem to which he then applied standard methods of stochastic control theory. We shall present this method in Section 4 (of course preceded by an excursion on optimal stochastic control). On the basis of the stochastic control method, new methods for treating portfolio problems under transaction costs were developed during the last years (see [**KORN 97**]).

The so-called martingale method represents the second main approach for solving the continuous-time portfolio problem. It was introduced by Cox & Huang (see [**CO/HU 89**]), Karatzas, Lehoczky & Shreve (see [**K/L/S 87**]), and Pliska (see [**PLIS 86**]) in different variants during the eighties. A common feature of these variants is the decomposition of the portfolio problem into the determination of the optimal payments (consumption and / or final wealth) by methods of convex analysis followed by the determination of the corresponding portfolio process. In the complete market model of Section 2.3 the existence of this portfolio process is ensured by Theorem 2.63. We shall present the martingale method in Section 2. In Section 3 we shall give an application to a portfolio problem where options are traded instead of stocks.

Formulation of the problem. To judge the advantages of a payment stream in an objective way, we introduce a functional J which measures the utility of such a payment stream. A "good" payment stream is then characterized by a large value of J. So for a given initial wealth $x > 0$ an

5.1. Introduction and Formulation of the Problem

investor looks for a self-financing pair $(\pi, c) \in \mathcal{A}(x)$ which maximizes the expected utility from consumption and / or terminal wealth,

$$(5.1) \qquad J(x; \pi, c) = E\left(\int_0^T U_1(t, c(t))\, dt + U_2(X(T))\right)$$

Here, $X(t)$ is the wealth process corresponding to x and (π, c). U_1 and U_2 are assumed to be utility functions in the sense of the following definition.

Definition 5.1. (1) Let $U : (0, \infty) \to \mathbb{R}$ be a strictly concave and continuously differentiable function satisfying

$$U'(0) := \lim_{x \downarrow 0} U'(x) = +\infty, \quad U'(\infty) := \lim_{x \to \infty} U'(x) = 0.$$

Then U is called a *utility function*.

(2) A continuous function $U : [0, T] \times (0, \infty) \to \mathbb{R}$ such that for all $t \in [0, T]$ the function $U(t, .)$ is a utility function in the sense of part (1), is also called a *utility function*.

Examples of utility functions.

(1) $U(x) = \ln(x)$
(2) $U(x) = \sqrt{x}$
(3) $U(x) = x^\alpha$ for $0 < \alpha < 1$
(4) $U(t, x) = e^{-\rho t} \cdot U_1(x)$, $\rho > 0$ with U_1 a utility function as in (1) or (2).

Remark 5.2. (1) By the above definition, a utility function is strictly increasing. Thus, each additional unit of wealth leads to additional utility. Moreover, we require a utility function to be strictly concave. This in particular implies that $U'(x)$ is strictly decreasing. Thus we have a decreasing marginal utility, i.e. the gain of utility from one additional unit of money decreases with increasing x. The marginal utility in $x = 0$ is infinite, which can be paraphrased as "a tiny bit is much more than nothing" while the vanishing marginal utility in $x = \infty$ models a saturation effect.

(2) The methods of portfolio optimization presented in the following can also be applied to a wider class of utility functions as the one given in Definition 5.1. This wider class would also contain the popular but highly criticized quadratic utility function

$$U(x) = -\frac{1}{2}(x-a)^2.$$

However, this would need a more complicated notation. For the treatment of such utility functions we refer to [**KORN 97**].

Note that for an arbitrary $(\pi, c) \in \mathcal{A}(x)$ the expectation in $J(x; \pi, c)$ is not necessarily defined. We could now restrict the class of self-financing pairs (π, c) to all those for which the expectation in $(\pi, c) \in \mathcal{A}(x)$ is finite. However, an infinite positive expected utility is an investor's dream if it can be reached. We shall therefore allow for such a possibility by only requiring the following weak integrability condition for a feasible pair (π, c).

Definition 5.3. The problem

$$(5.2) \qquad \max_{(\pi,c) \in \mathcal{A}'(x)} J(x; \pi, c)$$

with

$$\mathcal{A}'(x) = \left\{ (\pi, c) \in \mathcal{A}(x) \,\middle|\, E\left(\int_0^T U_1(t, c(t))^- \, dt + U_2(X(T))^- \right) < \infty \right\}$$

is called the *continuous-time portfolio problem*.

Remark 5.4. (1) By restricting to the set $\mathcal{A}'(x)$, the integral in (5.2) is always defined. Also, the expectation exists but can be equal to infinity.

(2) In the case of positive utility functions, $U_1(t,.) > 0$ and $U_2(.) > 0$, the equality $\mathcal{A}(x) = \mathcal{A}'(x)$ is trivially satisfied.

In the following we shall present two methods for solving the portfolio problem. The first such method, the so-called martingale method, relies heavily on the completeness of the market. The second method, the so-called stochastic control method, is an application of standard methods of stochastic control theory to the portfolio problem (5.2).

5.2. The Martingale Method

General assumptions for this section:
Additionally to the general assumptions for this chapter we will use the notation of Section 2.3, p. 65. In particular, we have $d = m$. Thus, all assumptions of Theorem 2.63, "completeness of the market", are satisfied.

5.2. The Martingale Method

The main idea. The martingale method is mainly based on a separation of the dynamical (with respect to time) problem (5.2) into a static optimization problem ("determination of the optimal payoff profile") and a representation problem ("compute the portfolio process corresponding to the optimal payoff profile").

Motivation. We start by looking at a portfolio problem without consumption (i.e. we assume $c \equiv 0$, $U_1 \equiv 0$). Let the self-financing pair $(\pi, 0)$ be admissible for an initial wealth of $x > 0$. By Theorem 2.63, completeness of the market, we have for each corresponding wealth process $X^\pi(T)$

$$E(H(T) X^\pi(T)) \leq x \text{ for } T \geq 0.$$

Let the final payment $B \geq 0$ be $\mathcal{F}_T$-measurable with $E(H(T)B) = x$. Of course such random variables exist. A trivial example is

$$B := \frac{x}{E(H(T))}.$$

By Theorem 2.63 there exists a portfolio process $(\pi, 0) \in \mathcal{A}(x)$ with $B = X^\pi(T)$ P-a.s. Now define

$$\mathcal{B}(x) := \left\{ B \geq 0 \mid B \ \mathcal{F}_T\text{-measurable}, \ E(H(T) B) \leq x, \ E\left(U_2(B)^-\right) < \infty \right\}.$$

Obviously, $\mathcal{B}(x)$ represents the set of all final wealths with $E(U_2(B)^-) < \infty$ that can be generated by trading in the securities starting with some initial wealth $y \in (0, x]$ and satisfying $E(U_2(B)^-) < \infty$. So, for determining the optimal final wealth $X^\pi(T)$ in our portfolio problem

$$(5.3) \qquad \max_{(\pi,0) \in \mathcal{A}'(x)} E(U_2(X^\pi(T))),$$

it is enough to maximize over all random variables $B \in \mathcal{B}(x)$, i.e. it is sufficient to solve the problem

$$(5.4) \qquad \max_{B \in \mathcal{B}(x)} E(U_2(B)).$$

Note that in (5.4), we only have to optimize over a set of random variables. The time appearing in (5.3) (note that we optimized over a class of stochastic processes!) has disappeared. Therefore, we call (5.4) a static optimization problem. If now B^* is an optimal final wealth in (5.4), then to solve the portfolio problem completely we have to solve the representation problem

- Find a $(\pi, 0) \in \mathcal{A}'(x)$ with $X^\pi(T) = B^*$ a.s. P.

First we shall present the solution of the optimization problem (5.4). To motivate it we give a brief review of the Lagrangian method of (deterministic) non-linear constrained optimization.

Solving optimization problems with the help of the Lagrangian method. Let the function $f : \mathbb{R}^n \to \mathbb{R}$ be strictly concave, let $g : \mathbb{R}^n \to \mathbb{R}^k$ be convex, and let $f, g \in C^1$. Then we have

$\hat{x}$ solves the optimization problem
$$\max_{x \in \mathbb{R}^n} f(x)$$
$$\text{subject to} \quad g(x) = 0$$
$\Leftrightarrow$ there exists a $\hat{\lambda} \in \mathbb{R}^k$ such that $(\hat{x}, \hat{\lambda}) \in \mathbb{R}^{n+k}$ satisfies

$$\frac{\partial}{\partial x_i} f(x) - \sum_{j=1}^{k} \lambda_j \frac{\partial}{\partial x_i} g(x) = 0, \ i = 1, ..., n$$
$$g_i(x) = 0, \ i = 1, ..., k.$$

In words: $(\hat{x}, \hat{\lambda}) \in \mathbb{R}^{n+k}$ is a zero of the derivative of the Lagrangian function

$$L(x, \lambda) = f(x) - \lambda' g(x).$$

The Lagrangian method for the portfolio problem - motivation. We now set up an analogue to the above Lagrangian function in the setting of the optimization problem (5.4),

$$L(B, y) := E(U_2(B) - y \cdot (H(T)B - x))$$

with $y > 0$. Formally differentiating L with respect to B and y and interchanging the expectation with the differentiation process yields the equations

$$0 = L_B(B, y) = E(U_2'(B) - yH(T)),$$
$$0 = L_y(B, y) = x - E(H(T)B).$$

We will not justify this differentation, but use it only to derive the form of the optimal terminal wealth heuristically (of course we shall prove optimality later!). A random variable B satisfying

$$U_2'(B) - yH(T) = 0 \text{ a.s. } P$$

would solve the first equation. As by assumption the range of $U_2'(.)$ equals $\mathbb{R}^+$ and as $U_2'(.)$ is strictly decreasing, it can be inverted on $\mathbb{R}^+$ and we obtain

(5.5) $$B = (U_2')^{-1}(yH(T)).$$

Putting this into the second equation yields

$$0 = x - \underbrace{E\left(H(T) \cdot (U_2')^{-1}(y \cdot H(T))\right)}_{=:\chi(y)}.$$

5.2. The Martingale Method

Now, if we can solve this equation uniquely for y then we have found a possible candidate for the optimal final wealth via equation (5.5). Therefore we define

$$Y(u) := \chi^{-1}(u), \quad I_2 := (U_2')^{-1}$$

and obtain as a possible candidate for the optimal final wealth

$$B^* = I_2(Y(x) \cdot H(T)) > 0.$$

Now it will be our aim to prove that B^* is indeed the optimal final wealth.

Notation. Going back to the general optimization problem we define in analogy to the above considerations:

$$I_2(y) := (U_2')^{-1}(y) \quad \text{for } y \in (0, \infty),$$

$$I_1(t, y) := (U_1')^{-1}(t, y) \quad \text{for } y \in (0, \infty), t \text{ fixed},$$

$$\chi(y) := E\left(\int_0^T H(t) I_1(t, y \cdot H(t)) \, dt + H(T) I_2(y \cdot H(T))\right)$$

where $U_1'(.,.)$ denotes the partial derivative with respect to x, the second component.

The properties of $\chi(y)$ will be summarized in the following lemma.

Lemma 5.5. *Assume $\chi(y) < \infty$ for all $y > 0$. Then χ is continuous on $(0, \infty)$, strictly decreasing and satisfies*

$$\chi(0) := \lim_{y \downarrow 0} \chi(y) = \infty, \quad \chi(\infty) := \lim_{y \to \infty} \chi(y) = 0.$$

Proof. (1) Continuity of χ follows from continuity of H, I_1, I_2 and the dominated convergence theorem.

(2) $I_1(t,.), I_2(.)$ are both strictly decreasing on $(0, \infty)$. As we have $H(t) > 0$ for all $t \in [0, T]$ we thus also have that $\chi(y)$ is strictly decreasing in y.

(3) Due to

$$\lim_{y \downarrow 0} I_1(t, y) = \lim_{y \downarrow 0} I_2(y) = +\infty,$$

$$\lim_{y \to \infty} I_1(t, y) = \lim_{y \to \infty} I_2(y) = 0,$$

and the monotonicity of I_1, I_2 the assertions on $\chi(0)$ and $\chi(\infty)$ are a consequence of the dominated convergence theorem.

□

Remark 5.6. Lemma 5.5 in particular implies the existence of
$$Y(x) := \chi^{-1}(x)$$
on $(0, \infty)$ with
$$Y(0) := \lim_{x \downarrow 0} Y(x) = +\infty \quad \text{and} \quad Y(\infty) := \lim_{x \to \infty} Y(x) = 0.$$

The following simple lemma will prove to be quite useful for the proof of the main theorem of the martingale method, Theorem 5.8.

Lemma 5.7. Let U be a utility function with $I := (U')^{-1}$. Then we have
$$U(I(y)) \geq U(x) + y(I(y) - x) \quad \text{for } 0 < y,\ x < \infty.$$

Proof. As U is concave we have
$$U(I(y)) \geq U(x) + U'(I(y))(I(y) - x) = U(x) + y(I(y) - x).$$
$\square$

Now we are ready to give the solution of the portfolio problem.

Theorem 5.8 (Optimal consumption and optimal terminal wealth). *Consider the portfolio problem (5.2). Let $x > 0$ and $\chi(y) < \infty$ for all $y > 0$. Set $Y(x) := \chi^{-1}(x)$. Then, for*
$$B^* := I_2(Y(x) \cdot H(T)), \qquad \text{``optimal terminal wealth''}$$
$$c^*(t) := I_1(t, Y(x) \cdot H(t)), \qquad \text{``optimal consumption''}$$
there exists a self-financing portfolio process $\pi^*(t)$, $t \in [0,T]$, such that we have
$$(\pi^*, c^*) \in \mathcal{A}'(x), \quad X^{x,\pi^*,c^*}(T) = B^* \ \text{a.s. } P.$$
and such that (π^*, c^*) solves the portfolio problem (5.2). Here, $X^{x,\pi^*,c^*}(t)$ is the wealth process corresponding to the pair (π^*, c^*) and the initial wealth x.

Proof. i) By definition of B^* and $c^*(t)$ we have
$$E\left(\int_0^T H(t) c^*(t)\, dt + H(T) B^*\right) = x.$$

Note that we have $Y(x) \cdot H(t) > 0$ and that due to $I_1, I_2 > 0$ also B^* and c^* are positive. The existence of a portfolio process π^* corresponding to the payoff profile $(c^*(t), B^*)$ satisfying $(\pi^*, c^*) \in \mathcal{A}(x)$ is implied by Theorem 2.63 on complete markets.

ii) Next, we show that the unique (up to indistinguishability) portfolio process π^* even satisfies $(\pi^*, c^*) \in \mathcal{A}'(x)$. By Lemma 5.7 we have
$$U_1(t, c^*(t)) \geq U_1(t, 1) + Y(x) \cdot H(t) \cdot (c^*(t) - 1),$$

5.2. The Martingale Method

$$U_2(B^*) \geq U_2(1) + Y(x) \cdot H(T) \cdot (B^* - 1).$$

From this, the obvious relation $a \geq b \Rightarrow a^- \leq b^- \leq |b|$, and the fact that $Y(x) \cdot H(t)$, B^* and c^* are positive, we conclude the following chain of inequalities

$$E\left(\int_0^T U_1(t, c^*(t))^- \, dt + U_2(B^*)^-\right)$$

$$\leq E\left(\int_0^T (|U_1(t,1)| + Y(x) \cdot H(t)(c^*(t) + 1)) \, dt \right.$$

$$\left. + |U_2(1)| + Y(x) \cdot H(T)(B^* + 1)\right)$$

$$= |U_2(1)| + \int_0^T |U_1(t,1)| \, dt$$

$$+ Y(x) \left(x + E(H(T)) + \int_0^T E(H(t)) \, dt\right) < \infty.$$

To see the last inequality note that $U_1(t,x)$ is continuous and that the expected value $E(H(t))$ is bounded on $[0,T]$.

iii) Finally, we prove optimality of (π^*, c^*). Therefore, consider an arbitrary pair $(\pi, c) \in \mathcal{A}'(x)$ with wealth process $X^{x,\pi,c}$. From

$$U_1(t, c^*(t)) \geq U_1(t, c(t)) + Y(x) \cdot H(t)(c^*(t) - c(t))$$

$$U_2(B^*) \geq U_2(X^{x,\pi,c}(T)) + Y(x) \cdot H(T)(B^* - X^{x,\pi,c}(T))$$

we conclude

$$E\left(\int_0^T U_1(t, c^*(t)) \, dt + U_2(B^*)\right)$$

$$\geq J(x; \pi, c) + Y(x) \cdot \left(E\left(\int_0^T H(t) c^*(t) \, dt + H(T) B^*\right)\right.$$

$$\left. - E\left(\int_0^T H(t) c(t) \, dt + H(T) X^{x,\pi,c}(T)\right)\right)$$

$$= J(x;\pi,c) + Y(x) \cdot \underbrace{\left(x - E\left(\int_0^T H(t) c(t) \, dt + H(T) X^{x,\pi,c}(T)\right)\right)}_{\geq 0}$$

$$\geq J(x;\pi,c).$$

To see the last inequality use part (1) of Theorem 2.63 on complete markets. □

Example: "Logarithmic utility". We now consider the special choice of the logarithmic utility function. Note that values smaller than 1 have a negative utility! We then have

$$U_1(t,x) = U_2(x) = \ln(x)$$

$$\Rightarrow I_1(t,y) = I_2(y) = \frac{1}{y}$$

$$\Rightarrow \chi(y) = E\left(\int_0^T H(t) \cdot \frac{1}{y \cdot H(t)} \, dt + H(T) \cdot \frac{1}{y \cdot H(T)}\right) = \frac{1}{y}(T+1)$$

$$\Rightarrow Y(x) = \chi^{-1}(x) = \frac{1}{x}(T+1).$$

With this and Theorem 5.8 both the optimal consumption and the optimal final wealth are given by

$$c^*(t) = I_1(t, Y(x) \cdot H(t)) = \frac{x}{T+1} \cdot \frac{1}{H(t)},$$

$$B^* = I_2(Y(x) \cdot H(T)) = \frac{x}{T+1} \cdot \frac{1}{H(T)}.$$

In this special example, we can even calculate the portfolio process explicitly. To do so, note that by the proof of part (2) of Theorem 2.63 we have

$$(5.6) \quad H(t) \cdot X^{x,\pi^*,c^*}(t) = E\left(\int_t^T H(s) c^*(s) \, ds + H(T) B^* \,\Big|\, \mathcal{F}_t\right)$$

$$= x \cdot \frac{T-t+1}{T+1}.$$

This implies

$$x = x \cdot \frac{T-t+1}{T+1} + x \cdot \frac{t}{T+1} = H(t) \cdot X^{x,\pi^*,c^*}(t) + \int_0^t H(s) c^*(s) \, ds.$$

5.2. The Martingale Method

Application of Itô's formula to the product $H(t) \cdot X^{x,\pi^*,c^*}(t)$ on the right-hand side of the above equation yields (compare with the proof of part (2) of Theorem 2.63)

$$x = x + \int_0^t \underbrace{H(s) \cdot X^{x,\pi^*,c^*}(s) \left(\pi^*(s)' \sigma(s) - \theta(s)'\right)}_{=:f(s)} dW(s).$$

Hence we must have

$$f(s) = 0 \text{ a.s. } P \text{ for all } s \in [0,T].$$

As $H(s) \cdot X^{x,\pi^*,c^*}(s)$ is positive we thus obtain

$$\pi^*(t) = \left(\sigma(t)'\right)^{-1} \theta(t) \text{ for all } t \in [0,T].$$

In the special case of $d = 1$ and constant coefficients r, b, σ we get

$$\pi^*(t) = \frac{b-r}{\sigma^2} \quad \text{``local risk premium for stock investment''}.$$

Here, it is important to point out that the simplicity of the form of $\pi^*(t)$ is a bit misleading. Following a constant portfolio process indeed means that we have to trade at each time instant as stock and bond prices move in different ways. The constant quotient $(1-\pi)/\pi$ of bond wealth divided by stock wealth would immediately be no longer valid if one would not do the suitable trading ("rebalancing") actions. Note that from (5.6) we obtain another representation of the consumption rate

$$c^*(t) = \frac{1}{T-t+1} X^{x,\pi^*,c^*}(t).$$

So, the consumption rate is proportional to the current wealth of the investor and inversely proportional to the remaining time $(T-t)$.

The method of determining π^* in the above example can be generalized. Indeed, we have:

Theorem 5.9 (Solution of the representation problem (5.2)). *Let the portfolio problem (5.2) be given. Let $x > 0$ and assume $\chi(y) < \infty$ for all $y > 0$. Further, c^* and B^* should be given as in Theorem 5.8. If there exists a function $f \in C^{1,2}([0,T] \times \mathbb{R}^d)$ with $f(0,0,...,0) = x$ and*

$$\frac{1}{H(t)} \cdot E\left(\int_t^T H(s) c^*(s) \, ds + H(T) B^* \,\Big|\, \mathcal{F}_t\right) = f(t, W_1(t),..., W_d(t)),$$

then for all $t \in [0,T]$ we have

$$\pi^*(t) = \frac{1}{X^{x,\pi^*,c^*}(t)} \sigma^{-1}(t) \nabla_x f(t, W_1(t),..., W_d(t)).$$

Here, $\nabla_x f$ denotes the gradient of $f(t, x_1, ..., x_d)$ with respect to the x-coordinates.

Proof. Application of the multi-dimensional Itô-formula, Theorem 2.52, yields

$$\frac{1}{H(t)} \cdot E\left(\int_t^T H(s) c^*(s) \, ds + H(T) B^* \Big| \mathcal{F}_t\right) = f(t, W_1(t), ..., W_d(t))$$

$$= f(0, ..., 0) + \sum_{i=1}^d \int_0^t f_{x_i}(s, W_1(s), ..., W_d(s)) \, dW_i(s)$$

$$+ \int_0^t \left(f_t(s, W_1(s), ..., W_d(s)) + \tfrac{1}{2} \sum_{i=1}^d f_{x_i x_i}(s, W_1(s), ..., W_d(s)) \, ds \right).$$

On the other side, as in the proof of Theorem 2.63 on complete markets, we also have

$$\frac{1}{H(t)} \cdot E\left(\int_t^T H(s) c^*(s) \, ds + H(T) B^* \Big| \mathcal{F}_t\right) = X^{x,\pi^*,c^*}(t)$$

$$= x + \int_0^t \left((r(s) + \pi^*(s)'(b(s) - r(s) \cdot \underline{1})) X^{x,\pi^*,c^*}(s) - c(s) \right) ds$$

$$+ \int_0^t X^{x,\pi^*,c^*}(s) \pi^*(s)' \sigma(s) \, dW(s).$$

To see the last equality, note that (π^*, c^*) is an admissible, self-financing pair, and thus the wealth process obeys the wealth equation (2.22). Comparison of the integrands of the stochastic integrals of both representations yields the assertion by uniqueness of the representation of an Itô process. $\square$

With the help of the proof of Theorem 5.8 we can also give the solution of both the pure consumption and the pure terminal wealth maximization problem.

Corollary 5.10. (1) *The optimal terminal wealth B^* of the problem*

(5.7) $$\max_{(\pi, 0) \in \mathcal{A}'(x)} E(U_2(X^{x,\pi}(T)))$$

is given by

$$B^* := I_2(Y(x) \cdot H(T))$$

where in the definition of $\chi(y)$ we then have to set $I_1(t, y) \equiv 0$.

(2) *The optimal consumption process $c^*(t)$ of the problem*

(5.8) $$\max_{(\pi,c)\in\mathcal{A}'(x)} E\left(\int_0^T U_1(t,c(t))\,dt\right)$$

is given by

$$c^*(t) := I_1(t, Y(x) \cdot H(t))$$

where in the definition of $\chi(y)$ we then have to set $I_2(y) \equiv 0$.

5.3. Optimal Option Portfolios

As an application of the martingale method for portfolio optimization in the complete market which has just been introduced in the preceding section, we shall now consider a portfolio problem where instead of stocks we are only allowed to trade in options on these stocks (see [**KO/TR 99**]).

> **General assumptions for this section:**
> We use the same notations as in Chapter 2, Section 3, p. 65. Further, we assume $d = m$. Thus, the assumptions of Theorem 2.63 on complete markets are satisfied. Further on, we restrict ourselves to the case of constant market coefficients r, b, σ.

Description of the market model. We consider a market where a bond, d stocks, and d options on these stocks are traded. However, we assume here that we are only allowed to hold a portfolio consisting of the bond and the options. We further assume that the options have a price process of the form

(5.9) $$f^{(i)}(t, P_1(t), ..., P_d(t)), \quad i = 1, ..., d, \quad f \in C^{1,2},$$

and where the option prices satisfy the requirements of Proposition 3.19 (this is particularly satisfied for European puts and calls in the Black-Scholes model). Let

$$\varphi(t) = (\varphi_0(t), \varphi_1(t), ..., \varphi_d(t))$$

be an admissible trading strategy in bond and options. I.e. the integrals

$$\int_0^t \varphi_0(s)\,dP_0(s)$$

$$\int_0^t \varphi_i(s)\,df^{(i)}(s, P_1(s), ..., P_d(s))$$

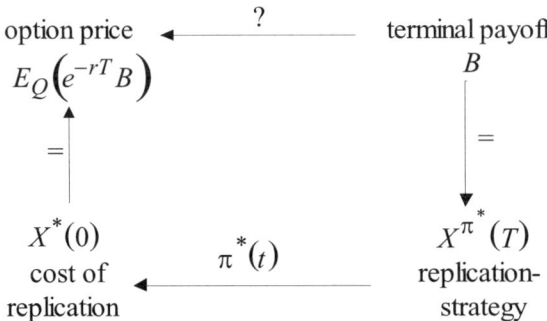

Figure 5.1. Scheme 1: Option pricing

are assumed to be defined and $\varphi(t)$ is assumed to be $\mathcal{F}_t$-progressively measurable. The corresponding wealth process $X(t)$ is given by

$$X(t) = \varphi_0(t) P_0(t) + \sum_{i=1}^{d} \varphi_i(t) f^{(i)}(t, P_1(t), ..., P_d(t)).$$

Let U be a utility function. We look at the problem

(5.10) $$\max_{\varphi} E(U(X(T)))$$

Motivation. To motivate the solution of the problem (5.10), we first take a look at the following diagrams representing the solution of the option pricing problem via the replication approach and the solution of the portfolio problem via the martingale approach. This will then inspire the third diagram showing the solution of problem (5.10).

Figure 5.1: Option pricing
Starting out from the final payment B of an option, we are looking for the option price. To find it, we first replicate the final payment via following a suitable portfolio strategy leading to a final wealth that coincides with the final option payment. Then the costs of setting up the cheapest replication strategy yield the option price.

Figure 5.2: Portfolio optimization with stocks
We are given an initial wealth of x. This will be invested according to a portfolio process $\pi^*(t)$ with the aim to obtain a terminal wealth which promises the highest possible utility (we ignore the possibility of consumption here). To do so, we first determine an optimal final payoff B^* and then look for a replication strategy for B^*.

Figure 5.3: Portfolio optimization with options
As in the stock portfolio problem above, we look for an optimal final wealth

5.3. Optimal Option Portfolios

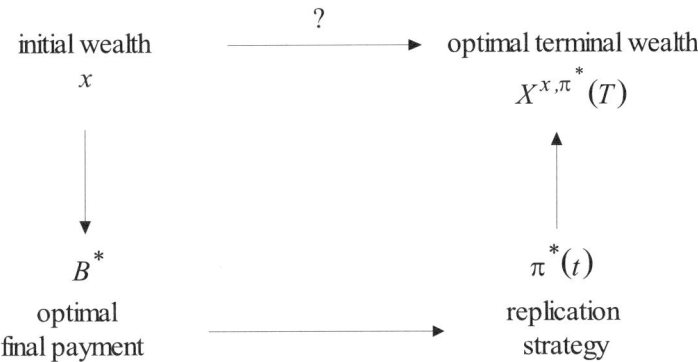

Figure 5.2. Scheme 2: Portfolio optimization with stocks

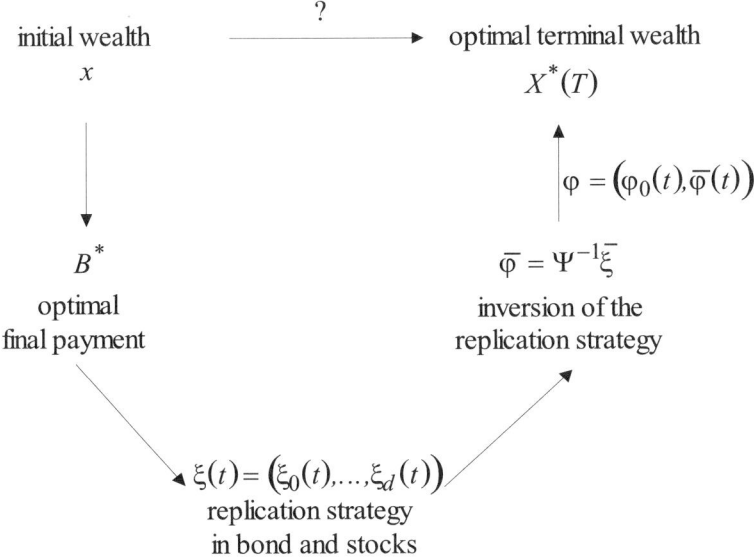

Figure 5.3. Scheme 3: Portfolio optimization with options

starting with an initial capital of x. To do so, we first determine an optimal payoff B^* and then a replication strategy $\xi(t) = (\xi_0(t),...,\xi_d(t))$ in bond and stocks for the payoff B^*. As stocks should not appear in our portfolio, we have to replicate the stock position by bond and options. This so-obtained bond and option strategy yields the optimal terminal wealth $X^*(T)$. This is formalized in the following theorem.

Theorem 5.11. *Let the Delta matrix* $\Psi(t) = (\Psi_{ij}(t))_{ij}$, $i,j = 1,...,d$, *with*

$$\Psi_{ij} := f_{p_j}^{(i)}\left(t, P_1(t),...,P_d(t)\right)$$

be regular for all $t \in [0,T)$. Then the option portfolio problem (5.10) possesses the following explicit solution:

(1) The optimal terminal wealth B^* coincides with the optimal terminal wealth of the corresponding stock portfolio problem (5.2).

(2) Let $\xi(t) = (\xi_0(t), ..., \xi_d(t))$ be the optimal trading strategy in the corresponding stock portfolio problem (5.2). Then, the optimal trading strategy $\varphi(t) = (\varphi_0(t), \varphi_1(t), ..., \varphi_d(t))$ in the option portfolio problem (5.10) is given by

$$\bar{\varphi}(t) = \left(\bar{\Psi}(t)'\right)^{-1} \cdot \bar{\xi}(t),$$

$$\varphi_0(t) = \frac{\left(X(t) - \sum_{i=1}^{d} \varphi_i(t) f^{(i)}(t, P_1(t), ..., P_d(t))\right)}{P_0(t)},$$

with $\bar{\varphi}(t) := (\varphi_1(t), ..., \varphi_d(t))$ and $\bar{\xi}(t) := (\xi_1(t), ..., \xi_d(t))$.

Proof. i) By Proposition 3.19 we have

$$f^{(i)}(t, P_1(t), ..., P_d(t)) = \sum_{j=0}^{d} \Psi_{ij}(t) \cdot P_j(t), \; i = 1, ..., d,$$

where

$$\Psi_{i0} := \frac{f^{(i)}(t, P_1(t), ..., P_d(t)) - \sum_{j=1}^{d} \Psi_{ij}(t) P_j(t)}{P_0(t)}.$$

As the trading strategy $(\Psi_{i0}(t), \Psi_{i1}(t), ..., \Psi_{id}(t))$ is self-financing we also have

$$df^{(i)}(t, P_1(t), ..., P_d(t)) = \sum_{j=0}^{d} \Psi_{ij}(t) \, dP_j(t).$$

Let now φ be an admissible and self-financing trading strategy in bond and options. Then, the corresponding wealth process satisfies

$$dX(t) = \varphi_0(t) \cdot dP_0(t) + \sum_{i=1}^{d} \varphi_i(t) \, df^{(i)}(t, P_1(t), ..., P_d(t)).$$

5.3. Optimal Option Portfolios

With the above representation of the option prices we obtain

$$dX(t) = \left(\varphi_0(t) + \sum_{i=1}^{d} \varphi_i(t) \Psi_{i0}(t)\right) dP_0(t)$$
$$+ \sum_{j=1}^{d} \left(\sum_{i=1}^{d} \varphi_i(t) \Psi_{ij}(t)\right) dP_j(t)$$
$$=: \zeta_0(t) \, dP_0(t) + \sum_{j=1}^{d} \zeta_j(t) \, dP_j(t).$$

Hence, the trading strategy ζ in bond and stocks is self-financing. As φ is admissible for the option portfolio problem (and as Ψ is a replication strategy) this implies that ζ is admissible for the stock portfolio problem.

ii) Let $\xi(t)$ be the optimal trading strategy of the corresponding stock portfolio problem with optimal wealth process $X(t)$. Then we get

$$X(T) = B^* \text{ a.s. } P,$$

$$dX(t) = \xi_0(t) \, dP_0(t) + \sum_{i=1}^{d} \xi_i(t) \, dP_i(t).$$

To obtain a trading strategy in bond and options admitting the same wealth process $X(t)$, we make the ansatz

$$dX(t) = \varphi_0(t) \, dP_0(t) + \sum_{i=1}^{d} \varphi_i(t) \, df^{(i)}(t, P_1(t), ..., P_d(t))$$

and obtain similarly to part (1) of the proof

$$dX(t) = \left(\varphi_0(t) + \sum_{j=1}^{d} \varphi_j(t) \Psi_{j0}(t)\right) dP_0(t)$$
$$+ \sum_{i=1}^{d} \left(\sum_{j=1}^{d} \varphi_j(t) \Psi_{ji}(t)\right) dP_i(t).$$

Comparison of the coefficients of the dP_i-terms of both representations of $X(t)$ yields the desired form of the last d components of $\varphi(t)$. Comparison of the dt-coefficients of both representations of $dX(t)$ yields

$$\xi_0(t) = \varphi_0(t) + \sum_{j=1}^{d} \varphi_j(t) \cdot \Psi_{j0}(t).$$

Due to

$$\xi_0(t) = \frac{X(t) - \sum_{i=1}^{d} \xi_i(t) P_i(t)}{P_0(t)} = \frac{X(t) - \sum_{i=1}^{d} \left(\sum_{j=1}^{d} \varphi_j(t) \Psi_{ji}(t) \right) P_i(t)}{P_0(t)}$$

we also have

$$\varphi_0(t) = \frac{X(t) - \sum_{i=0}^{d} \sum_{j=1}^{d} \varphi_j(t) \Psi_{ji}(t) P_i(t)}{P_0(t)}$$

$$= \frac{X(t) - \sum_{j=1}^{d} \varphi_j(t) \sum_{i=0}^{d} \Psi_{ji}(t) P_i(t)}{P_0(t)}$$

$$= \frac{X(t) - \sum_{j=1}^{d} \varphi_j(t) f(t, P_1(t), ..., P_d(t))}{P_0(t)}.$$

This shows that $(\varphi_0(t), \varphi_1(t), ..., \varphi_d(t))$ is self-financing. To show that $\varphi(t)$ is admissible it is enough to show that the stochastic integrals

$$\sum_{i=1}^{d} \int_0^t \varphi_i(s) \, df^{(i)}(s, P_1(s), ..., P_d(s))$$

are defined. Using the representation of the df-terms, the explicit form of $\varphi(t)$, and the admissibility of the strategy $\xi(t)$ in the stock portfolio problem, we get the admissibility of $\varphi(t)$ for the option portfolio problem.

iii) As we have shown in ii), following the bond and option strategy $\varphi(t)$ leads to the same utility as by using $\xi(t)$ in the stock portfolio problem. On the other hand, we cannot obtain a higher expected utility in the option portfolio problem. To see this, note that the existence of a strategy with a higher utility in the option portfolio problem would induce the existence of a bond and stock strategy ζ (as in i)) yielding a higher expected utility as ξ in the stock portfolio problem. But this would contradict optimality of $\xi(t)$. □

Remark 5.12. (1) Under the given assumptions, the optimal final wealth only depends on the utility functions but not on the choice of the tradable securities.

(2) The optimal strategy depends heavily on the traded options via the delta matrix (more precisely: via the replication strategy for the options).

5.3. Optimal Option Portfolios

Example: "Logarithmic utility". Let us choose the utility function
$$U(x) = \ln(x).$$
We specifically consider the Black-Scholes model with $d = 1$. From the example "logarithmic utility" in the previous section we know that the stock position in the optimal trading strategy is given by
$$\xi_1(t) = \frac{\pi^*(t) \cdot X(t)}{P_1(t)} = \frac{b-r}{\sigma^2} \cdot \frac{X(t)}{P_1(t)}.$$
Thus, the optimal trading strategy in bond and options is given in dependence of the delta-matrix as
$$\varphi_1(t) = \frac{b-r}{\sigma^2} \cdot \frac{X(t)}{\Psi_1(t) \cdot P_1(t)}.$$
If we now introduce the option portfolio process $\pi_{opt}(t)$, then we obtain the remarkable consequence

$$(5.11) \quad \pi_{opt}(t) := \frac{\varphi_1(t) \cdot f^{(1)}(t, P_1(t))}{X(t)} = \frac{b-r}{\sigma^2} \cdot \frac{X(t) \cdot f^{(1)}(t, P_1(t))}{X(t) \cdot \Psi_1(t) \cdot P_1(t)}$$
$$= \frac{b-r}{\sigma^2} \cdot \frac{f^{(1)}(t, P_1(t))}{f^{(1)}_{p_1}(t, P_1(t)) \cdot P_1(t)} = \pi_{stock}(t) \cdot \frac{f^{(1)}(t, P_1(t))}{f^{(1)}_{p_1}(t, P_1(t)) \cdot P_1(t)}.$$

Here, $\pi_{stock}(t)$ denotes the optimal portfolio process in the corresponding stock portfolio problem (5.2). The optimal portfolio process in (5.10) thus only differs from the one in (5.2) by the factor
$$\frac{f^{(1)}(t, P_1(t))}{f^{(1)}_{p_1}(t, P_1(t)) \cdot P_1(t)}.$$

In particular we have

Proposition 5.13. *With the choice of $U(x) = \ln(x)$, in the Black-Scholes model with $d = 1$ we have*

(1) $\pi_{opt}(t) = \pi_{stock}(t)$ *for all* $t \in [0, T]$
$\Leftrightarrow f^{(1)}(t, P_1(t)) = k \cdot P_1(t)$ *for a constant* $k \in \mathbb{R} \setminus \{0\}$.

(2) *In the case of a European call option we have*
$$\pi_{opt}(t) < \pi_{stock}(t) \text{ for all } t \in [0, T].$$

Proof. (1) Follows directly from the above relations (5.11) between π_{opt} and π_{stock}.

(2) We have
$$f^{(1)}(t, P_1(t)) = \Phi(d_1(t)) \cdot P_1(t) - \Phi(d_2(t)) \cdot e^{-r(T-t)} \cdot K$$
$$< \Phi(d_1(t)) \cdot P_1(t) = f^{(1)}_{p_1}(t, P_1(t)) \cdot P_1(t).$$

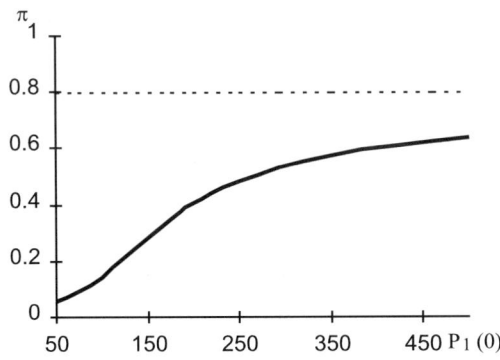

Figure 5.4. Portfolio with options

Together with (5.11) this yields the assertion as we also have

$$\frac{f^{(1)}(t, P_1(t))}{f^{(1)}_{p_1}(t, P_1(t)) \cdot P_1(t)} < 1.$$

□

Remark 5.14. Part (1) of Proposition 5.13 states that in the Black-Scholes model, $\pi_{opt}(t)$ is constant if and only if we have the degenerate case that the payoff of the contingent claims simply is a multiple of the underlying stock price. Part (2) says that with the choice of a European call option, in the option portfolio problem the optimal capital which is invested in the risky asset is always smaller than the corresponding risky position in the stock portfolio problem.

Example. We now look at a European call and the market coefficients

$$r = 0, \quad b = 0.05, \quad \sigma = 0.25, \quad T = 1, \quad K = 100, \quad P_0(0) = 1.$$

Figure 5.4 shows that part of the wealth which is optimally invested in the stock or in the option in the stock portfolio problem or in the option portfolio problem, respectively. More precisely, $\pi_{opt}(0)$ (bold line) and $\pi_{stock}(0)$ (dotted line) are given as functions of the underlying stock price $P_1(0)$. We observe:

- The deeper the option is in the money (i.e. $P_1(0) > K$), the closer $\pi_{opt}(0)$ gets to the optimal stock portfolio component $\pi_{stock}(0)$.
- The more the option is out of the money (i.e. $P_1(0) < K$), the smaller $\pi_{opt}(0)$ gets.

Excursion 8: Stochastic Control

> **General assumptions for this section:**
> Let $X(t)$ be an n-dimensional Itô process.

A stochastic differential equation of the form

$$(5.12) \qquad dX(t) = \mu(t, X(t), u(t))\, dt + \sigma(t, X(t), u(t))\, dW(t)$$

where $W(t)$ is an m-dimensional Brownian motion and where $u(t)$ is a d-dimensional stochastic process that we are free to choose – the so-called *control* – is called a *controlled stochastic differential equation*. The main task in stochastic control consists of determining an optimal control, i.e. a control process $u(t)$ which is optimal with respect to a certain cost functional. Before we make the notion of a control more precise and formulate suitable requirements on the coefficient functions of the stochastic differential equation, we look at a simple but illuminating example.

Example - maximizing the expected value in the presence of quadratic control costs. Let the controlled process $X(t)$ be of the form

$$X(t) = x + W(t) + \int_0^t u(s)\, ds$$

where $W(t)$ is a one-dimensional Brownian motion. As possible control action we are allowed to choose the intensity $u(t)$ of the drift process at each time instant $t \in [0, T]$; in aggregate we can choose

$$\int_0^t u(s)\, ds.$$

We now assume that the choice of $u(t)$ also results in costs of the form $a \cdot u^2(t)$. It is not only our aim to obtain a high value of $X(T)$ via choosing a suitable control $u(t)$, but also to take into account the control costs. Therefore, we consider the problem to minimize the difference

$$E\left(\int_0^T a \cdot u^2(t)\, dt - b \cdot X(T)\right)$$

with $a, b > 0$ by choosing the control process $u(t)$ optimally. As we can easily see, under suitable requirements on $u(t)$ we have

$$E\left(X\left(T\right)\right) = x + E\left(\int_0^T u\left(s\right) ds\right).$$

Hence, the above difference can be rewritten as

$$E\left(\int_0^T \left(a \cdot u^2\left(t\right) - b \cdot u\left(t\right)\right) dt - b \cdot x\right).$$

Minimizing the function in $u(t)$ under the integral leads to the optimal choice of

$$u^*\left(t\right) = \frac{b}{2a}.$$

However, for reasons of demonstration we shall solve this example in the following, this time via application of the methods of stochastic control (although those methods seem to be somewhat over-dimensional). Further applications of stochastic control will then be given in Section 5.3.

General assumptions for this section:
For $n, d \in \mathbb{N}$ let

$$Q_0 := [t_0, t_1) \times \mathbb{R}^n \text{ with } 0 \leq t_0 < t_1 < \infty$$
$$\bar{Q}_0 := [t_0, t_1] \times \mathbb{R}^n$$
$$U \subset \mathbb{R}^d \text{ closed.}$$

Further, let the coefficient functions in (5.12)

$$\mu : \bar{Q}_0 \times U \to \mathbb{R}^n$$
$$\sigma : \bar{Q}_0 \times U \to \mathbb{R}^{n,m}$$

be continuous with $\mu(.,.,u)$, $\sigma(.,.,u)$ in $C^1(\bar{Q}_0)$ for $u \in U$. Finally, for some constant $C > 0$ let

$$|\mu_t| + |\mu_x| \leq C, \quad |\sigma_t| + |\sigma_x| \leq C$$
$$|\mu\left(t, x, u\right)| + |\sigma\left(t, x, u\right)| \leq C \cdot \left(1 + |x| + |u|\right)$$

where $|.|$ are suitable norms (more precisely: Euclidean and spectral norm).

Explicit examples for coefficient functions which satisfy the above assumptions are given by (in the case of $n = 1$):

$$\mu\left(t, x, u\right) = ax + bu, \quad \sigma\left(t, x, u\right) = c_1 x + c_2 u,$$

or by
$$\mu(t, x, u) = a \cdot x \cdot u, \quad \sigma(t, x, u) = c \cdot x \cdot u,$$
if U is bounded.

Notation. If the process $X(s)$ solves the controlled stochastic differential equation (5.12) with an initial value of x at the starting time t, then we indicate this by denoting its expectation at time t by
$$E^{t,x}(X(s)).$$
A similar notation will be used for (expectations of) functions of $X(s)$ (see p. 117).

Definition 5.15. Let $(\Omega, \mathcal{F}, \{\mathcal{F}_t\}_{t \in [t_0, t_1]}, P)$ be a probability space equipped with a filtration. A U-valued progressively measurable process $u(t)$, $t \in [t_0, t_1]$ will be called an *admissible control*, if for all values $x \in \mathbb{R}^n$ the stochastic differential equation (5.12) with initial condition $X(t_0) = x$ possesses a unique solution $\{X(t)\}_{t \in [t_0, t_1]}$ and if we have

$$(5.13) \qquad E\left(\int_{t_0}^{t_1} |u(s)|^k \, ds\right) < \infty$$

for all $k \in \mathbb{N}$ and

$$(5.14) \qquad E^{t,x}\left(\|X(.)\|^k\right) := E^{t,x}\left(\sup_{s \in [t, t_1]} |X(s)|^k\right) < \infty$$

for all $k \in \mathbb{N}$.

Remark 5.16. (1) The above definition of an admissible control is more restrictive than the usual one given in stochastic control theory (see e.g. [**FL/RI 75**] or [**FL/SO 93**]). The main reason for that has its origin in the fact that assertions on existence of solutions of controlled stochastic differential equations require the notion of weak solutions of a stochastic differential equation if we want to use the weaker requirements on a control process. However, for our applications we do not need either the notion of a weak solution or that of a general control, so we simply omit their presentation.

(2) Examples of admissible stochastic controls in the sense of Definition 5.15 are progressively measurable and bounded processes with continuous paths and values in U. For these controls existence and uniqueness of a solution to the corresponding controlled stochastic differential equation is ensured by Theorem 3.22. The other requirements on an admissible control are trivially satisfied due to the boundedness of the control. However, for more examples

of admissible controls we usually need more general existence and uniqueness results for stochastic differential equations with measurable coefficient functions $\mu(t,x,u)$, $\sigma(t,x,u)$, or we require explicit assumptions on the form of $\mu(.,.,.)$, $\sigma(.,.,.)$ (see Section 2.6 in [**KRYL 80**] or Section 5.4 in [**FL/RI 75**]). With the help of such general existence and uniqueness assertions we can show that requirement (5.13) and our general assumptions imply requirement (5.14) (see [**KRYL 80**]).

Technical terms and formulation of the problem. Now we consider a more general problem where the process $X(t)$ will only be controlled as long as it stays in some given open set $O \subseteq \mathbb{R}^n$. For this, let either be $O = \mathbb{R}^n$ or an open set such that its boundary ∂O forms a compact, $(n-1)$-dimensional C^3-manifold. (note that $\bar{O} = O \cup \partial O$). Let

$$Q := [t_0, t_1) \times O$$
$$\bar{Q} := [t_0, t_1] \times \bar{O}$$
$$\tau := \inf\{t \geq t_0 \mid (t, X(t)) \notin Q\}$$

We look at the *cost functional*

$$J(t, x; u) = E^{t,x}\left(\int_t^\tau L(s, X(s), u(s))\, ds + \Psi(\tau, X(\tau))\right)$$

with continuous functions L, Ψ that satisfy the polynomial growth conditions

$$|L(t, x, u)| \leq C\left(1 + |x|^k + |u|^k\right),$$

$$|\Psi(t, x)| \leq C\left(1 + |x|^k\right),$$

for some $k \in \mathbb{N}$ on $\bar{Q} \times U$ or on $\bar{Q}$, respectively. Here, the costs

$$L(s, X(s), u(s))$$

are called *running costs* and

$$\Psi(\tau, X(\tau))$$

are called *terminal costs*.

Given initial values of $(t_0, x) \in Q$ it will be our aim to determine an admissible control $u(.)$ that minimizes the above cost functional, i.e. we try to solve the problem

Excursion 8: Stochastic Control

> (5.15) $$\min_{u \in \mathcal{A}(t_0,x)} J(t_0, x; u)$$
>
> with
> $$J(t_0, x; u) = E^{t_0,x}\left(\int_{t_0}^{\tau} L(s, X(s), u(s))\, ds + \Psi(\tau, X(\tau))\right)$$
>
> where $\mathcal{A}(t_0, x)$ denotes the set of all admissible controls $u(.)$ with start in $(t_0, x) \in Q$, i.e. the controlled process starts at time t_0 with a value of $X(t_0) = x$.

The function
$$V(t, x) := \inf_{u \in \mathcal{A}(t,x)} J(t, x; u), \quad (t, x) \in Q,$$
is called the *value function* of the minimization problem. It describes the evolution of the minimal costs in (5.15) as a function of the initial parameters (t, x), the starting time and the starting value of the process to control.

Heuristic derivation of the HJB-equation. The classical tool to solve the stochastic control problem (5.15) is the so-called *Hamilton-Jacobi-Bellman-equation* (for short: *HJB-equation*). We shall first derive it in a heuristic way. A formal proof of the relation between the value function of (5.15) and the HJB-equation will be given later.

For simplicity we assume $O = \mathbb{R}^n$. To derive the HJB-equation, we look at the following relation, the so-called *Bellman principle*:

$$V(t, x) = \inf_{u \in \mathcal{A}(t,x)}\left(E^{t,x}\left(\int_{t}^{\theta} L(s, X(s), u(s))\, ds + V(\theta, X(\theta))\right)\right)$$

$$V(t_1, x) = \Psi(t_1, x) \text{ for all } x \in \mathbb{R}^n,$$

for $t \in [t_0, t_1]$, $\theta \in [t, t_1]$. The Bellman principle states that we can get the minimal cost $V(t, x)$ by taking the infimum over the combined strategy "Choose the control $u(.)$ on $[t, \theta]$", which results in costs of

$$E^{t,x}\left(\int_{t}^{\theta} L(s, X(s), u(s))\, ds\right)$$

and "behave optimally on $[\theta, t_1]$ starting at time θ in $X(\theta)$", which leads to costs of $V(\theta, X(\theta))$. We shall prove the Bellman principle later. Here, we shall assume that it is valid. Further, we shall assume that all operations and manipulations done below (such as interchanging of limits) are allowed and that all stochastic integrals appearing have an expectation of zero. If inside the Bellman principle we apply the multi-dimensional Itô formula, Theorem 2.52, to $V(\theta, X(\theta))$, then this results in

$$V(t,x) = \inf_{u \in \mathcal{A}(t,x)} E^{t,x}\left(\int_t^\theta L(s, X(s), u(s))\, ds + V(t,x) \right.$$

$$+ \int_t^\theta \Big[V_t(s, V(s)) + V_x(s, V(s)) \mu(s, X(s), u(s))$$

$$\left. + \tfrac{1}{2} \cdot tr\big(\sigma(s, X(s), u(s)) \sigma(s, X(s), u(s))' V_{xx}(s, X(s))\big) \Big]\, ds \right)$$

if V is a $C^{1,2}$-function which we here assume. Using the notation of $a := \sigma\sigma'$, subtracting $V(t,x)$ on both sides of the above equation, dividing it by $(\theta - t)$ and taking the limit of $\theta \downarrow t$, we (formally) arrive at

$$0 = \inf_{u \in \mathcal{A}(t,x)} E^{t,x}\left(\lim_{\theta \downarrow t} \frac{1}{\theta - t} \int_t^\theta \Big[L(s, X(s), u(s)) \right.$$

$$+ V_t(s, X(s)) + \tfrac{1}{2} \cdot tr\Big(a(s, X(s), u(s)) \cdot V_{xx}(s, X(s))\Big)$$

$$\left. + V_x(s, X(s)) \cdot \mu(s, X(s), u(s)) \Big]\, ds \right)$$

$$= \inf_{u \in \mathcal{A}(t,x)} E^{t,x}\bigg(L(t, X(t), u(t))$$

$$+ V_t(t, X(t)) + \tfrac{1}{2} \cdot tr\Big(a(t, X(t), u(t)) \cdot V_{xx}(t, X(t))\Big)$$

$$+ V_x(t, X(t)) \cdot \mu(t, X(t), u(t)) \bigg).$$

Because at time t we know both the value of $X(t)$ and that of the control $u(t)$, we can drop the expectation operator in the last equation. We also only have to perform the minimization over all admissible initial values of the control, i.e. only over all $u \in U$ and not over all control processes $u(.)$, as only the initial values of the controls enter the above equation. So we arrive at

$$0 = \inf_{u \in U} \bigg(L(t, x, u) + V_t(t, x)$$

$$+ \tfrac{1}{2} \cdot tr\big(a(t, x, u) \cdot V_{xx}(t, x)\big) + V_x(t, x) \cdot \mu(t, x, u) \bigg),$$

which is the so-called HJB-equation for (5.15). Note that as a consequence of our manipulation no random terms appear in the HJB-equation! We can now obtain the value function $V(t,x)$ by first performing the minimization in the HJB-equation (in dependence of the unknown functions V_t, V_x, V_{xx}), then inserting the so-obtained minimizer u^* into the HJB-equation, dropping the infimum operator, and finally solving the partial differential equation with boundary condition

$$V(T,x) = \Psi(x) \text{ for all } x \in \mathbb{R}^n.$$

We then obtain an optimal strategy $u^*(.)$ – if the infimum is attained – by choosing $u^*(t)$ as an element of the argument of the infimum for $(t,x) = (t, X(t))$ which also is progressively measurable (if this choice is possible!).

Now we are in the position to give a rigorous proof for the relation between the value function $V(t,x)$ and the HJB-equation, a so-called verification theorem.

Notation.
(1) For $G \in C^{1,2}(Q)$, $(t,x) \in Q$, $a := \sigma\sigma'$, $u \in U$ let

$$A^u G(t,x) := G_t(t,x) + \tfrac{1}{2}\sum_{i,j=1}^n a_{ij}(t,x,u) \cdot G_{x_i x_j} + \sum_{i=1}^n \mu_i(t,x,u) \cdot G_{x_i}(t,x).$$

(2) $\partial^* Q := ([t_0, t_1) \times \partial O) \cup (\{t_1\} \times \bar{O})$.

Theorem 5.17 (Verification theorem for solutions of the HJB-equation). *Let $G \in C^{1,2}(Q) \cap C(\bar{Q})$ with $|G(t,x)| \leq K\left(1 + |x|^k\right)$ for some suitable constants $K > 0$, $k \in \mathbb{N}$, be a solution to the Hamilton-Jacobi-Bellman equation:*

$$\begin{aligned}
(5.16) \qquad & \inf_{u \in U}\left(A^u G(t,x) + L(t,x,u)\right) = 0, \quad (t,x) \in Q, \\
(5.17) \qquad & G(t,x) = \Psi(t,x), \qquad\qquad\qquad (t,x) \in \partial^* Q.
\end{aligned}$$

Then we have

(1) $G(t,x) \leq J(t,x;u)$ *for all* $(t,x) \in Q$ *and* $u(.) \in \mathcal{A}(t,x)$.

(2) *If for all* $(t,x) \in Q$ *there exists a* $u^*(.) \in \mathcal{A}(t,x)$ *with*

$$u^*(s) \in \arg\min_{u \in U}\left(A^u G(s, X^*(s)) + L(s, X^*(s), u)\right)$$

for all $s \in [t, \tau]$, where $X^*(s)$ is the controlled process corresponding to $u^*(.)$ via (5.12), then we obtain

$$G(t,x) = V(t,x) = J(t,x;u^*).$$

In particular, $u^*(t)$ is an optimal control and $G(t,x)$ coincides with the value function.

Remark 5.18. (1) Note that the value $X^*(s)$ does not depend on $u^*(s)$ but of course on $u^*(r)$, $r \in [t_0, s)$. Therefore, the definition of $u^*(s)$ in part (2) is an explicit one and not an implicit one.

(2) As the stochastic value function $V(t,x)$ of a stochastic control problem is unique (the minimal costs are unique, but not necessarily the minimizing strategy), there is at most one classical solution of the HJB-equation which satisfies the polynomial growth function.

Proof of Theorem 5.17.
(1) Let $(t, x) \in Q$. We show that for each stopping time θ with $t \le \theta \le \tau$ and each admissible control we get

$$(5.18) \qquad G(t,x) \le E^{t,x}\left(\int_t^\theta L(s, X(s), u(s))\,ds + G(\theta, X(\theta))\right).$$

As we have $G(s,y) = \Psi(s,y)$ for $(s,y) \in \partial^* Q$, then with the choice of $\theta = \tau$ relation (5.18) yields the assertion of part (1) above.

i) First assume that O is bounded:

As G is a solution of the HJB-equation we have

$$(5.19) \qquad 0 \le A^{u(s)} G(s, X(s)) + L(s, X(s), u(s))$$

for each admissible control $u(.)$, $t \le s \le \tau$. Application of the multi-dimensional Itô formula, Theorem 2.52, to $G(\theta, X(\theta))$ yields

$$(5.20) \quad G(\theta, X(\theta)) - G(t,x) - \int_t^\theta A^{u(s)} G(s, X(s))\,ds$$

$$= \int_t^\theta G_x(s, X(s))\,\sigma(s, X(s), u(s))\,dW(s).$$

Due to the boundedness of O the expectation of the stochastic integral vanishes, as on one hand G_x is bounded on O and further due to the general assumptions on $\sigma(s,x,u)$ together with requirement (5.13) we also get

$$E^{t,x}\left(\int_t^\tau |\sigma(s, X(s), u(s))|^2\,ds\right) \le D \cdot E^{t,x}\left(\int_t^\tau \left(1 + |u(s)|^2\right)\,ds\right) < \infty$$

for a suitable constant $D > 0$. Taking expectations in equation (5.20) and using inequality (5.19) yields the claimed inequality (5.18).

ii) Now consider a general O:

We shall prove (5.18) by approximating O by bounded sets O_p. More precisely: Let

$$O_p := O \cap \left\{ x \in \mathbb{R}^n \mid |x| < p, \; dist(x, \partial O) > \frac{1}{p} \right\},$$

$$Q_p := \left[t_0, t_1 - \frac{1}{p} \right) \times O_p, \quad 0 < \frac{1}{p} < t_1 - t_0.$$

If τ_p is the exit time of $(s, X(s))$ from Q_p then we have (note that O_p is bounded!)

$$(5.21) \quad G(t,x) \leq E^{t,x} \left(\int_t^{\theta_p} L(s, X(s), u(s)) \, ds + G(\theta_p, X(\theta_p)) \right)$$

with

$$\theta_p := \min(\theta, \tau_p).$$

Due to $\theta_p \to \theta$ P-a.s. for $p \to \infty$, the polynomial boundedness of L, requirements (5.13) and (5.14), and the dominated convergence theorem, we obtain

$$\lim_{p \to \infty} E^{t,x} \left(\int_t^{\theta_p} L(s, X(s), u(s)) \, ds \right) = E^{t,x} \left(\int_t^{\theta} L(s, X(s), u(s)) \, ds \right).$$

Continuity of G further implies

$$\lim_{p \to \infty} G(\theta_p, X(\theta_p)) = G(\theta, X(\theta)) \text{ a.s. } P.$$

As we further have

$$|G(\theta_p, X(\theta_p))| \leq K \left(1 + |X(\theta_p)|^k \right) \leq K \left(1 + \|X(.)\|^k \right)$$

and

$$E^{t,x} \left(\|X(.)\|^j \right) < \infty \text{ for all } j \in \mathbb{N},$$

for each admissible control $u(.)$, we get for $j > k$ that

$$E^{t,x} \left(|G(\theta_p, X(\theta_p))|^\alpha \right)$$

is bounded with the choice of $\alpha = j/k$ and $p > 1/(t_1 - t_0)$. Hence, the family $\{G(\theta_p, X(\theta_p))\}_p$ is uniformly integrable which then implies

$$\lim_{p \to \infty} E^{t,x} \left(G(\theta_p, X(\theta_p)) \right) = E^{t,x} \left(G(\theta, X(\theta)) \right),$$

and thus the convergence of (5.21) against (5.18) by which the assertion follows. □

Remark 5.19. In the proof of Theorem 5.17 we also showed that given the existence of a $C^{1,2}$-solution to the HJB-equation (and of an optimal control $u^*(.)$), we have the following Bellman principle:
For all stopping times θ with $t \leq \theta \leq \tau$ we obtain

$$V(t,x) = \inf_{u(.)\in\mathcal{A}(t,x)} E^{t,x}\left(\int_t^\theta L(s, X(s), u(s))\, ds + V(\theta, X(\theta))\right).$$

Theorem 5.17 justifies the following algorithm to solve the stochastic control problem (5.15):

Algorithm: *Solution of the stochastic control problem*
Step 1:
Solve the minimization problem (5.16) in the HJB-equation depending on the unknown function G (and its partial derivatives).
Step 2:
Let
$$u^*(s) := u^*(s, x, G(s,x), G_t(s,x), G_x(s,x), G_{xx}(s,x))$$
be a solution of the minimization problem. Then solve the partial differential equation
$$A^{u^*(t)}G(t,x) + L(t,x,u^*(t)) = 0, \quad (t,x) \in Q,$$
$$G(t,x) = \Psi(t,x), \quad (t,x) \in \partial^* Q.$$
Step 3:
Check all assumptions made and needed!

Remarks on the existence of a solution. The existence of a "classical" $C^{1,2}$-solution of the HJB-equation in Theorem 5.17 cannot be ensured in general. Typical results on existence need very strong requirements on the coefficient functions μ, σ, the cost functions L, Ψ, and the form of O. To be able to apply results from the theory of parabolic partial differential equations, we assume uniform parabolicity, i.e. there exists a $c > 0$ with

(5.22) $\quad \xi^T a(t,x,u) \xi \geq c|\xi|^2$ for all $(t,x,u) \in Q_0 \times U, \xi \in \mathbb{R}^n$.

We only cite such an existence result, but we do not need it for our further applications.

Theorem 5.20 (Krylov (1980)). *Assume (5.22) and further*

(1) *U is compact,*

(2) *O is bounded (and ∂O is a C^3-manifold),*

(3) *the functions a, μ, L and their partial derivatives with respect to $t, x_i, x_i x_j$ are continuous on $\bar{Q} \times U$,*

(4) $\Psi \in C^3(\bar{Q}_0)$.

Then, the HJB-equation possesses a unique solution in $C_p(\bar{Q}) \cap C^{1,2}(Q)$, where $C_p(\bar{Q})$ denotes the set of all continuous functions on $\bar{Q}$ which admit at most polynomial growth.

If O is not bounded then there are similar existence results if a, μ, L, Ψ are bounded (see [**FL/SO 93**], IV.4). Further, the requirements on a, μ, L, Ψ can be weakened if we assume a special structure for a, μ (e.g. μ, σ linear in both x and u).

Continuation of the example. We now apply the just learned method to the (in fact already solved) example from the beginning of this section. The HJB-equation corresponding to the process

$$X(t) = x + W(t) + \int_0^t u(s)\, ds$$

and to the cost functional

$$J(x, t; u) = E^{t,x}\left(\int_t^T a \cdot u^2(s)\, ds - b \cdot X(T)\right)$$

admits the form

$$\min_{u \in \mathbb{R}} \left\{\tfrac{1}{2} G_{xx} + u \cdot G_x + G_t + au^2\right\} = 0, \quad (t, x) \in Q,$$

$$G(T, x) = -bx, \quad x \in \mathbb{R}$$

for $Q = [0, T] \times \mathbb{R}$, $U = \mathbb{R}$. We now proceed according to the algorithm described above.

Step 1:
Formal minimization yields the following candidate for the optimal control:

$$u^*(t) = -\tfrac{1}{2a} G_x(t, X(t)).$$

Step 2:
Inserting $u^*(t) = -\tfrac{1}{2a} G_x(t, x)$ into the HJB-equation results in the (non-linear) partial differential equation

$$\tfrac{1}{2} G_{xx} - \tfrac{1}{4a} G_x^2 + G_t = 0, \quad (t, x) \in Q$$

$$G(T, x) = -bx, \quad x \in \mathbb{R}.$$

To solve it, we choose the ansatz

$$G(t, x) = -bx + h(t).$$

This transforms the partial differential equation into the ordinary differential equation for $h(t)$

$$-\frac{1}{4} \cdot \frac{b^2}{a} + h'(t) = 0,$$
$$h(T) = 0,$$

which is obviously uniquely solved by

$$h(t) = \frac{1}{4} \cdot \frac{b^2}{a} (t - T).$$

Thus we obtain

$$G(t, x) = -bx + \frac{1}{4} \cdot \frac{b^2}{a} (t - T),$$
$$u^*(t) = \frac{b}{2a}.$$

Step 3:
An essential part of the complete solution of a stochastic control problem with the help of the HJB-equation is to check all requirements which are needed to apply Theorem 5.17. This is often forgotten in practical applications and can be quite complicated in particular examples. However, in our simple example this causes no problem:

- As a Brownian motion with drift $b/2a$ the process $X^*(t)$ is the unique solution to the stochastic differential equation corresponding to $u^*(t)$.
- $u^*(t) = b/2a$ obviously satisfies the moment condition (5.13) in Definition 5.15. As a constant function it is also progressively measurable. Condition (5.14) follows from Lemma 3.23.
- $G(t, x)$ lies in $C^{1,2}$ and obviously satisfies the polynomial growth condition. Thus, it coincides with $V(t, x)$.

Now, we shall state some more generalizations of the already developed theory. Therefore, we consider two further stochastic control problems (for proofs of the results we refer to Chapter II and IV in [**FL/SO 93**]).

Remark 5.21. (1) If the cost functional $J(t, x; u)$ admits the form

$$J(t, x; u) = E^{t,x} \left(\int_t^\tau \Gamma(s) L(s, X(s), u(s)) \, ds + \Gamma(\tau) \Psi(\tau, X(\tau)) \right)$$

with

$$\Gamma(s) = \exp\left(\int_t^s q(r, X(r), u(r)) \, dr \right)$$

Excursion 8: Stochastic Control

for a bounded, continuous function $q(s,x,u)$, then we have a result similar to Theorem 5.17 if instead of (5.16) we consider the equation

(5.23) $$\inf_{u \in U} \left(A^u G(t,x) + L(t,x,u) + q(t,x,u) G(t,x) \right) = 0.$$

This case also contains the case of discounted costs, i.e. the choice

$$\Gamma(s) = \exp(-\beta(s-t))$$

for some $\beta > 0$.

(2) In the case of an infinite time horizon (i.e. a controlled stochastic differential equation on the time interval $[0, \infty)$) we assume that the coefficient functions μ and σ are autonomous (i.e. are independent of t) and also satisfy the general assumptions of this section. For the cost functions $L(x,u)$ and $\Psi(x)$ we make the same assumptions. If now τ denotes the first exit time of $X(s)$ from O, then our aim is to minimize the following cost functional

$$J(x,u) = E^x \left(\int_0^\tau e^{-\beta s} L(X(s), u(s)) \, ds + e^{-\beta \tau} \Psi(X(\tau)) 1_{\{\tau < \infty\}} \right)$$

where $\beta > 0$ is a discount factor and where we set $\tau = \infty$ if $X(s)$ never leaves O. This is in particular the case if we have $O = \mathbb{R}^n$. We now call a progressively measurable, U-valued process $u(.)$ an admissible control if for $t_0 = 0$ it satisfies requirement (5.13) for all finite positive values of t_1. In analogy to Theorem 5.17 we get the following theorem.

Theorem 5.22 (Verification theorem for solutions of the HJB-equation with an infinite horizon). *Let $\beta > 0$, let $G \in C^2(O) \cap C(\bar{O})$ with $|G(x)| \leq K(1+|x|^k)$ for some constants $K > 0$, $k \in \mathbb{N}$, be a solution to the HJB-equation*

$$\inf_{u \in U} \left(\tfrac{1}{2} tr(a(x,u) G_{xx}(x)) + G_x(x) \mu(x,u) + L(x,u) - \beta G(x) \right) = 0$$

$$x \in O,$$

$$G(x) = \Psi(x), \quad x \in \partial^* O.$$

Then we have

(1) *$G(x) \leq J(x,u)$ for all $x \in O$ and all admissible controls u.*
(2) *If for all $x \in O$ there exists an admissible control u^* with*

$$u^*(s) \in \arg\min_{u \in U} \Big[\tfrac{1}{2} tr(a(X^*(s), u) G_{xx}(X^*(s)))$$

$$+ G_x(X^*(s)) \mu(X^*(s), u) + L(X^*(s), u) - \beta G(X^*(s)) \Big]$$

for all $s \in [0, \tau]$, *where* $X^*(s)$ *is the controlled process corresponding to* $u^*(.)$, *then we obtain*

$$G(x) = V(x) = J(x, u^*).$$

(3) *In the case of* $\beta = 0$ *the assertions of (1) and (2) remain valid if* O *is bounded and if for all admissible controls* u *the first exit time* τ *is almost surely finite.*

5.4. Portfolio Optimization via the Stochastic Control Method

The stochastic control approach to continuous-time portfolio optimization was introduced by Robert Merton in the late sixties (see [**MERT 69**], [**MERT 71**]). Its main underlying concept consists of the application of stochastic control theory (as presented in the preceding section) to the portfolio problem.

> **General assumptions for this section:**
> Here we restrict ourselves to a market with constant market coefficients r, b, and σ. We assume $m \geq d$ and that the matrix $\sigma \in \mathbb{R}^{d,m}$ has full rank.

Note that we can also consider the case of an incomplete market. This, however, is not really surprising as completeness played no role in our excursion on stochastic control theory.

Main idea. The main idea of Merton's approach is to identify the wealth equation of an investor with strategy (π, c) as a controlled stochastic differential equation of the form

$$dX^u(t) = \mu(t, X^u(t), u(t)) dt + \sigma(t, X^u(t), u(t)) dW(t)$$

where μ, σ, u have the special forms of

(5.24)
$$u = (u_1, u_2) := (\pi, c),$$
$$\mu(t, x, u) = (r + u_1'(b - r \cdot \underline{1})) x - u_2,$$
$$\sigma(t, x, u) = x\, u_1' \sigma.$$

Reflecting the different variants of the verification theorems in Excursion 8, we shall also consider different variants of the portfolio problem. We start with considering the usual problem (5.2).

5.4. Portfolio Optimization via the Stochastic Control Method

Optimal consumption and optimal terminal wealth with a finite horizon. It is our aim to maximize the utility functional

$$J(t, x; u) := E^{t,x}\left(\int_t^T U_1(t, u_2(t))\, dt + U_2(X^u(T))\right)$$

by the choice of $u = (\pi, c)$. Let therefore

$$V(t, x) = \sup_{u \in \mathcal{A}(t,x)} J(t, x; u)$$

be the value function of the portfolio problem. Then, the corresponding HJB-equation has the form

(5.25) $\max_{u_1 \in [\alpha_1, \alpha_2]^d,\ u_2 \in [0, \infty)} \Big\{ \tfrac{1}{2} u_1' \sigma \sigma' u_1 x^2 V_{xx}(t, x)$

$+ \left((r + u_1'(b - r \cdot \underline{1}))x - u_2\right) V_x(t, x) + U_1(t, u_2) + V_t(t, x) \Big\} = 0$

$$V(T, x) = U_2(x)$$

for given constants $-\infty < \alpha_1 \leq \alpha_2 < +\infty$.

Remark 5.23. (1) Note that in the definition of an admissible control we only required the existence and uniqueness of the solution of the controlled stochastic differential equation, but not that this solution $X^u(t)$ should be non-negative. However, this is an essential feature of the definition of an admissible strategy $(\pi, c) \in \mathcal{A}(x)$ of our portfolio problem. Therefore, it could happen that an optimal control would, at least sometimes, lead to a negative wealth. However, in our examples we shall see that this is not the case. All the optimal controls appearing there yield a strictly positive wealth process. Thus, a non-negativity constraint could be added to the problem later without changing its optimal solution!

(2) While the form of the HJB-equation (5.25) is a result of a direct application of the verification theorem, Theorem 5.17 (with the choice of $Q = [0, T] \times \mathbb{R}$ and the substitution of "inf" by "sup"), the requirement

(5.26) $$\pi(t) = u_1(t) \in [\alpha_1, \alpha_2]^d$$

needs an explanation. The reason for this additional requirement is the applicability of the verification theorem. There, the requirements

$$|\mu_t| + |\mu_x| \leq C,\ |\sigma_t| + |\sigma_x| \leq C,$$
$$|\mu(t, x, u)| + |\sigma(t, x, u)| \leq C \cdot (1 + |x| + |u|)$$

can only be satisfied for coefficients of the form (5.24) with an unbounded range of x if the value set for the admissible controls

$u_1(t)$ is bounded. However, in the following examples, we shall show that – at least there – requirement (5.26) is not a real restriction if we choose the interval $[\alpha_1, \alpha_2]^d$ in an appropriate way.

Solution of the corresponding HJB-equation. Now we solve the portfolio problem (5.2) for the special choices of

$$(5.27) \qquad U_1(t,c) = \frac{1}{\gamma} e^{-\beta t} c^\gamma, \quad U_2(x) = \frac{1}{\gamma} x^\gamma$$

with $\beta > 0$, $\gamma \in (0,1)$.

Step 1: Solve the (formal) maximization problem.
Under the assumption that $V(t,x)$ is strictly concave in x and that the wealth process is strictly positive (both these assumptions have to be checked later!), the maximization in the HJB-equation (5.25) leads to the candidates

$$(5.28) \qquad u_1(t) = -\left(\sigma\sigma'\right)^{-1} (b - r \cdot \underline{1}) \cdot \frac{V_x(t,x)}{x \cdot V_{xx}(t,x)}$$

$$(5.29) \qquad u_2(t) = \left(e^{\beta t} \cdot V_x(t,x)\right)^{\frac{1}{\gamma-1}}$$

where we additionally assume that we always have $(u_1, u_2) \in [\alpha_1, \alpha_2]^d \times [0, \infty)$. Note further that for the maximality of u_1, u_2 according to (5.28), (5.29), it is sufficient under the above conditions that u_1, u_2 are the zeros of the corresponding partial derivatives.

Step 2: Solve the partial differential equations.
If we insert u_1, u_2 of the form (5.28) into the HJB-equation (5.25) then this results in the following partial differential equation for $V(t,x)$

$$(5.30) \quad 0 = -\tfrac{1}{2} (b - r \cdot \underline{1})' (\sigma\sigma')^{-1} (b - r \cdot \underline{1}) \frac{V_x^2(t,x)}{V_{xx}(t,x)} + r \cdot x \cdot V_x(t,x)$$
$$+ V_x^{\frac{\gamma}{\gamma-1}}(t,x) \cdot e^{\frac{\beta t}{\gamma-1}} \cdot \left(\frac{1-\gamma}{\gamma}\right) + V_t(t,x).$$

For the solution of (5.30) the final condition $V(T,x) = \frac{1}{\gamma} x^\gamma$ suggests the following separation approach:

$$(5.31) \qquad V(t,x) = f(t) \cdot \frac{1}{\gamma} x^\gamma, \quad f(T) = 1.$$

Now we compute all the partial derivatives of this special (5.30), insert them into (5.30), divide by x^γ, and we arrive at the ordinary differential equation

$$(5.32) \quad 0 = \left[-\tfrac{1}{2}(b - r \cdot \underline{1})'(\sigma\sigma')^{-1}(b - r \cdot \underline{1}) \cdot \frac{1}{\gamma-1} + r\right] \cdot f(t)$$
$$+ \frac{1-\gamma}{\gamma} e^{\frac{\beta t}{\gamma-1}} f(t)^{\frac{\gamma}{\gamma-1}} + f'(t).$$

5.4. Portfolio Optimization via the Stochastic Control Method

Note that to obtain this form it is essential that the quotient $V_x^2(t,x)/V_{xx}(t,x)$ has a very simple form with the ansatz (5.31). With the abbreviations

$$a_1 := -\tfrac{1}{2}(b - r \cdot \underline{1})'(\sigma\sigma')^{-1}(b - r \cdot \underline{1})\frac{1}{\gamma - 1} + r,$$

$$a_2(t) := \tfrac{1-\gamma}{\gamma} e^{\frac{\beta t}{\gamma-1}},$$

equation (5.32) has the form

(5.33) $$f'(t) = -a_1 f(t) - a_2 f(t)^{\frac{\gamma}{\gamma-1}}$$

with final condition $f(T) = 1$. The substitution

(5.34) $$g(t) = f(t)^{\frac{1}{1-\gamma}}$$

yields

(5.35) $$g'(t) = f'(t) \cdot \frac{1}{1-\gamma} f(t)^{\frac{\gamma}{1-\gamma}}.$$

Plugging (5.34) into (5.33) followed by a division by $(1-\gamma) \cdot f(t)^{\frac{1}{1-\gamma}}$ leads to the following linear differential equation for $g(t)$:

(5.36) $$g'(t) = -\frac{a_1}{1-\gamma} g(t) - \frac{a_2(t)}{1-\gamma}, \quad g(T) = 1.$$

Explicit solution of (5.36) via variation of constants yields

(5.37) $$g(t) = e^{\frac{a_1}{1-\gamma}(T-t)} + \frac{1-\gamma}{\gamma(a_1-\beta)}\left(e^{\frac{a_1-\beta}{1-\gamma}T} - e^{\frac{a_1-\beta}{1-\gamma}t}\right) e^{\frac{a_1}{1-\gamma}(T-t)}.$$

This then translates into the corresponding form for $f(t)$ via (5.34). $V(t,x)$ is then obtained from representation (5.31). The right-hand side of (5.37) can be simplified, but the above form has the advantage that we can easily infer the strict positivity of $g(t)$ from it. To see this, note in particular that both a_1 and β are positive and the sign of the term in braces equals the sign of its multiplying factor. Another consequence of the existence of a solution of the HJB-equation admitting the form (5.31) is the form of (π, c) as

(5.38) $$\pi(t) = u_1(t, X^u(t)) = \frac{1}{1-\gamma}(\sigma\sigma')^{-1}(b - r \cdot \underline{1}) =: \pi^*,$$

$$c(t) = u_2(t, X^u(t)) = \left(e^{\beta t} \cdot f(t)\right)^{\frac{1}{\gamma-1}} \cdot X^u(t).$$

Step 3: Check the assumptions.
i) $V(t,x)$ of the form (5.31) is obviously strictly concave as $f(t)$ is strictly positive. Further, $V(t,x)$ is a classical $C^{1,2}$-solution which satisfies the polynomial growth conditions.

ii) Due to (5.38) the wealth process $X^u(t)$ corresponding to the optimal $u(t)$ satisfies the stochastic differential equation

$$dX^u(t) = X^u(t)\left[(r + \pi^{*\prime}(b - r \cdot \underline{1}) - \left(e^{\beta t} \cdot f(t)\right)^{\frac{1}{\gamma-1}})\, dt + \pi^{*\prime}\sigma\, dW(t)\right],$$
$$X^u(0) = x.$$

In particular, this equation admits a unique solution which is strictly positive. Due to Lemma 3.23 it also satisfies the required moment condition (5.14).

iii) Due to the positivity of $X^u(t)$ and $f(t)$, the function $c(t)$ according to (5.38) is also positive. π^* is even constant. We now choose α_1, α_2 such that we have

$$\pi^* \in \left[\tfrac{\alpha_1}{2}, \tfrac{\alpha_2}{2}\right]^d.$$

Hence, requirement (5.26) is satisfied for the optimal π^*. In particular, that constraint is not binding. Then, for big values of α_1, α_2, requirement (5.26) can be ignored without changing the optimal strategy. As small values of α_i play no role in the unconstrained portfolio problem (5.2), we have therefore not only solved the stochastic control problem but also the portfolio problem (5.2).

Proposition 5.24. *The portfolio problem*

$$(5.39) \qquad \max_{(\pi,c)\in\mathcal{A}(x)} E\left(\int_0^T e^{-\beta t}\tfrac{1}{\gamma}c(t)^\gamma\, dt + \tfrac{1}{\gamma}X(T)^\gamma\right)$$

is solved by the strategy (π^*, c^*) according to

$$\pi^*(t) = \tfrac{1}{1-\gamma}\left(\sigma\sigma'\right)^{-1}(b - r\cdot\underline{1}),$$
$$c^*(t) = \left(e^{\beta t}f(t)\right)^{\frac{1}{\gamma-1}}X(t),$$

where $f(t)$ is given by (5.37) and (5.34).

Remark 5.25. (1) In general, it is difficult to give statements on the existence of a regular solution of (5.25).

(2) Similar to the partial differential approach of option pricing, the optimal strategy is a side product of the determination of the optimal utility in the stochastic control approach. However, we only get this "side product" explicitly if we can solve the partial differential equation explicitly.

(3) It is remarkable that the form of the optimal portfolio process is independent of the time. The form of the optimal consumption can be interpreted that the consumption rate (the consumption "speed") is proportional to the current wealth $X(t)$ where the factor of proportionality depends on time.

5.4. Portfolio Optimization via the Stochastic Control Method

Optimal consumption with an infinite horizon. We shall now solve a so-called life-time consumption problem. More precisely, we consider the problem

$$(5.40) \qquad \max_{(\pi,c)\in\mathcal{A}(x)} E^x\left(\int_0^\infty e^{-\beta t}\frac{1}{\gamma}c(t)^\gamma \, dt\right)$$

with $\beta > 0$, $\gamma \in (0,1)$, $x > 0$.

To transform this problem into an equivalent stochastic control problem, we have to note that the requirement

$$X(t) \geq 0 \text{ for all } t \geq 0$$

(which is contained in $(\pi,c) \in \mathcal{A}(x)$) implies that the investor has to sell all his securities immediately if the wealth process $X(t)$ reaches zero. Let therefore

$$\tau := \inf\{t > 0 \mid X(t) = 0\}.$$

Then, in analogy to the consumption and terminal wealth example we consider the control problem given by its value function

$$(5.41) \qquad V(x) = \sup_{u\in U(x)} E^x\left(\int_0^\tau e^{-\beta t}\frac{1}{\gamma}c(t)^\gamma \, dt\right).$$

Here, $U(x)$ is the set of all admissible controls with initial wealth of x and which are characterized by the requirements
(5.42)
$$u_1(t) \in [\alpha_1,\alpha_2]^d, \quad u_2(t) \geq 0 \text{ for all } t \geq 0 \text{ with } u(t) = (u_1(t), u_2(t)).$$

Of course, the other requirements on an admissible control should also be met. As in the case of the unbounded random horizon of Excursion 8, we set up the corresponding HJB-equation as

$$(5.43) \qquad \max_{(u_1,u_2)\in[\alpha_1,\alpha_2]^d\times[0,\infty)} \left\{ \tfrac{1}{2}u_1'\sigma\sigma'u_1 x^2 V''(x) \right.$$

$$\left. + \left((r + u_1'(b - r\cdot\underline{1}))x - u_2\right)V'(x) - \beta V(x) + \frac{1}{\gamma}u_2^\gamma \right\} = 0.$$

Again, we go through the usual steps:

<u>1. Maximization</u>
The usual assumptions that V is in C^2, strictly concave and strictly increasing yields the following candidates for the optimal controls:

$$u_1^*(t) = -\left(\sigma\sigma'\right)^{-1}(b - r\cdot\underline{1})\frac{V'(x)}{x\cdot V''(x)},$$

$$u_2^*(t) = V'(x)^{\frac{1}{\gamma-1}}.$$

Again, we assume that (u_1^*, u_2^*) satisfies requirement (5.42). Inserting u_1^*, u_2^* into (5.43) leads to the differential equation

$$(5.44) \quad 0 = -\frac{1}{2}(b - r \cdot \underline{1})' (\sigma\sigma')^{-1} (b - r \cdot \underline{1}) \frac{V'(x)^2}{V''(x)} + r \cdot x \cdot V'(x)$$

$$- \beta \cdot V(x) + V'(x)^{\frac{\gamma}{\gamma-1}} \cdot \left(\frac{1-\gamma}{\gamma}\right).$$

2. Solution of the differential equation

The requirement of a polynomially bounded solution of (5.44) in the verification theorem suggests the ansatz

$$V(x) = \frac{1}{\gamma} A x^\gamma$$

with a positive constant A. Inserting this ansatz and the corresponding derivatives of $V(x)$ into (5.44), then dividing all terms by the common factor Ax^γ yields the following equation for A:

$$0 = -\frac{1}{2}(b - r \cdot \underline{1})' (\sigma\sigma')^{-1} (b - r \cdot \underline{1}) \cdot \frac{1}{\gamma - 1} + r - \beta \cdot \frac{1}{\gamma} + \frac{1-\gamma}{\gamma} A^{\frac{1}{\gamma-1}}.$$

This equation has a positive solution A if and only if we have

$$(5.45) \quad \beta > r \cdot \gamma - \frac{1}{2}(b - r \cdot \underline{1})(\sigma\sigma')^{-1}(b - r \cdot \underline{1}) \cdot \frac{\gamma}{\gamma - 1},$$

i.e. the discount factor β has to be chosen sufficiently large. In this case we get

$$A = \left(\frac{\gamma}{1-\gamma} \left[\frac{\beta}{\gamma} - \left(r - \frac{1}{2(\gamma - 1)} (b - r \cdot \underline{1})' (\sigma\sigma')^{-1} (b - r \cdot \underline{1}) \right) \right] \right)^{\gamma - 1}.$$

3. Checking the assumptions

i) Under assumption (5.45) $V(x) = \frac{1}{\gamma} A x^\gamma$ is obviously a C^2-solution of (5.44) and thus of (5.43) which satisfies the above conditions.

ii) Further, for a suitable choice of α_1, α_2 the candidates $u_1^*(t), u_2^*(t)$ are admissible (and thus optimal!) controls as they have the explicit forms of

$$u_1^*(t) = \frac{1}{1-\gamma} (\sigma\sigma')^{-1} (b - r \cdot \underline{1}),$$

$$u_2^*(t) = A^{\frac{1}{\gamma-1}} \cdot X(t).$$

5.4. Portfolio Optimization via the Stochastic Control Method

This leads to the following representation of the optimal wealth process

$$X^*(t) = x \cdot \exp\left(\left(r + \frac{1}{1-\gamma}(b-r\cdot\underline{1})'(\sigma\sigma')^{-1}(b-r\cdot\underline{1}) - A^{\frac{1}{\gamma-1}}\right)t \right.$$
$$- \frac{1}{2}\left(\frac{1}{1-\gamma}\right)^2 \left\|(b-r\cdot\underline{1})'(\sigma\sigma')^{-1}\sigma\right\|^2 t$$
$$\left. + \frac{1}{1-\gamma}(b-r\cdot\underline{1})'(\sigma\sigma')^{-1}\sigma W(t)\right).$$

In particular, this is strictly positive and satisfies the required moment conditions.

Thus, in total we obtain the following result in the case of an infinite horizon with the help of the verification theorem

Proposition 5.26. *Under assumption (5.45), the life-time consumption problem (5.40) is solved by the pair (π^*, c^*) with*

$$\pi^*(t) = \frac{1}{1-\gamma}(\sigma\sigma')^{-1}(b-r\cdot\underline{1}),$$
$$c^*(t) = A^{\frac{1}{\gamma-1}} \cdot X(t).$$

Remark 5.27. (1) The two main differences to the foregoing portfolio problem which are caused by the infinite time horizon are:
First, the time dependent factor of proportionality of the optimal consumption has now turned into the constant $A^{1/(\gamma-1)}$.
Second, for ensuring the convergence of the infinite integral over the utility of consumption the discount factor β has to be sufficiently large.

(2) In general we cannot expect the optimal strategies (π^*, c^*) to have such simple forms as in the foregoing example. Even more, we have the relation

$\pi^*(t) \equiv const, \; c^*(t) = \delta X(t)$ solve the problem

$$\max_{(\pi,c)\in\mathcal{A}'(x)} E^x\left(\int_0^\infty e^{-\beta t} U(c(t))\, dt\right)$$
$$\Leftrightarrow U(c) = \alpha c^\gamma + d \text{ for suitable } \gamma \in (0,1),\, \alpha, d > 0$$

(see e.g. Proposition 3.39 on p. 54 in [**KORN 97**]).

(3) If the growth condition (5.45) is not satisfied then we cannot ensure that the value function is finite.

Exercises

(1) Use the martingale method to solve the portfolio problem (5.2) in the case of constant market coefficients and with the utility functions

$$U_1(t,x) = U_2(x) = \frac{1}{\gamma} x^\gamma \text{ for } \gamma \in (0,1) \text{ fixed.}$$

(a) First, determine the optimal consumption $c^*(t)$ and the optimal final wealth B^*.
(b) Determine the optimal portfolio process $\pi^*(t)$.

(2) Use the martingale method to solve the consumption problem (5.8) with the utility functions

$$U_1(t,x) = \frac{1}{\gamma} e^{-\beta t} x^\gamma, \quad \gamma \in (0,1), \quad \beta > 0 \text{ fixed.}$$

How do the optimal strategies (π^*, c^*) depend on β?

(3) Consider the example "logarithmic utility" of Section 5.3 with an option with the final payoff

$$B = |P_1(T) - K|.$$

(a) Determine the price of B and the corresponding replicating trading strategy $\Psi(t) = (\Psi_0(t), \Psi_1(t))$.
(b) Show that with the above option Theorem 5.11 remains valid if (with the usual notations) we set

$$\varphi_1(t) := \begin{cases} \dfrac{\xi_1(t)}{\Psi_1(t)} & \text{if } \Psi_1(t) \neq 0, \\ 0 & \text{otherwise.} \end{cases}$$

(c) For fixed $t \in [0,T]$ regard the optimal portfolio process $\pi_{opt}(t)$ as a function of $P_1(t)$. What happens at that value of $P_1(t)$ for which $\Psi_1(t)$ vanishes?

(4) For $T > 0$ solve the following stochastic control problem

$$\min_{u(\cdot)} E^{0,x} \left(\int_0^T \left(M \cdot X(s)^2 + N \cdot u(s)^2 \right) ds + D \cdot X(T)^2 \right)$$

with

$$dX(s) = (A \cdot X(s) + B \cdot u(s)) \, ds + \sigma \, dW(s),$$
$$X(0) = x \in \mathbb{R},$$

and $M, N, D > 0, A, B, \sigma \in \mathbb{R}$, and $U = \mathbb{R}$.
Hint: To solve the HJB-equation use the ansatz $v(t,x) = f(t)x^2 + g(t)$ in step 2 of the solution algorithm.

(5) For $T > 0$ solve the stochastic control problem
$$\max_{u(.)} E\left(X(T)^\gamma\right)$$
with
$$dX(t) = a \cdot u(t) \, dt + u(t) \, dW(t)$$
$$X(0) = x > 0$$
and $x > 0$, $a \in \mathbb{R}$, $0 < \gamma < 1$, $U = \mathbb{R}$, $O = (0, \infty)$ and $\tau = \inf\{t \in [0, T] \mid X(t) = 0\} \wedge T$.

In particular, show that the optimal strategy $u^*(t)$ and the value function $V(t, x)$ have the forms
$$u^*(t) = \frac{a}{1 - \gamma} X(t),$$
$$V(t, x) = \exp\left(a^2 \cdot \frac{\gamma}{2(1 - \gamma)} (T - t)\right) \cdot x^\gamma.$$

(6) Show that in the market with constant coefficients and an infinite horizon the problem
$$\max_{(\pi, c) \in \mathcal{A}'(x)} E^x\left(\int_0^\infty e^{-\beta t} U(c(t)) \, dt\right), \quad \beta > 0,$$
admits the optimal solution pair of the form
$$\pi^*(t) \equiv \pi \in \mathbb{R}^d,$$
$$c^*(t) = \delta \cdot X(t),$$
for suitable constants $\pi \in \mathbb{R}$, $\delta > 0$ if and only if we have
$$U(c) = \alpha \cdot c^\gamma + d$$
for suitable $\gamma \in (0, 1)$, $\alpha, d > 0$.

(7) Solve the terminal wealth maximization problem (5.7) via the stochastic control approach in the case of constant coefficients for $d = m = 1$,
$$U_2(x) = \frac{1}{\gamma} x^\gamma,$$
if instead of the bond a stock with price
$$P_0(t) = p_0 \cdot \exp\left(\left(b_0 t - \tfrac{1}{2}\sigma_0^2\right) t + \sigma_0 W(t)\right)$$
is traded.

(8) Show that the market model of Exercise (7) is complete (without using Theorem 3.47).

Hint: First, find a combination of both stocks that generate a riskless portfolio.

Bibliography

[BACH 00] L. Bachelier, *Théorie de la spéculation*, Annales Scientifique de l'École Normal Superieure 17, 1900, pp. 21–86.

[BAUER 90] H. Bauer, *Maß- und Integrationstheorie*, de Gruyter, Berlin, 1990.

[BECH 98] D. Becherer, *The numeraire portfolio for unbounded semimartingales*, preprint, Technische Universität Berlin, 1998.

[BILL 68] P. Billingsley, *Convergence of Probability Measures*, J. Wiley & Sons, New York, 1968.

[BI/KI 98] N. H. Bingham, R. Kiesel, *Risk-neutral Valuation: Pricing and Hedging of Financial Derivatives*, Springer, Berlin, 1998.

[BL/SC 73] F. Black, M. Scholes, *The pricing of options and corporate liabilities*, Journal of Political Economics 81, 1973, 637–659.

[CH/DO 65] K. L. Chung, J. L. Doob, *Fields, optionality and measurability*, American Journal of Mathematics 87, 1965, 397–424.

[CO/HU 89] J. C. Cox, C. F. Huang, *Optimal consumption and portfolio policies when asset prices follow a diffusion process*, Journal of Economic Theory 49, 1989, 33–83.

[C/R/R 79] J. C. Cox, S. A. Ross, M. Rubinstein, *Option pricing: a simplified approach*, Journal of Financial Economics 7, 1979, 229–263.

[D/SCH 94] F. Delbaen, W. Schachermayer, *A general version of the fundamental theorem of asset pricing*, Mathematische Annalen 300, 1994, 463–520.

[FL/RI 75] W. H. Fleming, R. W. Rishel, *Deterministic and Stochastic Optimal Control*, Springer, Berlin, 1975.

[FL/SO 93] W. H. Fleming, M. H. Soner, *Controlled Markov Processes and Viscosity Solutions*, Springer, Berlin, 1993.

[F/SCH 91] H. Föllmer, M. Schweizer, *Hedging of contingent claims under incomplete information*, in: Applied Stochastic Analysis (eds: M.H.A Davis and R.J. Elliott), Stochastics Monographs 5, Gordon & Breach, New York, 1991, 389–414.

[F/SON 86] H. Föllmer, D. Sondermann, *Hedging of non-redundant claims*, in: Contributions to Mathematical Economics: Essays in Honour of G. Debreu (eds: W. Hildenbrand and A. MasColell), North-Holland, Amsterdam, 1986, 205–223.

[GI/MU 78] P. E. Gill, W. Murray, *Numerically stable methods for quadratic programming*, Mathematical Programming 14, 1978, 349–372.

[GO/ID 83] D. Goldfarb, A. Idnani, *A numerically stable dual method for solving strictly convex quadratic programs*, Mathematical Programming 27, 1983, 1–33.

[GRUN 98] B. Grünewald, *Absicherungsstrategien für Optionen bei Kurssprüngen*, Gabler Verlag, Wiesbaden, 1998.

[HA/PL 81] J. M. Harrison, S. R. Pliska, *Martingales and stochastic integrals in the theory of continuous trading*, Stochastic Processes and Applications 11, 1981, 215–260.

[HA/PL 83] ———, *A stochastic calculus model of continuous trading: Complete markets*, Stochastic Processes and Their Applications, 15, 1983, 313–316.

[HELLW 87] K. Hellwig, *Bewertung von Ressourcen*, Physica Verlag, Heidelberg, 1987.

[HULL 93] J. Hull, *Introduction to Futures and Options Markets*, Prentice Hall, Englewood Cliffs, 1993.

[J/L/L 90] P. Jaillet, D. Lamberton, B. Lapeyre, *Variational inequalities and the pricing of American options*, Acta Applicandae Mathematica 21, 1990, 263–289.

[JA/TU 96] R. Jarrow, S. Turnbull, *Derivative Securities*, South-Western College Publishing, Cincinnati, 1996.

[K/L/S 87] I. Karatzas, J. P. Lehoczky, S. E. Shreve, *Optimal portfolio and consumption decisions for a "small investor" on a finite horizon*, SIAM Journal on Control and Optimization 27, 1987, 1157–1186.

[KA/SH 91] I. Karatzas, S. E. Shreve, *Brownian Motion and Stochastic Calculus*, Springer, New York, 1991.

[KA/SH 98] ———, *Methods of Mathematical Finance*, Springer, New York, 1998.

[KORN 97] R. Korn, *Optimal Portfolios*, World Scientific, Singapore, 1997.

[KORN 98] ———, *Value preserving portfolio strategies and the minimal martingale measure*, Mathematical Methods of Operations Research 47(2), 1998, 169–179.

[KO/TR 99] R. Korn, S. Trautmann, *Optimal Control of Option Portfolios*, OR-Spektrum 21, 1999, 123–146.

[KRYL 80] N. Krylov, *Controlled Diffusion Processes*, Springer, Berlin, 1980.

[LAM/L 96] D. Lamberton, B. Lapeyre, *Introduction to Stochastic Calculus Applied to Finance*, Chapman and Hall, London, 1996.

[LONG 90] J. B. Long, *The numeraire portfolio*, Journal of Financial Economics 26, 1990, 29–69.

[LUEN 98] D. Luenberger, *Investment Science*, Oxford University Press, Oxford, 1998.

[MARK 52] H. Markowitz, *Portfolio selection*, Journal of Finance 7, 1952, 77–91.

[MERT 69] R. C. Merton, *Lifetime portfolio selection under uncertainty: the continuous case*, Reviews of Economical Statistics 51, 1969, 247–257.

[MERT 71] ———, *Optimum consumption and portfolio rules in a continuous time model*, Journal of Economic Theory 3, 1971, 373–413.

[MERT 90] ———, *Continuous-Time Finance*, Blackwell, Cambridge, MA, 1990.

[MU/RU 97] M. Musiela, M. Rutkowski, *Martingale Methods in Financial Modelling*, Springer, Berlin, 1997.

[MYNE 92] R. Myneni, *The pricing of the American option*, Annals of Applied Probability 2, 1992, 1–23.

[OKS 92] B. Øksendal, *Stochastic Differential Equations*, 3rd edition, Springer, Berlin, 1992.

[PETR 95] V. V. Petrov, *Limit Theorems of Probability Theory: Sequences of independent random variables*, Oxford University Press, 1995.

[PLIS 86] S. R. Pliska, *A stochastic calculus model of continuous trading: Optimal portfolios*, Mathematics of Operations Research 11, 1986, 371–382.

[R/YOR 91] D. Revuz, M. Yor, *Continuous Martingales and Brownian Motion*, Springer, Berlin, 1991.

[RO/ST 98] L. C. G. Rogers, E. S. Stapleton, *Fast accurate binomial pricing*, Finance and Stochastics 2, 1998, 3–18.

[RO/WI 87] L. C. G. Rogers, D. W. Williams, *Diffusions, Markov Processes and Martingales*, Volume II, Wiley, Chichester, 1987.

[RUBI 81] R. Y. Rubinstein, *Simulation and the Monte-Carlo Method*, Wiley, New York, 1981.

[SCHM 96] N. Schmitz, *Vorlesungen über Wahrscheinlichkeitstheorie*, Teubner, Stuttgart, 1996.

[SCHW 92] M. Schweizer, *Mean-variance hedging for general claims*, Annals of Applied Probability 2, 1992, 171–179.

[SHAR 85] W. F. Sharpe, *Investments*, Prentice-Hall, 1985.

[WE/WI 90] H. von Weizsäcker, G. Winkler, *Stochastic Integrals*, Vieweg Advanced Lectures, Braunschweig/Wiesbaden, 1990.

[WIEN 23] N. Wiener, *Differential space*, Journal of Mathematical Physics 2, 1923, 131–174.

[WIES 95] T. Wiesemann, *Wertorientiertes Portfoliomanagement : Ein Modell zur intertemporalen Portfoliowerterhaltung*, Dissertation, Universität Ulm, 1995.

[WIL 99] P. Wilmott, *Derivatives: The Theory and Practice of Financial Engineering*, John Wiley & Sons Ltd., Chichester, 1999.

[W/D/H 93] P. Wilmott, J. N. Dewynne, S. D. Howison, *Option Pricing: Mathematical Models and Computation*, Oxford Financial Press, Oxford, 1993.

[W/D/H 95] ———, *Mathematics of Financial Derivatives*, Cambridge University Press, Cambridge, 1995.

[ZHANG 97] P. G. Zhang, *Exotic Options*, World Scientific, Singapore, 1997.

Index

Admissible control, 225
American contingent claim, 130
Arbitrage bounds, 122
Arbitrage opportunity, 84, 85
Asian option, 154
Average option, 154

Barrier option, 154, 167, 184, 193
Bellman principle, 227
Binary option, 155
Binomial model, 8
Binomial tree
   algorithm, 179
Black-Scholes formula, 88
Bond, 11
Brownian filtration, 17
Brownian martingale, 71
Brownian motion, 17, 27
   multi-dimensional, 16
   one-dimensional, 16
   with drift, 19
Budget equation, 2
Bull spread, 149
Butterfly spread, 148

Call, 79
   European, 80
   European digital, 104
Cauchy problem, 106, 119
Characteristic operator, 118
Chooser option, 161
Complete market, 65
Compound option, 158
Consumption problem
   life-time, 241
Consumption process, 61

Consumption rate process, 61
Contingent claim, 86, 137
Continuous-time market model, 11, 56
Control, 223
   admissible, 225
Convergence in distribution, 171
Cost functional, 226
Cox-Ross-Rubinstein model, 8

Differential notation, 42, 44
Digital option, 155
Diversification effect, 5
Donsker's theorem, 174
   for triangular schemes, 174
Doob's inequality, 22

Equivalent martingale measure, 135
Exercise price, 79
Expiration date, 80
Expiry, 80

Fair price, 87
Feynman-Kac representation, 119
Filtration, 15
   canonical, 15
   natural, 15
Finite-difference methods, 190
Fundamental theorem of asset pricing, 137

Gap option, 156
Garman-Kohlhagen model, 151
Girsanov's theorem, 94
Growth optimum portfolio, 78

Hamilton-Jacobi-Bellman-equation, 227
Hedging strategy, 130

Increasing process, 26
Indexed option, 162
Indistinguishable, 16
Itô formula
  multi-dimensional, 51
  one-dimensional, 43
Itô integral, 37
Itô isometry, 34
Itô process
  n-dimensional, 42
  real-valued, 42

Lagrangian function, 208
Local martingale, 22, 41
Localizing sequence, 22
Lookback option, 169

Martingale, 18
Martingale measure
  equivalent, 99
Martingale method, 206
Martingale representation theorem, 71
Maturity, 80
Mean-variance approach, 1
Minimal martingale measure, 141
Modification, 16
Monte-Carlo simulation, 175

Natural price, 103
Novikov condition, 97
Numeraire, 143
Numeraire invariance, 147
Numeraire portfolio, 145

Objective measure, 103
One-period model, 1
Option
  American, 79
  call, 79
  European, 79
  put, 79
Optional sampling, 21

Partial integration, 52
Paylater option, 157
Payoff diagram, 80
Perfect hedge, 142
Portfolio
  return, 2
  vector, 2
Portfolio problem, 203, 206
Portfolio process, 62
  self-financing, 63
Product rule, 52
Put, 79
  European, 80
Put-call parity
  for American options, 128
  for European options, 125

Quadratic covariation, 43
Quadratic variation, 43

Realization of a stochastic process, 16
Replication principle, 83, 84
Replication strategy, 87
Return, 2
Risk-neutral market, 103
Risk-neutral measure, 103
Riskless portfolio, 105
Rogers and Stapleton
  algorithm, 191, 199
Running costs, 226

Sample path, 16
Self-financing, 59, 61
Simple process, 28
Stochastic differential equation, 53, 54
  controlled, 223
Stochastic integral, 37
  for simple processes, 29
  multi-dimensional, 40
Stochastic process, 15
  $H^2[0,T]$, 41
  $L^2[0,T]$, 33
  measurable, 32
  progressively measurable, 32
Stock price, 25
Stock price equation, 53
Stopped filtration, 20
Stopped process, 20
Stopping time, 20
Straddle, 148
Strangle, 149
Strike price, 79
Strong solution, 111
Sub-martingale, 18
Subjective measure, 103
Super-martingale, 18

Terminal costs, 226
Trading strategy, 60
Trinomial tree
  algorithm, 189

Usual conditions, 18
Utility function, 205
  logarithmic, 212, 221

Value function, 227
Variation of constants, 54
Vector of mean rates of stock returns, 25
Verification theorem, 229
Volatility, 19

Index

Volatility matrix, 25

Weak convergence, 171
  of stochastic processes, 171
Wealth equation, 62
Wealth process, 61
Writer
  of the option, 79